PRACTICAL BGP

Russ White
Danny McPherson
Sangli Srihari

Foreword by Yakov Rekhter

Addison-Wesley

BOSTON • SAN FRANCISCO • NEW YORK • TORONTO • MONTREAL
LONDON • MUNICH • PARIS • MADRID
CAPE TOWN • SYDNEY • TOKYO • SINGAPORE • MEXICO CITY

The publisher offers discounts on this book when ordered in quantity for bulk purchases and special sales. For more information, please contact:

U.S. Corporate and Government Sales
(800) 382-3419
corpsales@pearsontechgroup.com

For sales outside of the U.S., please contact:

International Sales
(317) 581-3793
international@pearsontechgroup.com

Visit Addison-Wesley on the Web: www.awprofessional.com

Library of Congress Cataloging-in-Publication Data

ISBN: 0321127005
Text printed on recycled paper
1 2 3 4 5 6 7 8 9 10
First printing, June 2004

Contents

Chapter 3
Scaling the Enterprise Using BGP   91

Chapter 4
Core Design with iBGP   130

Chapter 5
BGP Performance   161

Chapter 6
BGP Policy   184

Foreword

Over lunch at the 12th IETF meeting in January 1989, Len Bosack, Kirk Lougheed, and myself came up with a protocol we called "A Border Gateway Protocol." The outcome of what we produced was written on three napkins, giving BGP its unofficial title as the "Three Napkins Protocol." Following lunch, Kirk and I expanded the context of the napkins into few handwritten pieces of paper (see p. x). In less than a month after the meeting, we came up with the first two interoperable implementations of BGP.

BGP was built around few fairly simple ideas. The first idea was to provide loop-free routing by carrying information about the path that the routing information traverses, and using this information to suppress routing information looping. The second idea was to minimize the volume of routing information that has to be exchanged between routers by using the technique of incremental updates, in which a router, after an initial exchange of full routing information with a neighbor, exchanges only the changes to that information with the neighbor. Using incremental updates requires reliable transport of these updates between neighbors. The third idea was to use TCP as the necessary reliable transport, rather than (re)invent a new transport protocol. The last idea was to encode the information carried by BGP as a collection of attributes, with each attribute encoded as a <type, length, value> triplet. Doing this facilitates adding new features to BGP in an incremental fashion. All these ideas remain essential in today's BGP.

At the time of this writing, it has been fifteen years since BGP was originally designed. The evolution of BGP over these fifteen years came in several major "waves." The first wave produced support for IPv4 Classless Inter-Domain Routing (CIDR). The second wave produced such features as BGP Confederations, BGP Route Reflectors, BGP Communities, and BGP Route Dampening. The third wave produced such features as Multi-Protocol Extensions, and Capability Advertisement. The most recent wave produced such features as BGP/MPLS IP VPNs (also known as 2547 VPNs), BGP-based VPN auto-discovery, and BGP-based Virtual Private LAN Services (VPLS). It is precisely the last wave that expanded the scope of BGP well beyond supporting just inter-domain routing for the Internet.

During the first six years of its life (1989–1995), BGP changed its version number four times (from BGP-1 to BGP-4). However, since 1995, BGP has not changed its version number even once–in 2004 we still have BGP-4. This is because the introduction of Capability Advertisement provided a much more flexible mechanism for adding new, even backward incompatible features to BGP than did traditional version negotiation.

When BGP was originally designed in 1989, it was intended to be a short/medium term solution to Internet inter-domain routing. As a result the original design goals for BGP were fairly modest–to support inter-domain routing with a few thousand classful IPv4 routes without imposing any restrictions on the inter-domain topology (remember that BGP's predecessor, EGP-2, constrained inter-domain topology to a spanning tree).

Fifteen years later BGP remains the sole inter-domain routing protocol for the Internet. Yet current use of BGP extends well beyond its original design goals. From a protocol designed to support inter-domain routing in the Internet that had just a few thousand classful IPv4 routes BGP evolved into a protocol that supports inter-domain routing in the Internet with well over 120,000 thousands classless (CIDR) IPv4 routes.

Moreover, today's BGP is no longer restricted to simply distributing IPv4 (or IPv6) routes. BGP evolved from being an inter-domain routing protocol for the Internet to a protocol that supports constrained, loop-free distribution of information, both within a single autonomous system, as well as across multiple autonomous systems, while placing little to no restrictions on the type of the information that it distributes. This makes BGP well-suited for applications that require constraint-based loop-free distribution of information both within a single autonomous system, as well as across multiple autonomous systems, irrespective of whether the nature of this information is different or the same as IPv4 (or IPv6) routes. To illustrate the diversity of the applications that use BGP today just look at such applications as BGP/MPLS IP VPNs, BGP-based VPN auto-discovery, and BGP-based Virtual Private LAN Services (BGP-based VPLS), and the services provided by these applications. What makes such use of BGP attractive is that the reuse of a common protocol, BGP, enables service providers to lower the operational cost of introducing these services and enables equipment vendors to lower the development cost and shorten the time to market. It is precisely these factors that positioned BGP as an essential tool for building multi-service networks that support services such as IP VPNs, VPLS, and the Internet.

From its inception BGP generated a certain amount of controversy. The most recent being the use ofBGP for carrying information other than IPv4 (and IPv6) routes. To put all the controversy in proper perspective, it is important to keep in mind that, in general, a technology exists neither for its own sake, nor for the sake of fitting into a particular set of technical dogmas, but for the sake of solving a particular business problem. How could one judge how well a particular technology solves a particular business problem? To answer this question I would like to remind you of the saying, "the proof of the pudding is in the eating." In the context of this discussion this means that the ultimate judge is the marketplace. It is the market, and nothing else, that ultimately determines the suitability of a particular technology for solving a particular business problem; BGP, as a technology, is by no means an exception to this. In order to judge how well BGP solves a particular problem, look at the success (or failure) of such a solution in the marketplace.

As one of the co-inventors of BGP, I would be the first to admit that BGP is by no means a "perfect solution"—in fact it was never intended to be one. Those who look for a perfect solution should look elsewhere. From the beginning BGP was focused on solving practical problems, solving them in a timely fashion, and being satisfied with a "good enough," rather than a perfect solution. In other words, both the original design of BGP and the evolution of the original design over the past fifteen years have been firmly rooted in pragmatism and unconstrained by dogmas.

When asked about my opinion of the future of BGP, or any other technology for that matter, I usually say that I do not have a crystal ball, and therefore I do not predict the future in general, or the future of BGP in particular. In fact, I usually add that my past experience has shown over and over again how folks who were predicting the future turned out to be wrong. All I can say is that I hope that future BGP development will continue to be firmly rooted in pragmatism, and that in the end it is the market that will separate useful BGP development from useless BGP development.

Yakov Rekhter
March 2004

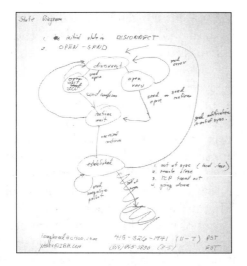

Early sketches of BGP design.

Preface

"Experience is the best teacher" is a valuable truism in network design, especially in designing a routed network using a protocol as widespread, and as little understood, as the Border Gateway Protocol (BGP). It's hard to grasp BGP at a high level, because network engineers tend to see only a small piece of the system they are interacting with–either their connection to the Internet, or their network backbone, or some other slice. From this perspective, it's hard to understand how BGP works in the real world, and what impact decisions in one small slice of the network will actually have in the larger internetwork.

How, for instance, does BGP express policy? And what is the difference between a routing protocol that expresses policy versus one that "just" provides routing information? When should I use BGP, and when should I not? What are the most common policy mechanisms used in BGP, and how are they expressed? What do I do when everything falls apart?

These, and many other questions, are the questions we set out to answer in this book. So, while this is a book about BGP, it's actually a book about network design and deployment. We hope, through this book, you can learn from our experience in deploying BGP, both our failures and our successes, in all types of environments, from small enterprise networks to large-scale service providers. In *Practical BGP,* you will find help in deciding where to use BGP and where not to, as well as techniques for designing, deploying, managing, and troubleshooting BGP networks.

We hope you enjoy the fruit of our labors and experience (and not just for its ability to put you to sleep).

Russ White
Danny McPherson
Sangli Srihari

Acknowledgments

There are many folks we'd like to thank for helping us find our way to the completion of this book. We'd like to thank Mary Franz for seeing this project through to completion, and Yakov Rekhter, for writing the Foreword and providing valuable feedback on the content. We'd also like to thank Enke Chen, Sam Ntac, Kevin Dilio, Rob Thomas and our technical reviewers for their insightful review and comments. And, of course, we'd like to thank Srihari's wife—for always answering the phone!

We'd also like to thank all of the great folks at Addison-Wesley that were involved in this project, for their usual diligence, professionalism, guidance, and most of all, unending patience.

Finally, we'd like to thank our employers, Arbor Networks, Cisco Systems and Procket Networks, for affording us the opportunity to have and expend our spare cycles on this project.

Dedications

I wish to dedicate this book to my daughters, Kortney and Ashli, for being such a positive influence in my life, and making the world a more beautiful place. *—Danny McPherson*

I wish to dedicate this work to my parents, who are responsible for what I am today. "Amma and Daddy, I am so blessed to have you both as my parents." *—Srihari Sangli*

I would like to dedicate this book to my two daughters, Bekah and Hannah—"Daddy, are you done yet?" I would like to thank God for giving me the opportunities and abilities many times over to work in an interesting and compelling field, and to write books. *—Russ White*

1

The Border Gateway Protocol

When networks were small, there was no concept of interior and exterior gateway protocols; a network ran a routing protocol, and that was the end of it. The Internet, for instance, ran the *Hello Protocol* on devices called fuzzballs (before they were called routers), until some problems in the Hello Protocol led to the development of RIP (Routing Information Protocol). RIP was run as the only routing protocol on the Internet for many years. Over time, however, the Internet grew (and grew and grew), and it became apparent that something more was needed in routing protocols—a single ubiquitous protocol couldn't do all the work that routing protocols were being required to do and scale in any reasonable manner.

In January 1989 at the 12th IETF meeting in Austin, Texas, Yakov Rekhter and Kirk Lougheed sat down at a table and in a short time a new exterior gateway routing protocol was born, the Border Gateway Protocol (BGP). The initial BGP design was recorded on a napkin rumored to have been heavily spattered with ketchup. The design on the napkin was expanded to three hand-written sheets of paper from which the first interoperable BGP implementation was quickly developed. A photocopy of these three sheets of paper (see Foreword) now hangs on the wall of a routing protocol development area at Cisco Systems in Santa Clara, CA.

From this napkin came the basis for BGP as we know it today. Now, with countless contributors and hundreds of pages in tens of documents, deployed in thousands of networks, interdomain routing in the Internet today is defined as BGP.

This book is about BGP, from the basics of the BGP protocol itself to information on deploying BGP in networks stretching from small and simple to very large and extremely complex. We'll begin with an overview of the BGP protocol itself here in Chapter 1. We'll then move into various deployment situations, starting with small enterprise networks using BGP internally and to connect to the Internet. From there we'll continue to move through ever-larger scale deployments of BGP, discussing how BGP and its extensive policy mechanisms fit into network architectures. We continue by providing details about finely tuning BGP to perform optimally and scale effectively in an array of deployment scenarios. We finish with in-depth discussions on debugging and troubleshooting various problems within the protocol and BGP networks.

Exterior and Interior Gateway Protocols

In order to understand why BGP is designed the way it is, you first need to understand where it fits in the world of routing protocols. Routing protocols can be divided along several axes, the first being Interior Gateway Protocols (IGPs) versus Exterior Gateway Protocols (EGPs). The primary difference between EGPs and IGPs is the place in the network where they provide reachability information; that is, within an administrative routing domain (intradomain) or between administrative routing domains (interdomain).

Routing Domains

Exactly what a routing domain is depends primarily on the context. In Intermediate System to Intermediate System (IS-IS) terminology, for instance, a *routing domain* is the area in which topology information is flooded. Open Shortest Path First (OSPF) simply refers to this as an *area*. Within the context of BGP, however, a routing domain is *the set of routers under the same administrative control*. In other words, there are routers your company, school, division, and so on can administer, configure, and manage, and there are routers beyond your control. Those routers under your control are typically said to be within your routing domain; those outside your control are outside your routing domain.

This definition isn't as precise as it sounds, since a particular router may be within the control of an entity, but not under the control of everyone who works for that entity or is a part of that entity. For example, a limited set of people within an organization may be able to configure the router that connects that organization to the Internet, but that doesn't necessarily mean this router is in a separate routing domain from the rest of the routers in the organization.

Within the world of BGP, those routers under a single point of administrative control are referred to as an *autonomous system (AS)*. Exterior routing, then, concerns itself with providing routing information between routing domains, or autonomous system boundaries while interior routing concerns itself with providing routing information within a routing domain or autonomous system.

Why Not Use a Single Protocol for Both Internal and External Routing?

If all routing protocols provide the same information—reachability and path information—why not use a single routing protocol for both interior and exterior routing? The simple answer is that routing protocols may not just provide reachability information—they may also provide policy information. There are several reasons why protocols designed to route within an autonomous system don't carry policy information:

- Within an autonomous system (AS), policy propagation generally isn't important. Since all the routers contained within the routing domain are under a single administrative control, policies can be implemented on all the routers administratively (through manual configuration). As such, the routing protocol doesn't need to propagate this information.

- Speed of convergence is a very important factor for routing protocols within an autonomous system, while it is not as much of a factor as stability between autonomous systems. Routing protocols providing reachability information within an autonomous system need to be focused on one thing: providing accurate information about the topology of the network as quickly and efficiently as possible. Open Shortest Path First (OSPF), Intermediate System to Intermediate System (IS-IS), and Enhanced Interior Gateway Protocol (EIGRP) all provide this sort of routing, expressly designed for intradomain routing.

> Some policy propogation is creeping into interior gateway protocols in the form of information about the quality of service across various paths within a network; even here, the definitions of interior and exterior routing becomes blurred.

Why is it so important to split the routing information learned from within your domain from the routing information learned from outside your domain? There are many reasons—for instance, in order to scope propagation of changes made within a routing domain so they don't impact external routing domains, or perhaps to provide the capability to hide specific information about your network from external entities. The reasoning behind these and many other possible responses will become more obvious as we proceed through the book.

Preventing Changes in Other Routing Domains from Impacting Network Operation

Let's examine the network illustrated in Figure 1.1 and consider how changes in one routing domain could have a serious negative impact on the operation of another routing domain.

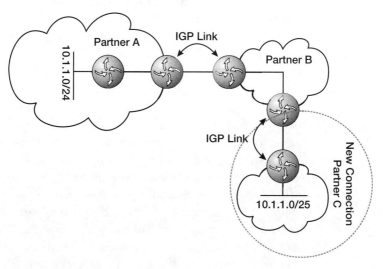

Figure 1.1
Unintentional consequences of bringing up a new link when sharing routing information.

In this network, the network administrators have decided to share routing information through an interior gateway protocol, including specific information about how to reach servers and hosts within each other's networks as needed. It's decided that 10.1.1.0/24 is one of the destinations that they need to share information about, so redistribution between the IGPs used in Partner A and Partner B's networks is set up to allow this information to leak between the two routing domains. In time, Partner B also partners with Partner C and again uses IGP redistribution to share information about reachable destinations between the two routing domains.

However, in this case, the routing information provided by Partner C into Partner B's routing domain, and thus leaked into Partner A's routing domain, overlaps (or conflicts) with the internal routing information in Partner A's routing domain. The result is that some destinations within Partner A's network will become unreachable to sources within Partner A's network—the actions of Partner B's network administrators have caused a fault in Partner A's network. This sort of problem is not only difficult to identify, it is also difficult to fix, since it will involve actions on the part of the network administrators from, possibly, all three routing domains.

Hiding Information about Your Network

The network illustrated in Figure 1.1 also uncovers another problem which can result when simple IGP redistribution is used to share information between autonomous systems; in this case, information about Partner C's internal network infrastructure is passed on to Partner A. If Partner A and Partner C are actually competitors, the information about Partner C's network could actually be used to compromise their competitive position. In general, it is always best to use policy-based rules to prevent information about your internal network from leaking beyond its intended bounds.

Policies between Domains

Examining the issues illustrated through Figure 1.1, it is apparent that some sort of policy implemented by Partner A, in the first case, and by Partner C, in the second case, would prevent the problems described. For instance, in the first case, a policy of not accepting routing information from outside the network that would interfere with internal routing information would resolve this problem, and all such future problems, without manually configuring a list of filters on a regular basis. In this example, simply filtering the routing information learned by Partner A from Partner B so that no prefixes with a prefix length longer than 24 bits be accepted would resolve this issue permanently if all the networks within Partner A's routing domain have a 24-bit length.

In the second case, if Partner C could somehow mark the routing information it is advertising to Partner B so that Partner B will not pass the information on to Partner A, this problem could also be resolved without resorting to manual lists maintained by Partner B. So two possible policies we would want to implement between routing domains would be to mark routes so they cannot (or should not) be advertised beyond the adjacent routing domain (Partner B) and to prevent leaking information that would provide a better route to internal networks than the internal routing information provides. What other sorts of policies would we want to implement through an Exterior Gateway Protocol (EGP)?

- Always take the closest exit point. If you want to allow traffic from other networks to traverse your network but you want to minimize the amount of bandwidth you need to provision in order to allow this, then you should be able to set up a policy of always taking the closest exit point out of your network, rather than the best path, toward the destination. This is typically referred to as *closest-exit* or *hot potato routing*.

- Take the closest exit point to the final customer. In some cases, in order to provide better service to customers who are reaching your network through another autonomous system, you want to be able to always choose the best, or shortest, path to the final destination rather than the shortest path out of your network. This is typically referred to as *best-exit routing*, though oddly it's sometimes also referred to as *cold potato routing*.

- Take the cheapest exit point. In some cases, you may have contracts requiring payment per a given amount of traffic sent on a particular link or set of links. If this is true, you may want to route traffic out of your autonomous system based on the cheapest exit point rather than the closest.

- Don't traverse certain networks. If you are running a network carrying secure or sensitive data, you might want to have some control over the physical forwarding path the traffic takes once it leaves your network. In reality, controlling the path your traffic takes is almost impossible, even with BGP, because IP packets are routed hop by hop, and thus anyone you send the packets to can decide to send them someplace you don't want them to go.

• Avoid accepting redundant or unstable routing information from other networks. In order to scope resource consumption within your network, you may want to impose policies that discard redundant routing information or suppress unstable route advertisement.

In some cases, combining two or more of these different policies may be required. For instance, you may want to take the closest cheap exit point, from you network, and not traverse certain other networks. These policy definitions are rather high level; they state goals rather than the implementation of goals. One of the more confusing aspects of deploying BGP is turning such goals into actual implemented policies within and at the borders of your network.

Distance Vector, Link State, and Path Vector

Routing protocols are effectively distributed database systems. They propagate information about the topology of the network among the routers within the network. Each router in the network then uses this distributed database to determine the best loop free path through the network to reach any given destination. There are two fundamental ways to distribute the data through a network:

• By distributing vectors, each router in the network advertises the destinations it can reach, along with information that can be used to determine the best path to each reachable destination. A router can determine the best vector (path) by examining the destinations reachable through each adjacent router or neighbor, combined with additional information, such as the metric, which indicates the desirability of that path. There are two types of vector-based protocols: distance vector and path vector.

• By distributing the state of the links attached to the routers, each router floods (or advertises to all other routers in the network, whether directly adjacent or not) the state of each link to which it is attached. This information is used independently by each router within the routing domain to build a tree representing a topology of the network (called a shortest path tree). Routing protocols that distribute the state of attached links are called link state algorithms.

Each of these data distribution methods is generally tied to a specific method of finding the best path to any given destination within the network. The following sections provide a quick overview (or review) of each of these types of routing protocols. Remember that a primary goal of routing protocol design is that routing protocols must be capable of determining loop free paths through the network. Generally, routing protocols assume that the best (or shortest) path through the network is also loop free.

Link State

Link state protocols, such as IS-IS and OSPF, rely on each router in the network to advertise the state of each of their links to every other router within the local routing domain. The result is a complete network topology map, called a shortest path tree, compiled by each router in the network. As a router receives an advertisement, it will store this information in a local database, typically referred to as the link state database, and pass the information on to each of its adjacent peers. This information is not processed or manipulated in any way before it is passed on to the router's adjacent peers. The link state information is *flooded* through the routing domain unchanged, just as the originating router advertises it.

As each router builds a complete database of the link state information as advertised by every other router within the network, it uses an algorithm, called the *shortest path first algorithm,* to build a tree with itself as the center of that tree. The shortest path to each reachable destination within the network is found by traversing the tree. The most common shortest path first algorithm is the Dijkstra algorithm.

Distance Vector

Routers running distance vector algorithms advertise the vector (path) and distance (metric) for each destination reachable within the network to adjacent (directly connected) peers. This information is placed in a local database as it is received, and some algorithm is used to determine which path is the best path to each reachable destination. Once the best path is determined, these best paths are advertised to each directly connected adjacent router.

Two common algorithms used for determining the best path are Bellman-Ford, which is used by the Routing Information Protocol (RIP and RIPv2), and the Diffusing Update Algorithm (DUAL), used by the Enhanced Interior Gateway Protocol (EIGRP).

Path Vector

A path vector protocol does not rely on the cost of reaching a given destination to determine whether each path available is loop free. Instead, path vector protocols rely on analysis of the path to reach the destination to learn if it is loop free. Figure 1.2 illustrates this concept.

A path vector protocol guarantees loop-free paths through the network by recording each hop the routing advertisement traverses through the network. In this case, router A advertises reachability to the 10.1.1.0/24 network to router B. When router B receives this information, it adds itself to the path and advertises it to router C. Router C adds itself to the path and advertises to router D that the 10.1.1.0/24 network is reachable in this direction.

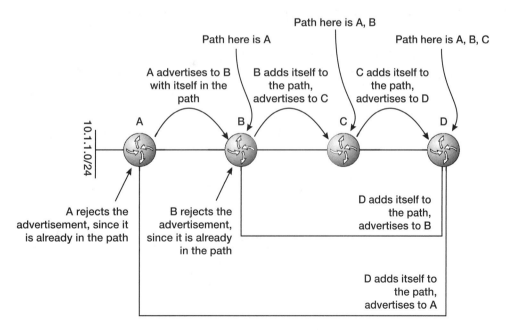

Figure 1.2
Simple illustration of path vector protocol operation.

Router D receives the route advertisement and adds itself to the path as well. However, when router D attempts to advertise that it can reach 10.1.1.0/24 to router A, router A will reject the advertisement since the associated path vector contained in the advertisement indicates that router A is already in the path. When router D attempts to advertise reachability for 10.1.1.0/24 to router B, router B also rejects it since router B is also already in the path. Anytime a router receives an advertisement in which it is already part of the path, the advertisement is rejected since accepting the path would effectively result in a routing information loop.

BGP Path Vector Implementation

BGP implements the path vector concept on a larger scale rather than treating a single router as a single point in the path to any given destination. BGP treats each autonomous system as a single point on the path to any given destination (Figure 1.3).

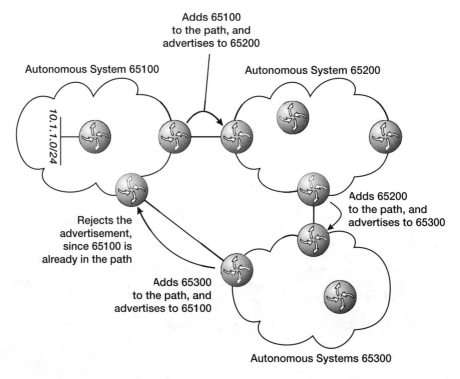

Figure 1.3
Path vector over a set of autonomous systems.

This case is identical to the case in Figure 1.2, except that each autonomous system is considered a point along the path rather than a single router. The network 10.1.1.0/24, typically referred to as a *prefix,* is advertised with the list of autonomous systems the update has passed through; this list of autonomous systems is called the *AS Path.* AS 65100 originates the prefix 10.1.1.0/24, adding itself to the AS Path and advertises it to AS 65200. AS 65200 adds itself to the AS Path, and advertises the prefix to 65300. When AS 65300 advertises the prefix 10.1.1.0/24 to AS 65100, the prefix will be rejected since the 65100 sees that its local AS is already included in the AS Path, and accepting the route would result in a routing information loop.

The primary reason BGP treats an entire autonomous system as a single hop in the AS Path is to hide topological details of the AS. AS 65200, for instance, cannot tell what the path through AS 65100 looks like, only that the destination is reachable through AS 65100. One interesting side effect of treating each autonomous system as a single entity with which the autonomous system path vector is associated is that without additional information or rules, BGP can only detect loops between autonomous systems: it cannot guarantee loop-free paths inside an AS (Figure 1.4).

Since every router within AS 65200 receives the prefix 10.1.1.0/24 with the same AS Path, and BGP relies on the AS Path to prevent loops from forming, it is obvious that BGP cannot provide loop-free routing within an AS. As a result, BGP must ensure that every router in the AS

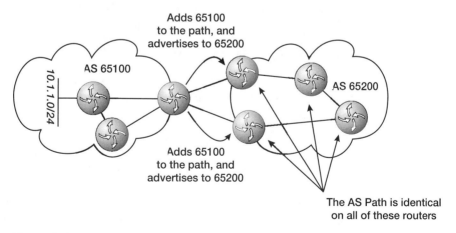

Figure 1.4
BGP routing within an AS.

makes the same decision as to which exit point to use when forwarding packets to a given destination and that a constrained set of route advertisement rules is used within the autonomous system. BGP then allows the interior gateway protocol running within the AS to determine the best path to each of the AS exit points.

BGP Peering

What are the mechanics of one BGP speaker peering with another speaker? What substrate protocols does BGP use to transport routing information? This section describes various aspects of BGP peering.

> While BGP is most often run on routers, which are also responsible for forwarding traffic, in some cases other devices may run BGP as well, whether to simply gather information about the routing tables being carried in BGP or to carry routing information between routers. Since this is the case, we will sometimes refer to *devices that are running BGP* rather than *routers* specifically. A device that is running BGP is called a *BGP speaker,* and two BGP speakers that form a BGP connection for the purpose of exchanging routing information are called BGP *peers* or *neighbors.*

BGP Transport

How does BGP carry information about reachable destinations between the devices (routers) running BGP? How is the information encoded when it's transported between peers?

Transporting Data between Peers

A Transmission Control Protocol (TCP) transport connection is set up between a pair of BGP speakers at the beginning of the peering session and is maintained throughout the peering session. Using TCP to transport BGP information allows BGP to delegate error control, reliable transport, sequencing, retransmission, and peer aliveness issues to TCP itself and focus instead on properly processing the routing information exchanged with its peers.

When a BGP speaker first initializes, it uses a local ephemeral TCP port, or random port number greater than 1024, and attempts to contact each configured BGP speaker on TCP port 179 (the well-known

BGP port). The speaker initiating the session performs an active open, while the peer performs a passive open. It's possible for two speakers to attempt to connect to one another at the same time; this is known as a *connection collision.* When two speakers collide, each speaker compares the local *router ID* to the router ID of the colliding neighbor. The BGP speaker with the higher router ID value drops the session on which it is passive, and the BGP speaker with the lower router ID value drops the session on which it is active (i.e., only the session initiated by the BGP speaker with the larger router ID value is preserved).

BGP Routes and Formatting Data

A BGP route is defined as a unit of information that pairs a set of destinations with the attributes of a path to those destinations. The set of destinations is referred to, by BGP, as the Network Layer Reachability Information (NLRI) and is a set of systems whose IP addresses are represented by one IP prefix.

BGP uses *update messages* to advertise new routing information, withdraw previously advertised routes, or both. New routing information includes a set a BGP attributes and one or more prefixes with which those attributes are associated. While multiple routes with a common set of attributes can be advertised in a single BGP update message, new routes with different attributes must be advertised in separate update messages.

There are two mechanisms to withdraw routing information in BGP: To withdraw routes explicitly, one or more prefixes that are no longer reachable (unfeasible) are included in the withdrawn routes field of an update message (the update message may contain one or more new routes as well). No additional information, such as associated path attributes (e.g., AS Path), is necessary for the routes being withdrawn. Alternatively, because a BGP speaker only advertises a single best route for each reachable destination, a BGP update message that contains a prefix that has already been advertised by the peer, but with a new set of path attributes, serves an implicit withdraw for earlier advertisements of that prefix.

A BGP update message is made up of a series of *type-length vectors* (TLVs). Attributes carried within the BGP message provide information about one or more prefixes that follow; attributes are described in the BGP Attributes section later in this chapter.

BGP data, as it's transported between peers, is formatted as shown in Figure 1.5.

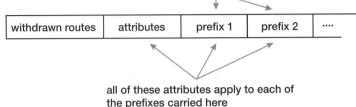

these are called network layer reachability
information (NLRI) in the BGP drafts, and
prefixes by common usage

all of these attributes apply to each of
the prefixes carried here

Figure 1.5
Encoding information in a BGP packet.

As previously noted, one interesting aspect of this packet format is
that while only a single set of attributes may be carried in each update
message, many prefixes sharing that common set of attributes may be
carried in a single update. This leads to the concept of *update packing,*
which simply means placing two or more prefixes with the same attributes in a single BGP update message.

Interior and Exterior Peering

Beyond the mechanics of building peering relationships and transporting data between two BGP speakers, there are two types of peering relationships within BGP: *interior peering* and *exterior peering.* BGP sessions
between peers within a single autonomous system are referred to as *interior BGP,* or iBGP, sessions, while BGP running between peers in different autonomous system are referred to as *exterior BGP,* or eBGP,
sessions.

There are four primary differences between iBGP and eBGP peering relationships:

- Routes learned from an iBGP peer are not (normally) advertised
  to other iBGP peers. This prevents routing loops within the autonomous system, as discussed in the previous section titled
  BGP Path Vector Implementation.
- The attributes of paths learned from iBGP peers are not (normally)
  changed to impact the path selected to reach some outside network. The best path chosen throughout the autonomous system
  must be consistent to prevent routing loops within the network.

- The AS Path is not manipulated when advertising a route to an iBGP peer; the local AS is added to the AS Path only when advertising a route to an eBGP peer.
- The BGP next hop is normally not changed when advertising a route to an iBGP peer; it is always changed to the local peer termination IP address when a route is being advertised to an eBGP peer.

These last two points–the BGP next hop is normally changed when advertising a route to an eBGP peer while it is left unchanged when advertising a route to an iBGP peer, and the addition of the local autonomous system in the AS Path are illustrated using Figure 1.6.

In Figure 1.6, the 10.1.1.0/24 prefix originates on router A with an empty AS Path list and a BGP next hop of router A. Router A then advertises this prefix to router B. Router B, when advertising the route to router C, adds AS65100 to the AS Path list and sets the BGP next hop to 10.1.3.1, because router C is an exterior peer (a peer outside the autonomous system). Router C then advertises the 10.1.1.0/24 prefix to router D without changing the AS Path or the BGP next hop, since

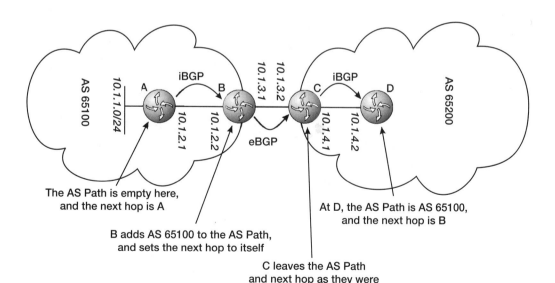

Figure 1.6
eBGP and iBGP peering.

router D is an interior peer (a peer within the same autonomous system). Router D will need a path to router B in order to consider this prefix reachable; generally, the BGP next hop reachability information is provided by advertising the link between B and C through an interior gateway protocol, or through iBGP, originating the link as a prefix from C into AS65100.

All BGP peers are connected over a TCP transport session. As such, IP reachability must exist before a pair of BGP speakers can peer with one another. For iBGP sessions, reachability between speakers typically is provided using an interior gateway protocol. EBGP peers are normally directly connected over a single hop (across a single link), with no intervening routers, and therefore require no additional underlying routing information. There are mechanisms for connecting eBGP peers across multiple hops; these are covered in more detail in Multipath section of Chapter 7.

Converting an understanding of BGP into practical, running configurations isn't always as easy at it seems, so we will often provide sample configurations for networks used as examples. These examples will be shown using Cisco IOS Software as the operating system. For the network in Figure 1.5, the following configurations, along with some explanation of the various parts of the configuration, are provided.

```
!
hostname router-a
!
router BGP 65100
! enables the BGP process and defines the local AS number
 network 10.1.1.0 mask 255.255.255.0
 ! the above line causes router-a to originate the 10.1.1.0/24
 ! prefix in BGP
 neighbor 10.1.2.2 remote-as 65100
 ! configures an iBGP session with router-b


!
hostname router-b
!
router bgp 65100
  ! The number following the router bgp command above is
  ! the local autonomous system number
 neighbor 10.1.2.1 remote-as 65100
 ! configures an iBGP session with router-a
```

```
neighbor 10.1.3.2 remote-as 65200
! configures an eBGP session with router-c; note the AS
! number in this command does not match the AS number of
! the local router

!
hostname router-c
!
router bgp 65200
 neighbor 10.1.3.1 remote-as 65100
 ! configures an eBGP session with router-b; note the AS
 ! number in this command does not match the AS number of
 ! the local router
 neighbor 10.1.4.2 remote-as 65200
 ! configures an iBGP session with router-d
 network 10.1.3.0 mask 255.255.255.0
 ! configures this router to advertise the 10.1.3.0/24
 ! prefix to router-d, so router-d will be able to reach the
 ! BGP nexthop towards 10.1.1.0/24; reachability could also
 ! be provided through an interior gateway protocol or static
 ! routing

!
hostname router-d
!
router bgp 65200
 neighbor 10.1.4.1 remote-as 65200
 ! configures an iBGP session with router-c
```

With these configurations in place, router D should learn the 10.1.1.0/24 prefix from router C, and install it as a reachable destination within its routing table.

BGP Notifications

Throughout the duration of a BGP session between two BGP speakers, it's possible that one of the two peers will send some data in error or send malformed data or data the other speaker doesn't understand. The easiest remedy in any of these situations is simply to shut down the BGP session, but a simple session shutdown doesn't provide any diagnostic information to the speaker that transmitted the information that triggered the peering session to shut down, and therefore no corrective

action can be taken. To provide the information needed to take corrective action, BGP includes *Notifications,* which should be sent by the
BGP speaker closing the session.

Notifications consist of three parts:

- A notification code
- A notification subcode
- A variable-length data field

The Notification code indicates what type of error occurred:

- An error occurred in a message header, error code 1.
- An error occurred in the Open message, error code 2.
- An error occurred in an Update message, error code 3.
- The hold timer expired, error code 4.
- An error occurred in the finite state machine, error code 5.
- Cease, error code 6.

The subcode provides more information about the error—for instance, where in the Open message the error was. The BGP speaker
transmitting the Notification can fill in the data field with information
such as the actual part of the Open message causing the error. While
the data field is variable in length, there is no length field in the Notification code format. This is because the length of the data field is im-
plied by the length of the complete message.

Message Header Errors

Message header errors generally indicate problems in the packet format. Since TCP is a reliable transport service, message header errors
should be very rare, although it is possible for an implementation of
BGP to malform a packet, causing this type of error. Three subcodes
are defined in the base BGP specification:

- Connection not synchronized
- Bad message length
- Bad message type

Open Message Errors

Notifications transmitted while two BGP peers are opening a session are generally the result of misconfiguration rather than packet-level errors or problems in a BGP implementation.

- Unsupported version number, which means the BGP peer has transmitted a BGP version this speaker does not support.
- Bad peer autonomous system; the peer has claimed an autonomous system number that isn't valid.
- Bad BGP Identifier; the peer has transmitted a BGP router ID that is invalid.
- Unsupported optional parameter; the peer has indicated it wants to use some optional parameter the receiver doesn't support.
- Authentication failure; the peer is sending packets that are encrypted or authenticated in some way, but the authentication check is failing.
- Unacceptable hold time.

Update Message Errors

As BGP peers exchange updates, a number of errors can occur that make it impossible for one speaker to process an update transmitted by the other speaker:

- Malformed attribute list; the list of attributes included in the update packet has some error that makes it unreadable by the receiver.
- Unrecognized well-known attribute; the sender is including an attribute the receiver must be able to process but does not recognize.
- Missing well-known attribute; the sender is not including a required well-known attribute.
- Attribute flags error; the flags included with an attribute are not formed correctly (generally flags carry various options that apply to the attribute).
- Attribute length error; an attribute is either too long or too short.

- Invalid Origin; the origin code attribute is set to an invalid value.
- Invalid Next Hop; the Next Hop attribute is set to an invalid value.
- Optional attribute error; an optional attribute is malformed.
- Invalid network field; a prefix included in the update is invalid.
- Malformed AS Path; the AS Path included in the update is invalid.

Cease

The Cease code indicates to the receiver that the peer for some reason has chosen to close the BGP connection. The Cease Notification is not sent if a fatal error occurs, but rather it provides a graceful mechanism to shut down a BGP connection.

BGP Capabilities

There are various extensions to BGP that, to function correctly, require support of both BGP speakers in a session. How does a BGP speaker know when another BGP speaker it's peering with supports these extensions to BGP? Through BGP capabilities, which are negotiated when a BGP session is started.

> The ability for one BGP speaker to advertise capabilities to a peer BGP speaker is described in RFC3392, Capabilities Advertisement with BGP-4. *draft-ietf-idr-dynamic-cap* describes a way in which these capabilities can be advertised dynamically not only on session startup but after a session is established.

When first initiating a session, a BGP speaker sends an Open message describing various parameters, including a set of *capability codes*, one for each optional capability it supports. Capability codes are defined for things such as

- Route refresh, capability code 0 and 2
- Multiprotocol extensions, capability code 1

- Cooperative route filtering, capability code 3
- Dynamic capability exchange, capability code 6
- Graceful restart, capability code 64
- Four octet autonomous system numbers

The applicability and value of these and other BGP capabilities and extensions will be discussed in later sections.

If a BGP speaker receives a capability code it does not support when enabling a peering with another BGP speaker, it will send a Notification message to its peer, which shuts down the session, with a notification subcode indicating that the peer requested a capability the local BGP speaker doesn't support. The receiving peer can either break off communications on receipt of a notification code indicating an unsupported capability, or it can attempt to peer again without that capability enabled.

The BGP Peering Process

There are a lot of elements to the BGP peering process; when a BGP speaker begins a session with a new peer, it must determine if it is peering with an external neighbor or an internal neighbor, it must negotiate capabilities, and it must do a number of other things. The BGP session state machine in Figure 1.7 illustrates the process in an attempt to bring all these different actions together in one place.

BGP Attributes

BGP attributes are a confusing array of information carried in a BGP update capable of indicating anything from path preference to various additional pieces of information about a route, either within an autonomous system or outside an autonomous system. There are four basic types of attributes:

- **Well-known mandatory attributes**; these attributes must be recognized by all BGP speakers and must be included in all update messages. Almost all of the attributes impacting the path decision process, described in the next section, are well-known mandatory attributes.

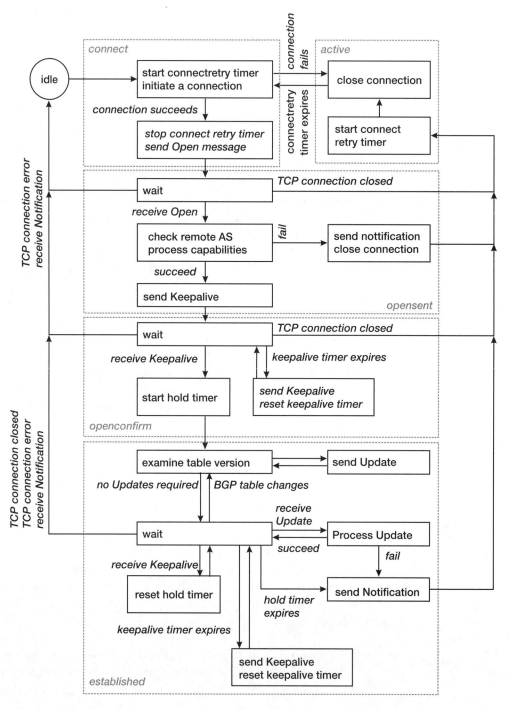

Figure 1.7
The BGP peering state machine.

- **Well-known discretionary attributes**; these attributes must be recognized by all BGP speakers and may be carried in updates but are not required in every update.
- **Optional transitive attributes**; these attributes may be recognized by some BGP speakers, but not all. They should be preserved and advertised to all peers whether or not they are recognized.
- **Optional nontransitive attributes**; these attributes may be recognized by some BGP speakers, but not all. If an update containing an optional transitive attribute is received, the update should be advertised to peers without the unrecognized attributes.

Figure 1.8 illustrates the way in which attributes are included in a BGP update message.

There are several other attributes not shown in Figure 1.8 but included in BGP, such as Communities and Extended Communities.

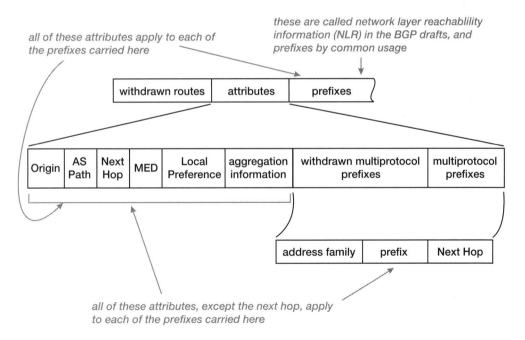

Figure 1.8
Carrying attributes within a BGP update.

Origin Code

The ORIGIN is a well-known mandatory attribute that indicates the origin of the prefix or, rather, the way in which the prefix was injected into BGP. There are three origin codes, listed in order of preference:

- IGP, meaning the prefix was originated from information learned from an interior gateway protocol
- EGP, meaning the prefix originated from the EGP protocol, which BGP replaced
- INCOMPLETE, meaning the prefix originated from some unknown source

The following configurations illustrate two of these origin codes using Cisco IOS Software.

```
!
hostname router-a
!
....
!
interface Ethernet1/0
 ip address 10.1.12.4 255.255.255.0
!
....
!
interface Serial3/0
 ip address 10.0.7.4 255.255.255.0
!
....
!
router bgp 65500
 no synchronization
 bgp log-neighbor-changes
 network 10.0.10.0
 redistribute static metric 10
 neighbor 10.0.7.10 remote-as 65501
 no auto-summary
!
ip classless
ip route 10.7.7.0 255.255.255.0 10.1.12.1
```

```
!
hostname router-b
!
....
!
interface Serial0/0
 ip address 10.0.7.10 255.255.255.0
!
....
!
router bgp 65501
 no synchronization
 bgp log-neighbor-changes
 neighbor 10.0.7.4 remote-as 65500
 no auto-summary
!

router-b#sho ip bgp
BGP table version is 3, local router ID is 10.0.16.10
Status codes: s suppressed, d damped, h history, * valid, > best,
i -internal, r RIB-failure
Origin codes: i - IGP, e - EGP, ? - incomplete

   Network          Next Hop        Metric  LocPrf Weight Path
*> 10.7.7.0/24      10.0.7.4            10        0  65500 ?
*> 10.0.10.0        10.0.7.4             0        0  65500 I
```

An Origin code of IGP typically suggests that the route was cleanly derived inside the originating AS. An Origin code of EGP suggests that the route was learned via the EGP protocol. Origin codes of Incomplete typically result from aggregation, redistribution, or other indirect ways of installing routes into BGP within the originating AS.

AS Path

The AS_PATH is a well-known mandatory attribute, and as described in the section BGP Path Vector Implementation earlier in this chapter, is the list of all autonomous systems the prefixes contained in this update have passed through. The local autonomous system number is added by a BGP speaker when advertising a prefix to an eBGP peer.

Next Hop

The BGP NEXT_HOP is a well-known mandatory attribute. As described in the section Interior and Exterior Peering earlier in this chapter, the Next Hop attribute is set when a BGP speaker advertises a prefix to a BGP speaker outside its local autonomous system (it may also be set when advertising routes within an AS; this will be discussed in later sections). The Next Hop attribute may also serve as a way to direct traffic to another speaker, rather than the speaker advertising the route itself, as Figure 1.9 illustrates.

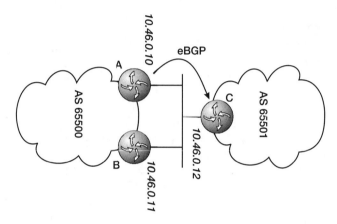

Figure 1.9
BGP third party Next Hop.

The following configurations from a router running Cisco IOS Software illustrate Router C using B as the BGP next hop for destinations in AS65500, even though Router C is learning these routes directly from A.

```
!
hostname router-a
!
....
!
interface FastEthernet0/1
 ip address 10.46.0.10 255.255.255.0
 duplex auto
 speed auto
!
....

!
```

```
router bgp 65500
 no synchronization
 bgp log-neighbor-changes
 network 10.46.12.0
 neighbor 10.46.0.12 remote-as 65501
 neighbor 10.46.0.12 route-map setnexthop out
 no auto-summary
!
....
!
access-list 10 permit 10.46.12.0
!
route-map setnexthop permit 10
 match ip address 10
 set ip next-hop 10.46.0.11
!

!
hostname router-b
!
....
!
interface FastEthernet0/1
 ip address 10.46.0.12 255.255.255.0
 duplex auto
 speed auto
!
....

!
router bgp 65501
 no synchronization
 bgp log-neighbor-changes
 neighbor 10.46.0.10 remote-as 65500
 no auto-summary
!

router-b#show ip bgp
BGP table version is 2, local router ID is 208.0.14.12
Status codes: s suppressed, d damped, h history, * valid, > best, i -
internal, r RIB-failure
Origin codes: i - IGP, e - EGP, ? - incomplete

   Network          Next Hop           Metric LocPrf Weight Path
*> 10.46.12.0       208.0.0.11              0           0 65500
```

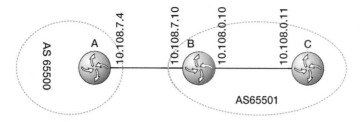

Figure 1.10
Setting the Next Hop to Self in iBGP.

Most BGP implementations deployed today also allow the network administrator to set the BGP next hop when advertising a route between iBGP peers; Figure 1.10, and the following configuration from a router running Cisco IOS Software, illustrates this fact.

```
!
hostname router-a
!
....
!
interface Serial3/0
 ip address 10.108.7.4 255.255.255.0
!
....
!
router bgp 65500
 no synchronization
 bgp log-neighbor-changes
 network 10.108.12.0 mask 255.255.255.0
 neighbor 10.108.7.10 remote-as 65501
 no auto-summary
!

!
hostname router-b
!
....
!
interface Serial0/0
 ip address 10.108.7.10 255.255.255.0
```

```
!
....
!
interface FastEthernet0/1
 ip address 10.108.0.10 255.255.255.0
 duplex auto
 speed auto
!
....
!
router bgp 65501
 no synchronization
 bgp log-neighbor-changes
 neighbor 10.108.0.11 remote-as 65501
 neighbor 10.108.0.11 next-hop-self
 neighbor 10.108.7.4 remote-as 65500
 no auto-summary
!

router-b#show ip bgp
BGP table version is 2, local router ID is 10.108.16.10
Status codes: s suppressed, d damped, h history, * valid, > best,
              i - internal, r RIB-failure
Origin codes: i - IGP, e - EGP, ? - incomplete

   Network          Next Hop          Metric LocPrf Weight Path
*> 10.108.12.0/24   10.108.7.4             0             0 65500 i

!
hostname router-c
!
....
!
interface FastEthernet0/1
 ip address 10.108.0.11 255.255.255.0
 duplex auto
 speed auto
!
....
!
router bgp 65501
 no synchronization
```

```
bgp log-neighbor-changes
neighbor 10.108.0.10 remote-as 65501
no auto-summary
!

router-c#show ip bgp
BGP table version is 2, local router ID is 10.108.13.11
Status codes: s suppressed, d damped, h history, * valid, > best,
              i - internal, r RIB-failure
Origin codes: i - IGP, e - EGP, ? - incomplete

    Network          Next Hop            Metric LocPrf Weight Path
*>i10.108.12.0/24    10.108.0.10              0    100      0 65500 i
```

The reason why a network administrator would want to do this is discussed in later sections.

Multiple Exit Discriminator (MED)

The MUTLI_EXIT_DISC (MED) is an optional nontransitive attribute that provides a mechanism for the network administrator to convey to adjacent autonomous systems to optimal entry point in the local AS; Figure 1.11 illustrates this concept.

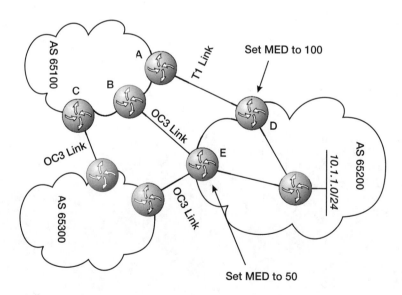

Figure 1.11
The Multiple Exit Discriminator.

Here, AS 65200 is setting the MED on its T1 exit point to 100 and the MED on its OC3 exit point to 50, with the intended result that the OC3 connection be preferred. However, the problem with using the MED in this way becomes apparent with this simple example. First, AS 65100 will receive three paths to 10.1.1.0/24, one through AS 65300 and two through AS 65200. The MED of the path through AS 65100 and the paths through AS 65200 will not be compared since their AS Path is not the same. If AS 65100 has set its BGP local preferences on router A, B, and C, to favor the path through AS 65300, then the MED from AS 65200 will have no impact as MED is considered after local preference in the BGP decision algorithm.

MEDs received from different autonomous systems are not compared as a default behavior, though many implementations provide a mechanism to enable comparing of MEDs between different autonomous systems. Benefits and offshoots of using MEDs and comparing them between different AS Paths will be discussed in later sections.

If the path through AS 65300 did not exist, or was not preferred over the path through AS 65200 for some other reason, the MEDs advertised by routers D and E might have some impact on the best path decision made by AS 65100. However, if AS 65100 sets some BGP metric with a higher degree of preference in the decision algorithm, such as the local preference, to prefer one path over the other, the MED would never be considered.

Local Preference

The LOCAL_PREF attribute is a well-known attribute that represents the network operator's degree of preference for a route within the entire AS. The larger the value of the local preference, the more preferable the route is; Figure 1.12 illustrates.

AS 65100 is receiving two possible paths to the 10.1.1.0/24 network, one of which is received through AS 65200 and the other of which is received through AS 65300. Although the path through AS 65200 is shorter—one AS hop rather than two—AS 65100's network administrator would prefer to send traffic destined to this prefix along the high-speed outbound OC3 connection rather than along the outbound T1. Setting the local preference on this prefix as it is received on router

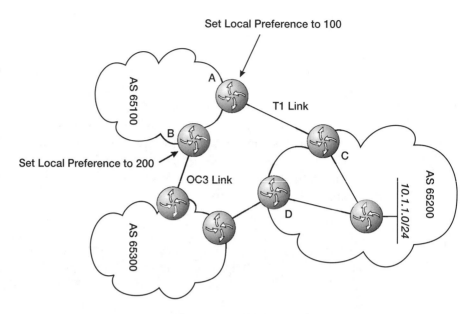

Figure 1.12
Local Preference.

A to 100, and on router B to 200, causes all of the BGP speakers within AS 65100 to prefer the path through B, thus preferring the higher-speed link.

Communities

The COMMUNITIES attribute is an optional transitive attribute. Communities are, effectively, tags that can carry almost any information about a route within or between autonomous systems. Communities are used to group routes sharing common characteristics that cannot be described using the other attributes. Communities generally are not directly used to determine policy or the best path to a destination. That is, while a community itself does not influence the BGP route selection algorithm, communities are typically used to trigger underlying policies that take effect based on the value of the associated community (e.g., communities can be used to match and modify one or more of the BGP attributes that do impact the results of the best path selection algorithm).

Several communities are defined as well-known, or global, communities, which should be recognized by all BGP implementations:

- The NO_EXPORT community, which states that the group of routes marked with this community should not be advertised outside of the local autonomous system.
- The NO_ADVERTISE community, which states the group of routes marked with this community should not be advertised to any BGP peer of the speaker that receives it.
- The NO_EXPORT_SUBCONFED community, which states the group of routes marked with this community should not be advertised outside a single autonomous system, even if that autonomous system is a part of a confederation of autonomous systems.

Communities are 32 bits (4 octets) long, with the following standards for using the community space:

- The communities numbered 0x00000000 through 0x0000FFFF and 0xFFFF0000 through 0xFFFFFFFF are reserved for future assignment of well-known communities.
- The recommended encoding for all other communities is the two-octet autonomous system number of the AS that attached the community to the route in the first two octets of the community number. The remaining two octets can be assigned based on policies internal to the AS.

RFC1997, BGP Communities Attribute, describes communities within BGP. RFC1998, An Application of the BGP Community Attribute in Multi-Home Routing, describes the use of the NO_EXPORT community in dual-homed environments, and the section Conditional Communities in Chapter 7 describes an extension of RFC1998.

Extended Communities

BGP extended communities, as their name implies, are an extension to BGP communities. The primary differences between communities and extended communities are as follows:

- Extended communities are 64 bits, or 8 octets, in length.
- The extended community number space is more structured than the standard community address space, as described next.

Figure 1.13 illustrates the extended community layout.

If the I bit is clear (0), the community type was assigned on a "first come, first served" basis through the Internet Assigned Numbers Authority (IANA). If the I bit is set (1), the community type is either experimental or was assigned through IETF consensus. If the type code indicates that a subtype (or low type) is included, the data field is 6 octets in length. If the type code indicates that a subtype is not included, the data field is 7 octets in length.

Extended communities defined in various drafts include the following:

- Autonomous System Specific (two octet), type 0x0 (or 0x4), which allows the local network administrator to carry communities specific to their autonomous system by setting the subtype to a value indicating the type of information being carried, the first two octets of the data portion to their autonomous system number, and the remaining four octets to the data carried.
- Autonomous System Specific (four octet), type 0x02 (or 0x42); this extended community is similar to the AS Specific extended community, except it allows four octets from the data field for the autonomous system number and two octets for the data carried.
- IPv4 Address Specific Type, type 0x01 or 0x41, which allows the owner of an IPv4 address block to encode some information in an extended community pertinent to this address space. The

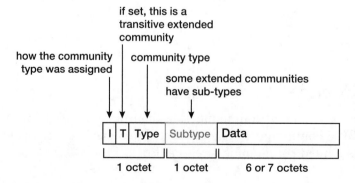

Figure 1.13
The extended community layout.

subtype field is set by the originator to indicate the type of information carried, the first four octets of the data field are set to the IPv4 address, and the last two octets of the data field are set to the pertinent information.

- Opaque, type 0x03 or 0x43, allows opaque data to be carried within an extended community. The subtype field is set to a value set according to consensus within the IETF or other Internet Addressing and Number Authority (IANA) rules.
- Route Target, which is a subtype of either the two octet AS specific, four octet AS specific, or IPv4 specific types, with the subtype set to 0x02. This extended community is described in further detail in Chapter 10, Deploying BGP/MPLS Layer-3 VPNs.
- Route Origin, which is a subtype of either the two octet AS specific, four octet AS specific, or IPv4 specific types, with the subtype set to 0x03. This extended community is described in further detail in Chapter 10, Deploying BGP/MPLS Layer-3 VPNs.
- Link Bandwidth, which is a subtype of the two octet AS specific type, with a subtype of 0x4. This community is described in more detail in Chapter 7, New Features in BGP.

BGP extended communities are described in the Internet Draft document, draft-ietf-idr-bgp-ext-communities, *BGP Extended Communities Attribute*, which should be progressed to RFC status sometime in the near future.

Multiprotocol Addresses

The original BGP packet format was formatted around IPv4 addresses, which are 4 octets in length. In order to carry new types of addresses, such as IPv6, MPLS Labels, VPN information, CLNS addresses, and others, special address family attributes were created to carry these address types. Each type of address is identified using an *Address Family Identifier* (AFI), and a *Subsequent Address Family Identifier* (SAFI). The ability of BGP to carry multiple address types is used in carrying MPLS VPN information, as described in Chapter 10, Deploying BGP/MPLS Layer-3 VPNs. This capability is also used to carry CLNS and IPv6 address, as described in the section Multiprotocol BGP, below.

> The ability to carry multiple address types and other information pertaining to virtual private networks, is outlined in the IETF Internet Draft draft-ietf-idr-rfc2858bis, which is currently in draft state and specifies an update and intended to oboselete RFC 2858.

Attributes and Aggregation

Aggregation, or summarization, not only hides reachability information, it also hides topology information. In BGP, this means hiding the AS Path and other attributes of the prefixes aggregated.

Aggregation and the AS Path

Figure 1.14 illustrates the interaction between the AS Path and aggregation.

In this network, routers C and D are advertising 10.1.2.0/24 and 10.1.3.0/24, respectively, to router B, which is in another autonomous system. Router B is aggregating these two advertisements toward router A, advertising the single prefix 10.1.2.0/23. But how does router B build the AS Path in the route it advertises to router A?

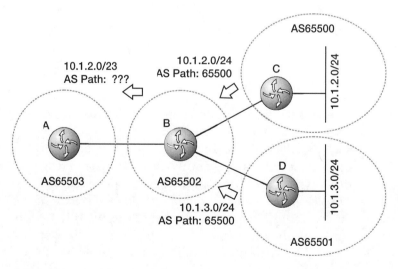

Figure 1.14
Aggregation's impact on route attributes.

It can't act as though AS65500 and AS65501 don't exist, since that would break the inherent loop detection qualities of the AS Path, and it would also break any policies based on the AS Path containing AS65500 or AS65501 in AS65503 (or downstream). It can't include both of these autonomous systems in the AS Path sequentially, since that would imply that the path to reach either of these networks passes through both of these autonomous systems.

The solution to this problem is to include both of the originating autonomous systems as an *AS Set*. An AS Set includes a set of autonomous systems possibly included in the path to a given advertised route, in no particular order. When advertising this aggregate, then router B would advertise (65502 {65500, 65501}) in the AS Path, grouping AS65501 and AS65500 into an AS Set, and prepending the local AS number, AS65500.

The Atomic Aggregate

Suppose we change the network slightly, so it now looks like the network in Figure 1.15.

Suppose router B is now receiving both 10.1.2.0/23 and 10.1.3.0/24; note that these two prefixes overlap. Router B only wants to advertise 10.1.2.0/23 toward A. Since it already has this prefix in its

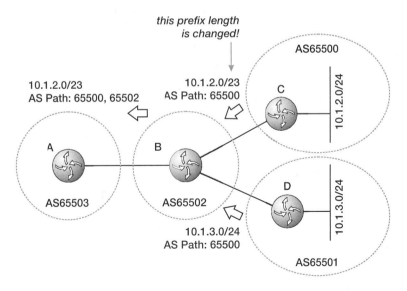

Figure 1.15
The Atomic Aggregate bit.

table, it can simply advertise the prefix as it was received from
AS65500. But this leaves out the information that part of this prefix,
10.1.3.0/24, is actually reachable in AS65501; in fact, AS65501 doesn't
appear in the AS Path of the advertisement to router A.

In this case, router B should include the *Atomic Aggregate* attribute in
the advertisement. This tells router A that while the AS Path, as presented, is loop free, there is some longer prefix length component within
this prefix reachable through an autonomous system not listed in the AS
Path. The Atomic Aggregate is a well-known discretionary attribute.

BGP's Best Path Algorithm

Interior Gateway Protocol Cost

BGP can also take into consideration the cost of reaching the exit point
from within the autonomous system (Figure 1.16).

At router C, the two paths advertised from AS 65200, and passed
via iBGP through routers A and D, look the same. From C's perspective, the cost of transmitting the packet from the exit point to the final
destination is the same, so it only makes sense to take the shortest path
to the exit point from the AS. The easiest way to determine the shortest
path to the exit point of the AS is to use interior gateway protocol metrics to compare the paths.

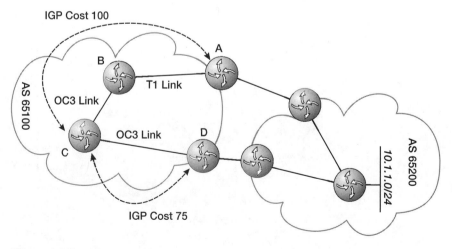

Figure 1.16
Interior Gateway Protocol cost in BGP metrics.

The IGP metric check assumes that the same IGP is running throughout the AS; if several different IGPs are running within the same AS, their metrics are not comparable, and the results of this check can actually produce suboptimal routing to the edge of the AS.

IGP metric allocation values are typically derived from a number of factors. For example, the number of "route miles" or "propagation delay" a particular connection uses may be factored. Other factors could include the available capacity of a link (e.g., a 1000-Mbps gigabit Ethernet connection would be 10 times more preferable than a 100-Mbps Fast Ethernet connection), or perhaps some multiple is used to reflect the reliability of the Physical Layer medium. The method used to derive IGP metrics varies widely among network operators and is influenced by many other factors as well (e.g., the available metric allocation range provided by the interior gateway protocol being used).

BGP Identifier

The BGP Identifier is a four-octet value exchanged with BGP peers in the Open message. The value of the BGP Identifier is determined on startup and is the same for all peers of the BGP speaker. If the value of the BGP Identifier changes all the BGP sessions must be reset and must be reinitiated using the new value. As such, the local BGP Identifier value is typically derived from an IP address associated with a loopback or other similar virtual system interface, so as to avoid potential instability introduced by interface or other hardware failures. Note that it is not a requirement that the value be derived from an active IP address on the local system, or that if it was, the address must remain active. However, the value must be unique within the routing system and not deriving the BGP Identifier value from an active system IP address may introduce conflicts. Typically, implementations first attempt to get the value from a virtual interface, though the value is often determined by using a value of the lowest IP address configured on any active interface on the BGP speaker.

The BGP Identifier is often referred to simply as router ID. The router ID of the advertising router is generally considered the "tie breaker" in the BGP bestpath algorithm; if multiple paths are identical in cost, using the router ID to break the tie allows the routing decision to be made deterministically throughout the autonomous system (hence the requirement for uniqueness of the value). If two paths have the same preferences throughout all of the other steps, the path through the advertising router with the lowest router ID will be considered the best path, installed in the local routing table, and advertised to peers.

Weight

Most implementations of BGP provide a mechanism that allows the network administrator to set the weight on a particular prefix such that it wins the local best path calculation without impacting the best path calculations used in the remainder of the network; this factor is normally referred to as the weight, and influences decisions only by the local router. Weight is not a defined BGP metric, and is not advertised as an attribute to a route in BGP, so it does not impact the routing decision at any other router in the network.

> Note that caution should be taken when manipulating weight as it only impacts path selection on the local system and may result in routing loops.

Review Questions

1. What is a routing domain from BGP's perspective? How is this different from a routing domain within IS-IS?
2. What are the two primary differences between an interior gateway protocol and an external gateway protocol?
3. What types of policies would you normally see implemented through BGP?
4. For what does BGP use the path information it carries through the network?
5. Why does BGP treat each autonomous system as a point on the connectivity graph? What does this imply about BGP's usefulness within an autonomous system?
6. What transport does BGP use to build a session to another BGP speaker? What local port number and remote port number does BGP use when initiating a connection?

7. How is a collision resolved between two BGP speakers attempting to open a connection at the same time?

8. Define *prefix, NLRI,* and *attribute.*

9. How many sets of attributes can a single BGP update contain? How many prefixes?

10. What are the four primary differences between eBGP peering relationships and iBGP peering relationships?

2

BGP at the Edge

When you are first examining BGP, it appears as though most of the work done by the protocol (along with the most complex configurations) would be between Internet service providers, rather than between Internet service providers and their customers—and to a large degree, this is true. But there are a lot of configuration options and issues at the edge, as well. For instance, a company connecting to the Internet through an Internet service provider might actually run BGP with the service provider. Why? That's what we'll cover in this chapter.

We'll first discuss the actual connection to the service provider: then we'll discuss, in separate sections, different ways of connecting to the Internet, including single homing to a single service provider, dual homing to a single service provider, and dual homing to two different service providers.

Connecting to a Service Provider

The first issue a company faces when connecting to the Internet is how to get started. Even those who work for a company already connected to the Internet generally don't understand how this piece of their network works, so just to demystify the process somewhat, we'll cover some basics here. There are three essential topics to be discussed: the physical connection, IP addressing, and security.

The Physical Connection

Generally, the Internet service provider (ISP) through which you connect to the Internet will be responsible for bringing in any physical connections to your business. The service provider will either bring a physical line into a room someplace in the business or contract with a local telephone service provider to do so. The type of line they bring in will depend on the amount of traffic you intend to send and receive–it could be anything from a 56-kbps ISDN connection to a 10-Gbps Ethernet or OC192 SONET connection.

This physical connection between the service provider equipment and the customer equipment is typically referred to as the local loop, and it terminates in a point called the DEMARC, which is short for the demarcation point. The demarcation point is the location where the maintenance of the physical line becomes the company's responsibility rather than the responsibility of the local telephone provider or the Internet service provider. Depending on the way the contract with the service provider is written, this demarcation point could actually be an Ethernet port on a router, a Network Interface Unit (NIU) that provides a connection to the customer's CSU, or perhaps a Ethernet switch that the service provider maintains. There are lots of options and services available here, and they're largely dependent on what your requirements are and what facilities are available or need to be provisioned to accommodate your requirements.

The service provider's side of the circuit also terminates into a DE-MARC within the provider's point of presence (POP). Generally, the physical cable will terminate into some sort of a router called a customer *aggregation router* or *edge router.*

IP Addressing

Once your physical connection to the Internet is established, where do you get an IP address the rest of the world can understand and route to? While it's possible to go through one of the various Regional Internet Registries (RIRs), generally these organizations cater only to larger users of IP addresses and typically require membership and charge fees. For instance, RIPE currently only allocates /19 address space blocks, which include up to 8192 hosts, or 32 class C networks. These organizations also assign Autonomous System (AS) numbers, which only a larger company with multiple connections to the Internet would need. So, if you don't go to one of the Regional Internet Registration authorities, where can you get an IP address? Your service provider, of course!

There are currently four Regional Internet Registries (RIRs): Réseaux IP Eu-
ropéens Network Coordination Centre (RIPE NCC) for European customers,
the American Registry for Internet Numbers (ARIN) for customers in the
Americas, the Latin American and Caribbean Internet Addresses Registry
for the Latin American and Caribbean (LAC) region, and the Asian Pacific
Network Information Centre (APNIC), catering to the Asian Pacific region.
RIRs are typically non-profit, fee-based membership organizations.
They're allocated blocks of IP addresses and Autonomous System Numbers (ASNs) from the Internet Assigned Numbers Authority (IANA).

Generally, service providers are allocated large blocks of addresses from one of the four Regional Internet Registries and then allocate subsets of those larger blocks to their customers. Many service
providers charge a fee when allocating address space to customers,
while others may consider it part of the Internet connection service itself and charge no additional fee (or perhaps bundle it inconspicu-
ously!). Many companies connecting to the Internet today use network
address translators (NATs), which enable them to pay for a small block
of addresses from the service provider and yet place a large number of
hosts behind those addresses.

Regional Internet Registries (RIRs) are often confused with Internet Routing Registries (IRRs). IRRs only serve as repositories for address, routing,
and policy information, whereas RIRs are responsible for allocation of IP
addresses and autonomous system numbers. Many service providers and
other organizations operate their own IRRs for customers and often require that customers register their address and policy information in public IRRs (e.g., LEVEL3). To confuse things more, APNIC, ARIN, and RIPE
also operate IRRs!

Security

A good number of people are very concerned with security, since there
are a large number of highly publicized hacking incidents, viruses, and
such that seem to come as part of a connection to the Internet. While
this book doesn't focus directly on host or even network security, we do
provide information relating to best current practices of securing BGP

networks. There are many good books published that do focus on network security, and there are many good products that can help to safeguard you against the attacks of hackers and the problems of virus infestation, worms, and so forth.

Single Homing to a Service Provider

Generally, for smaller companies not heavily dependent on their Internet connection, simply connecting to one service provider at one location, which is typically referred to as single homing, is sufficient. If losing that single connection to the Internet causes your business to stop functioning in some way—you regularly communicate with a large number of customers through e-mail or sell things on a Web server at your location, for instance—then single homing probably isn't a good option.

Single homed networks don't need to run BGP at all. The service provider can use a statically configured route to reach your addresses, and you can configure a static default route that passes all traffic to otherwise unknown destinations on to the service provider's network for carriage to the ultimate destination. There's a common misconception that BGP provides some great deal of added functionality to single homed networks—in reality, it only provides a good bit of unnecessary complexity.

Dual Homing to a Single Service Provider

If your connection to the Internet is more critical and your business has more than one location, then you can also connect to the same Internet service provider from two different locations, or perhaps to two different points in the same service provider's network. Figure 2.1 illustrates both of these connection situations.

Advantages

The first advantage of dual homing into a single service provider is that it's easy. There's only one set of technical support engineers to deal with, one set of salespeople to deal with (that should cut the number of phone calls you get in half, at least), one bill, and so on. The various issues with load balancing, which we will discuss in the next section, Dual Homing to Multiple Service Providers, becomes much easier, since you can deal with one set of engineers in working out the details.

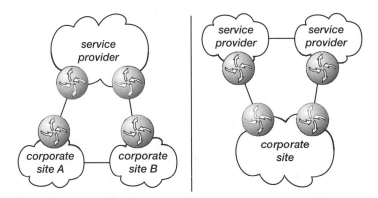

Figure 2.1
Dual homing to a single service provider.

By dual homing into the same service provider at two different locations, you are reducing your risk of a single router or link failure disrupting your connection to the Internet. While there is no requirement that each of the links be terminated on a separate router at the customer location, given that recurring cost of any reasonable size connection to the Internet far outweighs potential capital requirements for an additional router, it's likely well worth the investment!

Disadvantages

The primary disadvantage of connecting to the same service provider in two different places is the egg syndrome—you are placing all your eggs in one basket. While it's obvious that an interruption in the service provider's connection can also mean you've lost your connection to the Internet (which should be a rather rare situation or you've got larger problems), it's not so obvious that regional disruptions can also cause you to lose your connection to the Internet. Figure 2.2 illustrates one such situation.

Even though this business only has one office, it has decided to connect to the same service provider at two locations in order to provide redundancy in the event of router, power, or other failures. What the corporate network manager cannot see, however, is how the physical network is provisioned. While it appears, from a routing perspective, that the service provider has two links from each of these POPs into a single regional hub, in reality both of these links are carried over

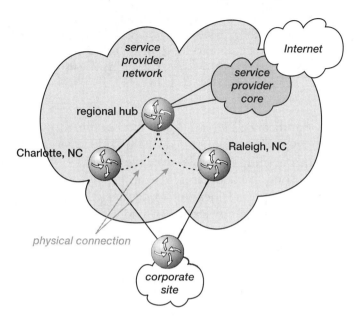

Figure 2.2
Dual homed to two regional points of presence.

the same physical cable (often a fiber optic connection), or even on two separate cables through the same physical trench or conduit. A backhoe cutting through this single cable or set of cables–called *backhoe fade*–causes the customer to lose all connectivity to the Internet.

This concept of physical diversity of cabling as well as logical diversity of connection points is a well-worn subject within design circles. Many service providers (including traditional telephone companies) are unwilling to tell customers what their physical network looks like and prefer simply to tell their customers where they can connect and how. As we'll see, physical diversity is just as important as logical diversity and should be considered in all network designs. If you're buying multiple connections to the Internet in order to protect against router or circuit failure, you should verify with your Internet provider that the circuits terminate on different routers within the service provider point of presence. You should also verify with your local loop provider that the circuits are (and remain) provisioned on separate physical cables between your location and the service provider locations.

> You should request circuit Design Layout Records (DLRs) from your provider; they typically provide physical cable identifiers that can be used to determine whether physical circuit diversity exists or not.

A significant disadvantage to dual homing to a single provider for a company that is all contained at the same physical site is also alluded to in the preceding example–any given service provider will generally only have one point of presence in a given area, and thus there will only be one optimal location to connect. In order to connect to two places within the same service provider's network, you must generally run a long-haul circuit (or backhauled local loop) to the second POP, which can often prove to be prohibitively expensive.

When Should You Run BGP?

While it is easy enough simply to configure static default routes toward each connection to the service provider, there are situations where running BGP is desirable. These will almost always relate to optimal routing and traffic flow considerations, which are covered in the next two sections, and detecting link or connectivity failure. Figure 2.3 illustrates one such situation.

In Figure 2.3, the connections from the corporate network to the service provider are over Ethernet segments through firewalls. Firewalls typically have very little ability to pass routing information from the routers that are peering to the service provider across the wide area links to the routers that are connected to the corporate sites; if one of these links or firewalls fails, the routers within the corporate network will have little information about this failure to trigger a change in their routing decisions.

Opening a hole in the firewall so BGP traffic can pass through it and passing a default route using a multihop eBGP session between the service provider edge and the corporate network provides the dynamic routing information the corporate site routers need to determine which path to take toward the Internet. Information on eBGP, multihop eBGP, and what routes to exchange where will be discussed in detail as we progress.

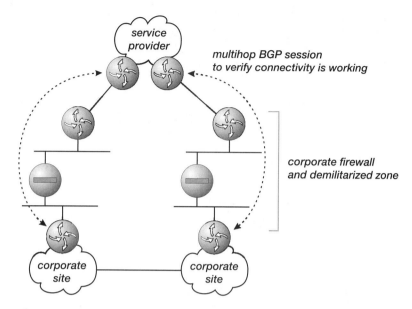

Figure 2.3
Using BGP when peering to a single service provider to verify link status.

Do You Need an Autonomous System Number?

If you do exchange BGP routes with your service provider, will you need to acquire an autonomous system number from a Regional Internet Registry? Generally, the answer is no. Instead of registering with an RIR to obtain an autonomous system number, you can use a private autonomous system number assigned by your service provider. The service provider will strip it out of the AS Path when advertising it toward the provider's peers. The Internet Assigned Numbers Authority (IANA) has defined autonomous system numbers 64512 through 65535 as private numbers, not to be advertised on the Internet backbone. Your service provider can assign one of these numbers to your network.

RFC 2270, *Using a Dedicated AS for Sites Homed to a Single Provider*, describes how private autonomous system numbers can be used by service providers. Be sure to check with your service provider to ensure that it supports private AS numbers if you intend to use them.

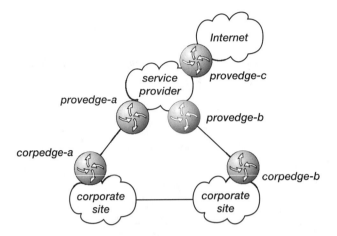

Figure 2.4
Dual homing with a private AS.

Figure 2.4 illustrates a dual homed connection to a service provider using one of these private autonomous systems; sample configurations for the routers shown follow.

```
hostname corpedge-a
!
interface serial 0
ip address 192.168.100.8 255.255.255.254
!
router bgp 64912
neighbor 192.168.100.9 remote as 100
neighbor 192.168.200.40 remote-as 64912
....
hostname corpedge-b
!
interface serial 0
ip address 192.168.200.40 255.255.255.254
!
router bgp 64912
neighbor 192.168.200.41 remote-as 100
neighbor 192.168.100.8 remote-as 64912
hostname provedge-c
!
router bgp 100
neighbor 172.30.8.10 remove-private-as
```

The provider uses the **remove-private-as** configuration, which is applied on egress, when peering with other service providers in order to strip the private autonomous system numbers out of the AS Path of each route it advertises. Service providers that allow customers to use private AS numbers typically enable **remove-private-as** on all eBGP sessions.

Inbound Traffic Flow Control

The next consideration when dual homing to a single service provider is the way the routes are received and processed by the service provider when you are exchanging BGP routes with them. Figure 2.5 illustrates how the prefixes the customer is advertising into the service provider will appear within the service provider's network.

Although both corpedge-a and corpedge-b are advertising the same prefix, and provcore is receiving each route from provedge-a and provedge-b, provcore will only install one path to the 192.168.80.0/23 range of addesses in its routing table; this is because BGP always chooses only one path to each destination. There are several ways you can control which path is chosen by your service provider, and there

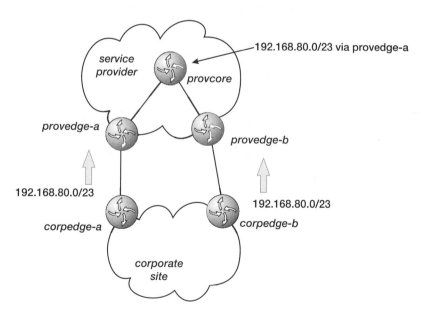

Figure 2.5
Inbound load balancing while dual homed to the same service provider.

are ways around the single best path nature of the BGP decision algorithm. In this section, we will cover the various methods.

The first way to control the link over which inbound traffic will flow is to set the multiple exit discriminator (MED) on the 192.168.80.0/23 route as you advertise it to the service provider. The MED is supposed to be a hint to a neighboring autonomous system indicating which inbound path you would prefer traffic traverse for a particular prefix. The problem with using the MED to ask the provider to prefer a particular link is that many service providers reset the MED values on prefixes they learn on the edges of their network—so the service provider may simply ignore or reset the MED value you send. Service provider policies vary widely with regard to whether MEDs are accepted from customers or peers and precisely how they're used in the BGP path selection process. Before deciding to use MEDs, you should discuss with your service provider what MED policies it supports.

Another way in which you can control the link over which inbound traffic flows is to send a community along with the prefix that the service provider can interpret as a request to set the BGP local preference to a given value. For instance, if you send the community 100 along with the 192.168.80.0/23 prefix from corpedge-b, the service provider may interpret this community as a request to set the local preference on the prefix to 100 on provedge-b, giving this path priority over the path learned through provedge-a. You would need to contact your service provider to find out about whether they provide support for such communities and what community semantics are required.

Finally, you could also prepend extra hops (additional autonomous system numbers) onto the AS Path to make one of the two paths preferred. Prepending extra hops onto the AS Path is a very common trick to attempt to load balance inbound traffic; we'll cover it in more detail in Chapter 3, Configuring BGP at the Edge, in the Load Balancing section.

RFC 1998, *An Application of the BGP Community Attribute in Multi-Home Routing*, describes a model for using BGP communities to set route preference policy within a service provider network. This functionality has been extended by many service providers such that communties can now also be used to trigger selective AS prepending by the service provider rather than the originating AS. Again, be sure to check with your service provider to learn what routing policy mechanisms it supports, as support for many routing policy features varies widely between networks.

One common misconception about IP traffic flows is that they're symmetric in nature, and by controlling the path taken by traffic in one direction, you can control the path taken by traffic in the other direction as well. In other words, by forcing packets routed to given destination to be passed along a particular link, you are forcing the packets transmitted from the destination back to the source to pass along that same link. However, this isn't true, as Figure 2.6 illustrates.

When forwarding IP packets, in fact, each device acts as an independent agent along the way; each router makes an independent decision on what interface and next hop a packet should use; for instance, packets traveling to the host in the service provider's network from the host in the corporate site may travel to corpedge-b, which then forwards along to provedge-b. Packets transmitted by the host in the service provider's network, representing the return traffic along this same session, could be routed along the provedge-a corpedge-a path.

Controlling packet flow in one direction has nothing to do with controlling the path the return traffic takes, and inbound traffic flow

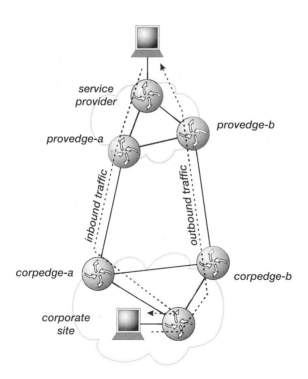

Figure 2.6
Assymetric traffic flow.

and associated policies must be considered independently of outbound traffic flow.

Inbound Load Balancing

Before doing any work to load balance inbound traffic over two connections to the same service provider, you should first check with the service provider to see if they will load balance over the two links without you having to do any configurations or additional work. It may turn out that the service provider will load balance into your network if you are not running BGP sessions with the provider to advertise your routes, so perhaps there's no real reason to run BGP between the service provider and the end customer.

BGP Multipath Inside the Service Provider's Network

However, once you've determined you need to peer with the service provider using BGP, you should check with your service provider to see if it has configured (or will configure) eBGP multipath in its network. EBGP multipath allows BGP to install two paths to the same destination with the same cost in the routing table, which will cause the router to load share between them, rather than select a single best path for each destination prefix as discussed earlier. An example of EBGP multipath is given in Chapter 4, Core Design with BGP, in the Load Balancing across the Backbone section.

Controlling Inbound Flow Using Longer Prefix Advertisements

If you need to peer with your service provider using BGP and the service provider is not running BGP multipath, then there is another method that might work, depending on what your service provider allows in the way of advertisements accepted from your router. This method is illustrated in Figure 2.7.

The corporate site has been assigned 192.168.80.0/23 by the service provider. Rather than advertising this one prefix, the customer has split the address range into two components and is advertising both to the service provider. Now there are two separate routes at provcore, so if the hosts and their associated bandwidth requirements are evenly dis-

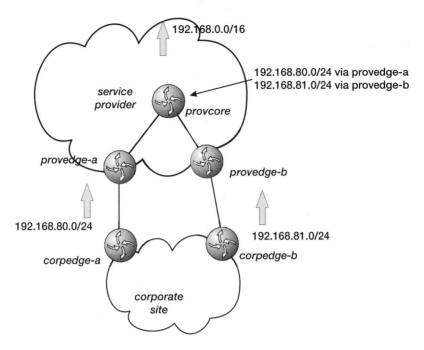

Figure 2.7
Load balancing by advertising longer prefixes into a single provider.

tributed between the two address ranges, the traffic directed into each path should be about equal. The number of addresses assigned by the service provider need not be large to advertise them as two sets of prefixes; just 4 IP addresses (i.e., a /30 prefix) can be divided into two advertisements with 31 bit prefix lengths. Even a range of two addresses can be advertised as two host routes (i.e., two /32 prefixes).

Deaggregating in this way will cause the service provider's routing tables to grow within their autonomous system but has no impact on the Internet at large, since the service provider will likely be aggregating all of the prefixes within a much larger range, say everything within 192.168.0.0/16, into one advertisement toward its peers. However, many service providers will only accept a single advertisement from customers for each block of contiguous address space. You should check with your service provider to see what route advertisement and prefix filtering policies it employs.

Dual Homing to Multiple Service Providers

Another option is to dual (or even triple) home to multiple service provider's networks. Since you aren't relying on a single service provider to connect your network to the Internet, there is less chance of a failure (theoretically). Dual homing presents more complicated problems in the area of controlling the traffic flowing in and out of your network

As with dual homing to a single service provider, you don't necessarily need to peer with the two service providers you are connecting through in order to use both inbound and outbound links. The reasons for running BGP inside your network are generally the same as the reasons for running BGP when you are dual homing to the same provider, given in the preceding When Should You Run BGP? section.

Controlling Inbound Traffic Flow

The methods described previously to load share or control the traffic inbound when peering with two different providers–relying on interior BGP multipath or advertising longer prefix lengths–generally won't work when peering with two different service providers. In fact, while there are ways to control inbound traffic flow when dual homing to two different providers, there is no way to control inbound traffic flow precisely enough to achieve real load sharing, in general.

Let's begin with the most essential problem–getting traffic to flow on both links at all–and then discuss how to adjust the amount of traffic flowing across those links.

Getting Traffic to Flow on Both Inbound Links

Figure 2.8 illustrates a simple dual homing arrangement between a corporation and two service providers, SP-A and SP-B.

The corporate customer has been assigned the 10.1.1.0/24 address space by SP-A, who is their primary service provider. However, they decided to obtain services with SP-B as well, and peer with SP-B's routers, while advertising the prefix they were assigned by SP-A out through SP-B. What the corporate site administrators cannot see, however, is that SP-A isn't actually advertising their 10.1.1.0/24 prefix toward their peers on the Internet backbone. Instead, SP-A is summarizing (or aggregating)

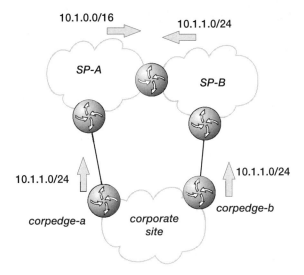

Figure 2.8
A simple dual homing configuration.

their prefix into a much larger block, 10.1.0.0/16, and advertising that toward their peers on the Internet backbone.

SP-B, however, doesn't control the 10.1.0.0/16 address space, so it cannot aggregate the customer's prefixes. Instead, it must advertise the individual prefix advertised by the corporate site. So the service providers peering with SP-A and SP-B will receive two paths toward the corporate site:

- 10.1.0.0/16 through SP-A
- 10.1.1.0/24 through SP-B

Since the longest prefix length (most specific route) always wins, all the service providers receiving these two advertisements will prefer the path through SP-B. This, of course, results in virtually all the traffic destined to the corporate site passing through SP-B, resulting in what could hardly be considered load sharing between the two links.

The most common solution for this situation has been for the customer to contact the service provider they were assigned addresses by and ask that they no longer include this particular prefix within the aggregates they are advertising. In this case, the corporate site network administrator would ask that SP-A *punch a hole* in their 10.1.0.0/16 aggregate by *leaking* the longer 10.1.1.0/24 prefix through it. The result is illustrated in Figure 2.9.

This appears to resolve the problem, getting traffic to flow over both links—but it's not quite as simple as this appears at first glance. Let's add another service provider into the picture and see what the result is; Figure 2.10 illustrates.

SP-C receives three routes, each of which will provide the information needed to reach the destination within the corporate site network. It will receive the 10.1.0.0/16 aggregate from SP-A, which it will keep, and it will receive two copies of the 10.1.1.0/24 prefix, one from SP-A, and the other from SP-B. SP-C will choose one of these two prefixes and keep it; the other prefix will be ignored or otherwise discarded.

If SP-C chooses the 10.1.1.0/24 prefix from SP-A, then the effect is the same as if SP-B had never advertised this longer prefix. All the traffic sourced from SP-C and SP-A will travel across corpedge-a, and only traffic originating within SP-B will travel across corpedge-b. If SP-C chooses the path through SP-B, then the opposite is true. There is no way to have SP-C split the traffic destined to 10.1.1.0/24 between the

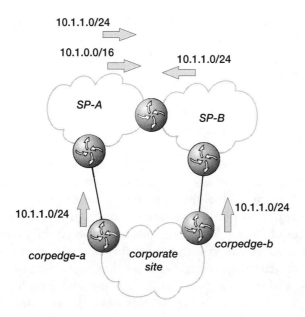

Figure 2.9
Dual homing with leaking through the aggregate.

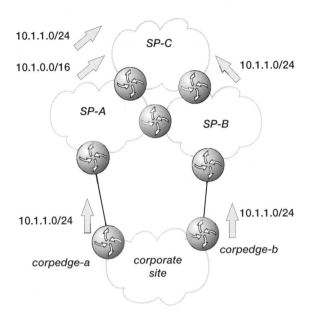

Figure 2.10
Leaking a prefix with a third service provider.

two different paths presented to it. Of course, most service providers peer with more than one or two other service providers, so there is some statistical chance that enough service providers are going to choose one path or the other to provide some amount of traffic on both links.

Although this might seem like an easy and straightforward solution for the corporate site customer, the impact of poking such holes on the Internet itself can be severe if enough customers request this service. For instance, at the time of this writing, the Internet backbone routing table contains about 140,000 reachable destinations. Of those, about 40,000 are prefixes added to the table either in error or in order to load balance between two connections to the Internet through two different service providers.

This practice has, at this point, significantly increased the size of the Internet routing tables and promises to be the fastest growing section of the Internet routing table into the future. There are some solutions being worked on to reduce this growth, all of which will impact the customer's ability to control the amount of traffic being received over a given set of links. Several of these are discussed in Chapter 4, Backbone Design with BGP.

Controlling the Choices Other Providers Make through AS Path Prepend

It is possible to influence, to some degree, which path is chosen by providers beyond the two service providers with which you are peering through the use of AS Path Prepending. To prepend your AS Path when you advertise your network toward your BGP peers means to make the networks you are advertising appear to be farther away in terms of the BGP AS hop count. Note, however, that there are many other metrics in the BGP decision algorithm before the AS Path is considered, such as local preference and the multiple exit discriminator. This will be placed in context after we discuss how prepending AS hops onto your advertisements affects the path chosen toward your network.

This is a rather rough method of working and may have no impact at all on inbound load levels across the two peering links. Figure 2.11 illustrates AS Path prepending.

Let's discuss what occurs at each of these service providers if the corporate site administrator prepends AS hops onto their advertise-

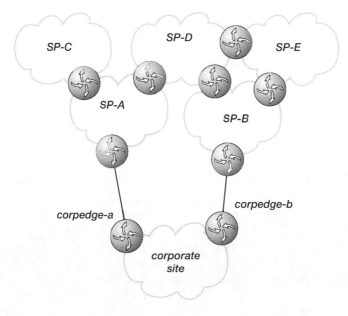

Figure 2.11
AS path prepend and its effects.

ments towards SP-A and SP-B; Table 2.1 outlines the routing choices made, considering only the AS path length (which is unrealistic, as we'll discuss later).

Prepending AS hops to the prefixes corpedge-a is advertising makes little difference until you reach the point where you are prepending four AS hops. When you add four AS hops, all the traffic shifts to the path through corpedge-b, including the traffic from SP-A. The only service provider's traffic that is shifted, SP-D, is shifted by the first AS hop addition. Let's look at the impact of adding AS paths at corpedge-b (Table 2.2).

The biggest impact is made when the second AS hop is prepended, and again when the fourth AS hop is prepended. From these two tables, you can see that if the biggest traffic generator is in SP-C, and you want to shift that traffic over to the link through corpedge-b, then the only way to do so is by shifting all the traffic over to the link through corpedge-b.

Table 2.1
Routing Choices Considering Only AS Path Length

	SP-A	**SP-B**	**SP-C**	**SP-D**	**SP-E**
No prepend	Chooses path via corpedge-a	Chooses path via corpedge-b	Chooses path via SP-A	Chooses path via either SP-A or SP-B	Chooses path via SP-B
Prepend one hop at corpedge-a	Chooses path via corpedge-a	Chooses path via corpedge-b	Chooses path via SP-A	Chooses path via SP-B	Chooses path via SP-B
Prepend two hops at corpedge-a	Chooses path via corpedge-a	Chooses path via corpedge-b	Chooses path via SP-A	Chooses path via SP-B	Chooses path via SP-B
Prepend three hops at corpedge-a	Chooses path via corpedge-a	Chooses path via corpedge-b	Chooses path via SP-A	Chooses path via SP-B	Chooses path via SP-B
Prepend four hops at corpedge-a	Chooses path via SP-D	Chooses path via corpedge-b	Chooses path via SP-A	Chooses path via SP-B	Chooses path via SP-B

Table 2.2

	SP-A	SP-B	SP-C	SP-D	SP-E
Prepend one hop at corpedge-b	Chooses path via corpedge-a	Chooses path via SP-B	Chooses path via SP-A	Chooses path via SP-A	Choose either the path through SP-D or the path through SP-B
Prepend two hops at corpedge-b	Chooses path via corpedge-a	Chooses path via SP-B	Chooses path via SP-A	Chooses path via SP-A	Chooses path via SP-E
Prepend three hops at corpedge-b	Chooses path via corpedge-a	Chooses path via SP-B	Chooses path via SP-A	Chooses path via SP-A	Chooses path via SP-E
Prepend four hops at corpedge-b	Chooses path via corpedge-a	Chooses path via SP-A	Chooses path via SP-A	Chooses path via SP-A	Chooses path via SP-E

Further, these tables only consider what happens if the AS Path is the deciding factor in making a routing choice. Often, the AS Path length is not the deciding factor for service provider routers choosing the best path out of their network. A service provider who strips out any duplicate autonomous systems when it receives routes or sets its local preference based on a preferred provider contract or service level agreement (SLA) will simply ignore the AS Path prepending done by the corporate site network administrators.

Again, this is a rather rough way of trying to adjust traffic levels. The results will be unpredictable at best; you probably won't ever achieve inbound load balancing over two links through two different service providers, at least not for any length of time, using this method. There is one other–more complicated–method that can be used, which revolves around forcing all the communications between your network and the rest of the hosts on the Internet to travel along symmetric paths–at least as far as the exit and entry points into your network are concerned. This is discussed in the Forcing Symmetric Routing section later in this chapter.

Using Only One Link at A Time

Rather than attempting to load balance inbound between the two service provider connections, you can also configure one link to be used only when the primary link fails. While RFC 1998 BGP community-based policies provide a mechanism to use only one link at a time between multiple service providers, there is, effectively, one way to use one service provide connection as a primary link and the second service provider link as a backup link today: conditional advertisement.

Conditional Advertisement

Conditional advertisement allows you to advertise a network to a BGP peer only when some network condition is met; generally, the condition used is the existence of another route in the routing table. Figure 2.12 illustrates a backup connection using BGP conditional advertisement; sample configurations follow.

The configurations for the routers and the output of **show ip bgp** on *corpedge-b* and *provedge-b* follow.

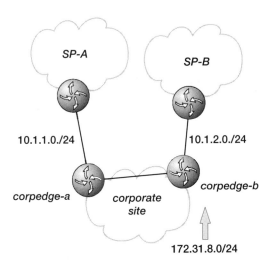

Figure 2.12
Conditional advertisement.

```
!
corpedge-b
!
router isis
 net 49.1111.0000.0000.0002.00
!
router bgp 65240
 no synchronization
 bgp log-neighbor-changes
 network 10.1.1.0 mask 255.255.255.0
 network 172.31.8.0 mask 255.255.255.0
 neighbor corpedge-a remote-as 65240
 neighbor provedge-b remote-as 65242
 neighbor provedge-b advertise-map advertmap non-exist-map nonexistmap
 no auto-summary
!
access-list 10 permit 172.31.8.0 0.255.255.255
access-list 20 permit 10.1.1.0 0.0.0.255
!
route-map advertmap permit 10
 match ip address 10
!
route-map notexistmap permit 10
 match ip address 20

corpedge-b#sho ip bgp
BGP table version is 4, local router ID is 10.1.2.1
Status codes: s suppressed, d damped, h history, * valid, > best
Origin codes: i - IGP, e - EGP, ? - incomplete

   Network          Next Hop            Metric LocPrf Weight Path
*> 172.31.8.0/24    corpedge-a               0           32768 i
*> 10.1.1.0/24      corpedge-a              20             200 i

provedge-b#sho ip bgp
BGP table version is 4, local router ID is 10.1.2.2
Status codes: s suppressed, d damped, h history, * valid, > best
Origin codes: i - IGP, e - EGP, ? - incomplete

   Network          Next Hop            Metric LocPrf Weight Path
*> 10.1.1.0/24      10.1.1.1                20             200 i
```

When corpedge-b loses its route to 10.1.1.0/24, the route falls out of its BGP table.

```
corpedge-b#sho ip bgp
BGP table version is 4, local router ID is 10.1.2.1
Status codes: s suppressed, d damped, h history, * valid, > best
Origin codes: i - IGP, e - EGP, ? - incomplete

   Network          Next Hop              Metric LocPrf Weight Path
*> 172.31.8.0/24    corpedge-a                 0            32768 i
```

Once this occurs, corpedge-b stops advertising 10.1.1.0/24, and corpedge-b begins advertising 172.31.8.0/24 towards provedge-b.

```
provedge-b#sho ip bgp
BGP table version is 4, local router ID is 10.1.2.2
Status codes: s suppressed, d damped, h history, * valid, > best
Origin codes: i - IGP, e - EGP, ? - incomplete

   Network          Next Hop              Metric LocPrf Weight Path
*> 172.31.8.0/24    10.1.1.1                   0            32768 i
```

Controlling Outbound Traffic Flow

We've discussed controlling inbound traffic flow while discussing peering with a single service provider or multiple service providers, since controlling inbound traffic flow is strongly tied with your peers' BGP and route aggregation policies. Outbound traffic flow control, however, is quite a bit simpler, since IP routing protocols are designed to control the adjacent next hop toward any given destination, and controlling the next hop taken toward any given destination also controls the exit path the traffic takes.

Controlling Outbound Traffic Flow Using Interior Gateway Protocols

Several methods can be used to control outbound traffic flow using the interior gateway protocol–such as EIGRP, IS-IS, and OSPF–you are already (most likely) running in your network. Figure 2.13 illustrates one method.

In this network, corpedge-a and corpedge-b are both advertising default routes (0.0.0.0/0) into the interior gateway protocol. Each router in the network receiving both routes will choose independently which of the two default routes is the best path out of the network.

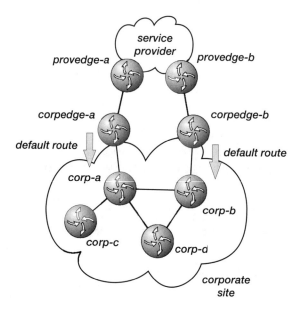

Figure 2.13
Load balancing outbound using default routes only.

- Corp-a will receive both default routes but will choose the path through corpedge-a.
- Corp-b will receive both routes as well but will prefer the path through corpedge-b.
- Corp-d will receive both default routes and will choose to load balance any traffic it receives through both of them.
- Corp-c will receive only one path to the default network, through corp-a, and will use that path.

By adjusting the metrics and locations from which the default route is advertised, you can control how much traffic is transmitted outbound on each link. It's also possible to be more granular than this in controlling outbound traffic flow; Figure 2.14 illustrates.

Here the corporate edge routers have been configured, using static routes, to advertise more than just the default route; the routes added actually cover the entire IP address space. By modifying the amount of address space each edge router advertises, the amount of outbound traffic passed over each link to the service provider can be adjusted, while the overlapping default provides a level of redundancy.

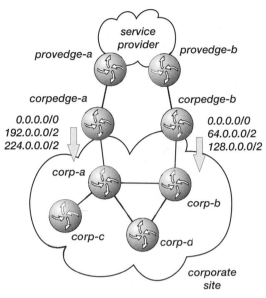

Figure 2.14
Load balancing outbound using interior gateway protocols and longer prefix advertisements.

Using BGP for Controlling Outbound Traffic Flow

Just as there are several ways to control outbound traffic flow using interior gateway protocols, there are also several ways to control outbound traffic flow using BGP. One major issue with using BGP to control outbound traffic flow is how deep into your network you need to run BGP to control outbound traffic flow. Figure 2.15 illustrates.

In this network, provedge-a and corpedge-a are peering through exterioir BGP, provedge-b and corpedge-b are peering through exterior BGP, and corpedge-a and corpedge-b are peering through interior BGP. Assume the best path chosen by corpedge-a to get to some destination, 172.20.9.40, is through corpedge-b, based on the information it has received through the BGP session.

As packets are received by corp-a destined to 172.20.9.40, they will be forwarded to corpedge-a, since corp-a believes this is the best default exit point from the network. When corpedge-a receives the packets, it will look up 172.20.9.40 in its routing table and discover the best path is through corpedge-b and the next hop toward corp-a. It will forward these packets to corp-a. This is a permanent forwarding loop

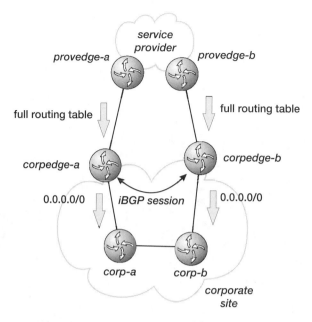

Figure 2.15
A simple BGP routing loop.

caused by the difference in the information the interior gateway protocol has available and the information BGP has available.

There are several ways to resolve this problem, one of which is to
enable synchronization within BGP on corpedge-a and corpedge-b.
BGP synchronization is designed to prevent this from happening by
preventing the propagation of routing information to iBGP peers if it is
determined that the routing information is not available via the interior
gateway protocol. In this case, if BGP synchronization is enabled, corpedge-b would not advertise the 172.20.9.40 prefix to corpedge-a, since
this destination is not reachable through the interior gateway protocol.
When corpedge-a receives packets destined to 172.20.9.40, it will find
there is only one valid path to this destination—out through provedge-a.
This resolves the problem by removing the prefix from corpedge-a's
routing table. However, this may not achieve the desired result, which
is to load balance traffic along the two outbound links.

Another possible way to resolve this is to redistribute the entire
BGP routing table into the interior gateway protocol at corpedge-a and
corpedge-b. Since this often results in large-scale network failures from

memory exhaustion, CPU resource consumption, and so forth, we wouldn't recommend this solution. As a matter of fact, we highly recommend that you never redistribute BGP routes into your IGP, or IGP routes into BGP, for that matter.

It's also possible to resolve this problem by running BGP on the corp-a and corp-b routers; when considering this possibility, remember that iBGP requires a full mesh to operate correctly. Thus

- Corpedge-a would need to peer with corpedge-b.
- Corpedge-a would need to peer with corp-a.
- Corpedge-a would need to peer with corp-b.
- Corpedge-b would need to peer with corpedge-a.
- Corpedge-b would need to peer with corp-a.
- Corpedge-b would need to peer with corp-b.

As you increase the number of routers in the core of the corporate network with the need for BGP routing information, the complexity of the full mesh increases. There are some solutions with less complexity, primarily route reflectors and BGP confederations. These are discussed in Chapter 4, Backbone Design with BGP. It's important to consider the memory and processor requirements on routers running BGP within the enterprise as well, since BGP can place significant resource requirements on routers.

Finally, it's also possible to resolve this problem by installing a link between corpedge-a and corpedge-b, as Figure 2.16 illustrates.

The addition of the link between corpedge-a and corpedge-b now means that traffic that needs to flow between the edge routers to load balance outbound will now pass across this direct path.

Once you've decided where and how to run BGP in order to control outbound traffic flow, you need to decide how you will actually control the preference for each prefix, adjusting the outbound flow of traffic.

It is *very* important that you consider some method to prevent traffic from transiting your autonomous system; techniques to prevent the ISPs from seeing your network as a possible alternate path to reach their peers are considered in the How Not to Transit Traffic section later in this chapter.

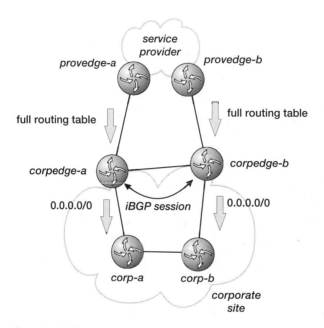

Figure 2.16
Adding an additional link to resolve routing loops within the corporate site.

Accepting Full Routes and Using Interior BGP Multipath or BGP Policies

It's also possible to load share between two possible BGP paths using interior BGP multipath configurations, which allow BGP to install more than one path into the routing table, given that they are equal paths in every respect (local preference, multiple exit discriminator, interior gateway protocol metric, etc.), but with two different BGP next hop addresses. Interior BGP multipath is discussed in Chapter 4, Core Design with BGP, in the Load Balancing Across the Backbone section.

If you are accepting full routes along both peering sessions, then you could also use normal BGP attribute policies, primarily Local Preference, to influence which paths packets take to which destinations. Figure 2.17 illustrates.

In this case, the policies could be configured so that about half of the destinations reachable within the Internet prefer to exit through corpedge-a, while the other half prefer to exit through corpedge-b. Any traffic that is received on corpedge-a and should prefer the corpedge-b exit would be sent over the link between the two routers, so this works

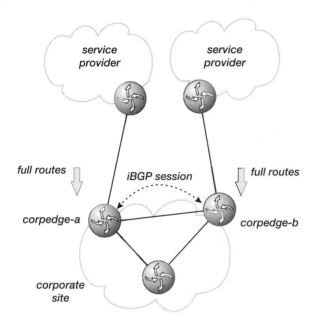

Figure 2.17
Accepting full routes and using policy to load balance outbound.

best if both corpedge-a and corpedge-b are in the same geographical building and can be connected by a single high-speed local area link.

Using policies to influence the BGP decision algorithm is discussed further in Chapter 3, Scaling the Enterprise Using BGP.

Using a Multihop BGP Session

It's also possible to load balance between several points in your network and the same BGP next hop; Figure 2.18 illustrates an example of this.

In Figure 2.18, corpedge-a has formed a multihop exterior BGP connection to provedge-a. It has been configured so the path to provedge-a through its connected link and the path to provedge-a through corpedge-b appear to be equal cost paths. Configurations for corpedge-a and provedge-a are provided as an example. 192.168.80.1 is the loopback address on provedge-a, while 192.168.100.1 is the loopback address on corpedge-a. Depending on your network, you may wish to dedicate a loopback interface and IP address for each multihop peering session. If you have more than one peering using ebgp multihop, this will allow you to move the IP/peering without interaction with your ISP.

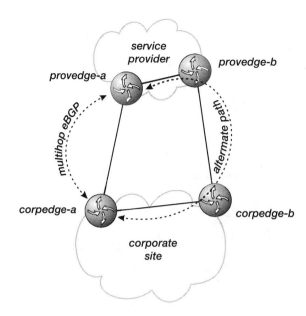

Figure 2.18
Using a BGP multihop session to load share outbound.

```
!
hostname corpedge-a
!
router bgp 65240
 no synchronization
 bgp log-neighbor-changes
 neighbor corpedge-b remote-as 65240
 neighbor 192.168.80.1 remote-as 65241
 neighbor 192.168.80.1 ebgp-multihop 5
 neighbor 192.168.80.1 update-source Loopback0
!
ip route 192.168.80.1 255.255.255.255 provedge-a
ip route 192.168.80.1 255.255.255.255 corpedge-b
!
int loopback 0
 ip address 192.168.100.1

!
hostname provedge-a
!
interface Loopback0
 ip address 192.168.80.1 255.255.255.255
```

```
!
router bgp 65241
 no synchronization
 bgp log-neighbor-changes
 redistribute static
 neighbor provedge-b remote-as 65241
 neighbor 192.168.100.1 remote-as 65240
 neighbor 192.168.100.1 ebgp-multihop 5
 neighbor 192.168.100.1 update-source Loopback0
 default-information originate
!
ip route 192.168.100.1 255.255.255.255 provedge-b
ip route 192.168.100.1 255.255.255.255 corpedge-a

corpedge-a#show ip bgp 0.0.0.0
BGP routing table entry for 0.0.0.0/0, version 2
Paths: (2 available, best #2, table Default-IP-Routing-Table)
  65241
    corpedge-b from corpedge-b (corpedge-b)
      Origin incomplete, localpref 100, valid, internal
  65241
    192.168.80.1 from 192.168.80.1 (192.168.80.1)
      Origin incomplete, metric 0, localpref 100, valid, external, best
```

From the output of **show ip route** on *corpedge-a,* you can see there is a single default route installed via 192.168.80.1:

```
corpedge-a#show ip route 0.0.0.0
Routing entry for 0.0.0.0/0, supernet
  Known via "bgp 65240", distance 20, metric 0, candidate default path
  Tag 65241, type external
  Last update from 192.168.80.1 00:10:51 ago
  Routing Descriptor Blocks:
  * 192.168.80.1, from 192.168.80.1, 00:10:51 ago
      Route metric is 0, traffic share count is 1
      AS Hops 1
```

Examining the available paths to the next hop address, 192.168.80.1, in the routing table, shows two paths to this next hop:

```
corpedge-a#show ip route 192.168.80.1
Routing entry for 192.168.80.1/32
  Known via "static", distance 1, metric 0
```

```
Routing Descriptor Blocks:
* corpedge-b
    Route metric is 0, traffic share count is 1
  provedge-a
    Route metric is 0, traffic share count is 1
```

Traffic routed through the default route will be load shared across these two paths to the next hop.

Accepting Partial Routes

Another option to manage and control outbound load is to accept partial routes through the BGP peering sessions with the service providers you are connected to. There are actually a few ways to achieve this; we'll use Figure 2.19 to illustrate this concept, and provide sample configurations.

The first decision to make when accepting partial routes is which routes to receive. There are two options in general: Accept the set of routes on each corpedge router that direct enough outbound traffic onto each link to balance the traffic, or accept the set of prefixes that will produce optimal routing and load balance the remainder of the traffic using some other method, such as a method based on an interior gateway protocol.

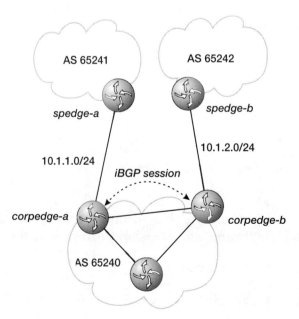

Figure 2.19
Accepting partial routes.

If you decide to accept the set of prefixes that will roughly balance outbound traffic, the easiest way to do this is to accept just the default route through one peering session and filter the prefixes accepted on the second connection until the traffic flow outbound on the two links is roughly equal. Configurations for corpedge-a and corpedge-b achieving this result are as follows:

```
!
hostname corpedge-a
!
router bgp 65240
 neighbor 10.1.1.1 remote-as 65241
 neighbor 10.1.1.1 prefix-list balance-list in
 neighbor corpedge-b remote-as 65240
!
ip prefix-list balance-list permit 0.0.0.0/1

!
hostname corpedge-b
!
router bgp 65240
 neighbor 10.1.2.1 remote-as 65242
 neighbor 10.1.2.1 prefix-list default-only in
 neighbor corpedge-a remote-as 65240
!
ip prefix-list default-only permit 0.0.0.0/32
```

The ip prefix list **balance-list** on corpedge-a permits half of the IP address space, while the ip prefix list **default-only** on corpedge-b permits only the default route. By adjusting the range of prefixes permitted in the **balance-list** prefix list on corpedge-a, you can balance the traffic sent across the two outbound links. Both corpedge-a and corpedge-b should generate a default route toward the corporate site routers behind them through an interior gateway protocol.

Accepting the set of prefixes that will produce optimal routing and using some other method to load balance the remainder of the traffic (typically some form of load sharing between the links based on the interior gateway protocol being used in the corporate site network) is another option. Why would you be concerned about optimal routing when connecting to the Internet? Looking at Figure 2.20, you can see that other customers are connected to the Internet using the same providers you are connecting to.

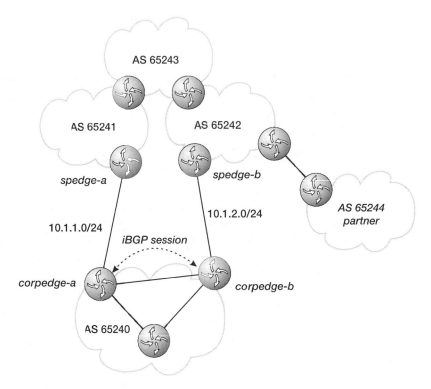

Figure 2.20
Accepting partial routes for optimum routing.

If AS 65244 represents a major partner (there is a good deal of traffic flow between AS 65240 and AS 65244), it doesn't make sense to send this traffic through AS 65241, since it will then need to travel through AS 65243, then AS 65242, to reach its destination. Instead, it makes more sense to accept the prefixes that are within the service provider's network, and possibly those prefixes that are one AS Path hop away from the service provider's network (the service provider's customers). For the remainder of the prefixes, assuming they are more than two AS Path hops away, you can load share traffic between the connections to the service providers based on some interior gateway protocol system within AS 65240.

Sample configurations for filtering so the service provider's prefixes and the service provider's customer's prefixes are accepted are as follows:

```
!
hostname corpedge-a
!
router bgp 65240
 neighbor 10.1.1.1 remote-as 65241
 neighbor 10.1.1.1 filter-list 10 in
 neighbor corpedge-b remote-as 65240
!
ip as-path access-list 10 permit ^[1-9]*_*65241$

!
hostname corpedge-b
!
router bgp 65240
 neighbor 10.1.2.1 remote-as 65242
 neighbor 10.1.2.1 filter-list 10 in
 neighbor corpedge-a remote-as 65240
!
ip as-path access-list 10 permit ^[1-9]*_*65242$
```

The as-path access-list, in each case, uses a regular expression to limit the prefixes accepted to those originated within the service provider's network and one AS Path hop beyond the service provider's network. Many service providers have fixed routing policies in place that allow customers to receive all routes, only customer routers, or default route. Where possible, allowing your service provider to assist in implementing these polices will reduce the load both on the provider's router for unnecessarily generating route updates, and your link and router for receiving and discarding updates. You should check with your service provider to see what policies it has in place in order to ease configurations required for you to obtain your desired scenario.

Forcing Symmetric Entry and Exit Points

Because BGP and other routing protocols primarily focus on the next hop toward a destination at each router or hop rather than a complete path, asymmetric routing is the normal, accepted behavior when dual homing to one or two service providers. However, there are situations where asymmetric traffic flow isn't desirable, such as the network connections illustrated in Figure 2.21.

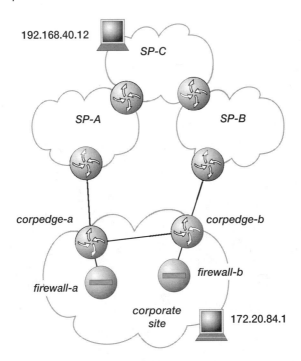

Figure 2.21
Forcing symmetric routing.

As you can see, there are a pair of firewalls, one behind each router that connects to an Internet service provider. Since firewalls generally inspect packets based on the flow to which the packets belong, traffic must be symmetrical for the firewalls to work correctly. For instance, suppose host 172.20.84.1, which is within the corporate site, initiates a TCP session with 192.168.40.12, which resides in SP-C. The initial connect packet passes along firewall-a; firewall-a creates some state based on this initial session packet and routes it out through corpedge-a. 192.168.40.12 transmits a return packet flowing through SP-B to corpedge-b and then to the firewall attached to corpedge-b. When firewall-b receives this packet, it will not have the state information that firewall-a set up when it received the initial packet of the session from 172.20.84.1, and it will reject the packet, possibly even logging it as an attack or intrusion attempt on the network.

Some firewall systems recognize this sort of problem and resolve it by programming the two firewalls to communicate with each other, sharing information about what state each firewall has on connections, address translations, and so on. If the two firewalls do not support this type of functionality, the network designer will be forced to choose between two alternatives: redesigning the network so all the traffic passes through a single firewall, or forcing the traffic across the corpedge-a and corpedge-b links to be symmetric.

Symmetric Paths versus Symmetric Entry and Exit Points

What is the difference between forcing traffic to take symmetric routing paths and forcing traffic to take symmetric entry and exit points? A great deal; symmetric routing means that each packet sourced from 172.20.84.1 destined for 192.168.40.12 will take the exact same path, link by link, router by router, as traffic originating at 192.168.40.12 and destined to 172.20.84.1. As we've noted before, symmetric routing is almost impossible to achieve when traverse the Internet or large service provider networks. This is a result of the inherent nature of the hop-by-hop routing paradigm that IP is based on.

However, it is possible to narrow the problem down to a smaller domain. In Figure 2.21, we are primarily interested in forcing the traffic for flows that pass through firewall-a to return through firewall-a, and the traffic for flows that pass through firewall-b to return through firewall-b. It doesn't matter if the traffic that passes out through corpedge-a returns through corpedge-a; in fact, if this traffic passes out through corpedge-a and returns through corpedge-b it's fine, as long as coredpge-b forwards the traffic to firewall-a through corpedge-a rather than to firewall-b. So we are concerned with forcing the entry and exit points into the network to be symmetric rather than the actual paths of the packets to be symmetric.

Using Two Address Pools

One possible solution to this problem is to use two separate pools of addresses. This is possible whether you are using global IP addresses (from the pool of IP addresses assigned by the service provider) for each PC, or if you are doing network address translation at each firewall, converting private internal addresses into public addresses assigned by the service providers. Figure 2.22 illustrates this concept with each firewall performing network address translation.

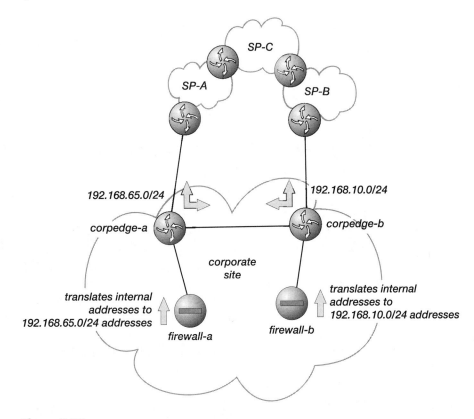

Figure 2.22
Forcing symmetric entry and exit points using two address pools.

Assume a host behind firewall-b sends a packet that initiates a session out to some server in SP-C. The server in SP-C transmits a packet back, but for some reason, the packet returns to the network through SP-A (this is possible if both service providers are advertising both address spaces). Corpedge-a would only have one route to 192.168.10.0 address in its routing table, though—through corpedge-b. It will forward the traffic across the link between the two; corpedge-b will then forward the packets on to firewall-b, and the entry and exit points would remain symmetric.

Using One Address Pool

It is also possible to force symmetric entry and exit points using a single pool of addresses by splitting the pool in half within the corporate site network. Figure 2.23 illustrates.

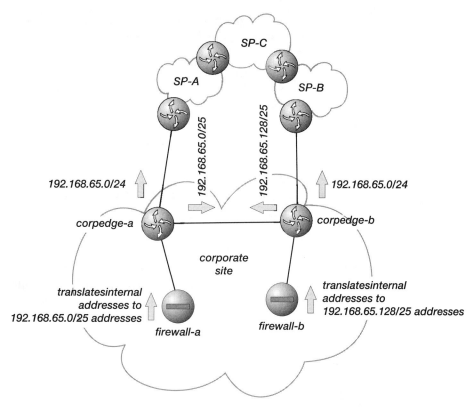

Figure 2.23
Symmetric entry and exit points using a single address pool.

Here there is a single address pool assigned by one service provider, advertised through both SP-A and SP-B. However, this single address pool has split into two smaller pools, which are used as network address translation pools on firewall-a and firewall-b. Packets belonging to a flow passing through firewall-a will always be routed to firewall-a, regardless of whether it is received through SP-A or through SP-B.

Intelligent Routing

So far, we've discussed somewhat static ways to manage the inbound and outbound traffic flow through multiple ISP connections. The principle behind intelligent routing is to measure the network's performance periodically and then to attempt to adjust the inbound and outbound traffic flows through your connections to service providers to provide optimal connectivity and/or the most accurate load sharing possible. We'll use Figure 2.24 to illustrate some principles of intelligent routing.

Generally, the intelligent routing controller is a special piece of software which resides on a host within the corporate site network. Every so often (or continuously), it samples the time it takes for a packet to travel from the intelligent routing controller to some set of sites on the Internet, using one of several methods:

- By pinging a given set of servers, such as well-known Web servers or a set of Web servers the customer specifies.
- By tracerouting to a given set of servers, such as well-known Web servers or a set of Web servers the customer specifies.
- By connecting to a set of hosts that it coorperates with; some providers of these services have servers scattered throughout the Internet to which these intelligent routing controllers can communicate.

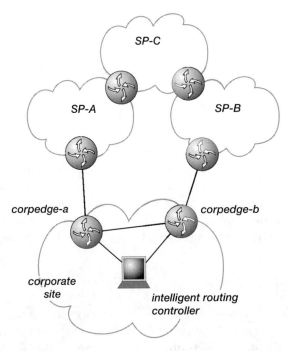

Figure 2.24
Intelligent routing concepts.

- By passively monitoring TCP performance of individual traffic flows.
- Through some other means.

The intelligent routing controller uses these periodic round-trip time measurements to determine which ISP the corporate site network should send traffic for particular servers or prefixes to, and then shifts the traffic to that service provider using some form of interaction with the router. The intelligent routing controller may peer with the corporate edge routers using BGP, or it may simply directly configure the corporate edge routers by manipulating static routes, BGP local preference through route maps, or some other method.

There are a number of companies developing software and/or appliances that perform intelligent routing functions. As the market for this type of functionality continues to evolve, more widely available solutions and products will be available in this space.

Considerations for All Service Provider Peering Situations

Whether you multihome to one service provider or many, there are several common configuration options and issues you should be aware of and make certain are handled properly.

How Not to Transit Traffic

The first of these issues is probably the most important—how not to transit traffic. Figure 2.25 illustrates a simple connection to two service providers.

Suppose AS 65240 is receiving a full routing table from AS 65241 and is then passing this full set of Internet routes on to AS 65242. What would prevent the routers in AS 65242 from preferring the path through AS 65240 for some destination within AS 65241 rather than through the Internet backbone? Nothing—which is why it's important for the routers at the edge of AS 65240 to filter their advertisements so that only those destinations reachable within AS 65240 itself are advertised through both of the eBGP peering sessions to AS 65241 and AS 65242. If you add to the equation the factor that most service providers prefer routes learned from customers over routes learned from peers, typically via BGP local preference, you'll realize that route leaks can quickly trigger negative results.

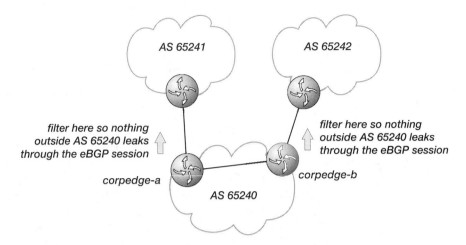

Figure 2.25
How not to transit traffic.

There are several ways to accomplish keep routes from being leaked via filtering; the first, and most direct, is to filter explicitly based on the prefixes AS 65240 actually owns (whether assigned by one of the service providers or through some address registry). Assuming that the 192.168.10.0/24 address range is within AS 65240, the following configurations will filter the advertisements from corpedge-a and corpedge-b so AS 65240 doesn't appear to be a transit path between AS 65241 and AS 65242.

```
!
hostname corpedge-a
!
router bgp 65240
 neighbor as-65241-edge remote-as 65241
 neighbor as-65241-edge prefix-list no-transit out
 neighbor corpedge-b remote-as 65240
!
ip prefix-list no-transit 10 permit 192.168.10.0/24 ge 24

!
hostname corpedge-b
!
router bgp 65240
 neighbor as-65242-edge remote-as 65242
 neighbor as-65242-edge prefix-list no-transit out
```

```
neighbor corpedge-a remote-as 65240
!
ip prefix-list no-transit 10 permit 192.168.10.0/24 ge 24
```

Each of the corporate edge routers uses a prefix list to filter out advertisements that are not in the 192.168.10.0/24 range of addresses.

Another option, which is actually simpler, is to filter the advertisements from corpedge-a and corpedge-b based on the origin autonomous system. Only those prefixes that originate within AS 65240 will be advertised to the AS 65241 and AS 65242 edge routers. The following sample configuration illustrates how to filter based on the origin autonomous system.

```
!
hostname corpedge-a
!
router bgp 65240
neighbor as-65241-edge remote-as 65241
 neighbor as-65241-edge filter-list 10 out
 neighbor corpedge-b remote-as 65240
!
ip as-path access-list 10 permit ^$


!
hostname corpedge-b
!
router bgp 65240
 neighbor as-65242-edge remote-as 65241
 neighbor as-65242-edge filter-list 10 out
 neighbor corpedge-a remote-as 65240
!
ip as-path access-list 10 permit ^$
```

AS Path filter list 10 only permits prefixes with an empty AS Path list—which means that they originated within the local autonomous system and denies all other prefixes. You could also use communities for this purpose, which we'll discuss in later sections.

Peering Techniques

When configuring a session with a BGP peer, should you peer from a loopback address or from the actual interface address connecting to that peer? There are good and bad things about each technique:

- Peering to loopback addresses means that as long as the peer can be reached, the BGP session will be up, and traffic will flow across it, removing dependencies on liveness of individual circuits, router interfaces, or linecards.
- If the route between two BGP speakers peering to their loopback addresses fails, it may take longer to recognize this failure since the interior gateway protocols must converge first and then the BGP processes on each speaker will recognize that the path between them has failed. There could be transient routing loops or black holes while the network converges.

Given these advantages and disadvantages, which one is better? As with all things in networking, it depends. If you are peering over a point-to-point link and won't have an alternative path to the peer router, then peering with the actual interface addresses makes more sense—BGP will discover, and route around, most failures more quickly. However, if you are peering two routers that are several hops apart, there are several alternative paths between the routers, and it isn't important which path between the routers is used to transit traffic between them, peering between the router's loopbacks makes more sense.

Given these guidelines, you will probably want to peer interface to interface when peering with external autonomous systems, and you will probably want to peer between loopback interface when peering between routers in the same autonomous system. Figure 2.26 illustrates both peering options.

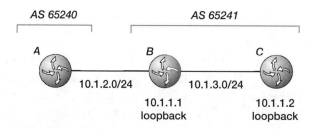

Figure 2.26
Loopback and interface-based peering.

The configurations required for loopback peering follow.

```
!
hostname A
!
router bgp 65240
 neighbor 10.1.2.2 remote-as 65241


!
hostname B
!
router bgp 65241
 neighbor 10.1.2.1 remote-as 65240
 neighbor 10.1.1.2 remote-as 65241
 neighbor 10.1.1.2 update-source loopback 0
!
interface loopback 0
 ip address 10.1.1.1 255.255.255.255
!
ip route 10.1.1.2 255.255.255.255 10.1.3.2


!
hostname C
!
router bgp 65241
 neighbor 10.1.1.1 remote-as 65241
 neighbor 10.1.1.1 update-source loopback 0
!
interface loopback 0
 ip address 10.1.1.2 255.255.255.255
!
ip route 10.1.1.1 255.255.255.255 10.1.3.1
```

Notice that the peering sessions are configured with **update-source loopback 0**. This instructs the router to establish the TCP transport connection using a source IP address of the routers loopback 0 interface rather than using the default egress interface IP address. As such, the remote router must be configured to peer with the loopback address of the router, rather than an interface address, and must have a route to the loopback address (hence the static route).

Route Origination

What's the best way to originate prefixes into BGP? There are two parts to this question: How do you get the prefixes into the routing table for BGP to advertise them, and then how do get the prefixes from the routing table into BGP so it will advertise them to its peers?

There are two ways to get a prefix into the routing table so BGP can pick it up and advertise it: through an interior gateway protocol, or through a static route to a logical interface on the router, such as a NULL interface. Considerations for both of these options include the following:

- Sourcing a prefix from an interior gateway protocol is more dynamic; if the path to the destination fails, then the route will be removed from the routing table and subsequently be withdrawn from BGP.
- Sourcing a prefix from a static route associated with a logical interface is more stable since the logical interface won't ever be down unless the router fails.
- Many service providers will probably suppress or dampen unstable BGP advertisements to them, so a wildly flaping IGP route may cause you to lose connectivity to the Internet for some length of time while the dampening penalty is reduced. BGP Dampening is disucssed in detail in later sections.

In general, for an enterprise it is better to source prefixes off a static route to a logical interface at BGP borders since this provides the most stability. The interior gateway protocol within the customer's network can be used to direct traffic around a failed link or the inability to reach a given edge router through a particular path in the network.

How routes are installed in BGP affects not only the stability of the route advertisement, it also impacts the value of the BGP Origin code. For example, paths picked up by BGP from the routing table through redistribution typically carry an Origin code of Incomplete(?), while routes installed in BGP via a static route and **network** command are listed with an Origin code of IGP(i). While the route Origin code is affected by the method used to bring the prefix into BGP, this decision point of the Origin code is low enough in the BGP decision algorithm that it typically makes little difference in actually determining which path is chosen among several available paths.

The primary difference between these two options is how the paths that are accepted into the BGP table is chosen—if you redistribute the paths, you must use filtering to make certain incorrect paths don't make it into BGP. If you use **network** statements, filtering isn't necessarily required, but each prefix you want to advertise requires a separate configuration line. Deciding which to use generally rests on which method of controlling the routes accepted into BGP the network administrator is most comfortable with.

Review Questions

1. What is the point at which the responsibility for a network connection transfers from the service provider to the customer?
2. Where would you normally get a block of addresses from if you are connecting to the Internet for the first time?
3. What are the primary advantages of dual homing to the Internet through the same Internet service provider?
4. How many routers should you use to peer with when dual homing to a single Internet service provider?
5. What is the primary disadvantage of dual homing to the same Internet service provider rather than to two different Internet service providers?
6. What other type of diversity is just as important as logical diversity?
7. What types of records can you request from your Internet service providers to determine whether or not you have enough diversity of the right types?
8. What are the primary considerations that would cause you to run eBGP with your Internet service providers?
9. How can you run BGP to an Internet service provider without a registered Autonomous System number?
10. What is the most common problem preventing traffic from flowing inbound on two links when dual homed to two different Internet service providers?
11. Can you control inbound traffic flow by controlling outbound traffic flow?
12. What methods could you investigate to balance inbound traffic flow through two different connections to the Internet?

13. What options could you consider if you only wanted to use one connection to an Internet service provider and only send traffic along a backup link when the primary link fails?

14. What are the primary means you have to control outbound traffic flow when dual homed to the Internet?

15. What is one of the major considerations when determining how to control outbound traffic flow across several connections to the Internet?

16. Why is it sometimes important to force traffic to enter and exit your network symmetrically?

17. What options can you consider when attempting to force traffic to enter and exit your network symmetrically?

18. How should you prevent your network from becoming a transit autonomous system if you are dual homing to the Internet?

3

Scaling the Enterprise Using BGP

While most network engineers think of BGP only in the context of the Internet or large-scale Internet service providers, BGP is commonly used to scale large and mid-sized enterprise networks as well. In fact, BGP may be the perfect fit in an organization where there are multiple groups or entities responsible for managing different pieces of the network, and the policies of each group are different or there are requirements for some administrative separation between each organization's routing domains. In this chapter, we'll discuss the use of BGP in large enterprise networks; where it fits in, how to connect an enterprise network using BGP to external networks, and how to use AS Confederations for BGP to scale an enterprise network.

BGP Cores

While a network using only interior gateway protocols for routing can grow to a very large size utilizing good design techniques such as well-conceived IP addressing and summarization plans, almost all networks become large enough that managing and scaling them using only an interior gateway protocol becomes difficult. If a network begins with a less than optimum design, the point where it can no longer be managed effectively becomes evident much more quickly.

In fact, splitting up a large, disorganized network managed by several different groups of administrators may be the best path to introducing better administrative control and scaling properties. Introducing

91

structure and additional policy mechanisms enabled by BGP will typically provide enough network compartmentalization to support implementation of a new network design through a series of smaller fixes, making what can sometimes appear to be a seemingly impossible task into a very solvable problem.

In this section, we'll discuss three networks that have reached the point where splitting them up into separate BGP domains will improve the network's performance and manageability.

A Large Network Split into Domains

A network can become so large its sheer size makes it difficult to manage, and difficult to achieve fast convergence and stability on, even though the network is well designed and the design is well executed. One possible situation of this type is illustrated in Figure 3.1.

In this large network, which is running OSPF for interior routing, all the routers not contained within an area are within area 0. As you can see from this diagram, the network is very large, having over 40 areas and over 50 routers in area 0. The network's addressing is well laid out; although there are over 4000 physical links, there are less than 500 routes in the routing table of any router in area 0.

This network could continue using OSPF for its routing needs, since the number of routers in area 0, the number of routes, and other indicators of a network that has become quite large are all well within reasonable ranges. However, the network administrators have noticed a few issues they would like to address.

- Areas 40 and 41 are actually two tiers deep, and several other areas are growing to the point where they will be multitiered as well. While they could be broken up into multiple areas, they would like some way to better organize these larger areas beyond placing them each in a single area or breaking them up into smaller areas and increasing the size of area 0 proportionality.

- The data center, with 27 networks where different servers and connections to larger systems reside, is actually 27 individual stub areas at the moment. Network administrators would like some way to terminate these without having to attach them all to area 0, primarily because this tends to be an area of the network which grows very quickly, especially as network security and stability becomes a larger concern in the center's daily operations.

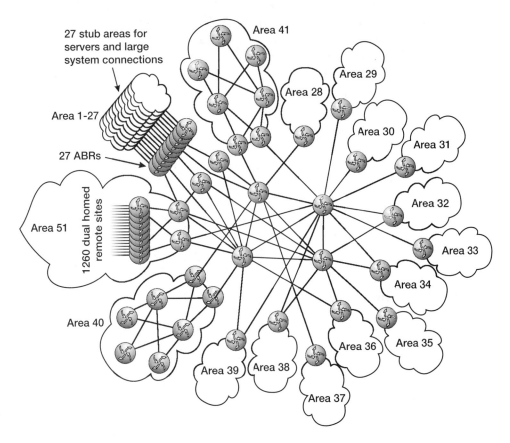

27 stub areas for
servers and large
system connections

Area 1–27

27 ABRs

1260 dual homed
remote sites

Area 51

Area 40

Area 41

Area 29

Area 28

Area 30

Area 31

Area 32

Area 33

Area 34

Area 35

Area 36

Area 37

Area 38

Area 39

Figure 3.1
A large network in need of a BGP core.

- There are 1260 remote sites, each dual homed, and over 50 routers connecting these dual homed remote sites, all in area 51. Administrators have noticed that the routing tables on each of the remote routers are growing, and convergence in this area is slowing down. They'd like some other way to organize these remote sites, but they've rejected the idea of making each of the 50 hub routers area border routers and placing each remote site in a separate stub area, as this would represent a major increase in the size of area 0.

Although administrators are aware that each of these issues could be addressed using OSPF virtual links, after many discussions within their network engineering and operations departments and consultations with outside networking experts, they have opted not to pursue this. What are their other options? Converting their core to BGP and creating separate OSPF domains within their network is one potential solution. Let's look at how converting the core of the network to run BGP could address each of these issues.

Areas 40 and 41

By dividing off areas 40 and 41 as separate OSPF processes and reconnecting them to the core of the network through BGP, we could allow these two areas to have their own area 0 and stub areas in order to organize the multitier environment in each one more clearly. Each of these new routing domains could advertise a single aggregate route into the core of the network through BGP and receive a default route only from the routers at the edge of the BGP core.

The Data Center

Currently, the data center is a mass of stub areas, each with an area border router connecting to area 0. These area border routers represent about half of the routers actually in area 0, so breaking the data center off as a separate OSPF routing domain, with its own smaller area 0, and connecting it back into the core of the network using BGP would drastically reduce the size of the current area 0. Both the data center and the rest of the network would now have a great deal of room to grow, for example, by providing additional stability and scalability properties such as scoping of OSPF LSA flooding, reduction in routing and forwarding table size, and a smaller number of OSPF nodes and routes resulting in a decrease in SPF computational complexity and improved convergence times. Figure 3.2 illustrates two possible ways of connecting these separate areas to a BGP core.

There are obvious advantages and disadvantages to each of these solutions. On the left side of Figure 3.2, each area border router must also be configured to run BGP, which could be a good deal of management overhead. However, there are no additional routers connecting each area to the core of the network, which could be important for some extremely delay-sensitive applications. There's no reason, however, that both types of connections can't be used, with some of the data center areas passing through an additional router toward the core and others connecting directly to the core.

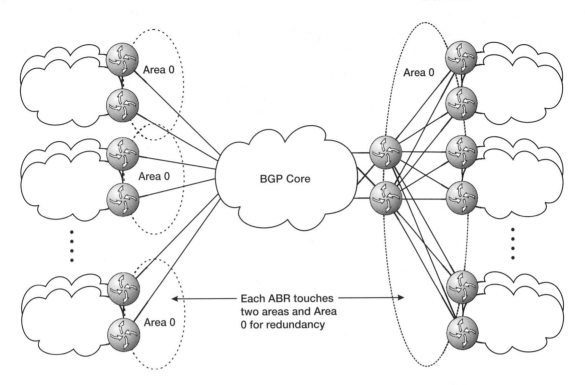

Figure 3.2
Two solutions to scaling the data center.

Area 51

Area 51 is the largest single area in this network, and it shows slow convergence times, frequent instability, and difficult maintenance issues. It's possible to resolve these issues by splitting up the area into multiple areas, each one attached to the current area 0, as Figure 3.3 shows.

While breaking off areas would certainly make this area of the network scale much better, it also requires breaking off areas on a regular basis; balancing the routers between the right areas appears to be a constant source of administrative overhead and effort. Instead, area 51 could be made into a separate OSPF routing domain and connected to a BGP core, which would allow more flexibility in managing the areas the remotes host sites are in, as Figure 3.4 illustrates.

With the configuration shown in Figure 3.4, areas may be created, and remote sites moved between areas, without impacting the core of the network in any way.

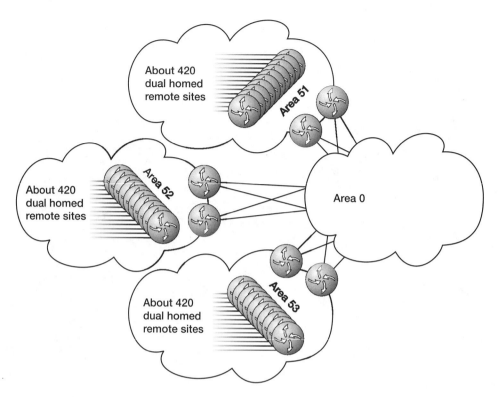

Figure 3.3
One solution to the area 51 problem.

The Smaller Areas
(Areas 28 through 39)

Finally, we come to the issue of what to do with the smaller areas, such as areas 28 through 39, which are not large enough to have more than a handful of routers in each and aren't large enough to need hierarchy within the areas. For these, a single area 0 is still a reasonable design, so the network administrators decide to leave these connected to the current area 0 and split off the other sections as described previously to build the new BGP core.

IBGP or eBGP?

Now that we've discussed each section of the network and determined how to fit them into a new BGP core, we have a network plan as illustrated in Figure 3.5.

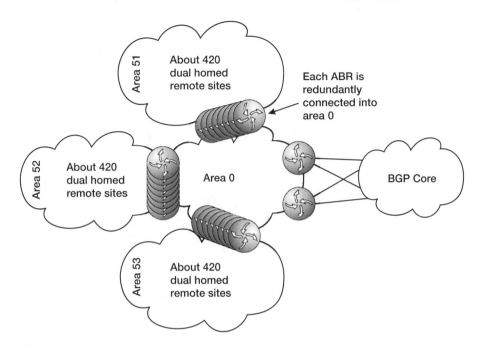

Figure 3.4
Connecting area 51 to a BGP core.

Examining Figure 3.5, you can see we've gained one more level of hierarchy within the network by using a BGP core. This allows the old OSPF areas 40 and 41 to be rebuilt into a routing domain containing its own level hierarchy. It also allows the remote sites to be divided up into three areas, with an area 0 that is independent from the core, and the data center, with its numerous networks, to be placed in a hierarchical network.

Using a BGP Core to Implement a Network Redesign

Throughout the last section, you were probably thinking to yourself, "This is all great if I had the most perfectly designed network and IP addressing plans in the world. Of course, I inherited a mess, so none of this will help me!" Well, even if you've inherited a mess, using a BGP core can be instrumental in splitting the network into a bunch of smaller more manageable networks, allowing it to continue to scale, while at the same time allowing each piece of the network to be addressed and

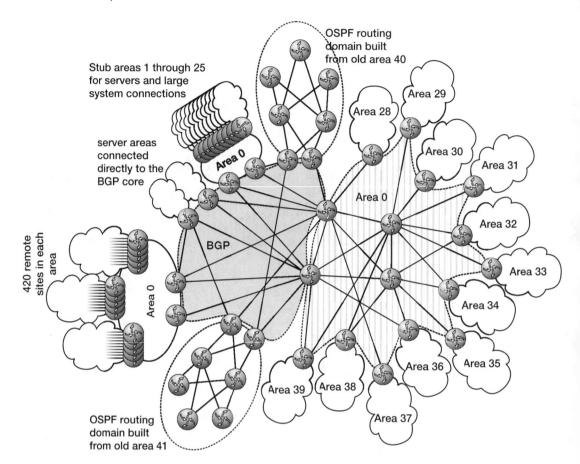

Figure 3.5
The network redesigned with an iBGP core.

redesigned as much as time and resources permit. We'll use the network illustrated in Figure 3.6 to describe how a BGP core can be used this way; although it's a small network in real terms, it does sufficiently illustrate the problems encountered in many much larger networks.

The network illustrated in Figure 3.6 started out running CLNS primarily and has been configured to support IP over time. The network runs IS-IS in dual mode, all in one large L1 routing domain, and IP addresses have been assigned on a seemingly random basis. A single ring of Packet Over SONET (POS) connections, originally a FDDI ring, serves as the network core. The network administrators have noticed that convergence is slow, router CPU consumption is high, and

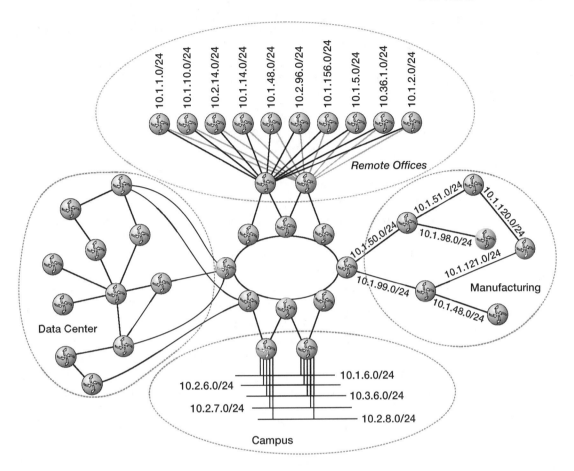

Figure 3.6
A poorly designed network.

sometimes connections to devices in the data center time out while the network converges. They'd like to start over, in some way, and make this network scale, but they don't seem to be able to convince all the necessary departments and management to allow them to perform any maintenance functions that may result in network downtime, such as re-assigning IP addresses and moving a few cables.

In this case, the network administrators would like to split up the network into different routing domains, rebuild the manufacturing area so the area is more hierarchical, and rebuild some parts of the data center network so it's easier to manage. They'd also like to reassign all the IP addresses in the entire network so they can summarize into the core of the network and better manage firewall, packet filtering, and other network security policies.

While all of this is possible taking a phased approach, the risk to the rest of the network while rebuilding the manufacturing network, for instance, due to network instability, is pretty high. A single mistake in the manufacturing rebuild could cause the campus network and remote offices to lose connectivity to the data center, for instance. How can we restructure the network in a very short period of time so each area of the network can be rebuilt at different times and reduce the risk of a total network outage while doing so?

We need some way to divide the network into smaller pieces. We could run BGP on the routers connected to the ring at the network core and stop running IS-IS across this ring. That would, in effect, separate each of the areas into a separate network, thereby allowing each area to be redesigned as needed, minimizing the potential for widespread instabilities or network outages. After each section of the network is rebuilt, readdressed, and otherwise is in satisfactory condition, the ring, running BGP, could be converted to an IS-IS L2 routing domain.

Using a BGP core, in this case, could be seen as a temporary measure, used to provide some network stability while the network is modified allowing the network to run with just an interior gateway protocol. In a very large network similar to the one shown in Figure 3.6, however, BGP may be a longer-term solution, allowing the older parts of the network to stabilize in their current condition and newer parts of the network to be designed independently of the older parts. In short, BGP can serve as a tool to separate the network, allowing each part of the network to be designed independently.

A Network Managed by Multiple Teams

As networks grow larger, their administration is often given to a group of teams, based on geographic regions, departments, or some other division. Sometimes competing requirements can make getting these teams to come to the same decision about how to design a particular piece of the network difficult since every team is trying to fulfill a different set of technical requirements. Putting a BGP core into a network that has several teams managing different parts of the network can help to divide the network, so each team can focus on the technical requirements they face and still produce a stable, scalable network. In this section, we'll discuss two places where BGP will help when dealing with a network that is managed through several teams: networks that are divided along geographic areas, and networks that are built when merging two different companies.

Networks Divided along Geographic Regions

When networks grow to a large size, they tend to be divided along geographic regions, with each region managed by a different team. The wide area network, often referred to as the network core or backbone, connecting these regions together is frequently managed by a separate team as well. Generally, in this arrangement, issues of how to appropriately segment and manage the network arise:

- Where is the edge of each region? Where does each regional network end and the core begin?
- Who should administer the routers at the edge of the core network since both the regional team and the core team have a vested interest in making certain these configurations are right?
- What routing protocol should be used throughout the network? A single interior gateway protocol may not fit all the needs of each region, so how do you build a large network with one interior gateway protocol, balancing the needs of each of these different regions?
- How can the hierarchy within the network (within the core) and the regions be maintained and the regions still be able to build hierarchy within the regions themselves?

These are typically difficult questions to answer, but using a BGP core can make answering them much easier. Let's look at Figure 3.7 as an example.

Running this sort of a network within a single interior gateway protocol routing domain would be a challenge. For instance, running an interior gateway protocol across transatlantic links could easily slow down convergence in other areas requiring very fast convergence. It's better, in this network, to place a BGP core along the wide area links and run each separate geographic area as an independent interior gateway protocol routing domain. Figure 3.8 illustrates.

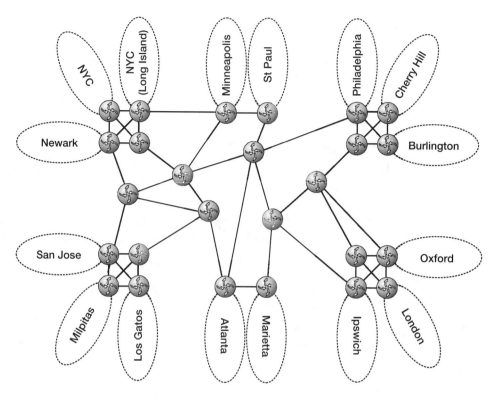

Figure 3.7
A large network divided geographically.

Now, each geographic region can manage its local part of the network without regard (pretty much) to its impact on the remainder of the network as a whole. A routing mistake in Minneapolis, for instance, likely wouldn't impact reachability between London and Newark, as long as the BGP core is managed properly. This sort of network design would also work well when a large-scale network with multiple locations is managed along divisional or political boundaries, and there needs to be some mechanism to separate the divisional pieces of the network so one network management team generally can't impact the operations of the other networks. Figure 3.9 illustrates this type of division.

Merging Networks with a BGP Core

It's not uncommon, when two companies merge, for their networks to merge as well. This typically occurs in order to decrease operational expenditures, such as circuit and staffing costs, associated with overlap-

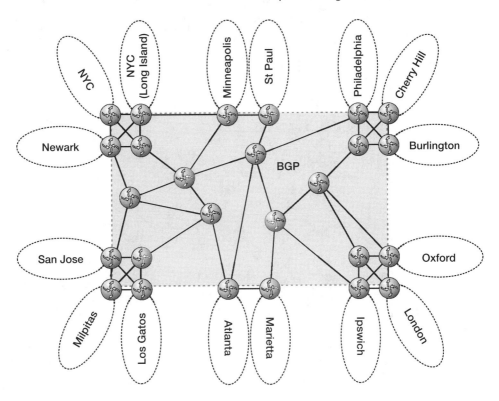

Figure 3.8
A geographically divided network with a BGP core.

ping or parallel deployments in certain markets. Generally, this is a very political, painful, and long-term exercise, and the end result isn't always an easily maintainable or manageable network. Quite often, it might be easier to continue managing the two networks as separate networks and merging smaller pieces of them over time, or implementing a new design to address all the needs of the new, merged organization. In this case, the BGP core could be treated as a longer-term (permanent) solution, which allows the network to scale, or it could be treated as a short-term solution, just to facilitate the merging of the networks.

Implementing a BGP Core

If building a BGP core is the right design choice, what is the next step? How would you go about implementing a BGP core? There are three fundamental issues that need to be addressed before discussing the

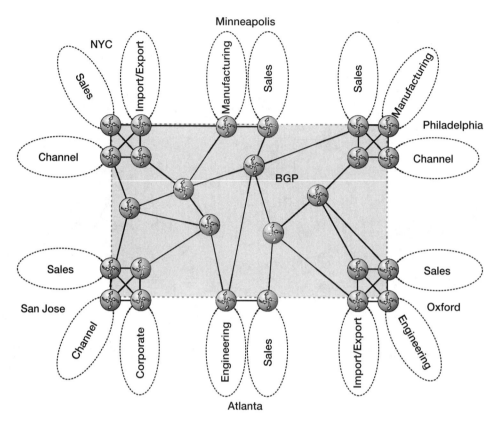

Figure 3.9
A network organized along divisional boundaries.

BGP core design itself: Should each separate routing domain within the network connect via eBGP, or should the core run iBGP to connect these separate routing domains; how should routing in the core itself be handled; and what sorts of information should be exchanged between the core of the network and each of the separate routing domains?

eBGP Cores versus iBGP Cores

The first issue we need to address is whether each routing domain will be in a separate autonomous system or they should all be in the same autonomous system. In other words, should eBGP connections be used to connect these various routing domains, or should iBGP? Figure 3.10 illustrates these two concepts.

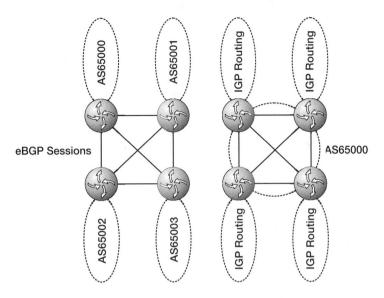

Figure 3.10
eBGP in the core versus iBGP in the core.

If each IGP routing domain within the network is configured as a separate autonomous system, then the core of the network must run eBGP to connect these separate autonomous systems. The core of the network could also be configured as a single BGP autonomous system, exchanging information between the IGP routing domains, each of which simply injects information into the iBGP core.

The primary advantage to using eBGP to interconnect these new routing domains is that the policies between the routing domains can be well defined; policy implementation can be placed above consistent routing decisions, as eBGP is guaranteed to be loop free at every point. If iBGP is used to interconnect these new routing domains, the routing decision at every point in the iBGP cloud must be the same in order to prevent routing information loops.

Using iBGP to interconnect these new routing domains presents a different set of advantages, though. For instance, it is possible to load share using multiple links across an iBGP cloud, which is difficult to do across eBGP connections. Further, the BGP community attribute can be used to propagate information such as policy through an iBGP cloud, and MPLS VPN services could be offered to connect the various domains across an iBGP cloud.

Which solution to use depends on the network itself. If you are splitting up an existing network using a BGP core, then it's probably best to use an iBGP core. If, however, you are merging networks that are already running BGP, for instance, it's probably best not to disturb the existing BGP infrastructure and run an eBGP core to interconnect these existing networks. On the other hand, one of the goals of merging the two networks may simply be for all the routers from the two networks to reside within the same autonomous system. As you can see, your options vary widely depending on the existing infrastructure and the goals of the network integration.

Routing within the Core

A BGP core, once it's built, may need an IGP to provide routing within the core, depending on how large the core is and whether the core is running iBGP or eBGP. The primary reasons a BGP core would need to run an IGP are to provide IP connectivity between BGP speakers so that BGP's underlying TCP Transport connection can be established, and to provide BGP next hop reachability information to all the BGP speakers within the core.

By default, when a BGP speaker attempts to establish a TCP Transport connection to a BGP peer, it uses the IP address of the egress interface used to reach that peer as the source address of the connection. As such, it must first be able to determine which egress interface it should use to reach the peer and therefore must have an IP routing table entry for the address of the peer. In addition, the peer must have a route back to the source IP address employed by the initiating BGP speaker and use as its source address the IP address the initiating peer expects.

A common configuration mistake is to configure a BGP connection between a set of peers with multiple paths between them and use the default source address selection behavior to establish the connections. If for any reason a different egress interface is selected to connect to the peer, the connection will fail—or it may have never been established!

Let's now examine why we might need to run an interior gateway protocol in the core in order to provide BGP next hop reachability, then examine how we can decide if we need to run an IGP within a BGP core. Figure 3.11 illustrates the reason we need to consider this decision.

In Figure 3.11, router A is advertising 192.168.1.0/24 to router B over an eBGP connection. The IP address the session between routers A and B is formed is 10.1.1.1. When Router B, in turn, advertises

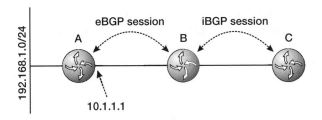

Figure 3.11
iBGP sessions and interior gateway protocols.

192.168.1.0/24 to router C, it leaves the next hop set to 10.1.1.1. In order to reach 192.168.1.0/24, then, router C must know how to reach 10.1.1.1; in other words, the route to 192.168.1.0/24 recurses through 10.1.1.1, and router C must resolve this recursion before forwarding any traffic to any host on the 192.168.1.0/24 network.

There are only two ways router C can learn 10.1.1.1 is reachable through router B: through manual configuration, such as a static route, or through an interior gateway protocol. With this in mind, let's examine an iBGP core in Figure 3.12 and determine if this core would need to run an IGP.

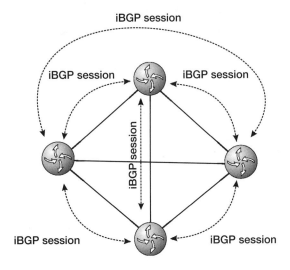

Figure 3.12
A simple iBGP core.

If all of the edge routers in this network originate, through redistribution or other means, all the routes within the routing domains attached to them, there is no need to run an interior gateway protocol within this core. This is because the next hop on each edge router is directly reachable through some physical connection between the routers themselves. Recursion is not required to reach any of the BGP next hops, and the core doesn't need to run an IGP. Another example, again purely iBGP, is shown in Figure 3.13.

In Figure 3.13, you'll notice that each of the routers at the edge of the iBGP core still has an iBGP peering session to every other router at the edge of the core. However, there is no longer a direct physical path between each pair of the routers. To reach 10.1.1.0/24, router A must be able to reach router D. Since there is no direct path from between Routers A and D, Router A must know its traffic has to pass through either routers B or C to reach router D; it could only learn this through manual configuration or through an IGP running between the routers in the iBGP core. A sample Cisco IOS Software configuration for this core is as follows:

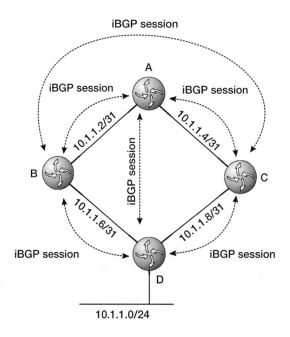

Figure 3.13
An iBGP core without a physical full mesh.

```
!
hostname A
!
router bgp 65000
 neighbor 10.1.1.3 remote-as 65000
 neighbor 10.1.1.5 remote-as 65000
 neighbor 10.1.1.8 remote-as 65000
 redistribute eigrp 200
!
router eigrp 100
 network 10.0.0.0
!


!
hostname B
!
router bgp 65000
 neighbor 10.1.1.2 remote-as 65000
 neighbor 10.1.1.5 remote-as 65000
 neighbor 10.1.1.6 remote-as 65000
 redistribute eigrp 300
!
router eigrp 100
 network 10.0.0.0
!


!
hostname C
!
router bgp 65000
 neighbor 10.1.1.3 remote-as 65000
 neighbor 10.1.1.4 remote-as 65000
 neighbor 10.1.1.8 remote-as 65000
 redistribute eigrp 400
!
router eigrp 100
 network 10.0.0.0
!


!
hostname D
!
router bgp 65000
```

```
 neighbor 10.1.1.2 remote-as 65000
 neighbor 10.1.1.5 remote-as 65000
 neighbor 10.1.1.7 remote-as 65000
 redistribute eigrp 500
 !
router eigrp 100
 network 10.0.0.0
```

Another core is shown in Figure 3.14. In Figure 3.14, each of the routers at the edge of the core has now been connected to routers outside the core with which they run eBGP. In this case, even though there is a direct connection between each of the routers running iBGP, some form of routing will be needed in the core to resolve the BGP next hops of each route learned through eBGP from these added eBGP peers around the edge.

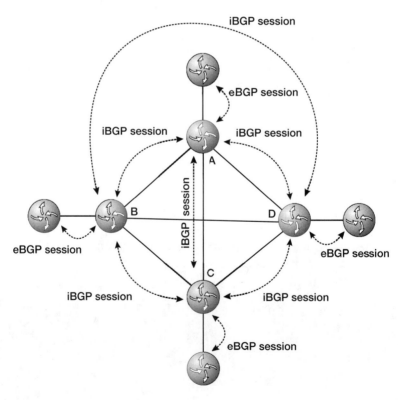

Figure 3.14
A more complex core.

It is possible to run this core without using an IGP to provide BGP next hop reachability by configuring each iBGP router at the edge with *next-hop-self,* as the following sample Cisco IOS Software configuration shows.

```
!
hostname A
!
router bgp 65000
 neighbor 10.1.1.2 remote-as 65000
 neighbor 10.1.1.2 next-hop-self
!


!
hostname B
!
router bgp 65000
 neighbor 10.1.1.1 remote-as 65000
 neighbor 10.1.1.1 next-hop-self
!
```

This will only work when the iBGP routers in the core are physically fully meshed and set the BGP next hop to that of the interconnecting interfaces, however; otherwise the problem depicted in Figure 3.13 will occur.

Originating Routes into the Core and the Domains

Once the BGP core is set up and running, how should you route among the different routing domains in the network? What types of routes should you allow into the core, how should you inject those routes, what types of routes should you allow into each routing domain, and how should you inject those routes? In general, once you've divided up the routing domain, you should inject the least amount of information (the lowest number of routes) possible from the core into each routing domain, and from each routing domain into the core. In a perfectly configured network, you should only need to inject one summary route from each routing domain into the core, and one route from the core into each routing domain, as Figure 3.15 illustrates.

Of course, the situations in which such a network will occur are generally limited to small lab environments. In most networks, you will

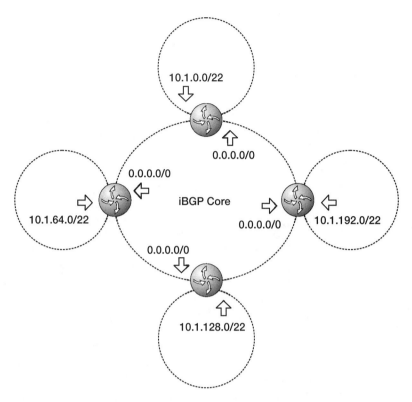

Figure 3.15
Minimal information into and out of the core.

need to inject a number of routes into the core to provide reachability to each of the attached routing domains, but you should still limit the number of routes injected from the core into the individual routing domains to the minimum number possible to provide stability to those routing domains. If you can't inject just a default route from the core into the attached routing domains, you should attempt to keep the number of routes injected to no more than a small percent of the total routes in the core of the network.

There are three general ways to inject routes into the core and into the attached routing domains; redistributing the routes, aggregating, and reoriginating the routes. Redistributing routes from the connected routing domains into the BGP core and from the BGP core into the connected routing domains is generally simple, given that the routes exist that you want to inject from one to the other.

Redistributing Route among the Core and the Routing Domains

Figure 3.16 illustrates redistribution from an attached routing domain into an iBGP core, and from the iBGP core into the interior gateway protocol running in the attached routing domain, and a sample Cisco IOS Software configuration follows.

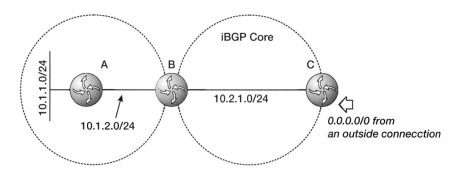

Figure 3.16
Simple redistribution between the core and a single routing domain.

```
!
hostname A
!
router eigrp 100
 network 10.1.0.0 0.0.255.255
!

!
hostname B
!
router eigrp 100
 network 10.1.0.0 0.0.255.255
 redistribute BGP 65000
 default-metric 10000 1 255 1 1500
!
router bgp 65000
 neighbor 10.2.1.1
 bgp redistribute-internal
 redistribute eigrp 100
```

```
!
hostname C
!
router bgp 65000
 neighbor 10.2.1.2
 ....
!
```

> Note the use of the command bgp redistribute-internal on Router B; Cisco IOS Software will not normally allow the redistribution of iBGP routes into any interior gateway protocol unless this command is configured. Since redistributing IGP routes into iBGP can cause routing infomation loops in some network designs, forcing the user to configure this command acts as a safegaurd against misconfigurations. It should only be used when the implications are fully understood.

While the network in Figure 3.16 shows a single redistribution point between the IGP (in this case EIGRP) and the BGP core, it's common to have two or more redistribution points so as to prevent having a single point of failure in the network. When mutual redistribution between two protocols occurs, it's very important to use some means to prevent a forwarding loops from forming from the interaction between the two routing protocols. Figure 3.17 illustrates a forwarding loop between BGP and OSPF; and explanation of how to prevent this loop follows.

In Figure 3.17, suppose router C is redistributing 10.1.1.0/24 from iBGP into OSPF. Now, when router B receives this external OSPF prefix, it will prefer the OSPF prefix over the iBGP learned prefix and set it's next hop to router C, or router A, depending on which one it learns the OSPF route from. If a packet is received by router A destined to some host on the 10.1.1.0/24 network, it will forward the packet to either router B or router C. Assume router A forwards the packet to router C. Router C will examine its local routing information, and discover that the next hop toward 10.1.1.0/24 is through B, so it will forward the packet to router B. Router B, on receiving the packet, will now examine its local routing table and determine the best path is either

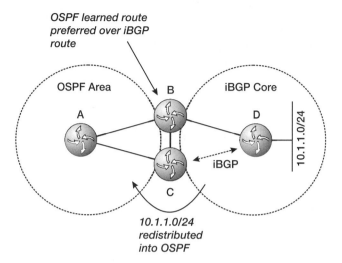

Figure 3.17
A routing loop through mutual redistribution.

through router A or through router C. This forms a complete forwarding loop.

In all cases where mutual redistribution between two routing protocols occurs, you should filter, in some way, the routes redistributed from one into the other so they cannot be redistributed back into the original routing protocol at some other redistribution point. Generally, this is done either through distribution lists, using some sort of route tagging, or not redistributing between the protocols themselves (reoriginating the routes instead).

Tagging Routes to Prevent Routing Loops

One way to tag routes in the iBGP core to prevent them from being redistributed back into the IGP is to use communities as route tags. Using the network depicted in Figure 3.18, the Cisco IOS Software configurations that follow use iBGP communities to tag the routes being learned through redistribution and then filter them out before being accepted by the other redistributing router.

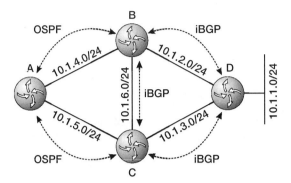

Figure 3.18
Redistribution example.

```
!
hostname A
!
router ospf 100
 network 10.1.4.0 0.0.0.255 area 0
 network 10.1.5.0 0.0.0.255 area 0


!
hostname B
!
router ospf 100
 network 10.1.4.0 0.0.0.255 area 0
 redistribute bgp 65000
 default-metric 10
!
router bgp 65000
 neighbor 10.1.2.1 remote-as 65000 route-map check-tags in
 neighbor 10.1.6.2 remote-as 65000 route-map check-tags in
 neighbor 10.1.2.1 send-community
 neighbor 10.1.6.2 send-community
 redistribute ospf route-map set-tags
 bgp redistribute-internal
!
route-map set-tags permit 10
 set community 100
!
route-map check-tags deny 10
 match community 100
```

```
route-map check-tags permit 20
 !


 !
hostname C
 !
router ospf 100
 network 10.1.5.0 0.0.0.255 area 0
 redistribute bgp 65000
 default-metric 10
 !
router bgp 65000
 neighbor 10.1.2.2 remote-as 65000 route-map check-tags in
 neighbor 10.1.6.1 remote-as 65000 route-map check-tags in
 neighbor 10.1.2.2 send-community
 neighbor 10.1.6.1 send-community
redistribute ospf route-map set-tags
 bgp redistribute-internal
 !
route-map set-tags permit 10
 set community 100
 !
route-map check-tags deny 10
 match community 100
route-map check-tags permit 20
 !
```

Again, BGP communities are only one way of accomplishing this. OSPF provides similar mechanisms to tag routes, and administrative route tag mechanisms have been defined for IS-IS as well. In addition, prefix lists could be used for this purpose, although they require manual updates each time a prefix is added or removed. As such, more dynamic mechanisms such as route tagging via communities are often preferable.

Aggregation

Rather than redistributing routes from the IGP routing domains into the BGP core, it's also possible to originate routes into the BGP core through aggregation; we'll use Figure 3.19 to illustrate.

From examining the network illustrated in Figure 3.19, you can see that 10.1.1.0/24, 10.1.2.0/24, 10.1.3.0/24, and 10.1.4.0/24 are all

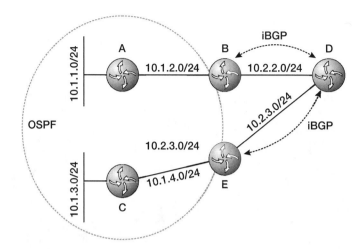

Figure 3.19
Using aggregation to originate routes into BGP.

"behind" the router at the edge of the iBGP core. Assuming 10.1.0.0/24 and 10.1.5.0 through 10.1.7.0 aren't used anyplace else, router B could advertise 10.1.0.0/21 into the core. This would, in effect, advertise the destinations that are reachable in the OSPF area into the core through aggregation rather than through redistribution, thereby resulting in a single /21 routing table entry rather than four /24 entries. Routers B and E would have the same configuration, as follows.

```
!
hostname B
!
router ospf 100
 network 10.1.0.0 0.0.7.255 area 0
 default-information origination always
!
router bgp 65000
 network 10.1.1.0 mask 255.255.255.0
 network 10.1.2.0 mask 255.255.255.0
 network 10.1.3.0 mask 255.255.255.0
 network 10.1.4.0 mask 255.255.255.0
 neighbor 10.2.2.1 remote-as 65000
 aggregate-address 10.1.0.0 255.255.248.0 summary-only
!
```

If you can aggregate the reachable destinations in the network, aggregation will provide you with routes that are only advertised as long as one of the component parts of the aggregate are reachable. For instance, in the network illustrated in Figure 3.19, if the 10.1.2.0/24 and 10.1.4.0/24 links both fail, the aggregate being advertised by router B would stop being advertised. This is useful when there are two entrance points into the routing domain.

Note also that the summary-only statement results in only the /21 prefix being advertised. If it's present, the /21, as well as the four /24 prefixes, would all be installed in the BGP routing table. The following CLI output illustrates the four /24 prefixes being suppressed by the **aggregate-address summary-only** statement:

```
r1#sh ip bgp
BGP table version is 21, local router ID is 10.0.0.1
Status codes: s suppressed, d damped, h history, * valid, > best,
i - internal,
              r RIB-failure, S Stale
Origin codes: i - IGP, e - EGP, ? - incomplete

   Network          Next Hop         Metric LocPrf Weight Path
*> 10.1.0.0/21      0.0.0.0                         32768 i
s> 10.1.1.0/24      0.0.0.0               0         32768 i
s> 10.1.2.0/24      0.0.0.0               0         32768 i
s> 10.1.3.0/24      0.0.0.0               0         32768 i
s> 10.1.4.0/24      0.0.0.0               0         32768 i
```

Reoriginating Routes

It's also possible to re-originate routes rather than redistributing them or aggregating them. This is illustrated in Figure 3.20, with a sample Cisco IOS Software configuration following.

```
!
hostname B
!
router ospf 100
 network 0.0.0.0 0.0.0.0 area 0
!
router bgp 65000
 network 10.1.0.0 mask 255.255.248.0
```

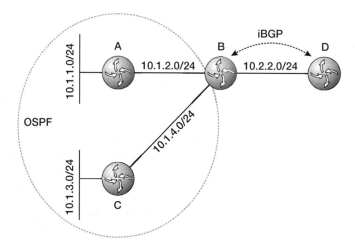

Figure 3.20
Reoriginating routes into the iBGP core.

```
 neighbor 10.2.2.1 remote-as 65000
!
ip route 10.1.0.0 255.255.248.0 null0
!
```

With this configuration, a static route for the /21 aggregate is configured on router B and is then injected into BGP through a network statement. In this case, the route is injected into the BGP core all the time, regardless of the originator's ability to actually reach the destinations within the area (i.e., regardless of the presence of the OSPF-learned route). This can provide stability in the network core, which can help the network avoid major failures in an individual area.

Which Origination Method Is Preferred by BGP?

The way in which a route is learned by BGP also impacts the algorithm BGP uses to determine the best path used to reach the destination network and determines which route should be installed in the BGP routing table. The next to the last decision point in the BGP best path algorithm considers the Origin Code associated with the route; routes that originate from an interior gateway protocol (for example, via a BGP network or aggregate-address command) are preferred over

routes learned from the Exterior Gateway Protocol (EGP), and routes
that are learned from an EGP are preferred over routes that are of an
undetermined origin (e.g., routes that are injected into BGP through redistribution).

For example, the following Cisco IOS Software output depicts
routes with three different BGP Origin codes:

```
r1#sh ip bgp
BGP table version is 29, local router ID is 10.0.0.1
Status codes: s suppressed, d damped, h history, * valid, > best,
i - internal,
            r RIB-failure, S Stale
Origin codes: i - IGP, e - EGP, ? - incomplete

   Network          Next Hop          Metric LocPrf Weight Path
*> 10.2.1.0/24      0.0.0.0                0         32768 65535
e
*> 10.2.2.0/24      0.0.0.0                0         32768 i
*> 10.2.3.0/24      0.0.0.0                0         32768 ?
```

Although all of the preceding routes were generated locally for
sake of example, the EGP route required that some EGP autonomous
system number (i.e., 65535) be specified in the path element in order to
avoid potential loops.

Suboptimal Routing with Restricted Reachability Information

Advertising a small number of routes into a given area of a network can
cause suboptimal routing to resources in the rest of the network; Figure
3.21 illustrates.

Assume that a host on the 10.1.1.0/24 network wants to open a session with a server on the 10.2.4.0/24 network. It would send its packets
to router A, which would then examine its forwarding information, and
find the closest match is the default route (0.0.0.0/0). Router A has two
equal cost default routes, one through router B and one through router
E. Since there is no way for router A to know which of these two paths
provides the shorter path, it will choose a path based on some load
sharing algorithm. It could choose the path through router E, which
would add an extra hop to the path. Router A no longer has the information necessary to choose the optimal path to the destination.

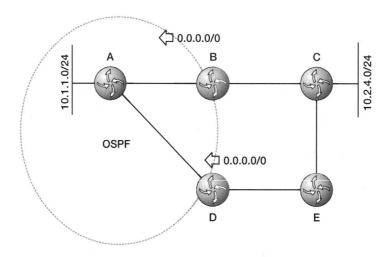

Figure 3.21
Suboptimal routing with restricted reachability information.

While this may not appear to be a major problem in the network illustrated in Figure 3.21, looks can be deceiving; for instance, router C could be in San Jose, and router E could be in London; the link between them could be a very long, low-speed link. To resolve this, you need to inject more routing information into the OSPF area. Figure 3.22 illustrates.

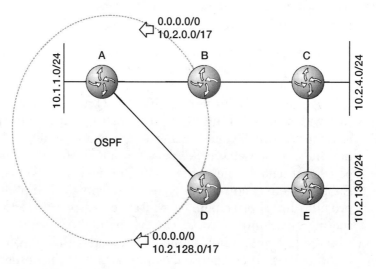

Figure 3.22
Advertising more specific summaries.

Instead of advertising just a default route into the OSPF area, two more specific summaries are added, providing enough information for router A to choose the most optimal route to each destination but still reducing the routing information advertised into the OSPF area. As you can see, router A now has sufficient information to determine the optimal path is via router D. You should also note that in the event of a failure of the path via router D, router A is still capable of forwarding packets via the route via router A because of the presence of the default route entry, 0.0.0.0/0.

External Connections

Once a large network is split up into smaller pieces, several other challenges arise; for instance, if you're using BGP within the core of your network, how do you connect the BGP core to networks in different companies, or the Internet?

Single Internet Connection

The simplest cases involve a single connection to an outside network with an iBGP core, such as the Internet, as Figure 3.23 illustrates.

If there is a single connection to an outside network, the easiest place to connect it is directly into the BGP core. A default route can be injected from this outside network, or from the edge of the BGP core

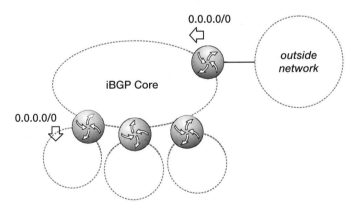

Figure 3.23
A single connection to an outside network.

and the outside network, and distributed throughout the rest of the network. Since there's only one connection between the internal and external network, this single default route will provide reachability to all the destinations inside and outside the network. An eBGP core with a single connection presents a slightly more difficult configuration, as shown in Figure 3.24.

There are two options when you are using an eBGP core to interconnect a number of smaller routing domains: reoriginating the internal routes at the border between the external and internal networks, or passing the routes through BGP and stripping off the internal autonomous systems. The following sample configurations illustrate how each of these options could be configured on the router at the edge between the networks using Cisco IOS Software.

The first configuration assumes that there are some number of routes within the 10.0.0.0/8 network in the routing table, and these can be aggregated into a single 10.0.0.0/8 route and advertised to the outside network.

```
!
router bgp 65000
 network 10.1.0.0 mask 255.255.0.0
 network 10.2.0.0 mask 255.255.0.0
 network 10.3.0.0 mask 255.255.0.0
 ....
 neighbor 192.168.100.1 remote-as <external AS>
```

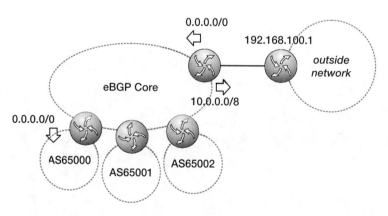

Figure 3.24
An eBGP Core with a single outside connection.

```
aggregate-address 10.0.0.0 mask 255.0.0.0 summary-only
neighbor 192.168.100.1 remove-private-as
!
router ospf 100
network 0.0.0.0 0.0.0.0 area 0
!
```

The configuration command **neighbor 192.168.100.1 remove-private-as** removes the private autonomous system numbers used for each of the smaller areas within the network. The second configuration shows how to configure the edge router to reoriginate the routes rather than redistributing them.

```
!
router bgp 65000
network 10.0.0.0 mask 255.0.0.0
....
neighbor 192.168.100.1 remote-as <external AS>
!
router ospf 100
network 0.0.0.0 0.0.0.0 area 0
!
ip route 10.0.0.0 255.0.0.0 null0
!
```

In this configuration, the 10.0.0.0/8 route will always be originated and advertised toward the outside network, regardless of whether or not any part of it is actually reachable through the edge router.

Multiple Internet Connections

Connections become more difficult when there are two or more connections to outside networks in several locations combined with an eBGP core. Figure 3.25 illustrates a network where there are multiple outside connections with an eBGP core.

While this network is slightly more difficult to manage from a routing perspective, the configuration options are the same as the configuration options for a single outside connection with an eBGP core: either reoriginating the routes at each edge, or aggregating and then advertising into the outside networks. Beyond stripping the private AS numbers, or reoriginating the internal routes, the remainder of the issues are similar to those addressed in Chapter 2, in Dual Homing to a Single Service Provider and Dual Homing to Multiple Service Providers.

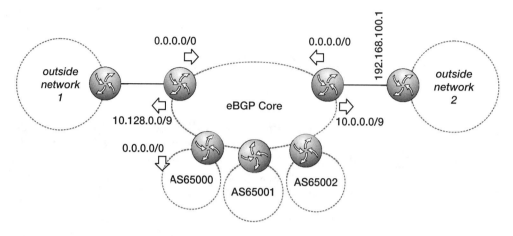

Figure 3.25
Multiple exit points with an eBGP core.

Multiple Connection Points and Confederations

The network illustrated in Figure 3.26 poses a more serious challenge; rather than the multiple connections coming into the core, each connection comes in through a different autonomous system outside the eBGP core.

Here there are two connections to an outside network from two different BGP autonomous systems connected through an eBGP core. If BGP isn't required between the outside networks and internal network, the simplest solution is to use static routes at the edges and run BGP within the network as a separate routing domain. However, if optimal routing with automatic failover between the connections to the outside networks is needed (as in the case of multiple connections to the Internet), then the only configuration that will really work is to configure the internal network as a BGP confederation.

When using BGP confederations, each sub-AS appears as a unique BGP autonomous system to all BGP routers that are members of the confederation. BGP confederation peer autonomous systems and the BGP confederation identifier are configured on each BGP speaker within the confederation. Sub-AS paths appear as a single autonomous system to nonconfederation eBGP peers, with the confederation's autonomous system value being derived from the BGP confederation identifier. BGP confederations introduce a new set of BGP attributes,

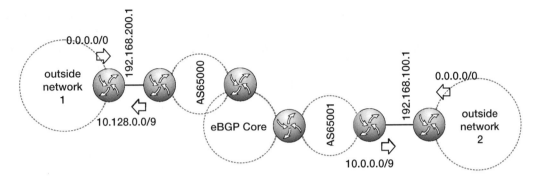

Figure 3.26
Multiple external network connections at multiple points in the network.

the AS Confederation Set and AS Confederation Sequence. These attributes are exchanged between BGP routers that are members of the confederation and, just as the AS Path is used to prevent loops with normal eBGP, provide a mechanism to prevent loops between BGP confederation peers. If a BGP speaker receives a BGP update containing an AS confederation sequence including its locally configured sub-AS in the path, it should discard the update.

Figure 3.27 illustrates this network, using a confederation to tie together the autonomous systems. Outside networks 1 and 2 both see the entire internal network as a single autonomous system, 65100, while AS65001 still sees AS65000 as connected through an eBGP connection

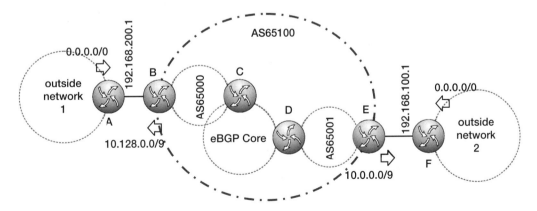

Figure 3.27
The internal network as a confederation.

across the core, AS65100. The configurations that follow provide an example of how this would be configured using Cisco IOS Software. Note that AS65100 is known as the Confederation identifier, and autonomous systems 65000, 65001 and 65100 are specified to be confederation member autonomous systems.

```
hostname b
!
router bgp 65000
 neighbor 192.168.200.1 remote-as 1
 neighbor <router c> remote-as 65100
 bgp confederation peers 65100
 bgp confederation identifier 65100
 network 10.128.0.0 mask 255.128.0.0
 ...
 ip route 10.128.0.0 255.128.0.0 null 0
!


hostname c
!
router bgp 65100
 neighbor <router b> remote-as 65000
 neighbor <router d> remote-as 65100
 bgp confederation peers 65000 65001
 bgp confederation identifier 65100
!


hostname d
!
router bgp 65100
 neighbor <router e> remote-as 65001
 neighbor <router c> remote-as 65100
 bgp confederation peers 65000 65001
 bgp confederation identifier 65100
!


hostname e
!
router bgp 65001
 neighbor 192.168.100.1 remote-as 2
```

```
neighbor <router c> remote-as 65100
bgp confederation peers 65100
bgp confederation identifier 65100
network 10.0.0.0 mask 255.128.0.0
...
 ip route 10.0.0.0 255.128.0.0 null 0
!
```

As you can see, all BGP routers are configured with **bgp confederation identifier 65100**, which is used to define the AS number used when peering with nonconfederation member eBGP peers. In addition, all peer autonomous system numbers representing members of the local confederation are specified via the **bgp confederation peers** command.

In addition, BGP confederation attributes must never be advertised to normal eBGP peers. Several broken implementations have advertised BGP confederation attributes to nonconfederation peers, resulting in continuous BGP session resets and widespread BGP instability.

Review Questions

1. What are some common reasons for splitting up a large enterprise network using BGP?
2. When merging two networks, should you consider using a BGP core as a permanent solution or a short-term solution?
3. What is the primary advantage of using eBGP within the core of an enterprise network versus iBGP?
4. What is one of the primary advantages of using iBGP to build a BGP core within an enterprise network?
5. What is the primary reason a BGP core will still need to run an IGP?
6. What are the three primary ways of originating routes into BGP?
7. What is one important consideration to consider when using two points of mutual redistribution between two routing protocols?

4

Core Design with iBGP

In the previous chapter we discussed using BGP to build or redesign a core for an enterprise network; this chapter builds on this by discussing the implementation of iBGP in a network core. Thus, we will be looking more in depth at the actual deployment of iBGP within the core of any network, enterprise, or service provider. We begin with a discussion of full mesh in iBGP and why it's necessary. Then we discuss the use of Route Reflectors and Confederations within an iBGP core to relax the requirement for a full iBGP mesh.

Full Mesh iBGP Cores

One possible way to design an iBGP core is to mesh fully each of the iBGP speakers in the core—each iBGP speaker must have a direct peering relationship with each other iBGP speaker. The first set of questions that comes to mind is, Why is this? What property of iBGP requires that all the iBGP speakers in a given autonomous system must be peered to one another? What impact does this rule have on the scaling of the iBGP core? These questions are discussed in the following sections.

Why Full Mesh?

There's a simple rule in BGP that states, *When a BGP speaker receives an UPDATE message from an internal peer, the receiving BGP speaker shall not redistribute the routing information contained in that UPDATE message to other internal peers.* As a result, in native BGP, all the iBGP speakers (devices running BGP within the same autonomous system) must be directly peered to one another in order to provide complete connectivity. Figure 4.1 helps to illustrate why this is the case.

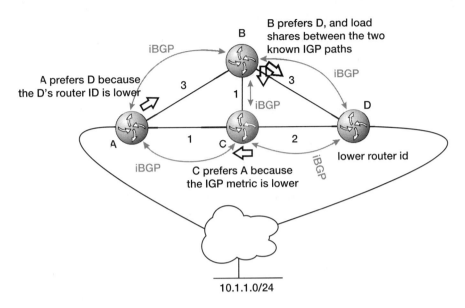

Figure 4.1
A possible routing loop using iBGP.

Assume for a moment that the preceding iBGP route advertisement rule didn't exist and that iBGP peers are permitted to announce routes learned via iBGP to other iBGP peers so long as they don't use the peer to reach the destination. In the network illustrated in Figure 4.1, all the routers (except router E) are within the same autonomous systems and iBGP peering only with immediately adjacent routers, so there is no full mesh of iBGP.

- Router E advertises 10.1.1.0/24 to router C.
- Router C advertises the route to routers A, B, and D.
- Router A advertises the route to router B, router B advertises the route to routers A and C, and router D advertises the route to router B.
- Router A prefers the path via router B to reach router C per the lower IGP metric value (4 versus 5).
- Router A therefore announces the route it learned from router B to router C because router C is not the peer that router A uses to reach the destination, nor is router C the peer that the route was learned from.

Router C has no mechanism to determine that the route announced by router A was actually originated by itself. As a result, a routing information loop is created (note the distinction of *routing information loop* here as opposed to *forwarding loop*). Given, this is a trivial example, but in complex topologies with lots of routing information, such duplication of routes and routing information loops not only result in unnecessary resource consumption but may also result in forwarding loops.

The fundamental reason for this routing information loop is BGP's use of the AS Path to guarantee a loop-free path between autonomous systems. Within an autonomous system, the AS Path does not change, and BGP has no mechanism to ensure loop-free paths. To resolve this, iBGP peers follow this simple rule–any route learned through iBGP is never advertised to any iBGP peer. Only routes learned through eBGP sessions or originated by the local system may be advertised to iBGP peers.

This implies that there cannot be more than one iBGP hop through an autonomous system; every iBGP router must be peered with every other iBGP router in the autonomous system. And, in fact, this is the way BGP was originally designed to operate, with all the iBGP speakers connected through a full mesh of BGP peering sessions. Figure 4.2 illustrates a full mesh version of the iBGP core illustrated in Figure 4.1.

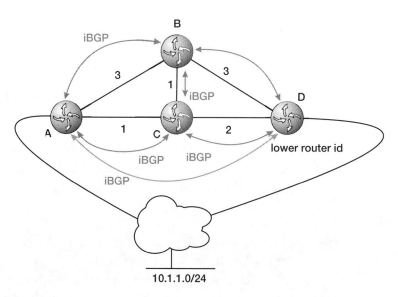

Figure 4.2
A full mesh iBGP core.

The physical network is still not a full mesh network, but the addition of an iBGP session between routers A and D completes the iBGP mesh. We can now apply the iBGP advertisement rule that no iBGP speaker should advertise a route to another iBGP speaker if the route was learned from an iBGP peer.

In Figure 4.2 all the routers now have the same routing information and will be making the same decisions, but the number of route advertisements is much lower and the possibility of routing information loops is removed by applying the iBGP route advertisement rule. Typically, smaller iBGP cores, and sections of larger iBGP cores, employ a full mesh of iBGP connections between routers within the network core.

Implications of Full Mesh Cores on Scaling

What are the implications of fully meshing iBGP peers in the core? Figure 4.3 illustrates three cores we can compare to determine this.

If we are running full mesh iBGP, each BGP speaker in the iBGP core with four routers will have three other peers. In the iBGP core with five routers, each BGP speaker will have four peers, and in the iBGP core with six routers, each BGP speaker will have five

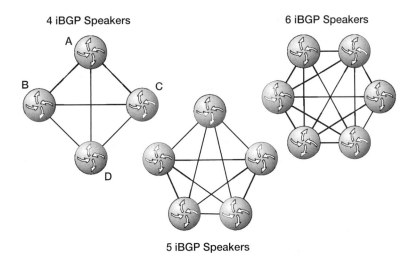

Figure 4.3
Three fully meshed iBGP cores.

peers. Thus, the number of iBGP peers each BGP speaker must maintain will increase in proportion to the number of routers in the iBGP core. This clearly isn't scalable from a network management perspective; if you have 99 routers in an iBGP core, you must configure all 99 existing routers in order to introduce one additional iBGP speaker to the core.

> To determine the number of sessions an iBGP speaker will be required to maintain in a fully meshed topology, simply multiply the number of routers (n) in the autonomous system by $n - 1$ (no session is required with itself) and then divide by 2; $n*(n - 1)/2$.

But speaker configuration and network management are only one part of the issue. A less obvious but more significant issue is the impact of a full mesh iBGP in the core of a network on the memory requirements and performance of the network. In Figure 4.3, for instance, assume each iBGP speaker in the core is receiving 1000 routes from some eBGP peer outside the core. Each iBGP speaker attached to the core is receiving the same 1000 routes. So, in the four-router network, routers A, B, C, and D are all receiving identical routes from some source outside the iBGP core. If each of these routers prefers the externally learned route over any other route received, then each iBGP speaker will advertise these 1000 routes to each of its peers.

Thus, router A would receive 1000 routes from some external peer, the same 1000 routes from router B, the same 1000 routes from router C, and the same 1000 routes from Router D. Router A will receive four copies of each route, incurring the cost of storing each of these routes, determining which path among those received is the best path, and transmitting some number of them to its peers. Router A will store, and handle, four copies of each known destination, 4000 prefixes, when only 1000 will be used.

As the network becomes larger, this waste of resources becomes worse. In the five-router iBGP core, each iBGP speaker will wind up holding 4000 routes they will not use; in the six-router iBGP core, each router will end up holding 5000 routes it will not use.

Route Reflectors

From the preceding sections on full mesh iBGP cores, and the scaling implications of iBGP cores, it's obvious that we should look for some way to eliminate the need for a full mesh among iBGP speakers in the same autonomous system. How could this be accomplished given the possibility of routing loops or reachability problems if we don't maintain a full mesh of connectivity? One possibility is *route reflection,* which reorganizes the iBGP core into a hierarchy and relaxes the iBGP route advertisement rules. Route reflection introduces the notion of *reflected routes,* which allows BGP speakers to break the rule of never advertising a route learned through iBGP to another iBGP peer in specific circumstances.

> Route Reflection is described in RFC 2796, *BGP Route Reflection—An Alternative to Full Mesh iBGP,* April 2002.

How Route Reflection Works

While the concept of route reflection is simple, the actual implementation of route reflection is a bit more difficult; reflected routes must not generate a routing information loop within the autonomous system. There are several changes to the way iBGP functions for route reflection, and each one must be present to make reflection work properly; each one of these changes is covered in the following sections.

Rules for Reflecting Routes

The first change required to make route reflection work is to define a set of rules defining which routes are reflected, which routes aren't, and what peers they're reflected to. To make things clearer, route reflection divides the iBGP peers of a route reflector into two groups: *client peers* and *nonclient peers.* A route reflector or set of route reflectors and its clients form what's referred to as a *route reflection cluster.*

Recall that BGP speakers only announce a single best route for any set of BGP paths for a given prefix. As such, the rules that a route reflector must use to determine where to reflect a route are applied after the BGP router has ran its best path selection algorithm. The route reflection advertisement rules are as follows:

- If the route was received from a nonclient peer, reflect the route to all client peers.
- If the route was received from a client peer, reflect the route to all nonclient peers and client peers.

Because a route reflector reflects routes learned from a client to nonclient and client peers, clients within a cluster need not be fully meshed. There are actually two options regarding client peering within a cluster. The common default behavior, intuitively referred to as *client-to-client reflection*, requires the route reflector to reflect routes learned from client peers to other client peers. The alternative option is not to use client-to-client reflection and maintain a full mesh of iBGP sessions within all the clients of a cluster. With the latter option, the second rule is modified slightly. We'll discuss both these configurations and the accompanying advantages and disadvantages as we progress.

Figure 4.4 illustrates a small set of routers we will use to describe the rules for reflecting routes.

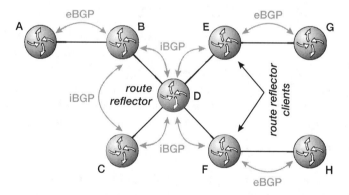

Figure 4.4
Route reflection.

In Figure 4.4 routers B, C, D, E, and F are in the same AS. Routers D, E, and F are in the same cluster, for which router D is the route reflector with E and F as clients. Routers B and C are nonclient iBGP peers of router D. Let's work through advertisements received from routers A, G, and H, as they pass through the route reflector, router D. We'll begin with an advertisement originating at router A:

- Router B receives the advertisement through eBGP from router A. Since the route is learned through eBGP, router B advertises the route to all of its iBGP peers, Routers C and D.
- When router C receives the route, it will not advertise it to any of its peers, since the only other peer it has, router D, is an iBGP peer, and the route was learned through iBGP from router B.
- When router D receives the route, it will not advertise the route to router C, since router C is a non-client peer, and the route was learned through iBGP from router B, who is a non-client peer. Router D will, however, *reflect* the route to routers E and F, since they are route reflector clients of router D.
- Subsequently, routers E and F will advertise this iBGP learned route to their eBGP peers, routers G and H.

As you can see, the rule used for advertising routes learned from an iBGP peer that is not a route reflector client is simple: the route reflector must not advertise routes learned from normal (non-client) iBGP peers to other (nonclient) iBGP peers that are not route reflector clients, but it must advertise the route to all route reflector clients. Let's consider an advertisement originating at router G.

- Router E receives the route through its eBGP peering session with router G. Since this route is learned through eBGP, router E will advertise it to each of its iBGP peers, which includes only router D.
- Router D receives the route through an iBGP session from a route reflector client. Normally, a route learned from an iBGP peer would not be advertised to any other iBGP peers, but since router D is a route reflector and the route was received from an iBGP client peer, router D will advertise the route to each of the iBGP clients, which includes only router F, and to each of its nonclient iBGP peers, which includes routers B and C.
- Since router F received the route through an iBGP session it will advertise the route to its eBGP peer, router H.
- When router B receives the route, it will advertise it to its only eBGP peer, router A. It will not advertise the route to router C because it peers with router C using normal iBGP, and the route was learned through iBGP.

In this case, the rule is simple, as well: A route learned from a route reflector client should be advertised to all iBGP peers (clients and nonclients), including other route reflector clients and nonclients. Finally, we will examine what happens when a route is originated through both routers G and H.

- Routers E and F both receive a route through their eBGP connections with routers G and H. They both advertise the route to their only iBGP peer, router D, since the route was learned through eBGP.
- Router D receives two copies of the route from its client iBGP peers. It runs its best path algorithm and selects one of the two routes as the best path toward this destination. Assume it chooses the path through router E.
- Router D now advertises the path through router E to the other route reflector clients through iBGP, which is only router F. Router F will continue to prefer the externally learned route to this destination. Router D also advertises the route to its nonclient iBGP peers, routers B and C.
- Router B receives the route from an iBGP peer and advertises it to its eBGP peer, router A. It will not advertise the route to router C, since the route was learned from an iBGP peer.
- Router C receives the route from router D, an iBGP peer, and does not advertise it to router B, since router B is also an iBGP peer.

The route reflector, in this case, must choose the best path among those received from route reflector clients and then advertise the best path to all other route reflector clients and all nonclient iBGP peers. Just as with any BGP router, the route reflector always runs the best path selection algorithm and selects only one best route for each prefix, regardless of whether the routes were received from client peers, nonclient peers, or both. As such, had the same route been learned by router D via routers A and B and routers G and E, router D would determine which path was best. If the path learned from router E is selected as best, the route advertisement rules associated with routes learned from clients would apply. If the path learned via router B was selected as best, the route advertisement rules associated with routes learned via nonclient iBGP peers would apply.

New Attributes Added
to Prevent Loops

Two new attributes are added to the routes reflected through a route reflector to prevent loops within the autonomous system: the *Originator
ID,* and the *Cluster List.* The purpose of these will become clear in the
following example.

Routers A, B, C, D, and E are all in the same autonomous system.
Router A is a route reflector client of router B. Router C is a route reflector client of router A. Routers D and E are route reflector clients of
router C. Let's assume a route is generated on router F, and follow it
through this example network.

- Router D receives the route through eBGP from router F and
  advertises it to its iBGP peers, which in this case is only router
  C.
- Router C receives the route from a route reflector client, so it
  advertises the route to router E, another route reflector client,
  and to routers A and B, both nonclient iBGP peers.
- Router B receives the route through a non client iBGP session
  and advertises the route to its route reflector clients, in this case
  only router A.

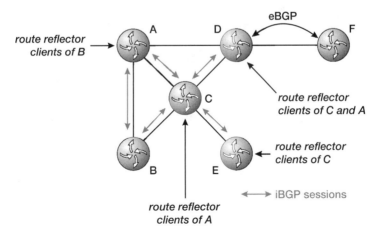

Figure 4.5
Attributes added to prevent loops in route reflection.

- Router A receives the route from a client iBGP peer with router B, and so router A advertises the route its route reflector clients, in this case router C.
- Router C received the route from a nonclient iBGP peer and will advertise the route to its clients, routers D and E.

We now have a routing information loop through simple reflection, even though we followed the rules of reflecting advertisements each step of the way. Given, the topology and configuration in the example could be modified to avoid this, but such loops are easily introduced in more complex topologies. This sort of loop is resolved by introducing two new BGP attributes associated with BGP route reflection, the Originator ID and the Cluster List.

The Cluster List contains a sequence of Cluster ID values and is used to record the reflection path traversed by the route as it passes through the autonomous system. The Cluster ID values are, by default, set to the Router ID of the reflecting route reflector, or to some otherwise explicitly configured value. A route reflector when receiving a route from a client peer sets the Originator ID to the value of the Router ID of the client from which the route was received.

Let's take another look at the sequence of events with these new attributes added.

- Router D receives the route through eBGP and advertises it to its peers, which in the example is only router C. Note that router D doesn't need to know it's a route reflector client of router C.
- Router C receives this route through an iBGP session with a route reflector client. Router C, as a route reflector, adds a Cluster List attribute to the route, and places its own router ID (or some explicitly configured value) in the Cluster List. Router C also places the router ID of router D into an Originator ID field now associated with the route.
- Router C advertises the route to its nonclient iBGP peers, routers A and B, and to each of its other route reflector clients, router E.
- Router B receives this route from a nonclient iBGP peer. Because it is a route reflector, before advertising the route to any of its peers, it prepends the locally configured Cluster ID (i.e., its router ID or some explicitly configured value) to the Cluster List router C created. The Originator ID added by router C is preserved.

- Router B advertises the route to each of its route reflector clients, which is only router A.
- Router A, as a route reflector, prepends its Cluster ID to the Cluster List router C originally created and reflects the route to each of its route reflector clients, which is only router C.
- Router C receives the route from router A. Upon receipt of the route from router A, router C examines the Cluster List attached to the route. Router C determines its Cluster ID is already in the Cluster List, so it discards the route.

Although not explicitly demonstrated in the preceding example, the purpose of the Originator ID is quite simple. Assume a session was configured between router A and router D, with router A as the route reflector and router D as the client. After receiving the route from router B, router A would advertise the route to router D. Upon receipt, router D would examine the routes attributes and realize that the Originator ID was equal to the local router ID, and therefore discard the route.

Effectively, the Cluster List provides path information within the autonomous system, much as the AS Path provides path information between autonomous systems. The Cluster List and Originator ID are both optional nontransitive BGP attributes, which means they are removed at the border of an autonomous system and should never be advertised to any eBGP peers.

> For backward compatibility, the first version of the Route Reflection specification, RFC 1966, did not require clients to check the Route Reflection attributes. Instead, it required route reflectors not to reflect routes to a client if the route was learned from the client, or if the Originator ID value is equal to the router ID of the client. However, the current version of the specification requires the client to check the Originator ID value. This is especially important as a widely deployed implementation, when performing client-to-client reflection, reflects the route back to all clients, including the client from which the route was received.

Modification of Other Attributes

When reflecting a route, a route reflector should never change the BGP Next Hop, Local Preference, Multiple Exit Discriminator, or the AS Path attributes associated with the route. Changing any of these can result in forwarding loops; Figure 4.6 illustrates a routing loop created when a route reflector changes the BGP Next Hop for a route it reflects.

Let's work through how router C can change the BGP Next Hop on a route learned from router A, thereby introducing a routing loop.

- Router A originates some route, advertising it to router B.
- Router B is a route reflector client of both router C and router D, although routers C and D are in different clusters. Router B advertises the route to each of its iBGP peers, both of which it is a client of.
- Router C receives this route from a client peer, router B. Its policy is configured to change the BGP Next Hop to itself when advertising routes to iBGP peers. As such, before it reflects the route learned from router B to router D, it adds the cluster list and originator ID and resets the BGP next hop to router C.
- Router D receives the route from router B as well. Its policy is also configured to change the BGP next hop to itself when advertising routes to iBGP peers. As such, before it reflects the route learned from router B to router C, it adds the cluster list and originator ID, and resets the BGP next hop to router D.

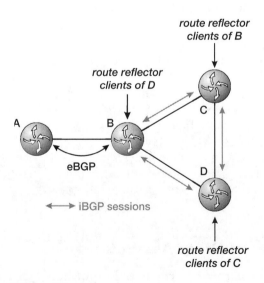

Figure 4.6
Route reflection loop created by changing the BGP next hop.

- Router D prefers the reflected path it receives from Router C over the path learned via router B because of the lower IGP metric (2) associated with reaching the BGP Next Hop. Router C prefers the path reflected from router D over the path learned via router B because of the lower IGP metric (2) associated with reaching the BGP Next Hop.

We now have a forwarding loop between routers C and D. Had we preserved the router B as the BGP Next Hop, routers C and D would have preferred the paths learned directly from router B and the forwarding loop would not have occurred.

Deploying Route Reflectors

How can route reflectors be used to increase the scalability of an iBGP core? The simple answer is through reducing the number of iBGP sessions required within the iBGP core and reducing the number of paths each iBGP speaker in the autonomous system must hold and process. There are also additional considerations when deploying iBGP route reflectors–for instance, redundancy within an iBGP core using route reflectors, which is covered in this section.

How Many Route Reflectors?

One of the largest concerns when deploying route reflectors is creating single points of failure within a network. Figure 4.7 illustrates a simple iBGP core using route reflection, along with several single points of failure.

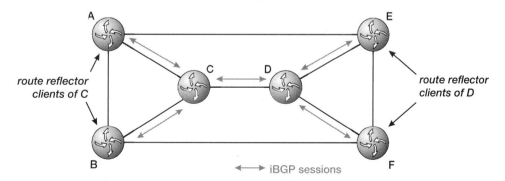

Figure 4.7
Single points of failure in a simple reflected iBGP core.

If either router C or D fails in this network, the entire network fails, even though physical connectivity still exists between the edge routers (the route reflector clients). To prevent a single router failure from causing the entire network to fail, a route reflector client may receive routes from more than one route reflector server; Figure 4.8 illustrates.

In this simple iBGP core, there are four route reflectors, each pair serving a set of edge routers within their respective cluster. If any one of the four route reflectors fails, the paths will still be available via the parallel route reflector, and therefore the network won't completely fail and the network is more fault tolerant. As you can see, adding more reflectors helps to increase the redundancy in the network.

Adding route reflectors also increases the number of redundant paths each of the edge routers must store and run through the best path calculation. At some point, you can add enough reflectors to create more work in the network than a simple full mesh would produce. Figure 4.9 illustrates.

- With no route reflectors, router B will need to build an iBGP peering session with routers A, C, and D. It will receive two copies of the advertisement for the 10.1.1.0/24 network, one from router A, and the other from router B.
- With one route reflector, router B will need to build a single iBGP peering session, with the route reflector. Router B will receive one copy of the advertisement for the 10.1.1.0/24 network,

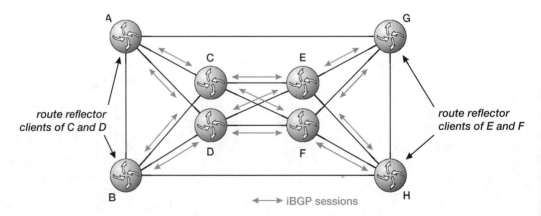

Figure 4.8
Redundancy in a simple iBGP reflected core.

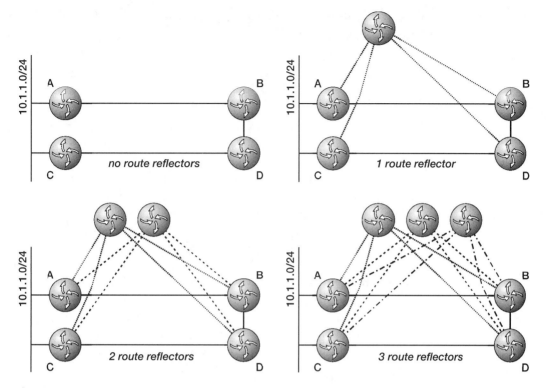

Figure 4.9
Increasing numbers of route reflectors.

from the route reflector. Note that as previously discussed, there is no redundancy in this model.

- With two route reflectors, router B will need to build two iBGP peering sessions, one with each route reflector. Router B will receive two copies of the advertisement for the 10.1.1.0/24 network, one from each route reflector.

- With three route reflectors, router B will need to build three iBGP peering sessions, one with each route reflector. Router B will receive three copies of the advertisement for the 10.1.1.0/24 network, one from each route reflector.

As you can see from this illustration, there is a limit to the number of useful route reflectors in an iBGP core; more reflectors do not imply a better design or less work being done in the network. Instead, you should carefully consider how much work route reflectors are saving in the network and balance this with redundancy requirements before deciding how many route reflectors there should be and where they should be placed.

Cluster IDs with Multiple Route Reflectors

When you have a multiple route reflectors serving the same set of clients, should the cluster ID be set to the same address on each of the route reflectors (placing both of the route reflectors in the same *route reflector cluster),* or should it be set to a different address on each route reflector? Let's use Figure 4.10 to consider these two options.

The question is, in its simplest form, should Routers A and B both be marking the updates that they receive with the same Cluster ID attribute? Let's examine what happens if they do not:

- Router C receives some route from router F, an eBGP peer. It advertises the route to routers A and B.
- Router A creates a new Cluster List attribute and inserts its router ID (or the otherwise explicitly configured cluster ID). It also sets the originator ID to the router ID of router C. Router A then advertises the route to routers B, D, and E.
- Router B, when it receives this update, examines the Cluster List attribute and discovers that its locally defined cluster ID is not in the list. It accepts the advertisement and prepends its cluster ID to the Cluster List.

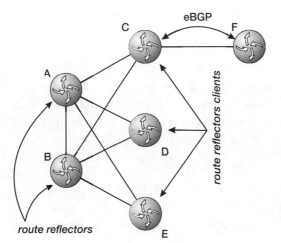

Figure 4.10
A simple route reflector cluster with two route reflectors.

- Router B also receives the update from router C, creates a new Cluster List attribute, and inserts its cluster ID. It also sets the originator ID to the router ID of router C. Router B then runs the best path algorithm and determines which of these two paths to use (i.e., the path learned via router A or the path via router C directly).
- Router B selects the path learned directly via router C as best and advertises this update to routers D, E and A.

Because routers A and B are using different identifiers to mark the Cluster List attribute on the update, routers D and E each receive two copies of the update. This means they need to install and maintain two copies of this update in their BGP routing table. However, if routers A and B were configured to insert the same cluster ID into the Cluster List attribute, the following would occur, instead:

- Router C receives some route from router F, an eBGP peer. It advertises the route to routers A and B.
- Router A creates a new Cluster List attribute and inserts its cluster ID (which is the same as the value configured on router B, rather than the default value obtained from the BGP router ID). It also sets the originator ID to the router ID of router C. Router A then advertises the route to routers B, D, and E.
- Router B receives this update and examines the Cluster List. Since its locally defined cluster ID is already in the Cluster List, router B discards the update.
- Router B also receives the update from router C, adds a Cluster List attribute, and inserts its cluster ID. Router B also sets the originator ID to the router ID of router C. Router B advertises this update to each of its route reflector clients, routers D and E, as well as its iBGP peer, router A. (Note: some implementations would reflect the route to router C as well, in which case router C should reject it since its router ID is listed in the Originator ID attribute.)
- When router A receives the update from router B, it discards it because the cluster list contains the locally configured cluster ID.

Now routers A and B are only required to store one copy of the route, even though routers D and E must store two copies. While this might not seem like a significant advantage, imagine a network with hundreds of redundantly deployed route reflectors with tens of thousands of routes. Using the same cluster IDs for multiple reflectors within a cluster could result in savings of tens of thousands of routes.

A significant problem can occur when you place routers A and B in the same route reflector cluster and configure them with the same cluster ID, however—it's relatively easy to create a situation where a destination doesn't appear reachable although simple topology changes would provide appropriate connectivity. Figure 4.11 illustrates a small reflector network of four routers we can use to explain this problem.

Router C announces 10.1.1.0/24 to router B, which advertises it to router A. Router A adds the cluster list and originator ID fields and inserts its configured cluster ID. Let's assume routers A and D are configured with the same cluster ID for a moment. When router A advertises the 10.1.1.0/24 route to router D, router D will discard the prefix because the cluster ID is the same as the locally configured value. To resolve this, we could configure routers A and D with different cluster IDs; then router D would accept the path from router A and pass it along to router E. However, this configuration still presents a single point of failure with either router A or router D.

The most typical configuration of this sort requires router B not only peer with router A as a route reflector client but that it peer with router D as a route reflector client as well. This would allow router D and router E to receive the 10.1.1.0/24 announcement from router B. However, if for some reason router D fails, router E will lose the route, even though a physical path still exists between routers E and B. Naturally, the sensible thing to do is to configure router E as a router reflector client of router A. This way, if router A or router D fails, then router

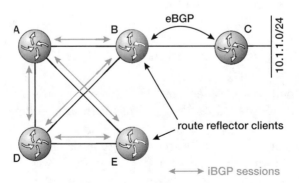

Figure 4.11
A simple network with reflection.

E and router B can still reach one another and learn of one another's destinations via BGP route reflection.

In the preceding scenarios, routes learned from a route reflector client are always advertised to other clients, assuming policy permits. This behavior is referred to as *client-to-client reflection.* There is another alternative, however. Rather than routers A and D reflecting the 10.1.1.0/24 learned route from router B to router E, a normal iBGP session could be configured between the two clients, allowing them to exchange routes directly. Then, so long as some path and connectivity exists between routers E and router B, they'll always be able to exchange routes. While this may seem like the optimal solution, it requires some additional consideration. If you intend to have direct iBGP peering sessions between clients in a cluster, you'll likely want to disable client-to-client reflection on the route reflectors serving the cluster. It'll also require that every time a client is added to the cluster sessions be configured between it and every other client in the cluster.

As a general recommendation, it's not a good idea to have mixed clusters that incorporate both client-to-client reflection and direct peering sessions between clients. You should either maintain a full mesh of client peering sessions within a cluster, or no peering sessions between clients and employ client-to-client reflection. Most implementations perform client-to-client reflection as a default behavior and don't provide a mechanism to configure mixed route reflection clusters.

Physical Topology versus Logical Topology

Since route reflection relaxes the route advertisement rules when advertising a route learned through an iBGP peer to another iBGP peer, it is possible to create routing information loops using route reflectors. The key, in most cases, is to make the logical reflection topology follow the physical topology: Anytime there is a wide variance between the physical topology and logical topology, when using route reflectors, it's very easy to end up with a loop in the network. Figure 4.12 illustrates one such topology and the resulting forwarding loop.

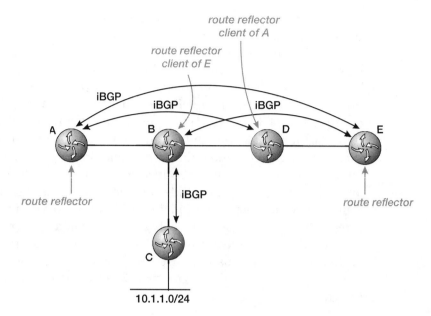

Figure 4.12
A hypothetical forwarding loop occurrence when physical and logical topologies do not match.

In Figure 4.12 routers B and E are route reflectors. Routers A and D are route reflector clients of router B; routers C and F are clients of router E.

- Routers A and F receive an advertisement for 10.1.1.0/24 from router G, an eBGP peer of both.
- Router A advertises the route to its only iBGP peer, the route reflector, router B. Router B, in turn, reflects the route to routers D and E.
- Router F advertises the route to its only iBGP peer, the route reflector, router E. Router E, in turn, reflects the route to routers C and B.
- Router B prefers the path learned from router A; router E prefers the path learned from router F.
- Router C prefers the path via router F and router D prefers the path via router A.

As a result of this configuration, a forwarding loop is introduced between routers C and D. This example describes a hypothetical situation where a forwarding loop would occur because the logical route reflection topology doesn't mirror the physical topology. In large networks with more complex topologies, configurations in which this may occur are much more realistic. As such, it's always a good idea to ensure that the physical and logical topologies are congruent.

Impacts of Reflection on the Best Path

Route reflection may also impact the outcome of the best path calculation, resulting in suboptimal route selection, even when the network is well designed. Figure 4.13 illustrates one such case.

Let's examine what each router would choose as its best path toward the 10.1.1.0/24 network if all the routers were configured as full mesh, and then examine the best paths chosen with a route reflector

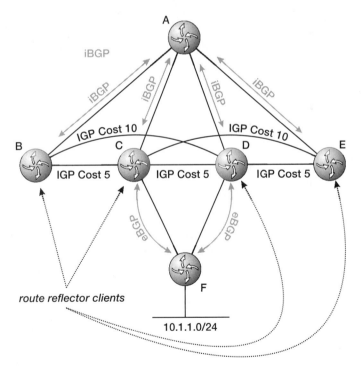

Figure 4.13
Route reflection impacts the outcome of the best path algorithm.

topology replacing the full mesh. If all of these routers were configured as an iBGP full mesh, and we assume that Multiple Exit Discriminator (MED) and Local Preference are both set equal on routers C
and D,

- Router B would choose C as its exit point because the interior
  gateway protocol metric is the lowest through this exit point.
- Router C would choose F as its next hop.
- Router D would choose F as its next hop.
- Router E would choose D as its exit point because the interior
  gateway protocol metric is lowest through this exit point.

However, with router A acting as a route reflector and routers B,
C, D, and E as route reflector clients, the process would be as follows:

- Router A would receive two copies of the update, one from
  router C and the other from router D, and would run the best
  path algorithm to determine which path is best. Assume router
  A chooses the path through C.
- Router A would then reflect this best path choice to each of its
  route reflector clients, routers B, D and E.
- Router B would choose C as its exit point.
- Router C would choose F as its next hop.
- Router D would choose F as its next hop.
- Router E would choose C as its exit point, even though router D
  is closer.

You could attempt to influence router A's best path choice so it
chooses router D as its exit point and reflects this choice back to B and E,
but then B would choose D as its exit point and would route suboptimally.
In most cases, the impact of changes in the best path chosen throughout
the network to reach any given destination caused by route reflection will
be minor, but network designers should be aware of the possible implications and design their networks with these implications in mind.

Hierarchical Route Reflectors

To increase further the scaling of an iBGP core, you can deploy route
reflectors in a hierarchy. Figure 4.14 illustrates a hierarchical route reflector iBGP core topology.

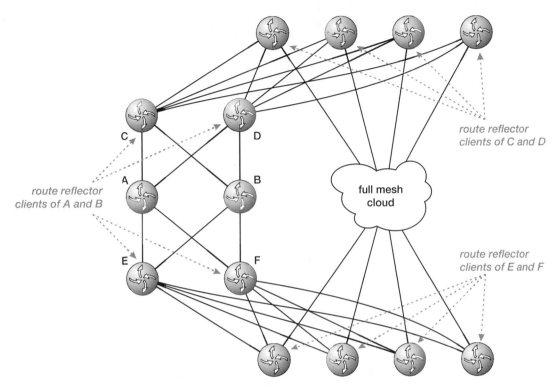

*route reflector
clients of C and D*

*route reflector
clients of A and B*

full mesh
cloud

*route reflector
clients of E and F*

Figure 4.14
An iBGP core using hierarchical route reflectors.

As illustrated in the diagram, there are three route reflection clusters. There's a root cluster for which routers A and B are the route reflectors and routers D, C, E, and F are clients. There are also two lower-level clusters, for which routers C and D and routers E and F are route reflectors, respectively.

When using hierarchical route reflectors in this way, you should be very careful that the route reflection follows the physical topology of the interconnected iBGP speakers. Not following the physical topology could lead to forwarding loops, as discussed earlier in this chapter.

BGP Confederations

As discussed in Chapter 3, another option to consider when scaling an iBGP core is splitting a single network into smaller routing domains and then gluing them back together as a *BGP confederation*. Simply put, a confederation is a set of autonomous systems that appear as single autonomous to those outside the confederation. Figure 4.15 illustrates a confederation.

- Router A peers with B using eBGP; from router A's perspective, B is in AS 65500, which is defined as the confederation ID.
- Router B peers with C using iBGP within the sub-AS 65200.
- Router C peers with D using eBGP (or what's often referred to as eiBGP); from router C's perspective, D is in AS 65300 (which again is a sub-AS of 65500).
- Router D peers with E using eBGP, peering with AS 65300. Router D also peers with C's sub-AS 65200.
- Router E peers with F using eBGP; from router F's perspective, E is in AS 65500.

Essentially, confederations allow the sub-AS members, AS 65200 and AS 65300, to appear as a single autonomous system, AS 65500, to both Routers A and F, which are outside the confederation. Within each confederated autonomous system (or sub-AS), route reflectors and other techniques may be used to scale the network further. Each sub-AS connects to the other autonomous systems within the confederation as

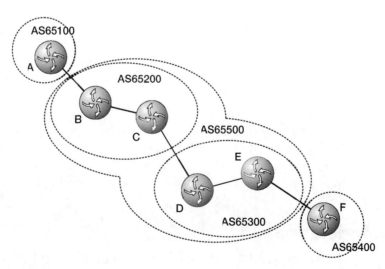

Figure 4.15
A simple confederation.

if they were external peers, using their sub-AS number as their local autonomous system. However, BGP speakers at the edge of the confederation appear to be part of the confederation autonomous system and strip all of the confederations information out of the AS Path when advertising routes.

How Confederations Work

When you first see a confederation of autonomous systems, the first thing you probably think is, "It must be confusing for the routers to understand what routes and routers belong where." While iBGP sessions are easy enough (they are just like iBGP sessions in a normal autonomous system), eBGP sessions are more complex. There needs to be some way to determine when an eBGP peer is part of the confederation or not and what information to strip out of a route when advertising it to a peer that is outside the confederation.

> Autonomous system confederations are described in RFC 3065.

New Attributes

Two new attributes are defined for BGP confederations:

- AS Confederation Sequence, which is a list of all the autonomous systems within a BGP confederation a particular route has passed through, in the order in which the autonomous systems were traversed.
- AS Confederation Set, which is a list of all the autonomous systems within a confederation a particular update has passed through, in no particular order.

> AS Confederation Sets, just as with AS Sets in normal BGP, are only used with aggregation to reduce the size of AS Path information. This is accomplished by listing each sub-AS only once, regardless of how many times the sub-AS may have appeared in multiple AS Paths that were aggregated.

These new attributes, carried as part of the AS Path, are used to prevent loops between autonomous systems that are members of the confederation. The rules for modifying an update for any BGP speaker within a confederation are as follows:

- If advertising the update to an iBGP peer, normal processing applies.
- If advertising to an eBGP peer within the same BGP confederation (shares the same confederation ID), prepend the sub-AS number to the list of sub-ASes in the AS Confederation Sequence.
- If advertising to an eBGP peer outside the BGP confederation (does not share the same BGP confederation ID), remove the AS Confederation Sequence and Set attributes, and prepend the confederation ID to the AS Sequence in the AS Path.

Tracking an Update Through a Confederation

The easiest way to understand how a confederation works is to track a route generated within one of the autonomous systems in the confederation through to where it exits from the confederation, and to track a route from one edge of the confederation to the other edge of the confederation. Figure 4.16 illustrates a route generated in the confederation and propagated to an external autonomous system.

- The update is originated by router A with an empty AS Path. Since the peer to which router A will be advertising this update, router B, is in the same BGP confederation but a different sub-AS, router A creates a new AS Confederation Set and inserts its sub-AS number, AS65100.
- Router B receives the update. Since router B is advertising this route to another member of the same BGP confederation, it prepends its local sub-AS number to the AS Confederation Set and advertises it to router C.
- Router C receives this update and processes it. Router C realizes that D is not a member of the BGP confederation, so it strips the AS Confederation Set from the AS Path, prepends the BGP confederation ID, 65400, to the AS Sequence of the AS Path, and advertises it to router D.

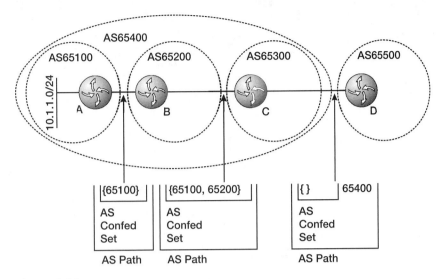

Figure 4.16
Tracking an update originated in a confederation.

Figure 4.17 illustrates the path of a route generated outside a confederation and then propagated through the confederation. The primary difference is in the AS Path itself rather than in the actions taken on the AS Confederation Set.

- Router A inserts its local autonomous system, 200, in the AS Sequence of the AS Path and advertises the prefix to router B.
- Router B, since it is advertising this route to a BGP speaker within the local BGP confederation but in a different sub-AS, creates a new AS Confederation Sequence, inserts its sub-AS number, 65100, and advertises it to Router C.
- Router C, since it is advertising this route to a BGP speaker within the local BGP confederation but in a different sub-AS, inserts its sub-AS number, 65200, in the AS Confederation Sequence and advertises it to router D.
- Router D receives this route from router C. Before router D can advertise the route to router E, which is an eBGP peer that is not a member of the local BGP confederation, router D must strip the AS Confederation Sequence attribute from the AS Path and prepend the Confederation ID, 65400, to the AS Sequence of the AS path.

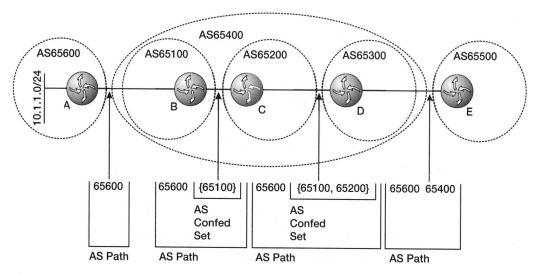

Figure 4.17
A route propagated through a confederation.

The path that Router E receives with the route only indicates one autonomous system (i.e., 65400) between AS100 and AS200, rather than three.

Deploying Confederations

If you are going to deploy confederations, there are several issues you should consider that will help you design the iBGP core and link the confederation autonomous systems. Some of these are discussed in following section.

First and foremost, how many sub-AS paths are going to be contained within the BGP confederation? This could depend on a number of things, such as the following:

- You're planning to deploy route reflection internal to each sub-AS for some additional hierarchy and scalability and therefore they might be larger than otherwise preferred.
- You might wish to use BGP confederations to scope BGP policy and administrative controls based on geographic or political boundaries.

- You're planning to run an independent interior gateway protocol within each sub-AS and are bounded by the existing IGP topologies or scalability thresholds.
- Transoceanic links and other physical topology characteristics of the network dictate constraints.
- You've acquired other networks and are going to employ BGP confederations as a first phase of full integration.

Clearly, there are lots of other possibilities that could arise. Generally, it's a good first step to determine what requirements and constraints exist and generate/overlay proposed topologies on network maps until something that accommodates the requirement set evolves.

Whether or not a single IGP is going to be used within the entire BGP confederation, you need to determine if you're going to preserve BGP next hops through the entire routing domain. If the answer is no, then you'll likely want to identify and generate configurations that only reset BGP next hops at sub-AS boundaries.

You'll also need to determine whether the multiexit discriminator (MED) attribute will be compared between sub-AS paths, normal autonomous systems, or both. This policy needs to be consistent throughout the entire BGP confederation. Different vendors and even software revisions from the same vendor behavior very differently when it comes to MED handling, especially MEDs as they relate to BGP confederations, so you'll need to verify your how your router vendor(s) behave and ensure policy is consistent across the BGP confederation.

BGP confederations don't provide support for hierarchy such as route reflection does. As a result, you'll need to ensure that your topology appropriately accommodates this. As previously discussed, route reflectors can be deployed within sub-AS paths, even hierarchically, if required.

Although not a strict requirement (though some implementations seem to disagree), sub-AS numbers are typically obtained from the reserved AS number pool. Reserved AS numbers designated for private use range from 64512 to 64534. Although any AS number should work for a sub-AS, using globally assigned numbers may generate confusion or configuration errors or may perhaps not be permitted by your implementation. Also, if any private-AS numbers are to be used with customers, you'll want to ensure that no conflicts occur. It's often a good idea to set up an internal assigned numbers authority to in order to consistently document and handle issues such as this, IP addressing, and so on. Finally, your BGP confederation number should be globally unique and is typically allocated by a Regional Internet Registry (RIR) such as ARIN or APNIC.

The entire list of AS number allocations can be found at the Internet Assigned Number Authorities (IANA) Web site: http://www.iana.org/assignments/as-numbers.

Review Questions

1. Why do iBGP peers only advertise routes learned from other iBGP peers to eBGP peers?

2. In a network with 100 iBGP peers, fully meshed, with a single peer receiving 1000 routes from an eBGP peer, how many routes would each iBGP peer receive and store?

3. If a route reflector receives a route from a nonclient peer, which peers would the route be reflected to?

4. If a route reflector receives a route from a client peer, which peers would the route be reflected to?

5. What is the Cluster ID?

6. What is the Cluster List?

7. What does the Cluster List provide?

8. Why should no other attributes be modified when a route reflector reflects a route?

9. How can we resolve issues with route reflectors being a single point of failure?

10. What is the primary disadvantage to consider when configuring each route reflector in a pair of redundant route reflectors with different Cluster IDs?

11. What is the primary disadvantage to consider when configuring each route reflector in a pair of redundant route reflectors with the same Cluster ID?

12. Why is it important to match the physical and logical topologies when using route reflectors?

13. What does a group of autonomous systems organized as a confederation appear as to routers outside the confederation?

14. What is the AS Confederation Sequence used for?

5

BGP Performance

Networks are getting faster. The size and speed of links used in networks is increasing rapidly, and routers and switches move packets at rates that would have been unthinkable in the not to distant past. Routing protocols are no exception to this general trend, with OSPF, IS-IS, and EIGRP all boasting of subsecond convergence in many large networks.

How does BGP fit in? BGP is often perceived as a slow but robust protocol, giving up its speed for stability, commonly measuring convergence times in minutes rather than seconds. But is the BGP protocol really slow, or has little work been done in this area because everyone assumes it's slow?

While BGP may never converge in large internetworks in the subsecond range, BGP can be optimized so convergence time is measured in seconds rather than minutes. This chapter discusses some optimizations used to improve BGP convergence time; other optimizations are still being worked on and should drive down BGP's convergence times even farther.

One of the hardest characterizations to make about BGP is the time it should take to converge two peers when they are initially connected; every implementation, in every release, makes improvements to convergence time. Beyond this, the number of prefixes exchanged between the peers, the number of paths available for each reachable destination, the speed of the peers, and the number of unique attributes in the table all impact the initial convergence time between two peers. While this initial convergence can take a long while (in terms of minutes in many cases), once it is completed, incremental convergence should be much faster.

Since there is no way to estimate the amount of time it will take to converge a set of BGP peers, it's best to take a baseline of the convergence time. Initialize the peers several times, if possible, and note the amount of time it takes to converge, and then watch incremental changes to see how long these take to propagate through the network. Only when you know what normal convergence looks like can you characterize specific times as being slow.

Peer Groups

Virtually every BGP implementation groups peers based on common outbound policies; Cisco IOS Software calls these groups of neighbors *peer groups*. Why do implementations group peers based on outbound policy toward the peers rather than in some other way? For the network administrator, this grouping can simplify configuration, allowing policies from a common group to be inherited by a number of neighbors rather than configuring each one independantly. Figure 5.1 illustrates, with a configuration from Cisco IOS Software following for router G, using peer groups to group eBGP peers with common outbound filtering policies.

In this example, the configuration isn't simplified by the use of peer groups (in fact, you could argue that the configuration is more complex because of peer groups). As your outbound policies become more complex, however, including filtering on communities, filtering out local private address space used, and other common filters, peer groups make the configurations much simpler to read and understand.

Impact on Convergence

Peer groups are not just a configuration convenience, however; they also impact BGP's convergence. To understand why, we have to delve a little into how BGP updates are generated by a process running on a router, which is, in the end, a computer program running on a computer.

One of the most expensive operations on any computer is the binary copy, the copying of a piece of data from one memory location to another. This is why many computer languages, including C, are so adroit at handling pointers; rather than move things around in memory, you point at things in memory and save the expensive copying of data from one place in memory to another place in memory unless it's really needed.

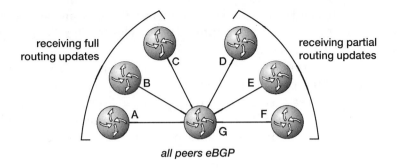

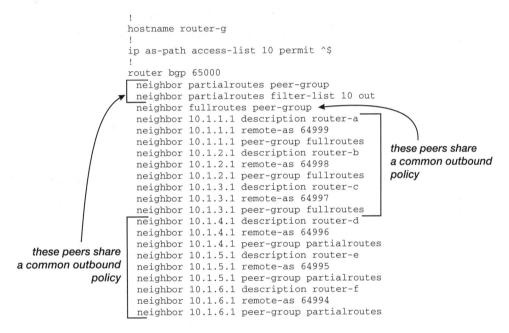

Figure 5.1
BGP peer groups.

If a single BGP process needs to send identical information to a large number of peers, what will it need to do? It will need to copy the information onto the output queue set up for each one of those peers. Since copying data from one place to another is a very expensive operation, copying update packets into multiple queues will be very expensive as well.

Instead, why shouldn't we leave the data in one place and copy from there when transmitting the packets? This is what peer groups allow the router to do; Figure 5.2 illustrates.

In using peer groups, we can eliminate one expensive copy of data in the processing of outbound updates transmitted to peers. What impact does this have on performance? Some testing with Cisco IOS Software illustrates the difference in convergence times with a number of peers configured independently and with those peers configured as a peer group.

The premise of this test is simple; router A advertises 100,000 routes to router B through iBGP. Once all 100,000 routes have been learned and installed by Router B, bring up a number of eBGP peers to which B must then readvertise the routes learned from Router A.

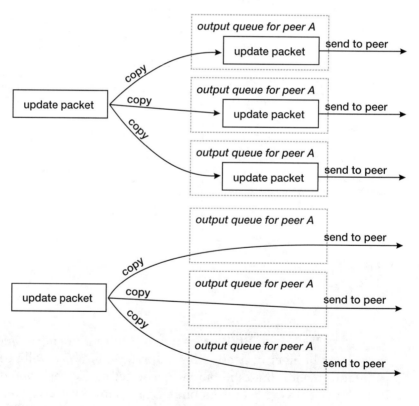

Figure 5.2
Peer group optimization of the packet transmission process.

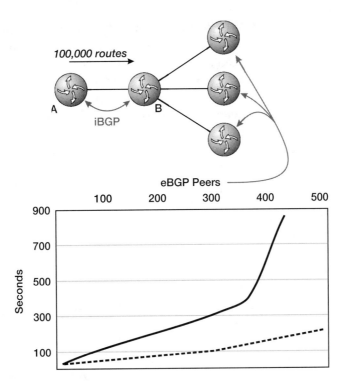

Figure 5.3
The impact of peer groups on BGP convergence.

Increase the number of peers, measuring how long it takes router B to finish advertising all 100,000 routes to all of the eBGP peers it has. The result of this test is illustrated as the solid line in the graph in Figure 5.3.

Introducing peer groups into router B's configuration makes a dramatic difference in the time it takes for the router to advertise all 100,000 routes, illustrated as the dotted line on the graph in Figure 5.3. Without peer groups, router B takes about 850 seconds to advertise all the routes to about 420 eBGP peers. With peer groups, router B can advertise the same routes to the same peers in about 120 seconds.

Update Groups and Peer Templates

The problem with peer groups, however, is obvious to anyone who has configured or managed a large-scale BGP network: Peer groups tie outbound policy to BGP performance. If you have complex outbound policies, your BGP performance will suffer. Further, while peer groups were originally designed to provide simpler, more compact configurations, they can make configurations more complex, by forcing the network administrator to consider performance issues when configuring their BGP processes. How do we resolve this problematic linkage between performance and policy? By unlinking them. But how could you delink these two closely related things?

Cisco IOS Software version 12.0(24)S introduced a pair of new features delinking performance from policy configuration from the network administrator's point of view: peer templates and update groups. Figure 5.4 illustrates peer templates.

Configuring peer templates in Cisco IOS Software is very similar to configuring peer groups. However, peer groups only cover one half of the problem, the simplification of policy configuration. What about the performance enhancements resulting from grouping peers with identical outbound policies?

Update groups provide this grouping. When update groups are enabled, the Cisco IOS Software BGP process will examine the outbound policy of each peer configured and will group those peers with identical outbound policies into update groups. Peers within update groups are treated in the same way peers in a peer group are treated; the same packet is copied to each peer rather than making several copies within memory.

Are Policy Configuration and Performance Really Unlinked?

It may appear, from the outside, that we have completely delinked BGP performance from configuration by splitting the two concepts into two pieces and implementing them separately; but when we examine the problem more closely, we see this isn't true. The ability of the BGP process to group neighbors based on outbound policy is still tied to the outbound policies configured, no matter what method is used to configure them.

To improve BGP performance, you should still try to define your outbound policies so any given peer will fall into one of a small number of policy settings. You can use two effective methods to control the complexity and variety of outbound policies in your network:

- Use a common set of filters on all your border routers for filtering out invalid route information.

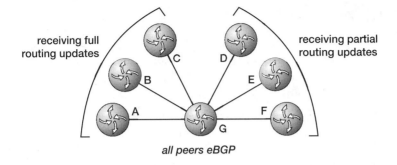

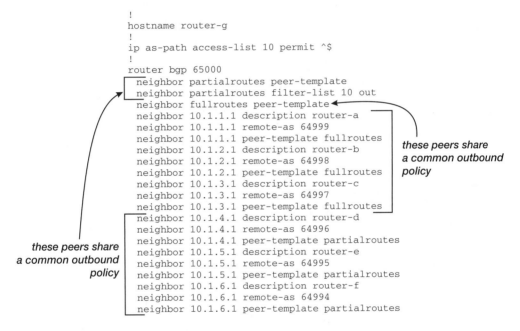

Figure 5.4
Peer templates.

• Use communities to characterize different types of peering relationships, marking routes with the correct communities as they are received or originated so they will be treated correctly at all borders.

The use of communities and filters at the edge are discussed in Chapter 6, BGP Policy.

Update Packing

BGP's packet format, as we discussed in Chapter 1, The Border Gateway Protocol, provides a set of attributes followed by the prefixes matching those attributes. Figure 5.5 illustrates.

Any group of prefixes sharing the same attributes can be packed into the same BGP update (as long as the BGP update doesn't exceed the maximum update size of 4096 octets). Assume a BGP process has the following set of information to send to a peer (using a single attribute, rather than all the attributes, to simplify the example somewhat):

- 10.1.1.0/24, with a community of 100
- 10.1.2.0/24, with a community of 100
- 10.1.3.0/24, with a community of 200
- 10.1.4.0/24, with a community of 100
- 10.1.5.0/24, with a community of 300
- 10.1.6.0/24, with a community of 200

Walking this table of routes to send from top to bottom, the BGP process would transmit

- community 100: 10.1.1.0/24, 10.1.2.0/24
- community 200: 10.1.3.0/24
- community 100: 10.1.4.0/24
- community 300: 10.1.5.0/24
- community 200: 10.1.6.0/24

This is five packets to transmit six routes to a peer. Since each packet transmitted requires a fixed amount of time to build, transmit,

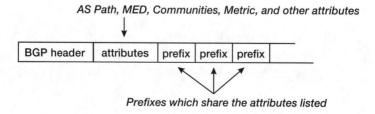

AS Path, MED, Communities, Metric, and other attributes

Prefixes which share the attributes listed

Figure 5.5
BGP update format.

and parse, it would make more sense to try to pack the prefixes into the updates more tightly. In this example, the BGP speaker could transmit three packets instead of five:

- community 100: 10.1.1.0/24, 10.1.2.0/24, 10.1.4.0/24
- community 200: 10.1.3.0/24, 10.1.6.0/24
- community 300: 10.1.5.0/24

This seems like a small change to make—how much difference would it really make in convergence times? The difference between an efficiently packing implementation and one that isn't can be huge. The test illustrated in Figure 5.6 shows the performance difference between Cisco IOS Software's performance with and without optimizations for update packing enabled.

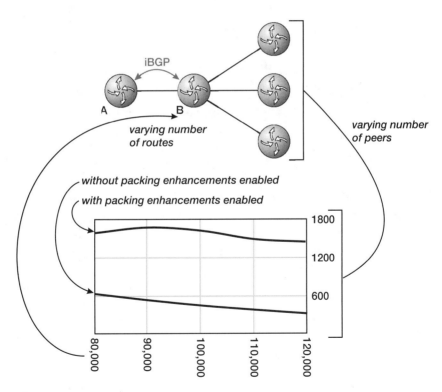

Figure 5.6
Update packing's impact on BGP performance.

This test is simple in concept: A number of routers are connected to router B, and configured as eBGP peers. A number of routes are advertised by router A, which router B must then readvertise to each of its peers. Ten minutes after router A begins advertising these routes to router B, B is checked to see if it has converged with all of its peers. If it has, the test passes, and the number of peers is increased. If router B has not yet converged with all of its peers, the test fails. We can see that router B can support a much larger number of peers with the enhancements to update packing enabled.

Timers

All routing protocols have timers, used to determine when an apparently inactive peering relationship should be dropped and the routes learned through that peering relationship should be no longer used. Routing protocols also have timers to prevent a network from never converging when faced with rapid changes in the network topology. We will examine both types of timers in the following sections.

Hold and Keepalive Timers

The hold and keepalive timers in BGP provide a simple test for peer aliveness. Since a BGP speaker only transmits information when its local databases change, there are no regular messages transmitted between two BGP peers. If a BGP speaker fails, there's no reason its peers should know it has failed, since a failure and a long stretch of time without any changes would look the same. To resolve this, BGP peers transmit periodic keepalive messages along their connections. Each peer also keeps track of the last time it received one of these keepalive messages from a peer and resets the peering session if a keepalive has not been received in some time. The amount of time a BGP speaker will wait to receive a keepalive before resetting a session is called the *hold time*.

BGP speakers advertise their configured hold time at the beginning of a session with another speaker. The hold time used for the session is determined by the lower of the two hold times advertised.

Connect Retry

The connect retry timer is designed to prevent a constantly flapping router from causing the network to fall into a state of continual churn; Figure 5.7 illustrates.

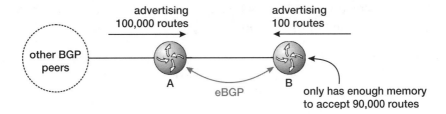

Figure 5.7
The connect retry timer prevents constant peer flapping from causing network failure.

Routers A and B are peering to each other through an eBGP connection; router A is advertising 100,000 routes to B, and B is transmitting 100 routes to A. Assume the peering takes place in this order:

- Routers A and B build their session.
- Router B advertises its 100 routes to A.
- A readvertises these routes to its other peers and then advertises its 100,000 routes to router B.
- Router B receives 90,000 of these routes and then fails due to memory exhaustion, resetting the session.
- When the session resets, A withdraws the 100 routes it has learned through router B.

Each time this process repeats, 100 routes are advertised into, then withdrawn from, the rest of the network behind router A. The network will never converge if routers A and B rebuild and tear down their BGP peering relationship fast enough.

To slow down the speed at which two peers can tear down and rebuild their peering sessions and to prevent this sort of situation from causing the rest of the network to fail to converge, a BGP peer is not allowed immediately to rebuild a peering session once it has failed. Instead, a BGP speaker must wait at least the connect retry interval before attempting to peer with a BGP speaker that was previously a peer.

Cisco IOS Software will wait for two minutes once an open attempt fails to retry opening a connection with a peer; it will accept an open from that peer during this time, however. Cisco IOS Software also allows the connect retry timer to be set specifically for a peer reset because it has transmitted too many routes. The amount of time it can be held in the down state before a connection attempt is made again is determined by the command

```
neighbor {ip-address or peer-group-name} maximum-prefix maximum
[threshold] [warning-only] [minimum restart time]
```

Open Delay

The open delay timer is used to prevent BGP speakers from attempting to actively open a BGP session at the same time; the process of opening a session between two BGP peers is described in Chapter 1, The BGP Protocol, in the BGP Peering Process section.

If two BGP speakers attempt to open a session with each other at the same time, a collision occurs. Collisions require complex processing to resolve, slowing down BGP convergence. To prevent collisions, the open delay timer is jittered, which means it is set to some number plus or minus some random amount; this prevents two routers with the same open delay from constantly colliding when they attempt to connect and backing off the same amount, only to collide again on their next attempted connection.

Minimum Origination Interval

The minimum origination interval determines how quickly a router may advertise changes in a route originating within the local autonomous system. This prevents rapid changes within a single autonomous system from causing constant turbulence throughout an internetwork, causing the entire internetwork to fail to converge; Figure 5.8 illustrates.

Every 30 seconds, router A reloads because of a power surge, causing the state of 10.1.1.0/24 to flap. Each time the state of 10.1.1.0/24 changes, router B advertises this change to C, and router C processes the change and passes it along to its neighbors. If the minimum origination interval on router B is set higher than 10 seconds, it would damp these changes, reducing the amount of work done on router C. Setting the minimum origination interval higher than 10 seconds will, of course, delay network convergence.

Cisco IOS Software doesn't implement the minimum origination interval. Exponential event dampening on the neighbor state between routers A and B would provide good damping for this type of event, as well, without the drawbacks of minimum origination interval.

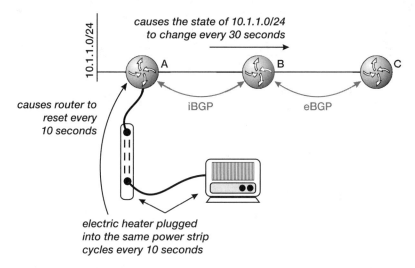

Figure 5.8
Electric heater based route origination flapping.

Minimum Route Advertisement Interval

The minimum route advertisement interval timer also acts to dampen instabilities in an internetwork. The minimum route advertisement interval is the amount of time a BGP speaker must wait before advertising any new information to its peers, no matter where the new information came from. Figure 5.9 illustrates.

At router A, the state of 10.1.1.0/24 changes once each second, a very fast flapping connection of some type; A has its minimum route advertisement set to 2 seconds.

- The first time the network comes back up, router A builds an update and sends it to C; it then sets its minimum route advertisement timer. Router C readvertises 10.1.1.0/24 to D and sets it minimum route advertisement timer as well.
- A moment later, 10.2.2.0/24 comes up, and router B advertises this change to C. Router C accepts this update but doesn't build a new update to D, since its minimum route advertisement timer is still running.
- 10.1.1.0/24 flaps again, but router A doesn't advertise this new instance of 10.1.1.0/24 to C, since its minimum advertisement timer is still running.

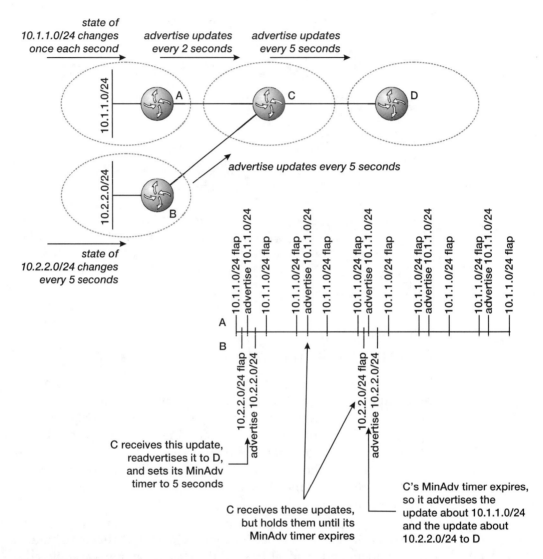

Figure 5.9
The impact of minimum route advertisement interval on update propagation.

- Five seconds after router C started its minimum advertisement timer, the timer expires. Router C examines its local BGP table and determines it needs to build updates for 10.1.1.0/24 and 10.2.2.0/24 toward router D. It builds and transmits these updates and then restarts it minimum advertisement timer.

- A moment later, 10.1.1.0/24 flaps again. When it comes back up, A advertises this information to C, since A's minimum route advertisement timer is not running. Router C again receives this information and holds it; it doesn't readvertise the change to router D because the minimum route advertisement timer is still running.

As you can see from this example, the minimum route advertisement timer effectively damps event change information. However, it also slows down convergence considerably. We'll use some tests run on the network illustrated in Figure 5.10 to examine the results of a 30-second minimum route advertisement interval versus having a minimum route advertisement interval. In this network, the route to 10.1.1.0/24 is withdrawn, and the routers are monitored to determine when they all agree this destination is no longer reachable.

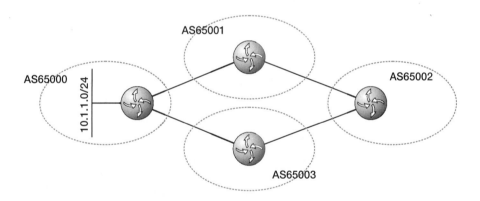

MinAdv	convergence time	updates	withdraws
30 seconds	59 seconds	11	14
0 seconds	<1 second	24	19

Figure 5.10
The impact of the minimum route advertisement timer on BGP convergence.

Convergence time in this small network is much shorter without the minimum advertisement timer set (or with the timer set to 0)—but we also see that without the timer, it takes a lot more network traffic to converge when the 10.1.1.0/24 route is withdrawn. Further testing in the small network has shown, however, that a good compromise is to set the minimum route advertisement timer to 1 second, dramatically reducing convergence time and resulting in a moderate increase in network traffic, rather than the much larger increase we see here.

> This testing also showed that being able to detect loops before you send a route to a peer, rather than detecting loops on receiving routes from peers, will reduce the number of messages sent in converging.
>
> For further information on this topic, and testing done in this area, see the paper *An Experimental Study of Internet Routing Convergence*, by Craig Labovitz et al., Microsoft Research, Technical Report MSR-TR-2000-8.

Transport-Level Issues

This section covers two transport-level issues relating to BGP performance: *fast external fallover* and optimizations in the Transport Control Protocol.

Fast External Fallover

BGP typically relies on recursive routing to find peers and learn their status; it cannot rely on direct knowledge at the IP layer for this peer status information. One optimization we can make in this area is to tie the state of a peer to the state of the interface the peer is reachable through; this optimization is called *fast external fallover*. Figure 5.11 illustrates.

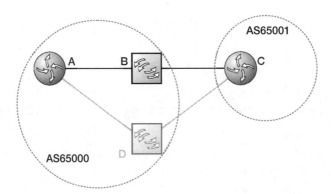

Figure 5.11
Fast external fallover.

Router A is eBGP peering with router C; it has one known path to router C, through the switched network with B. if the link between routers A and B fails, should A fail the peering relationship with C as well and remove all the routes it has learned through router C? There's no way for router A to tell if there's an alternate path available to C, so it will simply wait until it doesn't hear anything from router C for a full hold time.

This is precisely the situation fast external fallover is designed to address; if the network administrators know no backup path exists between routers A and C, they can configure the BGP process on router A to bring the peering relationship with C down if the interface through which C is reached fails. On routers running Cisco IOS Software, the command **bgp fast-external-fallover** is used to configure fast external fallover.

TCP Path Maximum Transmission Unit (MTU)

Since BGP relies on TCP to transport routing information between peers, TCP's operation can make a very large difference in BGP's performance. The TCP MTU size is the maximum segment size TCP will build before sending a packet down the IP stack for transmission. Generally, this is set to some small number, since TCP is a higher-level protocol and has no visibility to the MTU along an entire link. Figure 5.12 illustrates.

Since there is no way for TCP to know about the 1000-byte MTU link in the middle, TCP is normally set up (on routers) to default to a very small packet size and never attempt to increase it. This was probably a good tradeoff when the routing table was much smaller and the TCP flow required to converge BGP was short lived. In the current

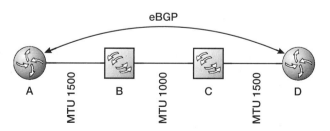

Figure 5.12
Path MTU in BGP.

Internet, with routing tables of 150,000 routes (and growing), the impact of just choosing a small MTU and hoping for the best is very large.

Let's consider why the MTU size would have such a large impact on BGP convergence. There are two issues to consider: BGP update packing, and the amount of return traffic transmitted to a BGP speaker in the form of packet acknowledgments. Let's work through an example.

Assume we have 1000 routes to send and can send them with packets of 500 bytes or packets of 1000 bytes. The attributes in each packet are going to take up some amount of space, let's say 250 bytes (though this is really variable, depending on the attributes), and each prefix is going to take up some space, let's say 4 bytes each.

If all the routes have the same attributes, then we can use the following formula to calculate the number of packets we will need to transmit:

```
Prefixes/((MTU - attribute size)/prefix size)
```

So:

```
1000/((500 - 250)/4) = 17
1000/((1000 - 250)/4) = 6
```

The impact of the MTU size is not proportional the change in the MTU size; as the MTU gets smaller, the amount of space taken by attributes becomes larger, so we need to send more packets to transmit the same number of prefixes. At the other end of the equation, if we are transmitting 17 packets, we are expecting to receive 17 acknowledgments, so every packet we need to send actually doubles the traffic on the wire between the two BGP peers. This, in turn, places more stress on the packet queues on the two routers.

A simple solution to this is to configure TCP path MTU detection on two routers running BGP. The impact of this change is shown in Figure 5.13.

The test is similar to the update packing test we discussed before; router A generates a varying number of BGP prefixes and advertises then to router B. Router B must readvertise all the routes learned from router A to a number of eBGP peers. Ten minutes after router A begins generating routes, router B is checked to determine if the network is converged. If it has, a higher number of peers or routes is chosen, and the test repeats. We can see from this simple test that enabling TCP

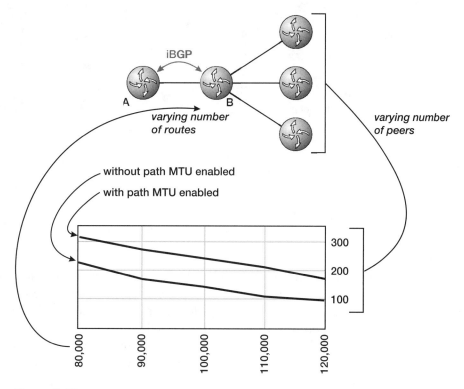

Figure 5.13
TCP path MTU discovery's impact on BGP performance.

path MTU discovery can double the performance of BGP when it is initially converging.

To enable TCP path MTU discovery on a router running Cisco IOS Software, use the command **ip tcp path-mtu-discovery,** which is not enabled by default in most versions.

TCP and Packet Buffer Overflows

BGP speakers, in large-scale networks, are typically peered with a large number of neighboring routers, as illustrated in Figure 5.14.

For each BGP update router A transmits to each of its peers, it will receive a large number of acknowledgments back. If any of these acknowledgments are dropped, the TCP session between router A and the peer that transmitted the acknowledgment will go into *TCP slow start*. When a TCP session goes into slow start, the amount of data

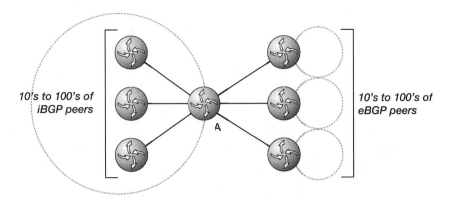

Figure 5.14
Typical peering rates in large scale networks.

transmitted across the session slows dramatically, and BGP convergence slows down with the decreased data flow. The key to preventing this slowdown in TCP is to prevent the acknowledgments from being dropped when router A receives them.

Where would router A drop packets when receiving them? Let's examine the processing of a BGP packet as router A receives it; Figure 5.15 illustrates.

When you execute the show interface command on a router running Cisco IOS Software, there is a counter for the *input queue* and the number of drops of the input queue. In reality, *interfaces do not have input queues under Cisco IOS Software*. Instead, processes that accept packets destined to the router itself, such as IP Input, have input queues. Why is the input queue counter shown per interface?

The size of a process's input queue is not limited. Instead, the number of packets any interface on the router may have waiting to be processed is limited. Thus, if an interface accepts 70 packets for IP, and 6 for Cisco Discovery Protocol, or the IS-IS protocol, the 76th packet will be dropped if none of the earlier packets is processed.

If a BGP speaker is receiving acknowledgment faster than the TCP process can process them, the interfaces are eventually going to run up against their input queue limits and start dropping packets. Packets dropped because an interface has overrun its limit on queue packets will be counted as drops in the output of **show interface.** This is a common problem when a BGP speaker is peered with more than 25 or 30 neighboring routers. Figure 5.16 illustrates how much

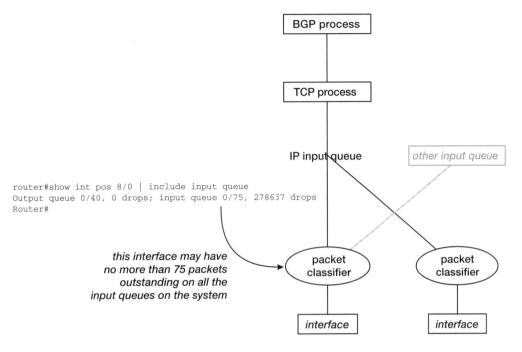

```
router#show int pos 8/0 | include input queue
Output queue 0/40, 0 drops; input queue 0/75, 278637 drops
Router#
```

Figure 5.15
Input queues on a router running Cisco IOS software.

impact increasing the input queue of an interface can make on BGP convergence times.

This test is similar to the one we discussed previously, in the TCP Path Maximum Transmission Unit section. Router A is feeding a varying number of routes to router B, which must then readvertise those routes to a varying number of eBGP peers. Ten minutes after router A has started advertising its routes to B, router B is checked to see if it has finished converging. If it has, the test is considered a success, and the number of routes or peers is increased.

The results indicate that with a large number of peers and a large number of routes, increasing the interface input queue size has a dramatic impact on BGP's convergence. But you shouldn't just run out and configure the input queue on all of your router interfaces to the maximum; it's better to determine what the right setting is rather than just setting them to the maximum possible.

On each interface, you should clear the counters and then monitor the interface for input queue drops. If you determine there are an

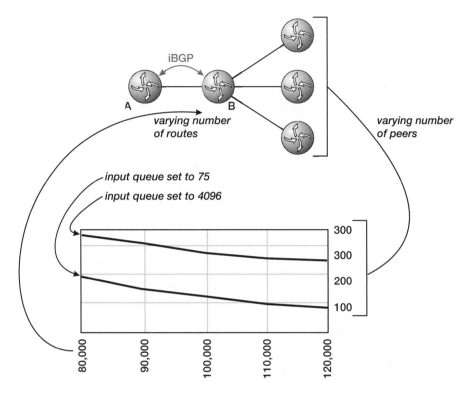

Figure 5.16
Impact of increasing the input queue size on convergence.

unacceptable number of input queue drops, you should increase the input queue by some small amount and clear the counters. Continue this process until you are comfortable with the number of drops the interface is recording.

Review Questions

1. How should you judge the performance of BGP in your network?
2. What inefficiency does grouping peers by outbound policy overcome?
3. What provides configuration grouping for outbound BGP policy without impacting BGP performance?
4. What provides BGP performance by grouping peers with similar outbound policies without impacting peer configuration?

5. How are BGP updates packed?

6. Which timer paces how often a BGP speaker will attempt to re-connect to a peer?

7. Which timer paces how often a BGP speaker will originate a route?

8. What is the minimum route advertisement interval supposed to suppress?

9. What property of the Transport Control Protocol does the input queue size of an interface interact with to impact BGP convergence times?

6

BGP Policy

While BGP provides routing information (information about the reachable destinations of prefixes and the loop-free paths available to reach them), it uses policy–rather than proximity–to determine which path is the best one to reach a given destination. This chapter describes the various policies a network administrator can configure to manipulate BGP attributes and the best path BGP will select. We also discuss where these attributes are normally derived from and some common uses for each of them. We'll complete this chapter with an extensive discussion of multiexit discriminator (MED) deployment considerations, many of which are directly influenced by a network operator's BGP policies.

> Throughout this chapter, we will work with policy configurations and feature sets available in Cisco IOS software; most of these same constructs and capabilities are found in all implementations of the BGP protocol.

Policy Instruments

Policy instruments are where the policies a network administrator would like to enforce are actually encoded. There are various mechanisms used to specify these policies, including access lists, prefix lists, community lists, AS path lists, and route maps; we could consider these *policy primitives*, since they are the basic building blocks through which a policy may be imposed on a BGP route and the various path attributes associated with it.

Table 6.1 provides a reference for CIDR and IP addressing; a fundamental understanding of this table is integral to successful policy instrumentation. While this table provides the values associated with traditional *classful* Internet address space, it's important to remember these classful boundaries no longer exist with the advent of Classless Inter-Domain Routing (CIDR).

Access Lists

The most basic, and familiar, policy instrument is the access list, which is a policy that defines a list of prefixes and associated wildcard bits.

> Access lists are commonly referred to as ACLs, we'll use the two interchangeably throughout this text.
>
> Reading this section, you may think it's much more terse than a full explanation of access lists as they relate to routing policy specification should be—and you're right! This was intentional, and the reasoning is simple. The next section discusses prefix lists, which are relatively new to Cisco IOS software. Prefix list are arguably much more intuitive than access lists when used to specify routing policy (primarily because they were designed to filter routing updates in the first place rather than IP addresses for packet filtering) and provide a number of additional advantages as well. If you're not burdened with existing deployments employing access lists for routing policy specification, but are interested in defining new routing policies, you may wish to skip this section and go straight to the prefix lists section.

Table 6.2 lists the various types of access lists, as well as a general description of each type of access list. For the purpose of this discussion we'll only be concerned with IP standard and extended access lists (or rather, we will only discuss numbered, and not named, access lists).

Access lists allow a network administrator to configure a list of prefixes that should either be permitted or denied for some operation. Standard IP access list syntax (as it relates to BGP routing policy specification) is as follows:

```
access-list access-list-number {deny | permit} prefix
[prefix-wildcard] [log]
```

Table 6.1
CIDR and IP Addressing Table

Prefix Length	Netmask	Inverse Netmask	Number of Unique IPs	Number of Class A Networks	Number of Class B Networks	Number of Class C Networks
/0	0.0.0.0	255.255.255.255	4,294,967,296	256	65,536	16,777,216
/1	128.0.0.0	127.255.255.255	2,147,483,648	128	32,768	8,388,608
/2	192.0.0.0	63.255.255.255	1,073,741,824	64	16,384	4,194,304
/3	224.0.0.0	31.255.255.255	536,870,912	32	8,192	2,097,152
/4	240.0.0.0	15.255.255.255	268,435,456	16	4,096	1,048,576
/5	248.0.0.0	7.255.255.255	134,217,728	8	2,048	524,288
/6	252.0.0.0	3.255.255.255	67,108,864	4	1,024	262,144
/7	254.0.0.0	1.255.255.255	33,554,432	2	512	131,072
/8	255.0.0.0	0.255.255.255	16,777,216	1	256	65,536
/9	255.128.0.0	0.127.255.255	8,388,608		128	32,768
/10	255.192.0.0	0.63.255.255	4,194,304		64	16,384
/11	255.224.0.0	0.31.255.255	2,097,152		32	8,192
/12	255.240.0.0	0.15.255.255	1,048,576		16	4,096
/13	255.248.0.0	0.7.255.255	524,288		8	2,048
/14	255.252.0.0	0.3.255.255	262,144		4	1,024
/15	255.254.0.0	0.1.255.255	131,072		2	512
/16	255.255.0.0	0.0.255.255	65,536		1	256
/17	255.255.128.0	0.0.127.255	32,768			128

Prefix	Subnet Mask	Wildcard	Addresses	
/18	255.255.192.0	0.0.63.255	16,384	64
/19	255.255.224.0	0.0.31.255	8,192	32
/20	255.255.240.0	0.0.15.255	4,096	16
/21	255.255.248.0	0.0.7.255	2,048	8
/22	255.255.252.0	0.0.3.255	1,024	4
/23	255.255.254.0	0.0.1.255	512	2
/24	255.255.255.0	0.0.0.255	256	1
/25	255.255.255.128	0.0.0.127	128	
/26	255.255.255.192	0.0.0.63	64	
/27	255.255.255.224	0.0.0.31	32	
/28	255.255.255.240	0.0.0.15	16	
/29	255.255.255.248	0.0.0.7	8	
/30	255.255.255.252	0.0.0.3	4	
/31	255.255.255.254	0.0.0.1	2	
/32	255.255.255.255	0.0.0.0	1	

187

Table 6.2
Access Lists Available in Cisco IOS Software

Access List Number	Description
1-99	IP Standard Access List
100-199	IP Extended Access List
200-299	Protocol Type-Code Access List
1300-1199	IP Standard Access List (extended range)
2000-2699	IP Extended Access List (extended range)
2700-2799	MPLS Access List

As you can see, there aren't many available parameters for standard IP access lists. You first specify the access list number, then the action to be taken (i.e., **permit** or **deny**). You then specify whether you want to match everything (you could use **any**, which is the same as stating an IP address of all zeros with an inverse mask of all ones: 0.0.0.0 255.255.255.255), a single /32 (**host**, which essentially specifies an IP address with an inverse mask of 0.0.0.0), or some range of addresses/prefixes (via **prefix** and **prefix-wildcard**). Wildcard bits only need to be specified if an IP address is provided; the **any** and **host** keywords don't require a wildcard. For instance, to deny 10.1.1.0/24 and 10.1.2.0/24 but permit prefixes within the remainder of 10.0.0.0/8, the following access list could be used:

```
!
access-list 10 deny 10.1.1.0 0.0.0.255
access-list 10 deny 10.1.2.0 0.0.0.255
access-list 10 permit 10.0.0.0 0.255.255.255
!
```

It isn't necessary for there to be a one-to-one correlation between the prefixes denied or permitted and the entries in the access list. This access list, for instance, would deny 10.1.1.0/25 and 10.1.1.128/25, as well as 10.1.1.0/24.

The simplest and most typical use of an access list for routing policy specification is in controlling the distribution of routes to BGP peers. For instance, suppose a network administrator would like to prevent the prefixes 10.1.1.0/24 and 10.1.2.0/24 from being advertised to a peer while allowing any other prefix in the 10.0.0.0/8 block of addresses to be advertised. The following sample configuration, coupled with the preceding access list, would accomplish this.

```
!
router bgp 65500
 neigbor 192.168.1.1 remote-as 65501
 neighbor 192.168.1.1 distribute-list 10 out
 ....
!
```

As you can see, an access list is applied via the **distribute-list** option on the **neighbor** command in the BGP router configuration mode. In the example, access list 10 is applied to all routes advertised (**distribute-list 10 out**) to our 192.168.1.1 BGP neighbor. An access list may also be applied as an inbound function (**distribute-list <number> in**), which filters incoming routes based on the policy defined in the access list. If an access list is applied to a BGP session as an inbound policy, for example, via the **neighbor 192.168.1.1 distribute-list 10 in** command, the BGP peer will not accept routes from the peer if they match **deny** statements in the access list.

There is a good deal of confusion over how the entries in an access list are matched against prefixes in this way; while they seem relatively simple when being applied to the source and destination addresses of packets (i.e., when employed in packet filtering application as opposed to routing policy specification), how are they applied to a prefix in a route advertisement? Essentially, the prefix is compared to the entry in the access list, and the prefix length, or subnet mask, is ignored. The wildcard bits are used to "mask out" parts of the prefix not compared to the access list entry. The examples shown in the Table 6.3 should provide some clarification.

Table 6.3

This access list entry	Matches
10.1.1.0 0.0.0.0	Any prefix of 10.1.1.0; for instance, 10.1.1.0/24, 10.1.1.0/25, 10.1.1.0/26, etc. This will not match 10.1.1.128/25, since the last octet must be all 0s.
10.1.1.0 0.0.0.255	Any prefix beginning with 10.1.1, with any number in the last octet. It will match 10.1.1.0/24, 10.1.1.0/25, 10.1.1.0/26, and also 10.1.1.128/25, or any other prefix with 10.1.1 as the first three octets, no matter what the prefix length is.

Access lists are evaluated beginning with the first entry; each entry is checked until a match is found, and the result from that match is returned as the filter result. For instance, in this access list,

```
!
access-list 10 permit 10.1.1.0 0.0.0.255
access-list 10 deny 10.1.1.128 0.0.0.127
!
```

If 10.1.1.0/25 were tested against this access list, it would first reach the permit line; since it matches the first line, the route would be permitted, and the second line of the access list would not be processed. This can sometimes trip you up when you're working with a very long access list, since you need to analyze the order in which routes are evaluated and make certain the right action is taken at the right times. It's also important to order your access list for the best performance; entries that are likely to be used more frequently should be specified as early in the access list as possible.

Finally, it's always a good idea to be as specific as possible when specifying policy. For example, in Table 6.3 the **10.1.1.0 0.0.0.255** access list is much less explicit than the **10.1.1.0 0.0.0.0** access list. That is, the **10.1.1.0 0.0.0.0** access list only matches a subset of the routes with the 10.1.1.0/24 address space, while the **10.1.1.0 0.0.0.255** access list matches the entire block of addresses.

Extended Access Lists

Extended access lists in Cisco IOS software, traditionally numbered 100 through 199, can be used to match prefixes as well, although this isn't as well documented; nor are they used as widely. The second address in the extended access list (used for filtering on destination addresses when used for packet filtering) matches the subnet mask of the prefix. The IP extended access list syntax (as it applies to BGP routing policy) is as follows:

> **access-list** access-list-number {**deny** | **permit**} *protocol* prefix prefix-wildcard network-mask network-mask-wildcard

With IP extended access lists, you first specify the access list number, then the action to be performed (i.e., **permit** or **deny**). You then specify the concerned protocol, which, when used for IP routing policy specifications, will always be **ip**. You then specify the prefix (this is the source when filtering packets), prefix-wildcard (this is the source wild-card when filtering packets), network-mask (this is the destination when filtering packets), and the network-mask-wildcard (this is the destination wildcard when filtering packets).

Table 6.4

This access list entry	Matches
`10.1.1.0 0.0.0.0 255.255.255.0 0.0.0.0`	This only matches 10.1.1.0/24; the prefix must have 10 in the first octet, 1 in the second octet, 1 in the third octet, and 0 in the last octet. The subnet mask, likewise, must be 255.255.255.0.
`host 10.1.1.0 host 255.255.255.0`	This behaves exactly as the statement above. The host directive simply provides a more intuitive mechanism to write explicit extended access list statements by removing the need to specify the associated wildcard bits.
`10.1.1.0 0.0.0.255 255.255.255.0 0.0.0.255`	10.1.1.0/24, and any subnet within that prefix. The prefix must begin with 10.1.1, but any number is accepted in the last octet. The subnet mask must start with 255.255.255, but any number is accepted in the last octet of the subnet mask.
`172.16.0.0 0.15.255.255 255.240.0.0 0.15.255.255`	This could be used to match the RFC 1918 prefix 172.16.0.0/12, or 172.16.0.0–172.31.255.255.

> The meaning of the various parts of an extended access list is not consistent between routing protocols on a router running Cisco IOS software. For packet filtering, the two sections refer to the source and destination addresses. When used to filter routing updates in BGP, they refer to the prefix and mask. When used to filter routing updates in EIGRP and RIP, they refer to the prefix and the source of the advertisement.

Application of Nonexistent Access Lists

If you apply an empty or nonexistent access list via the **distribute-list** function, or use it in a route map, what is the impact? Consider the following example:

```
!
hostname router-a
!
interface Serial3/0
 ip address 10.0.7.4 255.255.255.0
!
router bgp 65500
 no synchronization
 bgp log-neighbor-changes
 network 10.1.12.0 mask 255.255.255.0
 neighbor 10.0.7.10 remote-as 65501
 neighbor 10.0.7.10 distribute-list 10 out
 no auto-summary
!

!
hostname router-b
!
interface Serial0/0
ip address 10.7.10 255.255.255.0
!
router bgp 65501
 no synchronization
 bgp log-neighbor-changes
 neighbor 10.0.7.4 remote-as 65500
 no auto-summary
!

router-a#show ip bgp
```

```
BGP table version is 2, local router ID is 10.0.17.4
Status codes: s suppressed, d damped, h history, * valid, > best,
              i - internal, r RIB-failure
Origin codes: i - IGP, e - EGP, ? - incomplete


   Network          Next Hop            Metric LocPrf Weight Path
*> 10.1.12.0/24     0.0.0.0                  0            32768 I

router-b#show ip bgp
BGP table version is 4, local router ID is 208.0.16.10
Status codes: s suppressed, d damped, h history, * valid, > best,
              i - internal, r RIB-failure
Origin codes: i - IGP, e - EGP, ? - incomplete


   Network          Next Hop            Metric LocPrf Weight Path
*> 10.1.12.0/24     10.0.7.4                 0            0 65500 i
```

We can see from this example that router-a is advertising 10.1.12.0/24 to router-b, even though it has an inbound access list applied that subjects routes advertised to router-b to access list 10—an access list that hasn't been configured. router-b, however, is still receiving 10.1.12.0/24, so applying a nonexistent access list has no impact; it is effectively the same as an access list stating to permit all, or no **distribute-list** function being applied to the BGP peering session.

However, while this is true when filtering routing updates with an access list, it isn't true in other applications. A nonexistent access list permits everything when being used as a route filter in BGP, but a nonexistent access list denies everything in other applications (e.g., an interface configured to match all incoming packet to a nonexistent access list would result in all packets matching and all packets therefore being dropped!). That is, with most applications of access lists, a nonexistent access list serves as an implicit deny all.

Prefix Lists

While access lists were originally designed for packet filtering and were later adapted to the needs of route filtering, prefix lists were expressly designed for filtering routing information. As prefix lists were designed and implemented with route filtering in mind, they are more flexible than access lists in this role, and their structure and implementation in Cisco IOS software generally provide improved filtering performance. As you'll see, their syntax is also much more intuitive and things like support for incremental updates makes prefix lists more user-friendly than traditional access lists.

Prefix list syntax is as follows:

ip prefix-list list-name [**seq** seq-value] **deny|permit network/len** [ge ge-value] [le le-value]

When building a prefix list you first specify the prefix lists name and then provide an optional sequence number for the current entry. You then specify the action—**permit** or **deny**—and the prefix itself via a *network/mask length* notation. Prefix lists also provide the ability to specify *greater-than-equal-to* and *less-than-equal-to* values via the **ge** and **le** operators—we'll discuss this in a moment. If no **ge** or **le** operator is defined, the prefix must match the configured list entry exactly for the action specified to take place. An additional useful feature that prefix lists provide is the ability to specify a string of up to 80 characters that can be used to provide a description for the prefix list or its use. For example,

```
router(config)#ip prefix-list foo description ?
  LINE  Up to 80 characters describing this prefix-list

router(config)#ip prefix-list foo description
customer_A_BGP_filter
```

As discussed, sequence numbers allow you to update the prefix list incrementally, providing a mechanism to add or remove prefix list entries without having to rebuild the entire policy. If no sequence number is specified the value of the last entry is incremented by 5, and if this is the initial entry for the prefix list the sequence number value is set to 5, for example,

```
router(config)#ip prefix-list foo  ?
  deny         Specify packets to reject
  description  Prefix-list specific description
  permit       Specify packets to forward
  seq          sequence number of an entry
router(config)#ip prefix-list foo permit 1.2.3.4/32
router(config)#ip prefix-list foo permit 5.6.7.8/32
router#sh ip prefix-list foo
```

```
ip prefix-list foo: 2 entries
   seq 5 permit 1.2.3.4/32
   seq 10 permit 5.6.7.8/32

router(config)#ip prefix-list foo  seq 12 permit ?
  A.B.C.D  IP prefix <network>/<length>, e.g., 35.0.0.0/8

router(config)#ip prefix-list foo  seq 12 permit 1.1.1.1/32
router(config)#ip prefix-list foo permit 1.1.1.2/32
router(config)#ip prefix-list foo  permit 1.1.1.3/32
router#sh ip prefix-list foo
ip prefix-list foo: 5 entries
   seq 5 permit 1.2.3.4/32
   seq 10 permit 5.6.7.8/32
   seq 12 permit 1.1.1.1/32
   seq 17 permit 1.1.1.2/32
   seq 22 permit 1.1.1.3/32
router#conf t
Enter configuration commands, one per line. End with CNTL/Z.
router(config)#ip prefix-list foo seq 2 deny 1.0.0.0/32
router#sh ip prefix-list foo
ip prefix-list foo: 6 entries
   seq 2 deny 1.0.0.0/32
   seq 5 permit 1.2.3.4/32
   seq 10 permit 5.6.7.8/32
   seq 12 permit 1.1.1.1/32
   seq 17 permit 1.1.1.2/32
   seq 22 permit 1.1.1.3/32
```

As you can see, the default sequence numbers for the first and second entries are 5 and 10. The sequence number for the third entry is explicitly set to 12, and the fourth and fifth entries are both incremented in units of 5. Finally, a new entry with a sequence number of 2 is added, which places it in the first position of the prefix list. You can also remove individual entries or remove the entire prefix list, as the following example shows. The sequence number for an entry need not be specified when removing the entry.

```
router(config)#no ip prefix-list foo seq 10 ?
  deny    Specify packets to reject
  permit  Specify packets to forward
```

```
router(config)#no ip prefix-list foo seq 10 permit
5.6.7.8/32
router(config)#
router#sh ip prefix-list foo
ip prefix-list foo: 5 entries
    seq 2 deny 1.0.0.0/32
    seq 5 permit 1.2.3.4/32
    seq 12 permit 1.1.1.1/32
    seq 17 permit 1.1.1.2/32
    seq 22 permit 1.1.1.3/32
router#conf t
Enter configuration commands, one per line. End with CNTL/Z.
router(config)#no ip prefix-list foo

router(config)#
router(config)#ip prefix-list foo permit 1.0.0.0/8
router(config)#ip prefix-list foo permit 2.0.0.0/16
router(config)#ip prefix-list foo permit 3.0.0.0/24
router(config)#ip prefix-list foo permit 4.0.0.0/32
router(config)#ip prefix-list foo deny 0.0.0.0/0 le 32
router#sh ip prefix-list foo
ip prefix-list foo: 5 entries
    seq 5 permit 1.0.0.0/8
    seq 10 permit 2.0.0.0/16
    seq 15 permit 3.0.0.0/24
    seq 20 permit 4.0.0.0/32
    seq 25 deny 0.0.0.0/0 le 32
router(config)#no ip prefix-list foo permit 2.0.0.0/16
router#sh ip prefix-list foo
ip prefix-list foo: 4 entries
    seq 5 permit 1.0.0.0/8
    seq 15 permit 3.0.0.0/24
    seq 20 permit 4.0.0.0/32
    seq 25 deny 0.0.0.0/0 le 32
```

Automatic sequence number generation can be disabled with the configuration command **no ip prefix-list sequence-number**. If you suppress automatic sequence number generation, you must specify the sequence number value for each entry using the *seq-val* argument of the **ip prefix-list** command.

In addition to specifying an explicit prefix, you can specify ranges of prefixes to be matched using the **ge** and **le** operators. If no **ge** value is explicitly called out the range is expected to be a *ge-value* of 32, and if

no **le** is explicitly specified, then the range is prefix length to *le-value.*
The general rule for using the **ge** and **le** operators is as follows:

```
prefix length < ge-value <= le-value <= 32
```

Table 6.5 provides some sample prefix list definitions.

Table 6.5

Prefix List	Matches
ip prefix-list foo permit 10.0.0.0/8	Permit the prefix 10.0.0.0/8 only.
ip prefix-list foo deny 0.0.0.0/0 le 32	Deny everything.
ip prefix-list foo deny 192.168.0.0/8 ge 24 le 24	Deny all prefixes matching /24 within the 192.168.0.0/8 network.
ip prefix-list foo permit 0.0.0.0/0 ge 20 le 24	Permit all prefix from /20 to /24.

To build the same filters described in the access list example above
using a prefix list, we would use

```
!
ip prefix-list foo deny 10.1.1.0/24
ip prefix-list foo deny 10.1.2.0/24
ip prefix-list foo permit 10.0.0.0/8
!
```

In this example, we've used a name, rather than a number, to
specify the prefix list; this provides further flexibility in making routing
policy more readable. Overall, prefix lists provide much more flexibility than access lists for filtering routing updates, and they are more
readable, making policy configurations easier to understand.

> Prefix lists acnnot be used for packet filtering or in many update filtering
> situations in Cisco IOS software.

To apply a prefix list to the routes received from or sent to a BGP
peer, use the **prefix-list** keyword extension to the **neighbor** command
within the router BGP configuration mode.

```
!
ip prefix-list 10 deny 10.1.1.0/24
ip prefix-list 10 permit 10.0.0.0/8
!
router bgp 65500
 neighbor 172.16.35.1 remote-as 65501
 neighbor 172.16.35.1 prefix-list 10 out
!
```

You can also display the number of prefixes matching each entry in an applied prefix list (a prefix list that is actually being used for filtering routing updates) using the **show ip prefix-list detail** *list-name* command. The number of matches against a specific prefix list entry, called the hit count, or the hit counts for all the entries in the list can be reset using the **clear ip prefix-list** *list-name* **prefix**. If no prefix is specified, the hit count for all prefixes is reset. For example,

```
router#sh ip prefix-list detail foo
ip prefix-list foo:
   Description: customer_As_BGP_filter
   count: 4, range entries: 1, sequences: 5 - 25, refcount: 2
   seq 5 permit 1.0.0.0/8 (hit count: 3, refcount: 3)
   seq 15 permit 3.0.0.0/24 (hit count: 3, refcount: 1)
   seq 20 permit 4.0.0.0/32 (hit count: 3, refcount: 1)
   seq 25 deny 0.0.0.0/0 le 32 (hit count: 3, refcount: 1)
router#clear ip prefix-list foo 1.0.0.0/8
router#sh ip prefix-list detail foo
ip prefix-list foo:
   Description: customer_As_BGP_filter
   count: 4, range entries: 1, sequences: 5 - 25, refcount: 2
   seq 5 permit 1.0.0.0/8 (hit count: 0, refcount: 3)
   seq 15 permit 3.0.0.0/24 (hit count: 3, refcount: 1)
   seq 20 permit 4.0.0.0/32 (hit count: 3, refcount: 1)
   seq 25 deny 0.0.0.0/0 le 32 (hit count: 3, refcount: 1)
router#clear ip prefix-list foo
router#sh ip prefix-list detail foo
ip prefix-list foo:
   Description: customer_As_BGP_filter
   count: 4, range entries: 1, sequences: 5 - 25, refcount: 2
   seq 5 permit 1.0.0.0/8 (hit count: 0, refcount: 3)
   seq 15 permit 3.0.0.0/24 (hit count: 0, refcount: 1)
   seq 20 permit 4.0.0.0/32 (hit count: 0, refcount: 1)
   seq 25 deny 0.0.0.0/0 le 32 (hit count: 0, refcount: 1)
```

Empty Prefix Lists

If the updates advertised to a peer are filtered using a nonexistent prefix list, what are the results?

```
!
hostname router-a
!
interface Serial3/0
 ip address 192.168.7.4 255.255.255.0
!
router bgp 65500
 no synchronization
 bgp log-neighbor-changes
 network 192.168.12.0 mask 255.255.255.0
 neighbor 192.168.7.10 remote-as 65501
 neighbor 192.168.7.10 prefix-list 10 out
 no auto-summary
!

router-a#show ip bgp
BGP table version is 2, local router ID is 192.168.17.4
Status codes: s suppressed, d damped, h history, * valid, > best,
              i - internal, r RIB-failure
Origin codes: i - IGP, e - EGP, ? - incomplete

   Network          Next Hop          Metric LocPrf Weight Path
*> 192.168.12.0/24  0.0.0.0                0          32768 i

!
hostname router-b
!
interface Serial0/0
 ip address 192.168.7.10 255.255.255.0
!
router bgp 65501
 no synchronization
 bgp log-neighbor-changes
 neighbor 192.168.7.4 remote-as 65500
 no auto-summary
!

router-b#show ip bgp
BGP table version is 6, local router ID is 192.168.16.10
```

```
Status codes: s suppressed, d damped, h history, * valid, > best,
              i - internal, r RIB-failure
Origin codes: i - IGP, e - EGP, ? - incomplete

   Network          Next Hop           Metric LocPrf Weight Path
*> 192.168.12.0/24  192.168.7.4            0            0 65500
```

As you can see, application of a nonexistent prefix lists permit all prefixes by default, just as nonexistent access lists applied via a **distribute-list** action. If a given prefix does not match any entries of a prefix list, an implicit deny is assumed. Just as with access lists, if a prefix matches multiple entries in a prefix list, the entry with the lowest sequence number (i.e., the entry that appears earliest in the list) is used.

Regular Expressions

Regular expressions, while not a filter in their own right, are the basis for several other filter types, including some community lists and AS path access lists, which are covered in the following sections. While regular expressions can be very complicated, BGP's use of them is greatly simplified by the small numbers of symbols used in BGP—usually just numbers combined with one or two other operators. Table 6.6 provides the components of regular expressions, with notes on their application to the AS Path of a BGP update. From these basic regular expression components, you can make a regular expression matching any community, list of communities, an autonomous system, or list of autonomous systems. As you'll see when we apply these regular expressions in the following section, regular expressions are very powerful and a thorough understanding of them will make policy specification much simpler.

Community Lists

The BGP *Community* attribute provides a mechanism to group destinations (prefixes) that share some similar characteristics in order to latter apply common policy to those prefixes. A prefix can belong to multiple communities. By default, all destinations belong to the Internet community. The BGP community attribute itself is an optional, transitive, global BGP attribute in the numerical range of 1 to 4,294,967,296 (32 bits).

There are several default communities defined. Table 6.7 lists these communities.

Table 6.6

Component	Description
Range	A sequence of components contained within left and right square brackets (e.g., [123])
Atom	Any single character, such as
	. — Matches any single character
	^ — Matches the beginning of the input string
	$ — Matches the end of the input string
	\ — Matches the character
	- — Matches a comma(,), left brace (}), right brace (}), the beginning or end of the input string, or a space
Piece	An atom followed by one of the following symbols:
	* — Matches zero or more sequences of the atom
	+ — Matches one or more sequences of the atom
	? — Matches the atom or the null string
Branch	Zero or more concatenated pieces. For example,
	1* — Match any occurrence of the number 1, including none
	1+ — Match one or more occurrences of the number 1
	12?1 — Matches "11" or "121"
	_1_ — Matches " 1 ", ",1,", or ".1" A 1 with a space, period, or comma on either side. In the BGP AS Path, this would be "via AS 1."
	^1$ — Matches the beginning of the line, a "1," and the end of the line. This would math an AS Path with a 1 only in the path, which means directly and only from 1.
	^1_.* — Matches the beginning of the line, a "1," then a space, then any other combination of characters. This would match any BGP AS Path beginning with AS 1.
	^[1-3]_ — Matches the beginning of the line, any number between 1 and 3, and then a space. This would match any AS Path beginning with AS 1, 2 or 3.
	^$ — Matches an empty string. This would match any empty AS Path, which would be any update originating within the local AS.

Table 6.7

Community	Description
Internet	Advertise routes carrying this community to the Internet community. All BGP speaking routers belong to it.
no-export	Do not advertise routes carrying this community to eBGP peers. Routes carrying this community are advertised to eiBGP AS confederation peers.
no-export-subconfed (local-as)	Do not advertise routes carrying this community to external BGP peers (this includes peers in other member autonomous systems of the same BGP confederation)
no-advertise	Do not advertise this route to any BGP peer.

The recommended encoding for communities is of the form AA:NN, where AA represents the local autonomous system number and NN represents the network administrators assigned 2-octet value. The default display for communities in Cisco IOS software if of the form NNAA in decimal. In order to display communities in the more intuitive AA:NN format, **ip bgp-community new-format** must be configured.

> Even if a community is entered in the new AA:NN format it's not displayed this way unless **ip bgp-community new-format** is configured.

```
router(config)#ip community-list 1 permit 200:666
router#sh ip community-list 1
Community standard list 1
     permit 13107866
router(config)#ip bgp-community new-format
router#sh ip community-list 1
Community standard list 1
     permit 200:666
```

Community lists match one or more community attributes carried with a BGP route; they are generally used in route maps (described below) to filter routes or change some attribute to influence the best-path calculation. There are four general types of community lists:

```
router(config)#ip community-list ?
  <1-99>     Community list number (standard)
  <100-199>  Community list number (expanded)
  expanded   Add an expanded community-list entry
  standard   Add a standard community-list entry
```

Standard community lists match a given community per line:

```
router(config)#ip community-list 10 permit ?
  <1-4294967295>  community number
  aa:nn           community number
  internet        Internet (well-known community)
  local-AS        Do not send outside local AS (well-known community)
  no-advertise    Do not advertise to any peer (well-known community)
  no-export       Do not export to next AS (well-known community)
  <cr>
```

Expanded community lists match a list of communities against a regular expression:

```
router(config)#ip community-list 110 permit ?
  LINE  An ordered list as a regular-expression
```

The syntax of the community-list command is

```
ip community-list community-list-number {permit|deny} community-number
```

Community lists can be named, using a word, or numbered, using a number between 1 and 99 for standard community lists, and between 100 and 199 for expanded community lists. When defining community lists a single entry can contain one or more community values; however, in order to match the entry, the route must contain all the communities listed in the statement.

```
router(config)#ip community-list 1 deny 200:666
router(config)#ip community-list 1 permit 200:777 ?
  <1-4294967295>  community number
  aa:nn           community number
  internet        Internet (well-known community)
  local-AS        Do not send outside local AS (well-known community)
  no-advertise    Do not advertise to any peer (well-known community)
  no-export       Do not export to next AS (well-known community)
  <cr>
```

```
router(config)#ip community-list 1 permit 200:777 200:100 200:200
router#sh ip community-list 1
Community standard list 1
    deny 200:666
    permit 200:100 200:200 200:777
router(config)#ip community-list 1 permit 200:9999
router#sh ip community-list 1
Community standard list 1
    deny 200:666
    permit 200:100 200:200 200:777
    permit 200:9999
```

So in the preceding example, we'll only accept routes with two different sets of community values, 200:9999 or "200:100 200:200 200:777 (order independent)". As discussed, you can also define community lists based on regular expressions.

```
router(config)#ip community-list 100 permit ^200:.*
router(config)#ip community-list 100 deny :666$
router(config)#ip community-list 100 permit :777$
router#sh ip community-list 100
Community (expanded) access list 100
    permit ^200:.*
    deny :666$
    permit :777$
```

In the preceding example, community list 100 permits any community that starts with 200 or ends with 777. It denies any community that ends with 666—except 200:666 per the sequencing of the community list.

By default, *no* communities are sent to external or internal BGP neighbors. In order to send communities to BGP neighbors you must explicitly define **send-community** under the BGP **neighbor** command. It's generally a good idea to configure this for all internal BGP neighbors as a default policy. You may or may not want to send communities to external BGP peers; we'll further discuss this in later sections. Some examples of commonly used community-based filters and routing policies are given in the Communities in Practice section that follows.

One additional feature set that is useful with regard to BGP communities and communities lists is the ability to query the BGP routing to for routes matching a particular community or community list. The

show ip bgp community and **show ip bgp community-list** **<list-name>** commands provide this capability:

```
router#sh ip bgp community-list ?
  <1-199>  community-list number

router#sh ip bgp community ?
  aa:nn            community number
  exact-match      Exact match of the communities
  local-AS         Do not send outside local AS (well-known community)
  no-advertise     Do not advertise to any peer (well-known community)
  no-export        Do not export to next AS (well-known community)
  |                Output modifiers
  <cr>
```

As you'll see in the following sections, BGP communities provide a very powerful tool to scale routing policies in BGP networks.

Extended Communities

BGP extended communities provide an extended range of space, extending standard 32-bit communities to 64 bits (8 octets), helping to ensure that communities can be assigned for a plethora of uses (e.g., BGP/MPLS VPNs, as discussed in Chapter 10) without fear of overlap. They also introduce the notion of a Type field to the recommended community encoding in order to provide more structure of the community space. The extended community attribute is a transitive optional BGP attribute (Type Code 16).

Just as with standard communities, extended communities can be used to group sets of destinations that share some common characteristic. Configuring policies and advertisement of extended communities is Cisco IOS software is similar to configuring standard communities. It is important to realize that extended communities are a new BGP attribute and are totally independent of standard communities. As a result, extended and standard communities can either coexist or you can use only one type or the other.

To specify which type of communities are advertised to a BGP peer, the following BGP configuration parameters are used:

neighbor {ip-address | peer-group-name} send-community [both | standard | extended]

Community lists used to specification with extended communities behaves the same as with standard communities. You can either specify communities themselves or employ expanded community lists to match based on regular expressions.

AS Path Access Lists

AS path access lists match received or transmitted prefixes based on the list of autonomous systems in the route's AS path using a regular expression. They can be used in filtering the updates received from or transmitted to a peer, or they can be used as parts of a route map.

```
router(config)#ip as-path access-list ?
  <1-199>  Regular expression access list number
```

AS path access lists can be applied to filter updates sent to or received from a BGP peer using the **filter-list** keyword in the **neighbor** command under BGP. When using AS path access lists it's important to remember that the AS path is not added to a route until it's advertised to an external BGP peer. As such, if you're attempting to match routes originated from the local autonomous system, the correct regular expression would be ^$, as opposed to ^*as*$.

Empty AS Path Access Lists

If BGP is configured to filter routes based on an AS path list, but the As path filter list doesn't exist, will all the routes be permitted or denied?

```
!
hostname router-a
!
interface Serial3/0
 ip address 10.100.7.4 255.255.255.0
!
router bgp 65500
 no synchronization
 bgp log-neighbor-changes
 network 10.50.12.0 mask 255.255.255.0
 neighbor 10.100.7.10 remote-as 65501
 neighbor 10.100.7.10 filter-list 10 out
 no auto-summary
!
```

```
router-a#show ip bgp
BGP table version is 2, local router ID is 10.100.17.4
Status codes: s suppressed, d damped, h history, * valid, > best,
              i - internal, r RIB-failure
Origin codes: i - IGP, e - EGP, ? - incomplete

   Network         Next Hop            Metric LocPrf Weight Path
*> 10.50.12.0/24   0.0.0.0                  0          32768 i

!
hostname router-b
!
interface Serial0/0
 bandwidth 1100
 ip address 10.100.7.10 255.255.255.0
!
router bgp 65501
 no synchronization
 bgp log-neighbor-changes
 neighbor 10.100.7.4 remote-as 65500
 no auto-summary
!

router-b#show ip bgp

router-b#
```

An empty AS path filter list blocks all routes. AS path filter lists are commonly used to ensure only paths with the local autonomous system number, and customer autonomous system numbers are advertised to peers. For example, let's assume you want to define an AS path filter list permitting route advertisements originating in the local autonomous system (AS 100) and customer autonomous systems AS 200, AS 300, and AS400, but denying all other route advertisements. You could do this a number of ways. For example, the most straightforward way would be some along these lines:

```
router(config)#ip as-path access-list 1 permit ^$
router(config)#ip as-path access-list 1 permit ^200$
router(config)#ip as-path access-list 1 permit ^300$
router(config)#ip as-path access-list 1 permit ^400$
router#sh ip as-path-access-list 1
AS path access list 1
```

```
permit ^$
permit ^100$
permit ^200$
permit ^300$
permit ^400$
```

An alternative way to define the AS path filter list could be something along these lines:

```
router(config)#ip as-path access-list 1 permit ^$
router(config)#ip as-path access-list 1 permit
^(200|300|400)$
router(config)#ip as-path access-list 1 deny .*

router#sh ip as-path-access-list 1
AS path access list 1
    permit ^$
    permit ^(200|300|400)$
    deny .*
```

In the second example the pipe (|) is used to signify "or". Listing multiple entries on the same line of the filter not only makes the filter more intuitive, it helps to improve performance when the filter list is being processed. As you might suspect, there are numerous additional ways this simple policy could be expressed with regular expressions–further exploration in this area encouraged!

You can also use regular expression queries from the command line to search for matches to a particular AS path in the BGP routing table. For example,

```
router#sh ip bgp re ?
  LINE  A regular-expression to match BGP AS paths. Use "ctrl-v ?"
to enter "?"

router#sh ip bgp re ^1234_200$

router#
```

In the preceding example, we searched the BGP routing table for any routes with an AS path of "1234 200", where 200 would be the origin AS and AS 1234 for be the AS from which we learned the route.

Local Preference

Local preference is the "big stick" of metrics within an autonomous system; since it's at the beginning of the decision process (only subsequent to the local non-BGP *weight* attribute), setting the local preference to a high value typically causes a route to win the selection process regardless of the other attribute values (e.g., MED or AS Path) carried with the route. As such, local preference plays a key role in most well-designed routing policies.

The default local preference value for most implementations is 100. It's extremely important that this value be consistent on all BGP speakers within your autonomous system. The default local preference value can be altered by configuring **bgp default local-preference <value>** within the BGP router configuration mode.

```
router(config-router)#bgp default local-preference ?
  <0-4294967295>  Configure default local preference value
```

There are a number of general rules that typically apply to local preference value assignment. We'll further discuss how you go about assigning these values in the section titled Setting Routing Policy in Connected Autonomous Systems Using Communities.

Route Maps

Route maps gather up all the other policy instruments we've discussed thus far, allowing the network administrator to match on one or more attributes of a route, and set others, or simply filter routes based on multiple attributes. Figure 6.1 illustrates the syntax of a route map.

Route maps are made up of *clauses;* each clause begins with a **permit** or **deny** statement. Within each clause, there are **match** statements and **set** statements, with obvious implications.

Route Map Match Statements

A match statement checks the current prefix against the information, and determines if the prefix should be processed under this clause or not. If two conditions are listed within a single **match** statement, then a prefix will match if it matches either of the two conditions. If two conditions are listed under different **match** statements, then a prefix will only match if it matches both conditions; **match** statements may contain references to other policy instruments, such as access lists or prefix lists,

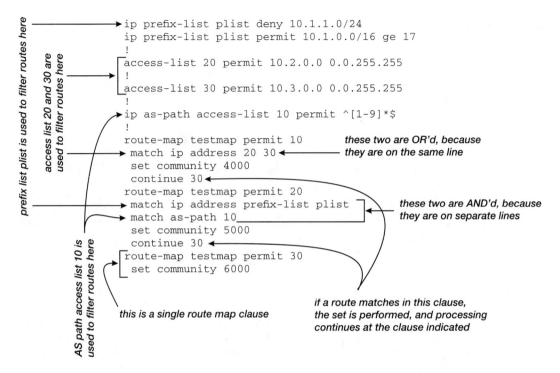

Figure 6.1
The anatomy of a route map.

or a **match** statement may contain a specific condition for matching, as
the following example shows.

```
route-map testmap permit 10
 ! matches prefixes against access list 10
 match ip address 10
 ! matches prefixes against the prefix list named aprefixlist
 match ip address prefix-list aprefixlist
 ! matches prefixes against the interface through which the BGP peer is
 ! reachable
 match interface FastEthernet0/0
 ! matches the MED value of 1000
 match metric 1000
 ! matches the route type
 match route-type external
 ! matches the route's AS Path against as path access list 10
 match as-path 10
```

```
! matches the route's communities against community list 10
match community 10
! matches the route's extended communities against the extended
! community list 10
match extcommunity 10
```

Some additional match clause available options are as follows:

```
r1(config-route-map)#match ?
  as-path        Match BGP AS path list
  community      Match BGP community list
  extcommunity   Match BGP/VPN extended community list
  interface      Match first hop interface of route
  ip             IP specific information
  length         Packet length
  metric         Match metric of route
  route-type     Match route-type of route
  tag            Match tag of route
```

One point of major confusion in handling route maps is in the combination of permits and denies in policy instruments, such as access lists, and the permits and denies in route maps. The following example illustrates how each pair of permits and denies will work using an access list as the policy instrument.

```
!
hostname router-a
!
access-list 10 permit 10.14.1.0 0.0.0.255
access-list 10 deny    any
access-list 20 deny    10.14.2.0 0.0.0.255
access-list 20 permit any
access-list 30 deny    10.14.3.0 0.0.0.255
access-list 30 permit any
access-list 40 permit 10.14.4.0 0.0.0.255
access-list 40 deny    any
!
route-map testmap permit 10
 match ip address 10
 set community 1000
!
route-map testmap deny 20
 match ip address 20
```

```
 set community 2000
!
route-map testmap permit 30
 match ip address 30
 set community 3000
!
route-map testmap deny 40
 match ip address 40
 set community 4000
!
router bgp 65500
 no synchronization
 bgp log-neighbor-changes
 network 10.14.1.0
 network 10.14.2.0
 network 10.14.3.0
 network 10.14.4.0
 neighbor 10.14.7.10 remote-as 65500
 neighbor 10.14.7.10 send-community both
 neighbor 10.14.7.10 route-map testmap out
 no auto-summary
!

!
hostname router-b
!
router bgp 65500
 no synchronization
 bgp log-neighbor-changes
 neighbor 10.14.7.4 remote-as 65500
 no auto-summary
!

router-b#sho ip bgp
BGP table version is 13, local router ID is 10.14.16.10
Status codes: s suppressed, d damped, h history, * valid, > best,
              i - internal, r RIB-failure
Origin codes: i - IGP, e - EGP, ? - incomplete
```

Network	Next Hop	Metric	LocPrf	Weight	Path
*>i10.14.1.0	10.14.7.4	0	100	0	i
*>i10.14.2.0	10.14.7.4	0	100	0	i

```
....
```

```
router-b#sho ip bgp 10.14.1.0
BGP routing table entry for 10.14.1.0/24, version 12
Paths: (1 available, best #1, table Default-IP-Routing-Table)
  Not advertised to any peer
  Local
    10.14.7.4 from 10.14.7.4 (10.14.17.4)
      Origin IGP, metric 0, localpref 100, valid, internal, best
      Community: 0:1000
router-b#sho ip bgp 10.14.2.0
BGP routing table entry for 10.14.2.0/24, version 13
Paths: (1 available, best #1, table Default-IP-Routing-Table)
  Not advertised to any peer
  Local
    10.14.7.4 from 10.14.7.4 (10.14.17.4)
      Origin IGP, metric 0, localpref 100, valid, internal, best
      Community: 0:3000
```

Since these results don't appear, on the surface, to be intuitive, we'll delve into this a little further and analyze why each prefix is either not sent from *router-a* to *router-b* or why they were sent with these communities. The policies on router-a are described in Table 6.8.

Let's follow each prefix advertised by *router-a* and see how the route-map processes them.

- 10.14.1.0/24 is permitted by access-list 10, so the **match** command in *testmap's* clause 10 succeeds. The clause itself is defined as a permit, so the **set** statement is performed, and processing

Table 6.8

	Access List	Route Map
10	permit 10.14.1.0/24	permit set community 1000
20	deny 10.14.2.0/24 permit any others	deny set community 2000
30	deny 10.14.3.0/24 permit any others	permit set community 3000
40	permit 10.14.4.0/24 set community 4000	deny

Table 6.9

	Route Map Permit	**Route Map Deny**
Policy Instrument Permit	Perform Set	Drop Route
Policy Instrument Deny	Move to the Next Route Map Sequence	Move to the Next Route Map Sequence

stops at this point. Thus, 10.14.1.0/24 is advertised to router-b with a community of 1000, as we see in the preceding output.

- 10.14.2.0/24 is not permitted by access-list 10, so processing moves to the next clause in the route map. 10.14.2.0/24 is denied by access-list 20, so, again, processing moves to the next clause in the route map. 10.14.2.0/24 is permitted by access-list 30, and the route map clause is a permit, so the **set** operation is performed, which sets the community to 3000.

- 10.14.3.0/24 is not permitted by access-list 10, so processing moves to the next clause in the route map. 10.14.3.0/24 is permitted by access-list 20, but the route map clause is a deny, so the route is not advertised to router-b.

- 10.14.4.0/24 is processed in the same way as 10.14.3.0/24 was processed.

As you can see from this explanation, the fourth route map clause isn't used at all by any of the routes. Table 6.9 describes the actions taken by the route-map code on each possible pair of permits and denies.

Route Map Set Statements

Set statements take actions on any prefixes that match the match statements in the route map clause. Route maps can set a number of attributes for any route:

```
router(config-route-map)#set ?
  as-path          Prepend string for a BGP AS-path attribute
  automatic-tag    Automatically compute TAG value
  clns             OSI summary address
  comm-list        set BGP community list (for deletion)
  community        BGP community attribute
  dampening        Set BGP route flap dampening parameters
  default          Set default information
```

```
extcommunity        BGP extended community attribute
interface           Output interface
ip                  IP specific information
ipv6                IPv6 specific information
level               Where to import route
local-preference    BGP local preference path attribute
metric              Metric value for destination routing protocol
metric-type         Type of metric for destination routing protocol
origin              BGP origin code
tag                 Tag value for destination routing protocol
weight              BGP weight for routing table
```

Not all of these possible set commands apply to BGP prefixes, of course. It is also possible to apply **set** statements without specify any match, which results in all routes to which the route map is applied to be subjected to the **set** actions.

Communities play a key role in the routing policy on many networks. When you're setting communities within a route map, you have two options: Add the communities you wish to add based on the match clause and leave the existing communities in place as well, or strip the old communities and only propagate the new community values. Recalling the discussion of Update Packing section in Chapter 5, BGP Performance, the more unique attributes attached to a given route the less efficient update packing and BGP performance will be. Because of this, it's generally recommended that if you don't intend to use the communities again you remove them from the route. The **additive** keyword in the community **set** clause of a route map can be used to preserve the existing communities; otherwise they're overwritten when the new community is added:

```
r1(config-route-map)#set community 1234:100 ?
  <1-4294967295>    community number
  aa:nn             community number in aa:nn format
  additive          Add to the existing community
  internet          Internet (well-known community)
  local-AS          Do not send outside local AS (well-known community)
  no-advertise      Do not advertise to any peer (well-known community)
  no-export         Do not export to next AS (well-known community)
  <cr>
r1(config-route-map)#set community 1234:100 additive ?
    <cr>
```

The Continue

The continue command causes the processing of a prefix to continue even though a match has been found in a given route map clause. Normally, the first time a prefix matches each of the policy instruments referenced in a route map clause, the **set** commands contained in that route map clause are executed, and the route map code finishes. If a **continue** command is used, however, the **set** commands are executed, and processing of the prefix continues with the indicated clause. It should be noted that one can only use the **continue** statement to proceed to a higher numbered statement in a route-map. This is done to prevent possible loops within the policy configuration.

Policy Lists

Policy lists in Cisco IOS software essentially allow the creation of common sets of filters that can be applied in a number of different route maps, much like peer groups help to ease BGP neighbor configuration overhead. This allows the network operator to build a common set of classification policies and apply those classification policies in several different filters. Figure 6.2 illustrates a policy list used in multiple route maps.

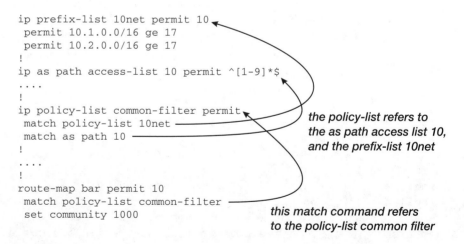

```
ip prefix-list 10net permit 10
 permit 10.1.0.0/16 ge 17
 permit 10.2.0.0/16 ge 17
!
ip as path access-list 10 permit ^[1-9]*$
....
!
ip policy-list common-filter permit
 match policy-list 10net
 match as path 10
!
....
!
route-map bar permit 10
 match policy-list common-filter
 set community 1000
```

the policy-list refers to
the as path access list 10,
and the prefix-list 10net

this match command refers
to the policy-list common filter

Figure 6.2
A policy list.

Communities in Practice—RFC 1998 and Other Routing Policies

You can think of communities as a way to tag a route with almost any policy or other information which might be useful in some way. For instance, communities are used, in various applications, to

- Tag routes coming from customers that you plan to advertise to peers
- Tag backbone routes that you plan to advertise to peers
- Tag peer routes or backbone (more-specific) routes that you don't intend to advertise to peers
- Indicate which routes belong to a particular virtual private network
- Tag routes coming from a given POP (point of presence) or geographic region in a network
- Convey the monetary cost of a link to an outside network.
- Carry the metrics of other protocols transparently through a virtual private network.
- Carry information about the advertising scope of a route.

Chapter 1 discusses the layout and transport of communities; in this section we discuss the use of communities for transporting policy.

Setting Routing Policy in Connected Autonomous Systems Using Communities

It's quite common for a single customer to be connected to two different service providers at the edge of the Internet; in this case, the customer may want to exercise some control over the routing from the service providers into their autonomous system. To provide this control, a service provider could manually configure their policies to set the Local Preference of a route in their autonomous system based on pervious instructions from the customer. Manual configuration, however, has many problems, including the administrative overhead required of the service provider in order to manually configure policies associated with each connection a customer has into their network, the incidence of human error when manual configuration is relied on for a primary means of setting policy, and the response time incurred when updates to the policy are required.

RFC 1998 describes the use of communities to allow a customer to indicate, within each path advertised to the service provider, the policy/route preference the customer desires to apply toward a given route. Generally, this means the customer advertises a community to the service provider and the service provider uses the community to set the local preference for the route. Figure 6.3 illustrates.

Router A is advertising the same route with two different communities; 65500:1200 toward AS65502, and 65500:1100 toward AS65501. When Router B receives 172.16.24.0/24, it sets the Local Preference to 100 and advertises the route to the rest of the routers within AS65501. Assuming AS5502 is passing the communities set by AS65500 through to AS65503, and AS65503 is passing them through to AS65501, when

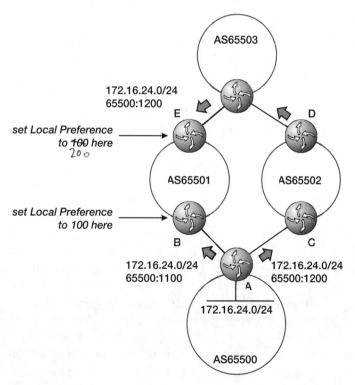

Figure 6.3
Using extended communities to influence provider route choice.

router E receives 172.16.24.0/24, it will set the Local Preference to 200, and advertise the route through to the rest of the autonomous system. The routers in AS65501 will prefer the route through router E, rather than the router through router B, to reach 172.16.24.0/24, because the Local Preference is set higher on the route through E. The following configurations for routers A, E, and F, using Cisco IOS software, show how this is set up.

```
!
router-a
!
....
router bgp 65500
 no synchronization
 bgp log-neighbor-changes
 network 172.16.24.0 mask 255.255.255.0
 neighbor 172.16.7.10 remote-as 65501
 neighbor 172.16.7.10 send-community both
 neighbor 172.16.7.10 route-map setcomm1 out
 neighbor 172.16.8.11 remote-as 65501
 neighbor 172.16.8.11 send-community both
 neighbor 172.16.8.11 route-map setcomm2 out
 no auto-summary
!
....
ip prefix-list matchprefer seq 5 permit 172.16.24.0/24
!
route-map setcomm2 permit 10
 match ip address prefix-list matchprefer
 set community 65500:1100
!
route-map setcomm1 permit 10
 match ip address prefix-list matchprefer
 set community 65500:1200
!

!
hostname router-e
!
....
router bgp 65501
 no synchronization
 bgp log-neighbor-changes
```

```
 neighbor 172.16.7.4 remote-as 65500
 neighbor 172.16.7.4 route-map setlocpref in
 neighbor 172.16.12.11 remote-as 65501
 no auto-summary
!
....
ip community-list 10 permit 65500:1200
!
....
route-map setlocpref permit 10
 match community 10
 set local-preference 200
....

router-e#sho ip bgp 172.16.24.0
BGP routing table entry for 172.16.24.0/24, version 9
Paths: (1 available, best #1, table Default-IP-Routing-Table)
  Advertised to non peer-group peers:
  172.16.12.11
  65500
    172.16.7.4 from 172.16.7.4 (172.16.17.4)
      Origin IGP, metric 0, localpref 200, valid, external, best
      Community: 65500:1200


!
hostname router-f
!
....
router bgp 65501
 no synchronization
 bgp log-neighbor-changes
 neighbor 172.16.8.4 remote-as 65500
 neighbor 172.16.8.4 route-map setlocpref in
 neighbor 172.16.12.10 remote-as 65501
 no auto-summary
!
....
ip bgp-community new-format
ip community-list 10 permit 65500:1100
!
route-map setlocpref permit 10
 match community 10
```

```
set local-preference 100
!
....

router-f#sho ip bgp 172.16.24.0
BGP routing table entry for 172.16.24.0/24, version 7
Paths: (2 available, best #1, table Default-IP-Routing-Table)
  Not advertised to any peer
  65500
    172.16.7.4 from 172.16.12.10 (172.16.16.10)
      Origin IGP, metric 0, localpref 200, valid, internal, best
  65500
    172.16.8.4 from 172.16.8.4 (172.16.17.4)
      Origin IGP, metric 0, localpref 100, valid, external
      Community: 65500:1100
```

Using Local Preference to Set Policy

There are a number of general rules that typically apply to local preference value assignment. For example, you want to first assign a default local preference value for the network, let's assume 100, since it's the default value used by most implementations. It's likely you'll want to prefer paying customer routes over similar routes learned from peers, so we'll set all routes learned from customers to 100 by default and all routes learned from peers to 80 by default. Now, you need to define some mechanism to allow customers that are multihomed to your network to select how their routes are preferred among their multiple connections to your network and perhaps how they're compared with routes learned from other networks and peers to which they may be connected as well. So your local preference assignment policy might look something like that shown in Table 6.10 (though likely more expansive):

Once you've decided what your polices are, you can now specify routing policy that allows customers to influence routing decisions on your network. You could define incoming route maps that are applied to all customer peering sessions. Let's assume, for this example, that your autonomous system number is 100 (Table 6.11).

Table 6.10

Local Preference Value	Purpose
70	Prefer this route less than routes learned from peers
80	Set this as the default value for all routes learned from peers
90	Prefer this route over routes learned from peers, but less than other customer routes
100	Default value assigned to all locally generated and customer advertised routes
110	Prefer this route over other customers and internal routes

> The AS path prepending functions included in Table 6.11 are often provided by service providers so their customers can influence path selection multiple AS hops away. The local preference can't be used for this, since the local preference attribute is only local to an AS and therefore has no direct impact on path selection beyond the local AS.

As you can see, we could add lots of additional community types and implement policy on the network to act on those communities. It's important for community values to be well documented and defined and all the advertisement policies you plan to use implemented consistently throughout the network.

Further, when using communities for routing policy specification, it's extremely important to be as explicit as possible about advertisement policies. For example, rather than assuming a route without a given set of communities attached means the route should be announced, write your policies so the route will only be announced if the "announce this route to this peer type" community is attached. This provides a seafety net; if the originating router is broken or misconfigured so the appropriate communities aren't attached to a route, the least possible damage will be done. That is, when global routing stability is a factor, it is a far better idea to not advertise a slew of garbage

Table 6.11

Received Community	Action
100:70	Set the local preference on this route to 70, strip this community, and add the standard customer community.
100:80	Set the local preference on this route to 80, strip this community, and add the standard customer community.
100:90	Set the local preference on this route to 90, strip this community, and add the standard customer community.
100:110	Set the local preference on this route to 110 (recall that 100 was skipped as it's the default value), strip this community and add the standard customer community.
100:1001	Preserve this community, add the standard customer community, and prepend AS 100 to the AS path of the route when advertising the route to external BGP peers.
100:1002	Preserve this community, add the standard customer community, and prepend AS 100 two times to the AS path when advertising the route to external BGP peers.
100:1003	Preserve this community, add the standard customer community, and prepend AS 100 three times to the AS path when advertising the route to external BGP peers.
100:666 or NO_EXPORT	Preserve this community and add the standard customer community.
NO_ADVERTISE	Preserve this community and add the standard customer community.

routes then to advertise them as a default policy. This same philosophy should be applied to prefix lists and even packets filters. Be as explicit as possible in permitting, and deny everything else.

The BGP community is defined in RFC 1997, *BGP Communities Attribute,* RFC 1998, *An Application of the BGP Community Attribute in Multi-Home Routing.* BGP extended communities are still in the specification stage within the Inter-Domain Routing (IDR) working group of the IETF, as well as a new form of community, the flexible community, which is covered in Chapter 7, New Features in BGP.

Sending and Accepting Communities

Typically, service providers don't send communities to peers or accept them from peers, which helps to limit the information carried in the global routing tables and provides efficiency gains on a number of planes. They also generally don't send communities to customers unless the customer requests the communities. One reason a customer might request to receive communities from their service provider is because they're multihomed and want to increase their local preference for a service and his customers via their direct connection but lower the preference for the service providers peers and prefer reaching them via an alternative route.

As discussed earlier in this chapter, Cisco IOS software requires that you explicitly enable sending communities to BGP peers.

Effects on Update Packing

While it's not obvious from general documentation about BGP, the use of communities can impact the speed at which BGP converges. This is because of the way in which BGP formats the routing information in each packet transmitted to a peer. A given set of attributes is carried in each packet along with the prefixes that share those attributes.

Since communities are attributes, setting, or simply accepting and propagating, a different community on each route will cause each prefix to be sent in a different packet, slowing down convergence dramatically. For more information on this, see the Update Packing section of Chapter 5, BGP Performance.

Safety Nets

There are a number of common filters all autonomous systems should place on their borders with other autonomous systems to prevent various sorts of invalid information from making it into or out of their networks. These filters act as *safety nets* against varying forms of attacks and misconfigurations that can occur from time to time on a network as large as the Internet, and they are also useful to protect your network in private peering relationships outside the context of the Internet.

Acceptable Advertisement Length

Normally, there is no reason to accept routes with very short or very long prefix lengths. When peering to another private network (such as peering to another company for directly exchanging access to servers in a partnership or merger and migrations, etc.), you would need to determine the range of acceptable prefix lengths by examining the routing table of the peering autonomous system. Generally, in private peering arrangements outside the Internet, acceptable prefix lengths are going to be within the /16 to /24 range, although it's going to depend on what it is you're trying to accomplish—in some cases, prefixes all the way down to /32s might be acceptable.

When connecting to the Internet, or at the peering point between two service providers, however, the best current practice for range of acceptable prefix lengths throughout the Internet is no shorter than 8 bits and no longer than 24 bits. Thus, most Internet service providers filter all routes at their borders so nothing less than a /8 is accepted, and nothing greater than a /24 is accepted. The easiest way to filter prefixes on prefix length is using a prefix list, as discussed earlier in this chapter; the following example will filter all prefixes with a prefix length less than 8 or a prefix length greater than 24.

```
ip prefix-list killbogons permit 0.0.0.0/0 ge 8 le 24
```

Alternatively, you could also use an extended access list applied as a distribute list (or within a route map) for this function:

```
access-list 101 deny any 255.255.255.128 0.0.0.127
access-list 101 permit any 255.0.0.0 0.255.255.255
```

It's possible to be more precise in filtering prefixes based on their length in the Internet, since blocks of addresses are assigned by Regional Internet Registries (RIRs). A list of the current prefix allocation lengths within each address blocks is available from each Registry. While this type of filtering can be very useful in reducing the amount of useless routing information received, it also has its dangers. Indiscriminate filtering on prefix length can destroy the utility of redundant links, making some destinations unreachable on a single link failure; Figure 6.4 illustrates.

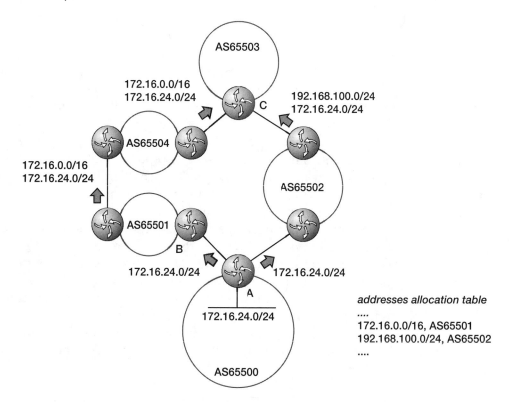

172.16.0.0/16
172.16.24.0/24

192.168.100.0/24
172.16.24.0/24

172.16.0.0/16
172.16.24.0/24

172.16.24.0/24   172.16.24.0/24

172.16.24.0/24

addresses allocation table
....
172.16.0.0/16, AS65501
192.168.100.0/24, AS65502
....

Figure 6.4
Filtering on allocation boundaries.

Router A is advertising 172.16.24.0/24 prefix to both AS65501 and AS65502, which are then advertising this prefix to AS65503. However, router C is filtering inbound prefixes based on the allocations of addresses shown in the external registry database; so it filters the inbound updates so only 172.16.0.0/16 and 192.168.100.0/24 are accepted.

This effectively cuts access off from AS65503 through AS65504 and AS65501. If the link between routers A and B fails, 172.16.0.0/16 will still be advertised into AS65503 but will not be reachable through AS65501, which is originating the aggregate. Since 172.16.24.0/24 is filtered inbound from AS65502, router C doesn't know there is an alternate path to this destination.

There are a large number of service providers that implement RIR-based acceptable advertisement filters in their networks. If you intended to announce more-specific prefixes from a registry allocated block, it's a good idea to understand which providers are currently filtering on what prefix boundaries; otherwise some loss of connectivity via certain networks may occur. The North American Network Operations Group (NANOG: *https://www.nanog.org*) often discuss these issues and their effect on Internet routing, and the Web site contains list (albeit sparse and quite dated) of some service providers filtering policies regarding acceptable advertisement lengths within a given address block.

In reality, the optimal prefix filtering model would require that all autonomous systems filter routes explicitly from each BGP peer. The problem with this is there's currently no up-to-date authoritative repository on the Internet describing what prefixes a given autonomous system is authorized to announce. Many service providers, such as Level3 Communications and Cable & Wireless (CW), maintain local Internet Routing Registries (IRR) that contain information on what prefixes a given customer is authorized to advertise and some policies associated with those prefixes. However, today most large service providers simply filter obviously bogus or otherwise critical address space explicitly from peers and openly accept all other routes. The result is a global routing system that's very susceptible to things like route high-jacking and unintentional route leaks adversely effecting Internet reachability and content security.

Some potential solutions to this problem are further in Chapter 9, BGP and Network Security.

Bogon Filters

There are several classes of bogons, or destinations, known to be invalid from sources outside BGP, which should be filtered at the edge of any autonomous system that is connected to the Internet:

- Private IPv4 Address Spaces. Private addresses are those IPv4 addresses are set aside as not routable on the Internet backbone in RFC 1918. These include 192.168.0.0/16, 172.16.0.0/12, and 10.0.0.0/8.
- Multicast Destinations. Unless a peering session is explicitly set up beforehand to allow multicast prefixes to be advertised in BGP, all multicast prefixes should be filtered, which includes the 224.0.0.0/5 address space.
- Unallocated Address Space. Each Regional Internet Registry maintains a list of allocated and unallocated addresses, as we've noted previously. Filtering all unallocated space on the edge of

an autonomous system can prevent a large portion of various denial of service attacks that are launched against networks. For example, a common trend of spammers involves advertising un-allocated address space, sending millions of spam messages from servers that are addressed within the space, and, finally, removing the routing advertisements.

Team CYMRU

CYMRU provides a list of bogons, as well as a number of services that are free of charge to the Internet community, that are updated continuously as each registry announces allocation changes within a given address block. Their current recommend filter list is shown in Table 6.12 (note that we've described bogons as included RFC 1918, etc. as well). Please note that this list does change over time, and thus it is important that network administrators monitor the list for changes. These can be readily incorporated into Cisco ACLs as the following (edited for brevity):

```
access-list 2010 deny ip 0.0.0.0 0.255.255.255 any
access-list 2010 deny ip 1.0.0.0 0.255.255.255 any
access-list 2010 deny ip 2.0.0.0 0.255.255.255 any
access-list 2010 deny ip 5.0.0.0 0.255.255.255 any
access-list 2010 deny ip 7.0.0.0 0.255.255.255 any
access-list 2010 deny ip 10.0.0.0 0.255.255.255 any
access-list 2010 deny ip 23.0.0.0 0.255.255.255 any
access-list 2010 deny ip 27.0.0.0 0.255.255.255 any
[ ... ]
```

The bogons can be filtered in BGP as well. This can be done with a Cisco prefix-list filter (edited for brevity):

```
ip prefix-list bogons description Bogon networks we won't accept.
ip prefix-list bogons seq 5 deny 0.0.0.0/8 le 32
ip prefix-list bogons seq 10 deny 1.0.0.0/8 le 32
ip prefix-list bogons seq 15 deny 2.0.0.0/8 le 32
ip prefix-list bogons seq 20 deny 5.0.0.0/8 le 32
ip prefix-list bogons seq 25 deny 7.0.0.0/8 le 32
ip prefix-list bogons seq 30 deny 10.0.0.0/8 le 32
ip prefix-list bogons seq 35 deny 23.0.0.0/8 le 32
ip prefix-list bogons seq 40 deny 27.0.0.0/8 le 32
[ ... ]
```

Table 6.12

0.0.0.0/8	1.0.0.0/8	2.0.0.0/8	5.0.0.0/8	7.0.0.0/8
10.0.0.0/8	23.0.0.0/8	27.0.0.0/8	31.0.0.0/8	36.0.0.0/8
37.0.0.0/8	39.0.0.0/8	41.0.0.0/8	42.0.0.0/8	49.0.0.0/8
50.0.0.0/8	58.0.0.0/8	59.0.0.0/8	71.0.0.0/8	72.0.0.0/8
73.0.0.0/8	74.0.0.0/8	75.0.0.0/8	76.0.0.0/8	77.0.0.0/8
78.0.0.0/8	79.0.0.0/8	85.0.0.0/8	86.0.0.0/8	87.0.0.0/8
88.0.0.0/8	89.0.0.0/8	90.0.0.0/8	91.0.0.0/8	92.0.0.0/8
93.0.0.0/8	94.0.0.0/8	95.0.0.0/8	96.0.0.0/8	97.0.0.0/8
98.0.0.0/8	99.0.0.0/8	100.0.0.0/8	101.0.0.0/8	102.0.0.0/8
103.0.0.0/8	104.0.0.0/8	105.0.0.0/8	106.0.0.0/8	107.0.0.0/8
108.0.0.0/8	109.0.0.0/8	110.0.0.0/8	111.0.0.0/8	112.0.0.0/8
113.0.0.0/8	114.0.0.0/8	115.0.0.0/8	116.0.0.0/8	117.0.0.0/8
118.0.0.0/8	119.0.0.0/8	120.0.0.0/8	121.0.0.0/8	122.0.0.0/8
123.0.0.0/8	124.0.0.0/8	125.0.0.0/8	126.0.0.0/8	127.0.0.0/8
169.254.0.0/16	172.16.0.0/12	173.0.0.0/8	174.0.0.0/8	175.0.0.0/8
176.0.0.0/8	177.0.0.0/8	178.0.0.0/8	179.0.0.0/8	180.0.0.0/8
181.0.0.0/8	182.0.0.0/8	183.0.0.0/8	184.0.0.0/8	185.0.0.0/8
186.0.0.0/8	187.0.0.0/8	189.0.0.0/8	190.0.0.0/8	192.0.2.0/24
192.168.0.0/16	197.0.0.0/8	198.18.0.0/15	223.0.0.0/8	224.0.0.0/3

From <http://www.cymru.com/Documents/bogon-bn-nonagg.txt>

Network administrators can remain informed on bogon changes through a variety of methods, including DNS, HTTP, e-mail, and even BGP itself.

The Bogon Route-server Project is one way Team Cymru provides updates in an automated manner. Through the use of eBGP multihop peering, the network administrator is provided with a redundant method of maintaining current filters on all border routers. Details on the bogon route-servers can be found at the following URL: *http://www.cymru.com/BGP/bogon-rs.html.*

The bogon prefixes are announced from the bogon route-servers with a specific ASN (65333) and community (888). So how does one use the community 65333:888 prefixes to generate a bogon filter? There are myriad methods, of course. One possible method is to use a route-map and a route with a next-hop of the null0 (Cisco) interface. For example,

```
! Remember to configure your Cisco router to handle the new style
! community syntax.
ip bgp-community new-format
!
! Set a bogon next-hop on all routers that receive the bogons.
ip route 192.168.1.1 255.255.255.255 null0
!
! Configure a community list to accept the bogon prefixes into the
! route-map.
ip community-list 10 permit 65333:888
!
! Configure the route-map. Remember to apply it to the proper
! peering sessions.
route-map CYMRUBOGONS permit 10
 description Filter the bogons we learn from the Cymru.com bogon route
servers
match community 10
set ip next-hop 192.168.1.1
!
```

The bogon-announce mailing list is another way to receive immediate notification of changes to the bogon list. Details for subscribing to the bogon-announce list can be found at the following URL: *http://puck.nether.net/mailman/listinfo/bogon-announce*.

The Team Cymru Bogon Reference Page includes all of these references, along with several additional references. It can be found at the following URL: *http://www.cymru.com/Bogons/*.

Maximum Prefixes

With several implementations of BGP, it's also possible to limit the number of prefixes a router receives from a peer; if the peer sends more routes than the limit, the router can either print a warning message or disable the peering session. The per peer maximum prefix limit is configured using the **maximum-prefixes** command under the **router BGP** submode in Cisco IOS software.

```
router(config-router)#neighbor 10.1.1.1 maximum-prefix 1000 ?
 <1-100>       Threshold value (%) at which to generate a warning msg
 restart       Restart bgp connection after limit is exceeded
 warning-only  Only give warning message when limit is exceeded
 <cr>
```

The warning-only keywords and the threshold value are mutually exclusive. If you configure the router to allow a maximum of 1000 prefixes and to produce a warning at 80% of that threshold, then the router will print a warning message to the console when it receives 800 routes and reset the session when it receives 1000 routes. Once the session is disabled as a result of exceeding the acceptable defined threshold, a **clear ip bgp** *neighbor ip* must manually be issued in order for the session to be reestablished.

It is possible to override this manual reset requirement by specifying the **restart** parameter, which requires a trailing argument defining the number of minutes (from 1 to 65,535) that should elapse before the session is automatically reestablished. Care must be taken when using this feature, however, as no policy or other action is taken beyond the session being restarted, and if the peer is still exceeding the maximum prefix once the session is established it will be disabled again until the restart timer expires and the session is reestablished–ad infinitum!

Where should you use this feature? On just about every peering connection you have with routers in another autonomous system–if you can't filter all prefixes learned from the peer explicitly. For instance, service providers could use this command to limit the number of routes learned from a given customer to less than 10, or perhaps 50 or 100. Enterprise networks accepting partial routes from a service provider can use this feature to keep some mistake at the service provider end of the circuit from causing their router to be overwhelmed with extra routing information. In general, it's a good idea to limit the number of prefixes a router is allowed to receive through BGP to some number you know is reasonable. However, it's still strongly recommended that routes be filtered explicitly if possible.

The AS Path

While the autonomous systems contained in the AS Path are not used in determining which path to use (i.e., the AS path length is a component of the bestpath calculation, not the AS Path itself), and it's not a good idea to use the AS path to set policy based on the existence of some distant autonomous system, there are still some common policies that are implemented based on the AS Path.

Remove Private AS

One common method use to dual home to two different service providers (or even to dual home to the same service provider) is to use a BGP private autonomous system number to peer to the service providers and let the service providers strip the private autonomous system numbers out of the path before they send them to their peers. The reason this is appealing is because in order to run BGP you would otherwise be required to become a member the Regional Internet Registry responsible for your region and pay membership fees for acquiring a unique autonomous system number. The command to strip out private autonomous systems in Cisco IOS software is

```
router(config-router)#neighbor 10.1.1.1 remove-private-AS ?
  <cr>
```

It's important to remember that this applies only to routes advertised to the specified peers and not to the routes when they're learned from the peering AS. As such, if you plan to employ routing policies utilizing private autonomous system numbers, it's generally a good idea to preconfigure this policy on all eBGP peering sessions.

RFC 1930, *Guidelines for Creation, Selection, and Registration of an Autonomous System (AS),* describes the requirements for getting an autonomous system number and what constitutes private AS space. RFC 2270, *Using a Dedicated AS for Sites Homed to a Single Provider,* describes one technique for using dedicated (private) AS number for this purpose.

Enforce First AS

Another common option is to disallow advertisements with an AS Path indicating that they are not from the peering autonomous system. Configuring this filter policy blocks the ability of an autonomous system to pretend to be another autonomous system, which can be used to source routes to nonexistent networks as a basis for denials of service or other attacks. Figure 6.5 illustrates using a configuration from Cisco IOS software.

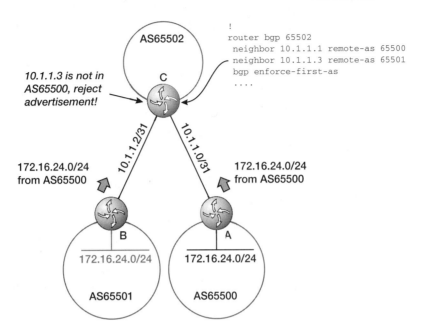

```
!
router bgp 65502
 neighbor 10.1.1.1 remote-as 65500
 neighbor 10.1.1.3 remote-as 65501
 bgp enforce-first-as
 ....
```

Figure 6.5
BGP enforce first AS.

In this network, AS65501 would like to advertise 172.16.24.0/24 for some reason, perhaps to try and steal traffic from AS65500, or misdirect that traffic, or it would like to source traffic from 172.16.24.0/24 and make the packets pass through reverse path forwarding checks at the edge of AS65502. One strategy AS65501 can use to advertise this route is to send the advertisement as though is originates from AS65500; in other words, router B advertises 172.16.24.0/24 with an AS path of [65500], even though it's not part of AS65500. When router C receives this advertisement, it checks the peer configuration, which states that router B is in AS65501, against the received advertisement, which claims to originate in AS65500, and notes that the next hop in the AS Path doesn't match the autonomous system the sending peer's autonomous system. Router C can safely discard this advertisement.

> In Cisco IOS software, the command that enables this checking, **bgp enforce-first-as,** was first available in the 11.1CC train of software. There are some releases later than this in which the command is not available. In future releases of software, this checking will be on by default.

Common AS Path Filters

Two other common AS Path filters are filtering out all learned routes (allowing only locally originated destinations) and the ability to filter on the actual number of autonomous systems listed in the AS Path. Each of these is covered in a section below.

Allowing Only Locally Originated Destinations

When a network is dual homed to two different service providers, it can become a valid transit path for traffic, even though this isn't the intent of the network administrator. Figure 6.6 illustrates.

In this network, AS65500 advertises 172.16.24.0/24 to AS65502, which then readvertises it to AS65503, one of its customers. AS65503 accepts this prefix and advertises it to its other upstream service provider, AS65504, which then prefers this path over the path learned through the backbone links, using AS65503 as a transit for 172.16.24.0/24. If AS65503 is a corporate or university network, they probably don't want to transit traffic in this way. How can they filter

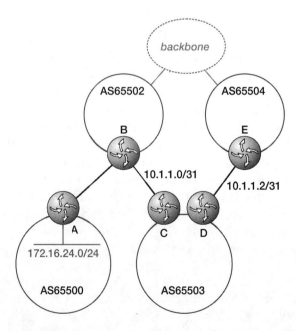

Figure 6.6
A simple case of multihoming and unintentional transit.

their routes so they don't appear to be a transit path for networks not originated within their autonomous system? The following configuration, using Cisco IOS software, provides this filtering.

```
!
hostname router-c
....
!
ip as-path access-list 10 permit ^$
....
!
router bgp 65503
 neighbor 10.1.1.1 remote-as 65502
 neighbor 10.1.1.1 filter-list 10 out
 ....

!
hostname router-d
....
!
ip as-path access-list 10 permit ^$
....
!
router bgp 65503
 neighbor 10.1.1.3 remote-as 65504
 neighbor 10.1.1.3 filter-list 10 out
```

These AS path access lists may not be intuitive when you first look at them; it appears they only permit routes with an empty AS Path–and that's exactly what they permit. They key is to understand where filtering takes place in the BGP implementation you're working with. In Cisco IOS software, filtering takes place before the local autonomous system number is prepended to the advertisement, so any routes that originate in AS65503 will have an empty AS Path when they are filtered. This may not be true in all BGP implementations, so you may need to include the local AS in the AS Path filter.

Filtering on the Number of Autonomous Systems in the Path

It's often useful to be able to filter on the number of autonomous systems in the AS Path rather than the length of the AS Path. What's the difference? Figure 6.7 illustrates.

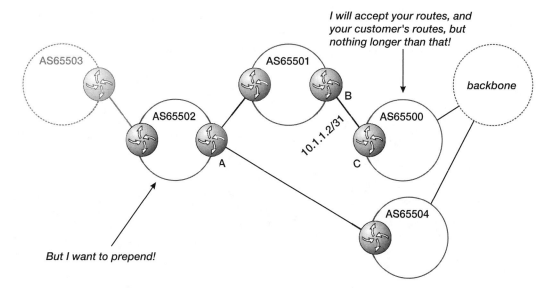

I will accept your routes, and your customer's routes, but nothing longer than that!

AS65503

AS65501

backbone

AS65502

B

10.1.1.2/31

AS65500

A

C

AS65504

But I want to prepend!

Figure 6.7
Filtering on the number of autonomous systems in the AS Path.

Assume that the network administrators of AS65500 sign a contract with AS65501's administrators to accept traffic from them, and any of their customers, and transit this traffic to the backbone. The challenge is to accept route from AS65501 and AS65502, but not from AS65503, which is potentially behind AS65502. The first attempt at a solution might look something like this:

```
!
hostname router-c
....
!
ip as-path access-list 10 permit ^[1-9]*_[1-9]*$
....
!
router bgp 65500
 neighbor 10.1.1.2 remote-as 65501
 neighbor 10.1.1.2 filter-list 10 in
....
```

This would limit the length of any AS Path accepted by router C to two hops, which seems to do what we want to do. The problem starts when AS65502, for some reason, wants to start prepending its autonomous system number into the AS Path. Now, router C will need to accept any AS Path with a length of three; the problem with accepting an AS Path of three is twofold:

- If AS65502 stops prepending its autonomous system number onto the path, AS65503's advertisements will now be accepted at router C.
- If AS65502 decides to prepend more than one onto the AS Path, the filter has to be changed at router C to accommodate this change in AS65502's policy.

Is there some other way around this problem? Yes, using the capability of a regular expression to recall a previous match, and using the recalled match to match another part of the compared string. The following configuration shows how this can be used.

```
!
hostname router-c
....
!
ip as-path access-list 10 permit ^([1-9]*_)\1*[1-9]*$
....
!
router bgp 65500
 neighbor 10.1.1.2 remote-as 65501
 neighbor 10.1.1.2 filter-list 10 in
....
```

To understand how the recall works in this context, let's look at how router C would process an advertisement prepended by AS65502.

- Router C receives some prefix from router B, say 172.28.1.0/24, with an AS Path of [65502 65502 65501].
- The AS Path is matched against the filter ^([1-9]*_)\1*[1-9]*$ to see if it should be accepted. The first match is against the beginning of line, and that passes.
- The second match is against the first autonomous system number in the path, which is 65502, followed by a space. This matches and is stored in the first "recall position" within the regular expression.

- The next match is for any number of reoccurrences of the first match, which is 65502, followed by a space. The regular expression engine finds one more of these, the second 65502 in the AS Path.
- Finally, the last match is for any autonomous system followed by an end of line, and this matches the final 65501, followed by the end of line.

Most regular expression engines no longer support the ability to recall previously matched items this way, so you need to check the documentation for the BGP implementation you are using to make certain it's supported before relying on this type of filtering.

Route Flap Damping

A large portion of the routing information propagated between BGP speakers on the Internet is the result of unstable or *flapping* routes. Route flaps continuously ripple through the Internet as a result of up and unstable paths or changes in attributes associated with a given path. These flaps result in wasted CPU, bandwidth and other network resources. RFC 2439, *BGP Route Flap Damping,* defines a mechanism by which the amount of routing state propagated via BGP can be reduced by reducing the scope of route flap propagation.

Several goals and assumptions are made with regard to route flap damping. One primary goal is that fast convergence must remain possible for normal route changes. The assumption is made that history predicts future behavior. That is, if a route is behaving badly consistently over some period of time it's likely to continue behaving badly. Likewise, if a route flaps considerably for a short amount of time and then stabilizes, it should no long be damped or suppressed but should be readvertised.

The general operation of route flap damping is depicted in Figure 6.8. Basically, route flap damping operates as follows:

- A fixed *penalty* is assessed for each flap. A flap can be either a route withdraw or update with an attribute change.
- If the penalty exceeds the *suppress-limit,* the route is not advertised (its advertisement is suppressed).

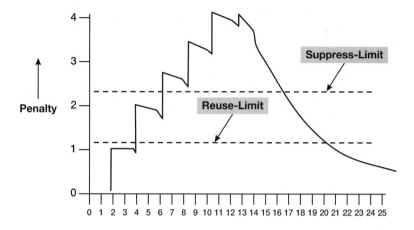

Figure 6.8
Route flap dampening.

- The penalty is exponentially decayed based on the *half-life* value.
- Once the penalty is decayed below the *reuse-limit,* the route is advertised.

Route flap damping is only applied to paths learned via external BGP. If a single route is dampened, other routes to that same destination may be used to forward traffic to the destination. Route flap dampening requires BGP speakers to maintain a history of the advertisement and withdraw of each BGP path implementations provide the capability to tune the suppress-limit, reuse-limit, and half-life values in order to control how long a misbehaving prefix is suppressed.

Cisco IOS software provides the capability to selectively damping routes at variable intervals based on characteristics such as community, prefix, prefix length, or AS Path. To enable route flap damping in Cisco IOS software, the **bgp damping** BGP configuration command is specified. You may also specify parameter values as follows:

```
bgp dampening <halflife-time> <reuse> <suppress> <maximum-suppress-time>
```

Cisco default BGP route flap damping parameters are as shown in Table 6.13.

Table 6.13

Description	Default Value
Penalty	1000 (penalty incurred for each flap)
Half-life	15 minutes (penalty is reduced by half at the end of each interval)
Suppress-Value	2000 (route advertisement is suppressed when penalty reaches this value)
Reuse	750 (route re-advertised)
Max-Suppress	60 minutes (4x suppress)

Alternatively, you can supply a route map argument via **bgp dampening route-map** *map-name* and specify custom flap damping parameters selective. Many service providers perform selective route flap damping on critical networks such as root Internet domain name service prefixes. Likewise, they often apply more harsh penalties for prefixes that are traditionally more unstable. For example, they may suppress a /24 prefix as a result of two flaps while they suppress /8 prefixes after four flaps occur. The following example will demonstrate how you might go about configuring selective route flap damping policies.

```
router bgp 65100
bgp dampening route-map selective-damping
!
ip prefix-list s-damping permit 0.0.0.0/24 le 32
!
route-map selective-damping permit 10
match ip address prefix-list s-damping
set dampening 30 125 2000 120
!
route-map selective-damping permit 20
set dampening 25 750 2000 45
!
```

As you can see, we defined a prefix list that matches all routes from /24 to /32. We then set the half-life to 30 minutes, the reuse-value to 125, the suppress-value to 2000, and the maximum suppress time to 120 minutes. For all other routes we set the half-life to 25 minutes, the reuse to 750, the suppress-value to 2000 and the maximum suppress time to 45 minutes. As a result, routes that are /24 or longer are suppressed much more quickly and remain suppressed for longer period of time than shorter prefixes.

The CLI command **show ip bgp dampened-paths** can be used to view the history of any routes that have flapped and are currently penalized or suppressed. Likewise, **clear ip bgp dampening [prefix]** can be used to clear the flap statistics associated a particular prefix or all prefixes that currently have penalties incurred.

Outbound Route Filtering

Outbound Route Filtering (ORF), described in IETF Internet-Drafts draft-ietf-idr-route-filter, draft-chen-bgp-prefix-orf, and draft-ietf-idr-as-path-orf, allows a BGP speaker to tell its peers what routes it will not accept based on local policy rules; this allows the speaker to not send those routes it knows will be discarded anyway, thereby saving resources on both sides on the connection. Figure 6.9 illustrates.

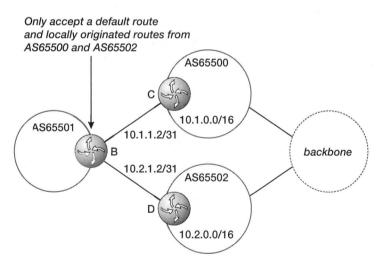

Figure 6.9
Outbound route filtering.

AS65501's network administrators are trying to receive enough
routes to optimally route along their two upstream providers but don't
want to accept full routes from both of them. This set of filters would
work:

```
!
hostname router-b
....
!
ip as-path access-list 10 permit ^65500$
!
ip as-path access-list 20 permit ^65502$
....
!
router bgp 65501
 neighbor 10.1.1.2 remote-as 65500
 neighbor 10.1.1.2 filter-list 10 in
 neighbor 10.2.1.2 remote-as 65502
 neighbor 10.2.1.2 filter-list 20 in
 ....
```

Each path router B receives will be filtered based on the autonomous system in the AS Path. If the AS Path contains more than just
the AS 65500 and the route is received from router C, the route will be
ignored. In the same way, any route learned from router D with more
than just the autonomous system 65502 in the AS Path will be ignored.
It would be more efficient, however, for routers C and D to not advertise these routes rather than advertising them just so router D can discard them.

This is precisely what outbound route filtering provides for: a set
of instructions that router B can send to routers C and D to indicate
what routes it is going to discard anyway, so routers C and D can filter
their advertisements before sending them to B. Equating the peering
autonomous systems with their address blocks, the equivalent configuration using ORF is as follows:

```
!
hostname router-b
....
!
access-list 10 permit 10.1.0.0 0.0.255.255
access-list 20 permit 10.2.0.0 0.0.255.255
```

```
....
!
router bgp 65501
 neighbor 10.1.1.2 remote-as 65501
 neighbor 10.1.1.2 capability orf prefix-list both
 neighbor 10.1.1.2 distribute-list 10 in
 neighbor 10.2.1.2 remote-as 65502
 neighbor 10.2.1.2 capability orf prefix-list both
 neighbor 10.2.1.2 distribute-list 20 in
 ....

!
hostname router-c
....
!
router bgp 65501
 neighbor 10.1.1.1 remote-as 65500
 neighbor 10.1.1.1 capability orf prefix-list both
 ....

!
hostname router-d
....
!
router bgp 65502
 neighbor 10.2.1.1 remote-as 65500
 neighbor 10.2.1.1 capability orf prefix-list both
 ....
```

Support for BGP ORF varies widely across Cisco IOS software versions and other BGP implementations. Likewise, many network operators prefer not to employ ORF because of the local requirements it places on their BGP routers. However, like other features, its support base continues to grow.

BGP MED Deployment Considerations

The BGP MED attribute provides a mechanism for BGP speakers to convey to an adjacent AS the optimal entry point into the local AS. While BGP MEDs function correctly in many scenarios, there are a number of issues that may arise when utilizing MEDs in dynamic or complex topologies. This section discusses implementation and deployment considerations

regarding BGP MEDs and provides information with which imple-
menters and network operators should be familiar.

The BGP MUTLI_EXIT_DISC (Multi-Exit Discriminator, or
MED) attribute, formerly known as the INTER_AS_METRIC, is currently defined in Section 5.1.4 of RFC 1771, as follows:

> MULTI_EXIT_DISC is an optional non-transitive attribute which is in-
> tended to be used on external (inter-AS) links to discriminate among
> multiple exit or entry points to the same neighboring AS. The
> MULTI_EXIT_DISC attribute is a four octet unsigned number which is
> called a metric. All other factors being equal, the exit point with lower
> metric SHOULD be preferred. If received over EBGP, the
> MULTI_EXIT_DISC attribute MAY be propagated over IBGP to other
> BGP speakers within the same AS. An MED attribute received from a
> neighboring AS MUST NOT be propagated to other neighboring au-
> tonomous systems.
>
> A BGP speaker MUST IMPLEMENT a mechanism based on
> local configuration which allows the MULTI_EXIT_DISC attribute to
> be removed from a route. This MAY be done prior to determining the
> degree of preference of the route and performing route selection (deci-
> sion process phases 1 and 2).
>
> An implementation MAY also (based on local configuration) alter
> the value of the MULTI_EXIT_DISC attribute received over EBGP.
> This MAY be done prior to determining the degree of preference of the
> route and performing route selection (decision process phases 1 and 2).

Section 9.1.2.2 (c) of RFC 1771 defines the following route selection criteria regarding MEDs:

> Remove from consideration routes with less-preferred MULTI_
> EXIT_DISC attributes. MULTI_EXIT_DISC is only comparable be-
> tween routes learned from the same neighboring AS (the neighboring AS
> is determined from the AS_PATH attribute). Routes which do not have
> the MULTI_EXIT_DISC attribute are considered to have the lowest
> possible MULTI_EXIT_DISC value.
>
> This is also described in the following procedure:

```
for m = all routes still under consideration
 for n = all routes still under consideration
  if (neighborAS(m) == neighborAS(n)) and (MED(n) < MED(m))
   remove route m from consideration
```

In the pseudo-code above, MED(n) is a function which returns the
value of route n's MULTI_EXIT_DISC attribute. If route n has no

MULTI_EXIT_DISC attribute, the function returns the lowest possible MULTI_EXIT_DISC value, i.e. 0.

If a MULTI_EXIT_DISC attribute is removed before re-advertising a route into IBGP, then comparison based on the received EBGP MULTI_EXIT_DISC attribute MAY still be performed. If an implementation chooses to remove MULTI_EXIT_DISC, then the optional comparison on MULTI_EXIT_DISC if performed at all MUST be performed only among EBGP learned routes. The best EBGP learned route may then be compared with IBGP learned routes after the removal of the MULTI_EXIT_DISC attribute. If MULTI_EXIT_DISC is removed from a subset of EBGP learned routes and the selected "best" EBGP learned route will not have MULTI_EXIT_DISC removed, then the MULTI_EXIT_DISC must be used in the comparison with IBGP learned routes. For IBGP learned routes the MULTI_EXIT_DISC MUST be used in route comparisons which reach this step in the decision process. Including the MULTI_EXIT_DISC of an EBGP learned route in the comparison with an IBGP learned route, then removing the MULTI_EXIT_DISC attribute and advertising the route has been proven to cause route loops.

Routes that have different MULTI_EXIT_DISC attribute SHALL NOT be aggregated.

With this in consideration, let's discuss some of the operational aspects with regard to BGP MEDs.

MEDs and Potatoes

In a situation where traffic flows between a pair of hosts, each connected to different transit networks, which are themselves interconnected at two or more locations, each transit network has a choice:

- Send traffic to the closest point in the local AS that peers with the adjacent transit network, or find the closest exit point from the local AS. This is called *hot potato routing*.
- Pass traffic to the interconnection location advertising the least cost path to the destination host. This is called *best exit routing*.

Hot Potato Routing

Hot potato (or *closest exit*) *routing* is called this because like a hot potato held in bare hands, and whoever has the packet tries to get rid of it quickly. Hot potato routing is accomplished by not passing the EGBP

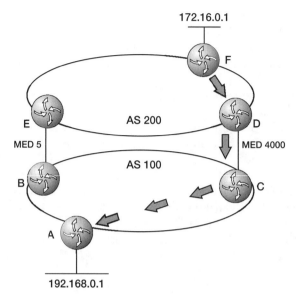

Figure 6.10
Hot potato (closest exit) routing.

learned MED into IBGP or by not accepting the EBGP learned MED at all, as is illustrated in Figure 6.10.

Rather than router F sending traffic to route E before it passes the traffic to AS 100, it forwards the traffic to router D because it consider router D more optimal based on some BGP or IGP metric. This minimizes transit traffic for the provider routing the traffic.

Cold Potato Routing

Far less common is *cold potato* (or *best exit*) *routing*, where the transit provider uses its own transit backbone capacity to get the traffic to the point that adjacent transit provider advertised as being closest to the destination. Cold potato routing is accomplished by passing the EBGP learned MED into IBGP. Figure 6.11 illustrates best exit routing.

Which Potato—Hot or Cold?

If one transit provider uses hot potato routing and another uses best exit, traffic between the two tends to be more symmetric. Depending on the business relationships, if one provider has more capacity or a significantly less congested backbone network, then that provider may

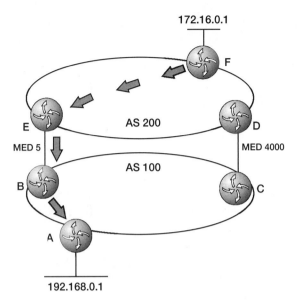

Figure 6.11
Cold potato (best exit) routing.

use best exit routing. An example of widespread use of best exit routing was the NSF-funded NSFNET backbone and NSF-funded regional networks in the mid-1990s.

In some cases a provider may use hot potato routing for some destinations for a given peer AS and best exit routing for others. An example of this is the different treatment of commercial and research traffic in the NSFNET in the mid-1990s. Today many commercial networks exchange MEDs with customers but not bilateral peers. However, commercial use of MEDs varies widely, from ubiquitous use of MEDs to no use of MEDs at all. Some service providers actually include "accept MEDs from all BGP peers" as collateral when selling Internet connectivity services. This probably isn't such a good idea, as we'll discuss in just a bit.

In addition, many deployments of MEDs today are likely behaving differently (e.g., resulting is sub-optimal routing) than the network operator intended, thereby resulting not in hot or cold potatoes, but, more likely, something akin to mashed potatoes! More information on unintended behavior resulting from MEDs is provided throughout this section.

Implementation and Protocol Considerations

There are a number of implementation and protocol peculiarities relating to MEDs that have been discovered that may affect network behavior. The following sections provide information on these issues.

MED Is an Optional Nontransitive Attribute

BGP MED is a nontransitive optional attribute whose advertisement to both IBGP and EBGP peers is discretionary. As a result, some implementations enable sending of MEDs to IBGP peers by default, while others do not send MEDs to IBGP peers as a default behavior. This behavior may result in suboptimal route selection within an AS. In addition, some implementations send MEDs to EBGP peers by default, while others do not. This behavior may also result in suboptimal interdomain route selection.

MED Values and Preferences

Some implementations consider an MED value of zero as less preferable than no MED value. This behavior will result in path selection inconsistencies within an AS. The current draft version of the BGP specification [BGP4] removes ambiguities that existed in RFC 1771 by stating that if route n has no MULTI_EXIT_DISC attribute, the lowest possible MED value (i.e. 0) should be assigned to the attribute. However, most deployed versions are not implemented to comply with this specification, a specification that has admittedly been all over the map with regard to how to handle missing MED values. For example, earlier versions of the specification called for a missing MED to be assigned the highest possible MED value (i.e., $2^{32}-1$).

In addition, some implementations have been shown to internally employ a maximum possible MED value ($2^{32}-1$) as an "infinity" metric (i.e., the MED value is used to tag routes as unfeasible) and would, upon on receiving an update with an MED value of $2^{32}-1$, rewrite the value to $2^{32}-2$. Subsequently, the new MED value would be propagated and could yet again result in routing inconsistencies or unintended path selections.

As a result of implementation inconsistencies and protocol revision variances, many attuned network operators today explicitly reset all MED values on ingress to conform to their internal routing policies (i.e., to include policy that requires that MED values of 0 and $2^{\wedge}32\text{-}1$ *not* be used in configurations, whether the MEDs are directly computed or configured) so as to not have to rely on all their routers having the same missing-MED behavior!

Comparing MEDs between Different Autonomous Systems

MED was intended for use on external (inter-AS) links to discriminate among multiple exit or entry points to the same neighboring AS. However, a large number of MED applications now employ MEDs for the purpose of determining route preference between like routes received from different autonomous systems.

A large number of implementations provide the capability to enable comparison of MEDs between routes received from different neighboring autonomous systems. For example, Cisco IOS software provides this capability via the **bgp always-compare-med** BGP configuration command. While this capability has demonstrated some benefit (e.g., that described in RFC 3345), operators should be wary of the potential side effects with enabling such a function.

Though this may seem a fine idea for some configurations, care must be taken when comparing MEDs between different autonomous systems. BGP speakers often derive MED values by obtaining the IGP metric associated with reaching a given BGP NEXT_HOP within the local AS. This allows MEDs to reasonably reflect IGP topologies when advertising routes to peers. While this is fine when comparing MEDs between multiple paths learned from a single AS, it can result in potentially "weighted" decisions when comparing MEDs between different autonomous systems. This is most typically the case when the autonomous systems use different mechanisms to derive IGP metrics, BGP MEDs, or perhaps even use different IGP protocols with vastly contrasting metric spaces (e.g., OSPF vs. traditional very small metric space in IS-IS).

MEDs, Route Reflection and AS Confederations for BGP

In particular configurations, the BGP scaling mechanisms defined in *BGP Route Reflection—An Alternative to Full Mesh IBGP* [RFC 2796] and

Autonomous System Confederations for BGP [RFC 3065] will introduce persistent BGP route oscillation [RFC 3345]. The problem is inherent in the way BGP works: A conflict exists between information hiding/hierarchy and the nonhierarchical selection process imposed by lack of total ordering caused by the MED rules. Given current practices, we see the problem most frequently manifest itself in the context of MED + route reflectors or confederations (see Chapter 8, Troubleshooting BGP).

One potential way to avoid this is by configuring inter-Member-AS or intercluster IGP metrics higher than intra-Member-AS IGP metrics and/or using other tie breaking policies to avoid BGP route selection based on incomparable MEDs. Of course, IGP metric constraints may be unreasonably onerous for some applications. Comparing MEDs between differing adjacent autonomous systems (which will be discussed in later sections), or not utilizing MEDs at all, significantly decreases the probability of introducing potential route oscillation conditions into the network.

Although perhaps "legal" as far as current specifications are concerned, modifying MED attributes received on any type of IBGP session (e.g., standard IBGP, AS confederations EIBGP, route reflection, etc.) is *not* recommended.

Route Flap Damping and MED Churn

MEDs are often derived dynamically from IGP metrics or additive costs associated with an IGP metric to a given BGP NEXT_HOP. This typically provides an efficient model for ensuring that the BGP MED advertised to peers used to represent the best path to a given destination within the network is aligned with that of the IGP within a given AS.

The consequence with dynamically derived IGP-based MEDs is that instability within an AS, or even on a single given link within the AS, can result in widespread BGP instability or BGP route advertisement churn that propagates across multiple domains. In short, if your MED "flaps" every time your IGP metric flaps, your routes are likely going to be suppressed as a result of BGP Route Flap Damping.

Deployment of MEDs may compound the adverse effects of BGP flap dampening behavior because it may cause routes to be readvertised solely to reflect an internal topology change.

Many implementations don't have a practical problem with IGP flapping, they either latch their IGP metric upon first advertisement or they employ some internal suppression mechanism. Some implementations regard BGP attribute changes as less significant than route withdrawals and announcements to attempt to mitigate the impact of this type of event. In addition, some vendors don't penalize MED changes at all.

Effects of MEDs on Update Packing Efficiency

As previously discussed, multiple unfeasible routes can be advertised in a single BGP Update message. In addition, one or more feasible routes can be advertised in a single Update message so long as all prefixes share a common attribute set.

The BGP4 protocol permits advertisement of multiple prefixes with a common set of path attributes to be advertised in a single update message, this is commonly referred to as "update packing." Update packing requires that all feasible routes within a single update message share a common attribute set, to include a common MULTI_EXIT_DISC value. As such, potential wide-scale variance in MED values introduces yet another variable and may result in a marked decrease in update packing efficiency.

Temporal Route Selection

Some implementations have had implementation defects (bugs) leading to temporal behavior in MED-based best path selection. These usually involve methods used to store the oldest route along with ordering routes for MED in earlier implementations that cause nondeterministic behavior on whether the oldest route would truly be selected or not. The reasoning for this is that "older" paths are presumably more stable, and thus more preferable. However, temporal behavior in route selection results in nondeterministic behavior, and, as such, is often undesirable.

Cisco IOS software provides the **bgp deterministic-med** BGP configuration command to disable temporal behavior from the BGP route selection process.

Effects of Aggregation on MEDs

Another MED deployment consideration involves the impact that aggregation of BGP routing information has on MEDs. Aggregates are often generated from multiple locations in an AS in order to accommodate stability, redundancy, and other network design goals. When MEDs are derived from IGP metrics associated with said aggregates, the MED value advertised to peers can result in very suboptimal routing. Figure 6.12 illustrates this.

In Figure 6.12 the aggregate route of 10.1.0.0/16 is originated by router F in AS 200. AS 200 advertises MEDs to AS 100 and derives their value from the IGP metric associated with reaching the BGP NEXT_HOP for a given route. As a result, router D advertises 10.1.0.0/16 to AS 100 with an MED value of 3 while router E advertises the route to AS 100 with an MED value of 2. AS 100 honors MEDs and as a result prefers the path via routers B and E, respectively. Now, a host on the 192.168.0.0/24 subnet connected to router A wishes to send information to a host on the 10.1.1.0/24 subnet connected to router G. Rather than taking router A-C-D-G path to reach the destination, the A-B-E-F-D-G path is used. If no MEDs were used in the topology, router A may have just as likely took the shorter path to reach router G.

As you can see, MEDs may result in very suboptimal route selection.

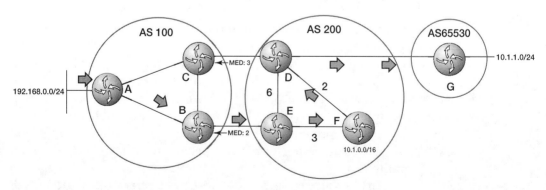

Figure 6.12
MEDs may break with aggregation.

MED Security Considerations

The MED was purposely designed to be a "weak" metric that would only be used late in the best-path decision process. The BGP working group within the IETF was concerned that any metric specified by a remote operator would only affect routing in a local AS if no other preference was specified. A paramount goal of the design of the MED was to ensure that peers could not "shed" or "absorb" traffic for networks that they advertise. As such, accepting MEDs from peers may in some sense increase a network's susceptibility to exploitation by peers.

Review Questions

1. What routes would you differentiate between using Local Preference?

2. What is the MED value often derived from when a route is advertised to another autonomous system?

3. What application of Communities is described in RFC 1998?

4. What mechanism is should be used to determine commonly accepted prefix lengths when peering to routers connected to the Internet?

5. What problems can filtering based on the address allocation tables provided by the Internet Registries cause?

6. Which RFC describes private address space that cannot be routed to or advertised on the Internet?

7. Beyond private address space, what other address spaces should be filtered at the edge of an autonomous system?

8. How does outbound route filtering reduce the number of prefixes advertised between two peers?

9. What's the difference between closest-exit and best-exit routing?

New Features in BGP

BGP is *not* a static protocol; new features are added almost yearly to the protocol to expand its capabilities in the face of a constantly changing world of internetworking. It may seem crazy to add new features to a protocol known for its overwhelming feature set, but each new feature is designed to meet a specific need or address a specific requirement in a large-scale environment. This chapter guides you through a number of these new capabilities and how they can be used in various network situations.

> This chapter provides information on a number of new features proposed for the BGP protocol; they may not all come into common use over time, nor may they all be implemented by the router vendors.

BGP Custom Decision Process

While the BGP best path algorithm described in Chapter 1 can be very complex, it doesn't address every possible route choice a network designer might want. One example is illustrated in Figure 7.1.

Autonomous system 65500's system administrator has a simple plan he'd like to implement for traffic being forwarded out of his network:

- Route through the shortest path, in terms of AS Path, to reach the destination.
- If both paths are equal length, route out the closest exit point.

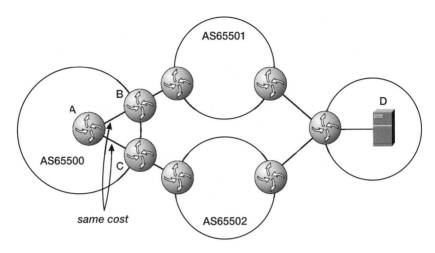

Figure 7.1
Custom metrics.

• If both exit points are equally distant, use the cheaper path (administratively defined, based on the cost of using the service provider).

Examining BGP's best path algorithm, we find the first two policies can be met using standard BGP attributes:

• Prefer highest Weight.
• Prefer highest Local Preference.
• Prefer locally originated routes.
• Prefer the route with the shortest AS Path; this meets the network administrator's first policy.
• Prefer routes originated within BGP over routes originated outside BGP.
• Prefer the lowest Multiple Exit Discriminator (also known as the MED, or the Metric).
• Prefer routes learned from external peers over routes learned from internal peers.
• Prefer the route with lowest interior gateway protocol (IGP) cost to the BGP next hop; this meets the network administrator's second policy.
• Prefer the older path, or prefer the path received from the router with the lower Router ID.

The challenge is to implement the third criteria, forwarding the traffic through the cheaper service provider. This cannot be implemented using the Local Preference, because setting the Local Preference based on the cost to use the service provider would negate the checks for the AS Path length and the cost to reach the exit point. The only real option within the normal BGP best path algorithm is to attempt to influence the Router ID the routes are learned through—a difficult task, at best.

The BGP Custom Decision Process, described in draft-retana-bgp-custom-decision, allows the insertion of custom decision points anyplace within the BGP best path algorithm, using a set of nontransitive communities (not transmitted outside the autonomous system). In this draft, a set of extended communities is set aside, called *cost communities* and used to insert custom metrics at any point in the BGP best path algorithm.

Each cost community consists of three parts:

- A one octet point of insertion, which describes where in the BGP best path algorithm the metric, or cost, carried in this community should be inserted in the best path algorithm.
  - A value of 128 in this field indicates the cost community should be considered before any other attribute of the route, including the Local Preference.
  - A value of 129 in this field indicates the cost community should be considered after the interior gateway protocol metric to the BGP next hop is considered.
  - A value of 130 in this field indicates the cost community should be considered after the selection is done between routes learned from internal and external peers.
  - A value of 131 in this field indicates the cost community should be considered after the Router ID's of the advertising router are compared.
- A one octet community ID, which differentiates between different cost communities of the same type.
- A four octet cost, which contains the metric assigned to this route.

With cost communities factored into the BGP best path algorithm, it becomes more flexible:

- Prefer highest Weight.
- If a cost community with a point of insertion of 128 is attached to these routes, prefer the route with the highest cost.

- Prefer highest Local Preference.
- Prefer locally originated routes.
- Prefer the route with the shortest AS Path; this meets the network administrator's first policy.
- Prefer routes originated within BGP over routes originated outside BGP.
- Prefer the lowest Multiple Exit Discriminator.
- Prefer routes learned from external peers over routes learned from internal peers.
- If a cost community with a point of insertion of 130 is attached to these routes, prefer the route with the highest cost.
- Prefer the route with lowest interior gateway protocol cost to the BGP next hop; this meets the network administrator's second policy.
- If a cost community with a point of insertion of 129 is attached to these routes, prefer the route with the highest cost.
- Prefer the path received from the router with the lower Router ID (or the older path).
- If a cost community with a point of insertion of 131 is attached to these routes, prefer the route with the highest cost.

Returning to the requirements within the preceding example, the challenge is in directing traffic to the cheapest service provider to route traffic through. The network administrator would like the traffic to choose the shortest AS Path and the closest exit point. In order to meet this set of requirements, the network administrator could attach a cost community with a point of insertion of 129 to the routes at the border, giving the route learned through the cheaper service provider a higher cost, so the cheaper route would be preferred if all other metrics are equal (except the router ID).

Controlling Redistribution at Remote Points

Redistribution Communities

In some rare situations, a network administrator may desire to control which autonomous systems a peer autonomous system may advertise certain routes to, or control the AS Path length (through AS Path prepending) at a remote autonomous system border. Figure 7.2 illustrates such a situation.

Assume AS65503's network administrator knows how AS65500, 65501, 65502, 65503, and 65504, are connected and has the following requirements:

- Traffic from AS65500 should prefer the route through AS65502 but should pass through AS65501 if the link to AS65502 fails.
- Traffic from the Internet should prefer the path through AS65502 and use AS65504 if the link to AS65502 fails.
- Traffic should never be routed from the Internet through AS65501.

This appears to be a simple set of requirements at first glance, but actually implementing them presents some problems. We are dealing with inbound traffic, so there's no way to use route preferences within

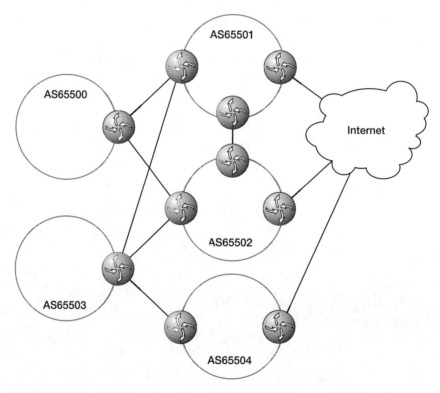

Figure 7.2
Controlling remote route distribution through communities.

the autonomous system to control this traffic flow; we must somehow mark the routes as they are advertised so AS65501, AS65502, and AS65504 know how to mark their advertisements to their peers so the correct inbound path is always chosen.

Let's begin with the first requirement and examine how this could be resolved. Traffic from AS65500 should prefer the route through AS65502, unless the link to AS65502 fails. One possible way to control the inbound traffic flow is by setting the MED when advertising these routes to AS65501 and AS65502. But this won't work for two reasons:

- AS65502 and AS65501 will strip the MED advertised by AS65503 when advertising these routes to AS65500, so AS65503's preferred entry point will not be passed along.
- Even if both of the routes advertised into AS65500 contained AS65503's MED, the two paths won't have the same AS Path, so the MED will be ignored.

Another option would be to use AS Path prepending to control the inbound traffic flow. Assume AS65501 prepends an extra hop onto the AS Path when advertising to AS65501. This would impact the best path algorithm in AS65500 so it would choose the path through AS65502 outbound, if all other factors are equal. Of course, if AS65501 prepends its AS Path when advertising its routes to AS65502, it will also force its inbound Internet traffic through AS65504, unless an even longer AS Path prepend is used on that peering session. This sort of cascading of policies is difficult to manage; it would be better to have some more specific way to manage them.

Controlling the redistribution of BGP routes, draft-ietf-ptomaine-bgp-redistribution-03.txt provides an alternative solution to this sort of problem; it allows a BGP speaker to attach nontransitive communities to a route that instructs the receiving autonomous system about how and where to redistribute the route to its peers. This draft describes how communities can be encoded with information describing which peers a receiving autonomous system should not readvertise this route to, and a number of times the receiving autonomous system should prepend its AS onto the AS Path of the route when readvertising it to certain peers.

In this case,

- A redistribution community can be applied to the routes advertised to AS65501 so AS65501 will prepend the AS Path when advertising them to AS65500. This would impact AS65500's route choice so it would choose to use AS65502 for outbound traffic when forwarding traffic destined to networks within AS65503.

- A redistribution community can be applied to the routes advertised to AS65501 so those routes are not readvertised to any of AS65501's peers than AS65500. This would prevent Internet traffic from using this path.
- Normal AS Path prepending can be used when advertising routes to AS65504, so this route is not preferred over the path through AS65502.

Redistribution communities provide a lot of flexibility in control over the AS Path chosen for inbound traffic, within a small radius of a highly connected internetwork, when the topology layout is well known.

No Peer

NOPEER community for BGP route scope control, draft-ietf-ptomaine-nopeer-02.txt, describes the ability to control the peers a receiving autonomous system may advertise a route to. For instance, in Figure 7.3, AS65500 wants to make certain its routes are not advertised

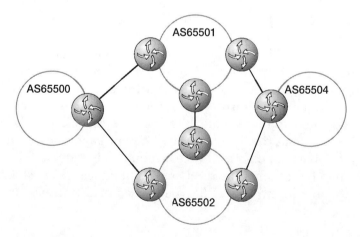

Figure 7.3
Using NOPEER to prevent traffic from following a backup path.

to AS65501 through AS65502; if the link between AS65500 and AS65501 fails, AS65500 doesn't want its traffic to be forwarded through AS65502. However, AS65500 does want its routes to be advertised to AS65504 from both AS65501 and AS65502.

AS65502 could mark the routes it's advertising to AS65502 with No Export, as well-known communities which would cause AS65502 not to advertise these routes to any of its external peers. This won't resolve our problem, however, since we do need the routes to be advertised from AS65502 to AS65504. We need some other way to mark the routes AS65500 is advertising to AS65502 so they won't leak through to AS65501.

The NOPEER draft describes a solution to this problem, a new nontransitive community with which AS65500 can mark its routes when advertising them to AS65502. This extended community encodes a list of autonomous systems the receiving AS should not advertise the route to. In this case, AS65500 could encode AS65503 as one of the peers AS65502 should not advertise its routes to when advertising them to AS65502. At the border of AS65502 and AS65003, the routes would be blocked because of this community.

Many Internet service providers offer some form of community that is similar in scope and purpose to the NOPEER community and even the res-distribution communities described in the last section. If you are interested in deploying these sorts of capabilities, consider discussing this with your ISP or other externally connected networks to determine if they are available today.

Multipath

When a pair of links, over which two eBGP sessions are configured and built, connects two autonomous systems, only one of the two paths will be used to forward traffic between the two autonomous systems. The BGP route selection algorithm will always select one path or the other as the best path, even if the paths are equal up to the point of the router ID of the advertising router. Thus, one link is the primary, and all traffic is carried on this link, and the other link is redundant, with little or no traffic carried along it.

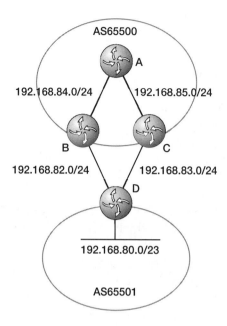

Figure 7.4
iBGP multipath.

Generally, the only way to use this second link is to direct traffic
outbound towards the Internet through it in some way, which normally
involves some method of splitting the outbound traffic using manual
configurations and monitoring the links to make certain the traffic is
fairly well divided between the two connections. Routers should be
able to receive two paths to each destination and share the load between the available paths. Some vendors have implemented a solution
to this problem, the ability to load share between two iBGP learned
paths. Figure 7.4 illustrates.

The following configurations are used on the routers in this network, which are all running Cisco IOS software.

```
!
hostname router-d
!

router bgp 65001
 bgp log-neighbor-changes
 redistribute static
 neighbor 192.168.83.3 remote-as 65000
 neighbor 192.168.82.4 remote-as 65000
```

```
!
ip route 192.168.80.0 255.255.255.0 Null0
....
!

hostname router-b
!
router ospf 100
 log-adjacency-changes
network 0.0.0.0 255.255.255.255 area 0
!
router bgp 65000
 no synchronization
 bgp log-neighbor-changes
 neighbor 192.168.83.10 remote-as 65001
 neighbor 192.168.85.5 remote-as 65000
!
hostname router-c
!
router ospf 100
 network 0.0.0.0 255.255.255.255 area 0
!
router bgp 65000
 no synchronization
 neighbor 192.168.82.10 remote-as 65001
 neighbor 193.168.84.5 remote-as 65000
!
!
hostname router-a
!
router ospf 100
 log-adjacency-changes
 network 0.0.0.0 255.255.255.255 area 0
!
router bgp 65000
 no synchronization
 bgp log-neighbor-changes
 neighbor 192.168.84.3 remote-as 65000
 neighbor 192.168.85.4 remote-as 65000
 maximum-paths ibgp  4
!
```

The command to focus on in this configuration is **maximum-paths bgp 4,** configured in the BGP router configuration mode on router A.

this command allows the BGP process to install more than one path into the local routing table, as long as all the metrics up to the interior gateway protocol cost to reach the BGP next hop are equal. The following output from router A illustrates the impact of this command.

```
router-a#show ip bgp 192.168.80.0
BGP routing table entry for 192.168.80.0/24, version 3
Paths: (2 available, best #2)
Multipath: iBGP
  Not advertised to any peer
  65001
    192.168.82.10 (metric 49) from 192.168.82.4 (192.168.82.4)
      metric 0, localpref 100, valid, internal, multipath
  65001
    192.168.83.10 (metric 49) from 192.168.83.3 (192.168.83.1)
      metric 0, localpref 100, valid, internal, multipath, best
....
```

Note the addition of the word **multipath** to the description of the route printed by BGP; this indicates that there is more than one path with the same Local Preference, MED, and AS Path length. When BGP in Cisco IOS software marks a route as a **multipath,** it also installs up to eight possible paths in the local routing table.

```
router-a#sho ip route 192.168.80.0
Routing entry for 192.168.80.0/24
  Known via "bgp 100", distance 200, metric 0
  Tag 300, type internal
  Last update from 208.0.3.10 11:08:03 ago
  Routing Descriptor Blocks:
  * 192.168.82.10, from 192.168.82.4, 11:08:03 ago
      Route metric is 0, traffic share count is 1
      AS Hops 1
    192.168.83.10, from 192.168.83.3, 11:08:03 ago
      Route metric is 0, traffic share count is 1
      AS Hops 1
```

When multiple paths are installed in the local routing table, Cisco IOS software loads shares traffic along the two available paths, placing different flows on different links by default.

Unequal Cost Multipath and the Exit Link Bandwidth

In some situations, there may be multiple exit points along links with different bandwidths, as Figure 7.5 illustrates.

Router A will receive two paths to 192.168.80.0/23, one through B and the other through C. The IGP cost to reach the next hop, router D, through C will be lower than the cost to reach D through B, so router A will choose the paths through B as the best path, installing the path through B in its routing table. It would be better, however, if router A could split the traffic along the outbound paths so both links are used rather than forwarding all the traffic along the path through router B; the Cisco IOS software BGP link bandwidth feature allows this type of load sharing.

On routers B and C, the bandwidth of the link to the next hop, router D, is carried as an extended community. When router A receives

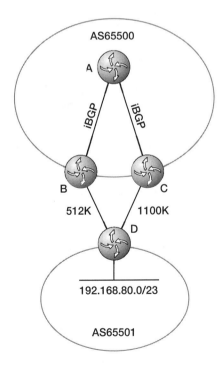

Figure 7.5
Unequal cost exit points.

these two advertisements, it will note the inclusion of these two extended communities and install both routes in the routing table, with costs that are proportional to the exit link bandwidths. The routing table will then compute a load sharing value between these two paths and allow the forwarding engine to split traffic along the two paths in proportion to the exit link bandwidths. The following configuration and show commands from Cisco IOS software illustrate the configuration and results of using BGP link bandwidth.

```
!
hostname router-d
!
....
!
interface Serial3/0
 ip address 10.1.7.4 255.255.255.0
 no ip route-cache
 no ip mroute-cache
 serial restart-delay 0
!
interface Serial3/1
 ip address 10.1.8.4 255.255.255.0
 no ip route-cache
 no ip mroute-cache
 serial restart-delay 0
!
....
!
router bgp 65501
 no synchronization
 bgp log-neighbor-changes
 network 10.1.3.0
 neighbor 10.1.7.10 remote-as 65500
 neighbor 10.1.8.11 remote-as 65500
 no auto-summary
!

!
hostname router-b
!
....
!
```

```
interface Serial0/0
 bandwidth 1100
 ip address 10.1.7.10 255.255.255.0
 delay 2000
!
....
!
router bgp 65500
 no synchronization
 bgp log-neighbor-changes
 neighbor 10.1.0.12 remote-as 65500
 neighbor 10.1.0.12 send-community both
 neighbor 10.1.7.4 remote-as 65501
 neighbor 10.1.7.4 dmzlink-bw
 no auto-summary
!

!
hostname router-c
!
....
!
interface Serial0/0
 bandwidth 500
 ip address 10.1.8.11 255.255.255.0
 delay 100
!
....
!
router bgp 65500
 no synchronization
 bgp log-neighbor-changes
 neighbor 10.1.0.12 remote-as 65500
 neighbor 10.1.0.12 send-community both
 neighbor 10.1.8.4 remote-as 65501
 neighbor 10.1.8.4 dmzlink-bw
 no auto-summary
!

!
hostname router-a
!
....
```

```
 !
 router bgp 65500
  no synchronization
  bgp log-neighbor-changes
  bgp bestpath dmzlink-bw
  bgp dmzlink-bw
  neighbor 10.1.0.10 remote-as 65500
  neighbor 10.1.0.11 remote-as 65500
  maximum-paths ibgp   4
  no auto-summary
 !
 ....
```

Once these configurations are in place, we can see that router A is treating these two paths as multipaths and recognizes the DMZ link bandwidth carried in the communities of each route.

```
router-a#sho ip bgp 10.1.3.0
BGP routing table entry for 10.1.3.0/24, version 7
Paths: (2 available, best #2, table Default-IP-Routing-Table)
Multipath: iBGP
  Not advertised to any peer
  65501
    10.1.7.4 from 10.1.0.10 (10.1.16.10)
      Origin IGP, metric 0, localpref 100, valid, internal, multipath
      Extended Community: 0x0:0:0
      DMZ-Link Bw 137 kbytes
  65501
    10.1.8.4 from 10.1.0.11 (10.1.13.11)
      Origin IGP, metric 0, localpref 100, valid, internal, multipath
  Extended Community: 0x0:0:0
  DMZ-Link Bw 62 kbytes
 ....
```

Since the BGP process on Cisco IOS software has marked both paths as **multipath,** it will now install them in the local routing table. But what will the routing table do with those link bandwidths?

```
router-a#sho ip route 10.1.3.0
Routing entry for 10.1.3.0/24
  Known via "bgp 65500", distance 200, metric 0
  Tag 65501, type internal
  Last update from 10.1.8.4 00:07:13 ago
```

```
Routing Descriptor Blocks:
* 10.1.7.4, from 10.1.0.10, 00:07:13 ago
    Route metric is 0, traffic share count is 2
    AS Hops 1
  10.1.8.4, from 10.1.0.11, 00:07:13 ago
    Route metric is 0, traffic share count is 1
    AS Hops 1
```

The routing table uses the DMZ link bandwidth to compute a *traffic share count,* which is then used to load share traffic over the two possible paths. The traffic share count is computed by walking all the available paths and finding the highest metric (highest cost) path among those installed in the routing table. The metric of the highest metric path is taken, and the metric of each path is then divided by the highest metric. The result is a traffic share count, which expresses the ratio of traffic that should be placed on the link.

In this case, one path has a traffic share count of 1, while the other path has a traffic share count of 2. For every 2 traffic flows placed along the lower cost path, 1 traffic flow will be placed on the higher cost path.

BGP Graceful Restart

A large number of the larger-scale routers used in networks, such as the Cisco 12000 and Cisco 10000, separates the control plane from the data plane; in other words, the control plane is not involved in the processes required to switch packets from one connected segment to another. Figure 7.6 illustrates this concept.

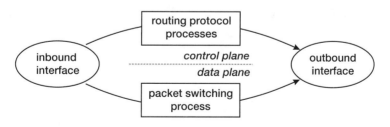

Figure 7.6
Separation of forwarding and control information.

If the control plane could restart without impacting the data used by the data plane, it should be possible to install new software, replace certain pieces of hardware, and perform other such tasks without causing the network to lose routing through the router. Beyond the local control plane and data plane in the router, however, we need to consider how the peers of this router will react if the local control plane, and the routing protocol processes along with it, are restarted. Figure 7.7 illustrates a small network we can use to explore the problems associated with a router restart.

In this network, router C would learn two paths for every reachable destination within or through AS65500, with router A chosen as the best path for each route. If the control plane on router A restarts, router C will continue forwarding traffic through router A until the BGP peering session fails, due to lost keepalives, for instance, between the two routers. At this point, router C would recalculate the best path for each route in its local tables, redirecting traffic to router B.

Under normal circumstances, this is what we would want; in fact, if router A fails, we would want router C to detect this failure as quickly as possible, and switch all of its traffic to router B as soon as it can. But if router A is still capable of forwarding traffic, because its data plane is capable of retaining the information required to continue forwarding traffic (through *NonStop Forwarding*, or NSF), then the extra network disturbance of detecting the failure and recalculating paths is undesirable. In some way, then, router A must keep router C from switching its best paths to router B. The most apparent way to accomplish this would

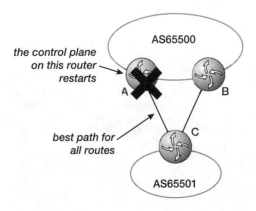

Figure 7.7
A multiple router network with graceful restart.

be for router A to continue sending keepalives to C while it is rebooting, or immediately on finishing its reload, so C will continue to forward traffic through router A. BGP protocol updates being transported over TCP include sequence numbers that are not easily (or impossible to be) maintained between system restarts.

There are two ways this problem can be addressed:

- By maintaining routing protocol state in some secondary memory within router A and referring to this state information while router A's control plane is restarting.
- By introducing some signaling within the routing protocol, which allows router A's routing process to recover the necessary state once it has restarted, including "I'll be back" signaling," which indicates a router is simply restarting and not being removed from the network.

Various network equipment vendors have pursued both of these options; there are positive and negative aspects to each one. For instance, maintaining state may reduce convergence time while the backup state information is being written, and if the state is the cause of the control plane to fail, the restarted process could be operating from the same invalid information, causing another failure. On the other hand, introducing signaling within the routing protocol requires the routers peering with the protected router to be upgraded as well as the protected router. We'll discuss the BGP extensions allowing peers to restart and resynchronize their information without disturbing routing in the remainder of the network.

draft-ietf-idr-restart, Graceful Restart Mechanism for BGP, defines the extensions to BGP discussed here.

There are two changes to the BGP protocol that are used to support graceful restart between two peers:

- A new capability that is used to indicate if a BGP speaker supports graceful restart, or can support a peer that is restarting, along with other information about the restart process.

- An End Of RIB marker, which indicates that a BGP speaker has finished sending all its local routing information. This is implemented as a simple empty withdraw packet.

The new Graceful Restart capability includes the following:

- The *Restart State* bit, indicating if this BGP speaker is currently restarting or not
- The *Restart Timer,* an indication of how long the speaker's peer should maintain state before declaring the graceful restart a failure, and resetting the BGP session
- A series of address family identifiers (AFIs) and subsequence address family identifiers (SAFIs), one for each address family the peers are exchanging routing information for
- For each address family, a Forwarding State bit indicating if forwarding state has been preserved for this address family

Figure 7.8 illustrates the process used by a pair of BGP speakers when one of them restarts.

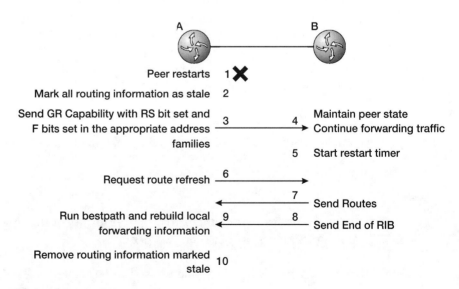

Figure 7.8
BGP graceful restart process.

1. Router A's control plane restarts; the forwarding tables used by the data plane are preserved.

2. When router A's control plane restarts, it marks any preserved routing or forwarding information as stale.

3. Router A sends the graceful restart capability along with the BGP Open message. It sets the restart bit in the graceful restart capability and includes a TLV for each address family it has preserved forwarding state for, with the forwarding bit set on each one.

4. When router B receives this BGP Open, it will examine its current open connections and realize that this Open is from a BGP speaker it is already peered to. Router B will maintain all the information it has received from router A, also maintaining forwarding state it built based on the received routing information.

5. Router B now starts its restart timer; if this timer expires before the peering relationship between routers A and B is fully formed, router B will reset the session.

6. Router A now sends a route refresh request to router B.

7. Router B begins sending the contents of its BGP table to A.

8. When router B has finished sending the contents of its BGP table to A, it transmits an End of RIB marker, to let router A know it has received a full compliment of information.

9. Router A, when it receives the End of RIB marker from B, runs BGP's best path algorithm across the information it has received and installs the required routing information into the local routing tables, which should also update the local forwarding tables.

10. Router A now removes any routing information that has not been refreshed by the route refresh.

Graceful Restart Deployment Considerations

When deploying graceful restart for any routing protocol, there are two issues you need to keep in mind: the impact of partial deployments, and the interactions between BGP and the underlying IGP if both are not capable of and configured for graceful restart. Figure 7.9 illustrates the issues that can occur in partial deployments of graceful restart.

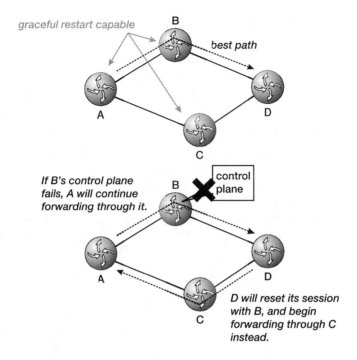

Figure 7.9
Partial graceful restart deployment.

In this network, we assume router D is not graceful restart capable, or it is not configured to respond to peers gracefully restarting. When B's control plane restarts, it signals router A so A doesn't reset its peering session and continues forwarding through router B. However, router D doesn't recognize this signaling, and it resets its session with B. Instead, it reconverges on the path through router C as the best path and drops traffic along the path until the reconvergence is complete. In this case, then, the path between B and D will become asymmetric; in other cases, it's possible to form a routing loop. It's also possible that router D will begin rejecting the traffic forwarded by router B because its unicast reverse path forwarding check will fail.

The solution to this problem is to make certain D is graceful restart capable, even if it's not configured to restart gracefully on failure (or isn't capable of it). Router D must be able to understand and respond correctly to router B's signals during a graceful restart to prevent network problems form developing.

If BGP is not capable of (or isn't configured for) graceful restart, but the underlying interior gateway protocol is, some amount of traffic can be dropped while BGP is reconverging after a control plane restart. Figure 7.10 illustrates.

Assume router A has chosen the routes learned through B as its best paths. When router B restarts, A will rest its BGP peering session with B, but it will continue learning the same information through C–in fact, C will be setting the next hop on the BGP routes it is learning to the same next hop as B did before it reset. Router A will not, however, reset its OSPF adjacency with B. Since OSPF is configured for graceful restart, it will believe that all paths reachable before the restart are still reachable through B, including the next hop for the routes it is learning through router C.

So router A will continue forwarding packets through router B, because router B is still the best path to the destinations learned through router C, based on the interior gateway protocol cost to the next hop,

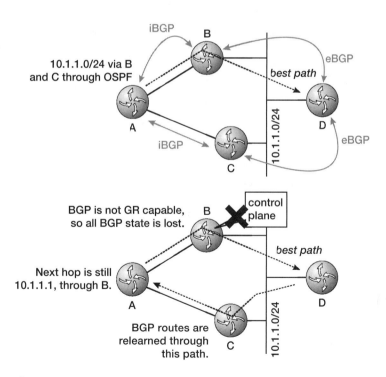

Figure 7.10
BGP interaction with interior gateway protocols during a graceful restart.

which is D. However, router B, when it receives these packets, may not have the forwarding information needed to forward them. Since the BGP process on router B has reset, it's likely that all the BGP learned routing information in the forwarding tables has been discarded, even though the OSPF learned forwarding information has been retained.

Router B, then, will drop all the BGP traffic forwarded along this path by router A. To resolve this problem, always make certain BGP and the underlying interior gateway protocols are both capable of and configured for graceful restart.

Interaction with Interior Gateway Protocols during Convergence

One perplexing problem with large-scale BGP deployments, particularly when BGP speakers are connected over multiple-hop networks within the autonomous system, is how to handle convergence time differentials between the interior gateway protocols. Figure 7.11 illustrates.

To understand how a differential in the convergence time between an interior gateway protocol and BGP can cause traffic to be dropped, let's work through a network event and the convergence that occurs afterward. Let's begin with router B not connected to the network at all,

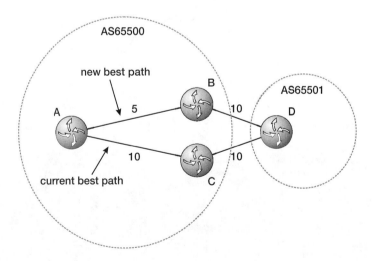

Figure 7.11
BGP Interaction with interior gateway protocols during convergence.

so the only path for router A to the networks reachable in and behind AS5501 is through router C.

When router B is first connected to the network (or powered on), the interior gateway protocol will advertise reachability to D through B rather quickly, probably on the order of seconds. However, it may take some time for the BGP process on router B to synchronize with D and learn all the paths available through AS65501. During this interval, router A will choose the path through B to reach D, because path through B has a lower interior gateway protocol metric.

As traffic is forwarded to router B from A, however, it will be dropped, since router B's BGP process has not learned all the paths D is advertising and has not installed them in its forwarding tables. The time period where router B will drop all the traffic destined to AS65501 will be the time difference between the interior gateway protocol convergence and BGP's convergence.

It would be nice to speed up BGP's convergence times to match those of the interior gateway protocols, but this probably isn't going to happen any time soon, since BGP is dealing with a much larger number of routes, and much more complicated decision algorithms, than the interior gateway protocols do. Further, if any improvement in convergence time is managed in BGP, there's no reason the same techniques couldn't be applied to the interior gateway protocols, making them faster still.

The other option, besides trying to speed up BGP's convergence times, is to slow down the interior gateway protocol's convergence. In this case, we would want router A to wait until BGP is converged on router B before using the new path to router D learned about through router B. There are, in fact, mechanisms for allowing OSPF and IS-IS to slow down convergence by advertising router B as not being available to transit traffic until BGP has converged.

OSPF "Stub Router" Advertisement

The OSPF process on router B, on starting, can advertise all connected stub interfaces (type 3 links, on which there are no other OSPF routers) with their interface cost, as normal and advertise all nonstub links, which have OSPF neighbors on them, as infinity (unreachable). This would make router B itself appear reachable, but no destinations attached to router B are reachable. When BGP converges on router B, it can signal the OSPF process, and OSPF can then readvertise its LSAs with the correct metrics, making it possible for router A to router through router B to reach D.

The Cisco IOS software command to configure the advertisement of an OSPF router as a stub until BGP has converged is **max-metric router-lsa on-startup wait-for-bgp.**

> RFC3137, OSPF Stub Router Advertisement, describes the use of OSPF stub router advertisements.

IS-IS Overload Bit

IS-IS defines an *overload bit,* which may be used whenever a router has been overloaded (for instance, when it runs out of memory or cannot forward traffic for some reason). If a router receives an LSP with the overload bit set, it will treat the originating router as a stub, which means the router itself is reachable, but no destinations behind the router may be reachable. While BGP is converging, an IS-IS process on router B could advertise its LSP with the overload bit set, which would prevent router A from routing through router B while allowing the BGP session to continue forming normally.

The Cisco IOS software command to set the overload bit in the router's LSP until BGP has converged is **set-overload-bit on-startup wait-for-bgp.** Another usage of the IS-IS overload bit is to enable it when one is performing disruptive maintenance on a router. Adding the command set-overload-bit can do this.

Inbound Route Summarization

One of the various problems facing the Internet today, as the world's largest internetwork, is the shear size of the Internet routing tables. It's not uncommon to find routers learning 180,000 or more reachable destinations, peering with multiple peers, and handling over 1 million possible paths for those destinations. This puts a considerable strain on the backbone routers of most Internet service providers, causing slower convergence times and various sorts of memory utilization problems. To make matters worse, the routing table in the Internet grows at a regular rate, as shown at *http://bgp.potaroo.net/,* for instance.

Why does the Internet table grow at this rate, and what can be done to slow it down? Various people have researched the reasons for the Internet table growth and have come to the conclusion that much of the Internet's table sizes are related to the number of dual-homed autonomous systems and the way in which prefixes are advertised by those dual-homed autonomous systems. Figure 7.12 illustrates one example of what how a dual-homed autonomous system impacts the Internet's routing table.

Before being dual homed, router A is advertising 10.1.1.0/24 to AS65500. Since AS65500 has been allocated the 10.0.0.0/8 address space, it aggregates this space at its border with AS65502, including router A's advertisement of 10.1.1.0/24. When router A is dual homed to both AS65500 and AS65501, AS 65501 begins receiving advertisements (or beings originating advertisements) for the 10.1.1.0/24 prefix. AS 65502 now receives an advertisement for 10.0.0.0/8 from AS65500,

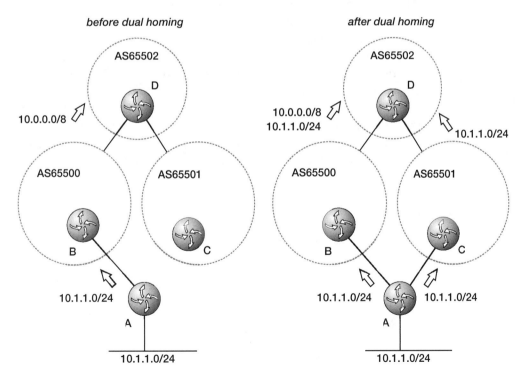

Figure 7.12
How dual homing impacts the Internet's backbone routing tables.

and an advertisement for 10.1.1.0/24 from AS65501, causing router A's traffic to be sent exclusively along the path through AS65501.

To correct this problem, the router A's administrator calls the network administrator in AS65500 and has them leak the 10.1.1.0/24 prefix through their aggregation. Now AS65502 receives two prefixes, 10.0.0.0/8 and 10.1.1.0/24, from two different peers. This increases the number of paths received and the overall size of the routing table. How can this issue be resolved?

One possible way of resolving this from router A's perspective is to advertise the 10.1.1.0/24 prefix conditionally, either only advertising the prefix when the path through AS65500 has failed or advertising it with a community that prevents it from being propagated onto AS65502; both of these concepts are explained in Chapter 2, BGP at the Edge. Considering Figure 7.13, however, we can see that beyond AS65502, the second advertisement of the 10.1.1.0/24 prefix no longer influences the path chosen by BGP.

Here we have simply taken the dual homed diagram from before, and extended one more autonomous system hop, to include AS65503. AS65500 is still advertising both 10.0.0.0/8 and 10.1.1.0/24; AS 65501 is still advertising 10.1.1.0/24. AS65502 still receives both of these sets of advertisements but chooses one of the two 10.1.1.0/24 routes as its best paths, and advertises only this single best path to AS65503.

AS65503 still receives two paths, the less specific /8 and the more specific /24, but the next hop is the same on both paths, so the /24 is imply redundant (and unnecessary) information. It's possible to bound the scope of the longer prefix, 10.1.1.0/24, by examining the routing

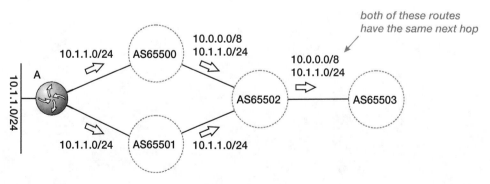

Figure 7.13
Overlapping prefixes beyond the second autonomous system hop.

tables in the edge routers, marking overlapping longer prefixes, and then dropping them. Let's examine Figure 7.14 to see how this would work.

In this network, router B is receiving both 10.0.0.0/8 and 10.1.1.0/24 from router A; router D is receiving 10.1.1.0/24. Router B, on detecting the two overlapping prefixes, can set the metrics on the longer prefix so it will win the best path decision through the rest of the network, and mark it so it's not advertised outside the domain. The easiest markings to use for this (although there are other markings possible) are the Local Preference on each route and the NO_EXPORT community.

- On receiving the overlapping prefixes, router B sets the Local Preference on the longer prefix to a high number based on its router ID. The reason the router ID is chosen for this is to account for the possibility of two routers at the edge detecting the overlap, to reduce the amount of information carried within the routing domain. It's possible to mark all overlapping longer prefixes with the same local preference, if the network administrator wants to carry more than one prefix in the autonomous system.
- Router B also marks the longer prefix routes with the NO_ EXPORT community.

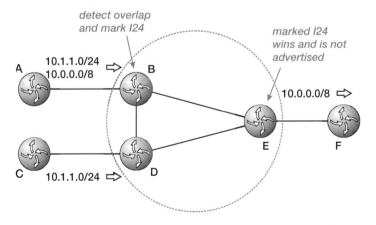

Figure 7.14
Bounding the longer prefix by detecting the overlap and marking it.

- Router D, on receiving the 10.1.1.0/24 route from router B, will prefer the path through B, blocking the advertisement of the 10.1.1.0/24 learned through router C into the rest of the autonomous system.
- Router E will prefer the 10.1.1.0/24 learned from router B, which is also marked with the NO_EXPORT community. This route will not be advertised to router F, since it is marked as NO_EXPORT.

draft-hardie-bounded-longest-match, Bounding Longest Match Considered, describes this approach to bounding the range of longer prefixes advertised for managing traffic flow.

Conditional Communities

In some cases, it's useful to be able to advertise a route with a community under some conditions and without that community otherwise. Figure 7.15 illustrates.

In this small internetwork, AS65000 would like to advertise its routes so it can reach the destinations in AS65002 through router C, but the system administrators would not like their routes advertised to AS65003 through AS65002 unless their link to AS65001 fails. This is a classic primary/backup scenario, where the primary link should be

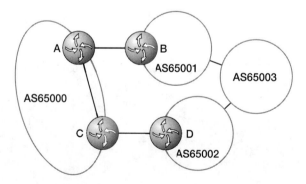

Figure 7.15
Conditional communities.

used for most traffic and the backup link used for those destinations within the autonomous system the backup link connects to. Allowing the system administrators in AS65000 to configure their routers in this way would reduce the routing table size at AS65003, unless the primary link fails.

Conditional communities would allow just such a configuration. Router C could be configured so the routes advertised to D would be marked with the No Export community as long as the link between routers A and B is operational. When AS65002 receives routes marked with the No Export community, it would not readvertise them to AS65003. However, when the link between routers A and B fails, C would remove this marking, and AS65002 would begin advertising these routes to AS65003, restoring connectivity.

Flexible Communities

Flexible BGP Communities, draft-lange-flexible-bgp-communities, describes a new type of community for BGP. Flexible communities build on extended communities, providing more options for marking BGP routes with policy information, and providing space for encoding IPv6 addresses within the community space.

Flexible communities introduce the concept of a *neighbor class,* which allows a network administrator to build policy based on the type of peering connection shared with an outside autonomous system. This is useful for both enterprise and service provider networks, as Figure 7.16 illustrates.

Service providers often connect to several different customers (and may even divide their customers by the types of routes they are receiving, the number of entry points the customer has, the types of services the customer is receiving, etc.), various public peering points, private transit peering relationships, and private nontransit peering relationships. Enterprise customers may have several connections to service providers and partners, plus other connections. Flexible communities, by allowing a network administrator to attach policies to routes to be acted on based on the class of a peering relationship, allows these relationships to be treated in a common manner throughout the entire network. Figure 7.17 illustrates the format of a flexible community.

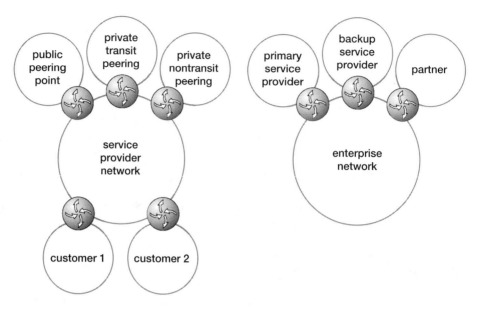

Figure 7.16
Classes of peering relationships for service providers and enterprise networks.

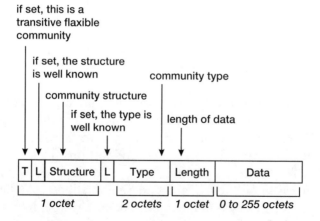

Figure 7.17
Flexible community formatting.

- The transitive bit denotes whether this community should be stripped at the border of the autonomous system or passed as an attribute of the route to other autonomous systems; if it is set to 0, the community is transitive; if it is set to 1, the community is no transitive. This field is set to 1 on any route received through an eBGP peering session, so flexible communities may only be passed to a connected autonomous system. If a flexible community is marked as transitive, the first four octets of the data field must contain the AS number of the autonomous system that attached the community to the route.
- The Structure L bit denotes whether the structure of the data field is well known; if this bit is set, the structure of the data field has been determined through the IETF process or some other process through which well-known flexible community structures may be defined.
- The community structure describes the structure of the data within the data field. For instance, the structure may note the data field is composed of IPv6 addresses, IPv4 addresses, or autonomous system/prefix pairs.
- The Type L bit denotes whether the type is well known; if this is set, the flexible community type is described in an IETF draft. If this is clear, the network administrator of this autonomous system has locally assigned the type code.
- The type describes the type of flexible community; for instance, a particular community may indicate that this prefix should not be exported to the entities listed in the data field.
- The length field describes the length of the data field in octets.

The structure and type fields act together to describe the correct action to take on a given route. For instance, the structure field may indicate the data field contains a list of neighbor classes, and the type field may indicate the action to take is to not export this prefix to the entities listed in the data field. The receiving BGP speaker would then interpret this to mean that this prefix should not be exported to the neighbor classes described in the data field.

One particular data field structure is defined with the flexible communities draft, the neighbor class. The high-order bit of the neighbor class is taken as a local/well-known indicator; if this bit is set, then the ncighbor class is well known. If it's clear, then the neighbor class has been locally defined within this autonomous system. Several neighbor classes are defined within the flexible communities draft:

- All neighbors
- A specific peer, which is normally applied to a nontransit peering relationship
- Customer peer
- Upstream peer
- Confederation peer

A number of well-known data field structure types are also defined in the flexible communities draft:

- Opaque
- A list of 2 octet autonomous system numbers
- A list of 4 octet autonomous system numbers
- A list of IP4 addresses
- A list of IPv6 addresses
- A list of neighbor classes

Outbound Route Filtering

Outbound route filtering (ORF) is a simple capability allowing a BGP speaker to advertise a set of filters to its peers. Why would you configure a BGP speaker to advertise filters? To save bandwidth between the speakers, and to save processing resources. For instance, if a BGP speaker is only going to accept 10,000 of 100,000 routes a speaker is sending, each of those prefixes still needs to be formatted, transmitted, received, and discarded. It makes more sense for the receiver simply to transmit its filters, so the sender filters the routes before they are formatted and sent. This is exactly what ORF does.

ORF is currently only defined for transmitting prefix and AS Path filters (not for filtering based on communities, although this may be included at some future time). Prefix-based ORF is available in Cisco IOS software versions 12.2(4)T, 12.2(14)S , 12.0(22)S, and above.

Review Questions

1. What capability does the cost community add to BGP?
2. What capability does the redistribution community add to BGP?
3. Where is the redistribution community most useful for implementing policy?
4. What capability does the No Peer community add to BGP?
5. What capability does iBGP multipath load sharing add to BGP?
6. What capability does the DMZ Link Bandwidth community add to BGP?
7. In what situations can BGP graceful restart be used to minimize the impact of a control plane restart on the network?
8. What new signaling methods are added to BGP to support graceful restart?
9. What two important issues do we need to consider when deploying BGP graceful restart?
10. Why would we want an interior gateway protocol to wait on BGP to converge before allowing its peers to route through the local router?
11. What problem within the Internet does inbound route summarization solve?

8

Troubleshooting BGP

BGP, as we saw in Chapter 1, The Border Gateway Protocol, is a complicated protocol, and troubleshooting BGP problems can be complicated, as well. In this chapter, we'll discuss some of the problems you might see when running BGP and how you can troubleshoot them, including establishing neighbors, missing routes, inconsistent routing, routing loops, and other issues.

Establishing Neighbors

Before you can actually exchange any routing information in BGP, you have to establish peering relationships with other BGP speakers. Lack of IP connectivity and neighbor setting mismatches are common reasons for a BGP peering session to fail.

No IP Connectivity

Perhaps the most common, and easiest to troubleshoot, problems involved in a failure to bring up a BGP session are simple lack of IP connectivity and mismatched endpoints. We'll use Figure 8.1 as an example.

We'll take the simplest case first, two routers not building a peering session. The first step is to examine the output of **show ip bgp summary** three or four times over a two- or three-minute interval.

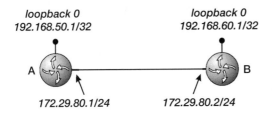

loopback 0
192.168.50.1/32

loopback 0
192.168.60.1/32

A   B

172.29.80.1/24   *172.29.80.2/24*

Figure 8.1
IP connectivity between BGP peers.

```
router-a#show ip bgp summary
....
Neighbor     V  AS MsgRcvd MsgSent TblVer InQ OutQ Up/Down State/PfxRcd
192.168.60.1 4  2       0       0      0   0    0 never            Idle
```

If router B's state remains *idle,* or it bounces between *idle* and *connected,* or *active* and *connected,* you should begin by verifying IP connectivity between the peers. We can examine the configuration on router A to determine what address on router B it is peering with.

```
!
hostname router-a
!
router bgp 65400
 neighbor 192.168.60.1 remote-as 65500
 neighbor 192.168.60.1 update-source 192.168.50.1
 neighbor 192.168.60.1 ebgp multihop 4
 ....
!
```

The IP address on router B we need to be able to reach is 192.168.60.1. There are two ways to determine if router A has connectivity to this address, by examining the routing table, or simply pinging it.

```
router-a#show ip route
....
Gateway of last resort is not set

192.168.60.1/32 is subnetted, one subnet
S       192.168.60.1/32 [1/0] via 172.29.80.2
```

```
172.29.80.2/24 is subnetted, one subnet
C       172.29.80.0/24 via Serial 0/0
....


router-a#ping 192.168.60.1

Type escape sequence to abort.
Sending 5, 100-byte ICMP Echos to 192.168.60.1, timeout is 2 seconds:
!!!!!
Success rate is 100 percent (5/5), round-trip min/avg/max = 1/1/1 ms
```

It appears that router A can reach 192.168.60.1, but we still don't know if router B can reach the IP address it's peering to on router A. But didn't we just ping router B from A? Yes, but routers typically source ping packets from the outbound interface listed in the routing table. So when we ping 192.168.60.1, router A automatically sources the ping from Serial 0/0.

When router B receives this ping, the source address is 172.29.80.1 rather than the actual source of the BGP session on router A, which is 192.168.50.1. Router B should certainly know how to reach 172.29.80.1, since it's directly connected to that subnet. How can test whether or not router B knows how to reach 192.168.50.1, without just logging in to router B and pinging from there? Most implementations of ping allow you to source the ping packet from a specific interface; we can source the ping from the loopback interface on router A.

```
router-a#ping
Protocol [ip]:
Target IP address: 192.168.60.1
Repeat count [5]:
Datagram size [100]:
Timeout in seconds [2]:
Extended commands [n]: y
Source address or interface: 192.168.50.1
Type of service [0]:
Set DF bit in IP header? [no]:
Validate reply data? [no]:
Data pattern [0xABCD]:
Loose, Strict, Record, Timestamp, Verbose[none]:
Sweep range of sizes [n]:
Type escape sequence to abort.
```

```
Sending 5, 100-byte ICMP Echos to 192.168.60.1, timeout is 2 seconds:
.....
Success rate is 0 percent (0/5)
```

If the ping sourced from the actual peering address fails, but the ping from the outbound interface succeeds, then the other BGP speaker, in this case router B, doesn't have a route to the BGP peering address.

eBGP Multihop

If IP connectivity exists between two eBGP peers, but they still won't form a peering session, the next step to check is their multihop status. BGP normally assumes eBGP peers will be directly connected, with no devices between them (the two peers will be one hop apart on the same subnet). Figure 8.2 illustrates, with configurations following.

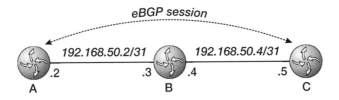

Figure 8.2
Multiple hops between eBGP peers.

```
!
hostname router-a
....
!
router bgp 65500
 neighbor 192.168.50.5 remote-as 65501
 ....
!
ip route 192.168.50.4 255.255.255.254 192.168.50.3
....

!
hostname router-b
....
!
router bgp 65501
```

```
    neighbor 192.168.50.2 remote-as 65500
    ....
    !
    ip route 192.168.50.2 255.255.255.254 192.168.50.4
    ....
```

By pinging router C from router A, we can see these two routers can reach one another through router B.

```
router-a#ping 192.168.50.5

Type escape sequence to abort.
Sending 5, 100-byte ICMP Echos to 192.168.50.5, timeout is 2 seconds:
!!!!!
Success rate is 100 percent (5/5), round-trip min/avg/max = 1/1/1 ms
```

Looking at the output of show ip bgp neighbors, however, we can see what the problem is.

```
router-a#show ip bgp neighbors
BGP neighbor is 192.168.50.5, remote AS 65501, external
link
    ....
  Number of unicast/multicast prefixes received 0/0
  External BGP neighbor not directly connected.
  No active TCP connection
```

Because the source address of BGP packets on this peer and the destination address listed in the neighbor statement are not in the same subnet, BGP marks this neighbor as unreachable. To resolve this, and to get these peers to build a session, configure them as *eBGP multihop peers*.

```
router-a#config terminal
router-a(config)#router bgp 65500
router-a(config-rtr)#neighbor 192.168.50.5 ebgp-multihop 3

router-b#config terminal
router-b(config)#router bgp 65501
router-b(config-rtr)#neighbor 192.168.50.2 ebgp-multihop 3
```

Mismatched Session Endpoints

This is a common problem when peering between the loopback interfaces on two routers, as Figure 8.3 illustrates.

```
!
hostname router-a
....
interface loopback 0
 ip address 192.168.50.1 255.255.255.255
 ....
!
ip route 192.168.60.1 255.255.255.255 172.29.80.2
....
router bgp 65500
 neighbor 192.168.60.1 remote-as 65501
 neighbor 192.168.60.1 ebgp-multihop 3
 ....


!
hostname router-b
....
!
interface loopback 0
 ip address 192.168.60.1 255.255.255.255
 ....
!
ip route 192.168.50.1 255.255.255.255 172.29.80.1
....
router bgp 65501
 neighbor 192.168.50.1 remote-as 65500
 neighbor 192.168.50.1 ebgp-multihop 3
 ....
```

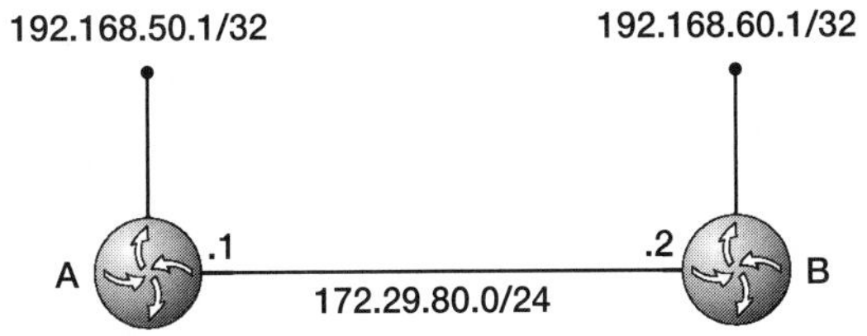

Figure 8.3
Peering between loopbacks.

Although these two routers are configured as eBGP multihop peers, and both routers can reach the other router's loopback interface, they still will not peer. Using debug ip tcp transactions, we see the following output.

```
router-b#debug ip tcp transactions
11:19:48: BGP: 172.29.80.1 open active, delay 9916ms
11:19:53: TCP: sending RST, seq 0, ack 3098129121
11:19:53: TCP: sent RST to 172.29.80.1:9719 from
172.29.172.29.80.2:179
```

Note that the address the reset (RST) was sent to on the last line of the debug output; this should be the address configured as a neighbor on router B, but it is, instead, router A's physical port address. This implies that router A is sourcing the session from the physical port rather than from the loopback address. The easy solution to this sort of a problem is to be certain the sessions are sourced and destined to the correct addresses on each router.

In this case, router A could be configured with the BGP router command update-source to make certain that the TCP session is sourced from the loopback interface rather than the physical port address.

```
router-a#config terminal
router-a(config)#router bgp 65500
router-a(config-rtr)#neighbor 192.168.60.1 update-source
loopback 0

router-b#config terminal
router-b(config)#router bgp 65501
router-b(config-rtr)#neighbor 192.168.50.1 update-source
loopback 0
```

It's possible for a pair of BGP speakers to form a multihop session as long as they are configured for the correct peering addresses, but only one of them is configured with the correct update source. This can cause problems with forwarding through the network, however; it's always best to configure both routers with the correct update source.

Open Parameters Mismatch

There are four pieces of information contained in the Open parameters used to set up a BGP session:

- Version
- Autonomous system
- Hold time
- Router identifier

A number of these can cause a session to fail if the parameters are mismatched. The following output of **debug ip bgp** from a router running Cisco IOS software provides an example of an autonomous system mismatch.

```
00:01:37: BGP: 192.168.60.1 open active, local address 192.168.50.1
00:01:37: BGP: 192.168.60.1 went from Active to OpenSent
00:01:37: BGP: 192.168.60.1 sending OPEN, version 4
00:01:37: BGP: 192.168.60.1 received NOTIFICATION 2/2
 (peer in wrong AS) 2 bytes FE4C
00:01:37: BGP: 192.168.60.1 remote close, state CLOSEWAIT
00:01:37: BGP: service reset requests
00:01:37: BGP: 192.168.60.1 went from OpenSent to Idle
00:01:37: BGP: 192.168.60.1 closing
```

The preceding notification message notes that this router has received a notification message because of an incorrect open parameter. Decoding the 2 bytes in this line (just converting from hexadecimal to decimal) yields the number 65100, which is the autonomous system of the local router. For more information about BGP notification codes, see the BGP Notifications section in Chapter 1.

Flapping Peers

If two BGP speakers are building a session and then dropping it constantly, there are several possible problems, generally all relating to lower-layer issues, that could be occurring. It's always best to have access to both BGP speakers in this situation, if possible, since debug output from both ends can be important in figuring out what is going on. Common problems include the following:

- Maximum Transmission Unit (MTU) problems along the link between the peers, especially in the case of multihop peers, either eBGP or iBGP.
- Rate limiting of BGP packets between the two peers, which can be a problem if quality of service is applied to a network in such a way to cause BGP packets to be frequently dropped in the network.
- Denial of service attack can be overloading router CPU or network congestion preventing the TCP session from staying established. This can be dangerous on upstream connections, as it will cause BGP flaps and dampening for your address space.
- Traffic shaping, and other quality of service systems applied to the network.

Two of the most useful commands in Cisco IOS software for tracking down and resolving these sorts of problems are **bgp log-neighbor-changes** and **show ip bgp summary.**

bgp log-neighbor-changes causes the reason for any neighbor reset to be logged to the console, where it can be captured in a console log or to a syslog server. These log messages can be very important in figuring out why a BGP peering session is flapping or failing on a regular basis. It is recommended to always configure bgp log-neighbor-changes as it becomes easier to determine why the sessions flapped historically rather than continue to suffer possibly service-affecting outages while debugging the problem. A typical log output is shown as follows.

```
%BGP-5-ADJCHANGE: neighbor 10.1.1.1 Down
   BGP Notification sent
%BGP-3-NOTIFICATION: sent to neighbor 10.1.1.1
   4/0 (hold time expired) 0 bytes
```

You can also view these log messages using the **show ip bgp neighbor** command, as long as **bgp log-neighbor-changes** is enabled.

```
router#show ip bgp neighbor 10.1.1.1 | include Last reset
 Last reset 00:01:02, due to BGP Notification
   sent, hold time expired
```

In Cisco IOS implementation of BGP, keepalive and update packets are both placed in a single per peer output queue; if keepalives are successfully transmitted between peers, but updates are not, the peers will constantly flap, forming an adjacency, then failing, and then forming another adjacency. Examining the output of **show ip bgp summary** for a specific neighbor can provide clues about the problems occurring between the peers.

```
router#show ip bgp summary | begin Neighbor
Neighbor V AS     MsgRcvd MsgSent TblVer InQ OutQ Up/Down  State/PfxRcd
10.1.1.1 4 65500      128      95  10167   0   15 00:03:04            0

router#show ip bgp summary | begin Neighbor
Neighbor V AS     MsgRcvd MsgSent TblVer InQ OutQ Up/Down  State/PfxRcd
10.1.1.1 4 65500      128      95  10167   0   16 00:03:04            0

router#show ip bgp summary | begin Neighbor
Neighbor V AS     MsgRcvd MsgSent TblVer InQ OutQ Up/Down  State/PfxRcd
10.1.1.1 4 65500      128      95  10167   0   17 00:03:04            0
```

From these sequential outputs on the same router, you can see the OutQ is increasing while the MsgSent column is not–even though packets are still being enqueued toward this peer, they are not being transmitted. If the packets are being enqueued at about the same rate as keepalives are sent, it appears that the keepalives are getting stuck behind updates in the output queue, so there is a problem with transmitting updates between the peers. If you suspect the problem may be related to large packets not being transmitted through the connection between the BGP peers, you can test this theory by using pings of various sizes.

Update Exchange

Once the BGP session is established, the peers exchange the contents of their BGP tables and use this information to build the tables needed to forward traffic through the connection. The following sections describe how to troubleshoot problems with incomplete reachability information being transmitted between peers and the information exchange process taking longer than it should.

Missing Prefixes

In most cases, problems with prefixes not received or not installed in the routing table can be traced to one of a few problems, such as synchronization, misconfigured or misapplied filtering, and next hop reachability. Each of these issues is covered in a section below.

Synchronization

Synchronization between BGP and the interior gateway protocol was originally designed to prevent forwarding packets into the interior of the network that will either loop or cannot be forwarded. Figure 8.4 illustrates.

192.168.48.0/24 is advertised through eBGP from E to D, through iBGP from D to B, then through eBGP from B to A. From router A, we try to ping some address on the 192.169.48.0/24 network, and find it is unreachable, although there is a valid entry in A's routing table, pointing to router B as the next hop. Examining the routing table on B, we find a valid entry as well, with the next hop pointing to router E; there is also an entry for router E in router B's routing table. Why can't we ping 192.168.48.0/24 from router A?

Tracing the path to 192.168.48.0/24 from router A, we find that routers B and C reply to the trace, but router D does not. Since we know router D has a valid routing table entry for the destination, there must be some problem at router C that is causing traffic to fail to reach 192.168.48.0/24 when sourced from router A.

Examining the routing table at router C, we see the problem immediately; since router C isn't running iBGP, it doesn't have a route to 192.168.48.0/24. This is the type of problem synchronization was

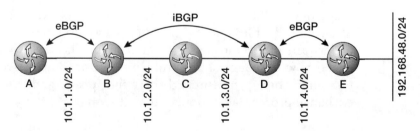

Figure 8.4
Synchronization in iBGP.

designed to solve, a router in the middle with an incomplete routing table stopping traffic from passing through an autonomous system.

Somehow, router D has to learn this route, so it can forward traffic between the two iBGP peers, routers B and D. There are two ways of allowing router C to learn these routes: by running iBGP on router C, or by redistributing the eBGP learned routes into the local interior gateway protocol at routers B and D so router C learns all possible destinations.

Synchronization assumes you will be redistributing the eBGP routes learned at the edges of the autonomous system into the interior gateway protocol. Thus any routes not learned through both iBGP and the interior gateway protocol at router B will not be advertised to router A, and the routing black hole at router C would not impact the network.

Current network design best practice, however, dictates that redistributing eBGP learned routes into an interior gateway protocol is not a good idea–interior gateway protocols are simply not designed to manage the number of routes learned through an eBGP connection–so router C should be made part of the iBGP mesh, and synchronization should be disabled.

Misconfigured or Misapplied Filtering

There are a lot of ways in which to filter routes in BGP, and therefore a lot of ways to mess up your filters so you're either not receiving all the routes you should receive, or you're receiving too many routes. We will cover some tools you can use to troubleshoot your filters in this section.

When trying to build a regular expression that will match a given set of autonomous system paths or communities, one fairly common technique is to build a small text file with the AS Paths you'd like to filter and then try various regular expressions using a command line utility like grep. Once you've fine tuned the regular expression using grep, you can then build an AS Path access list, or a community list, that mirrors the regular expression used in testing.

```
% more temp.txt
65500 65500 65501 65502
65320 65458 65512
% grep "^65320 [1-9]* [1-9]*" temp.txt
65320 65458 65512
% grep "^65500 .*" temp.txt
65500 65500 65501 65502
```

Note that the usefulness of this sort of testing is severely limited by inconsistencies in the various regular expression engines; for instance, in the preceding example, the space must be used to match a space, while Cisco IOS software matches an underbar (_) with a space, as well. However, most routers also have at least one way to test regular expressions on the router itself. For instance, in Cisco IOS software, under **show ip bgp,** we find a number of options to narrow the output based on a regular expression or a filter.

```
router#sho ip bgp ?
  A.B.C.D             IP prefix <network>/<length>, e.g., 35.0.0.0/8
  A.B.C.D             Network in the BGP routing table to display
  cidr-only           Display only routes with non-natural netmasks
  community           Display routes matching the communities
  community-list      Display routes matching the community-list
  dampening           Display detailed information about dampening
  filter-list         Display routes conforming to the filter-list
  inconsistent-as     Display only routes with inconsistent origin ASs
  neighbors           Detailed information on TCP and BGP neighbor
                      connections
  paths               Path information
  peer-group          Display information on peer-groups
  quote-regexp        Display routes matching the AS path "regular
                      expression"
  regexp              Display routes matching the AS path regular
                      expression
  summary             Summary of BGP neighbor status
  |                   Output modifiers
  <cr>
```

While these options are useful for finding specific entries in the BGP table, they are also useful for testing regular expressions and filters before putting them in place. For instance, if we wanted to see what impact filtering on the regular expression ^65501$ would have in the local BGP table, we could use **show ip bgp** with this regular expression as a modifier and see what routes match.

```
router#show ip bgp regexp ^65501$
BGP table version is 153800156, local router ID is 10.102.253.81
Status codes: s suppressed, d damped, h history, * valid, > best,
              i -internal
Origin codes: i - IGP, e - EGP, ? - incomplete
```

```
   Network               Next Hop                 Metric LocPrf Weight Path
*>i10.2.173.128/25     10.24.212.50                  0    100      0 65501 i
*>i10.43.66.0/25       10.24.212.50                  0    100      0 65501 i
```

Next Hop Reachability

Since BGP speakers don't change the next hop on routes learned through iBGP sessions, it's very common to see situations where routes are being learned, but the next hop, which could be several routers away, isn't reachable. Figure 8.5 illustrates.

At router C, the output of **show ip bgp 192.168.48.0** shows it is not reachable, because router C doesn't have a route to the link between A and B.

```
router-c#show ip bgp 192.168.48.0
BGP routing table entry for 192.168.48.0/24, version 3
Paths: (1 available, no best path)
Flag: 0x820
  Not advertised to any peer
  65500
    10.1.1.1 (inaccessible) from 10.1.2.1 (10.1.2.1)
      Origin IGP, metric 0, localpref 100, valid, internal
```

There are at least three different solutions to this problem. The first (and most obvious) is to include the link between routers A and B in the interior gateway protocol running between routers B and C. Router C would then learn the next hop, resolve the recursion, and install the route. Another option is to configure router B so it changes the next hop to itself.

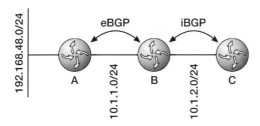

Figure 8.5
iBGP and unreachable next hops.

```
router-b#conf t
Enter configuration commands, one per line.  End with CNTL/Z.
router-b(config)#router bgp 65501
router-b(config-router)#neighbor 10.1.2.2 next-hop-self

router-c#show ip bgp 192.168.48.0
BGP routing table entry for 192.168.48.0/24, version 4
Paths: (1 available, best #1, table Default-IP-Routing-Table)
  Not advertised to any peer
  65500
    10.1.2.1 from 10.1.2.1 (10.1.2.1)
      Origin IGP, metric 0, localpref 100, valid, internal, best
```

> Another option is to advertise the network between routers A and B in iBGP to C.

```
router-b#conf t
Enter configuration commands, one per line.  End with CNTL/Z.
router-b(config)#router bgp 65501
router-b(config-router)#network 10.1.1.0

router-c#show ip bgp
BGP table version is 7, local router ID is 10.1.2.2
Status codes: s suppressed, d damped, h history, * valid, > best,
              i - internal, r RIB-failure
Origin codes: i - IGP, e - EGP, ? - incomplete
```

Network	Next Hop	Metric	LocPrf	Weight	Path
*>i192.168.48.0	10.1.1.1	0	100	0	65500 i
*>i10.1.1.0	10.1.2.1	0	100	0	i

```
2651B#show ip bgp 192.168.48.0
BGP routing table entry for 192.168.48.0/24, version 7
Paths: (1 available, best #1, table Default-IP-Routing-Table)
Flag: 0x820
  Not advertised to any peer
  65500
    10.1.1.1 from 10.1.2.1 (10.1.2.1)
    Origin IGP, metric 0, localpref 100, valid, internal, best
```

Local Origination Problems

Sometimes you don't receive routes because there are problems originating them; it's always important to make certain the BGP speaker originating the routes you're missing is actually advertising them. Most of the problems with route origination in Cisco IOS software involve a misconfiguration of the **network** or **aggregate-address** statements within the BGP process.

The **network** statement within Cisco IOS software configures the BGP process to take routes from the routing table and originate them; it acts differently if there is, or isn't, a **mask** included with the **network** statement. Table 8.1 summarizes the differences.

Table 8.1

Command	Explanation
network 10.0.0.0	Takes any entries in the routing table falling within the 10.0.0.0 through 10.255.255.255 range, regardless of the prefix length, and places them in the BGP table for advertising to peers. If no routes are advertised, check **show ip route 10.0.0.0 255.0.0.0 longer** to see if there are any components of this network.
network 10.1.1.0 mask 255.255.255.0	Looks for the 10.1.1.0/24 route in the routing table; if this route is present, places it in the BGP table for advertising to peers. If no routes are advertised, check **show ip route 10.1.1.0 255.255.255.0** to see if this route exists.
aggregate-address 10.0.0.0 255.0.0.0 summary-only	Looks for components of 10.0.0.0/8 within the local BGP table; if any are present, it aggregates the components into a single prefix and builds a local route to null0 to prevent routing loops. If no route is originated, check **sho ip bgp	include 10.** to make certain at least one component of the aggregate exists. Routes in the local routing table will not be used to build this aggregate, so a **network** statement must be included to pull routes from the routing table, in addition to the **aggregate-address** statement to create the aggregate.

Duplicate Router IDs

A BGP speaker will discard any routes originating from itself; as each route is received, the originator ID is compared to the local router ID, and if they match, the route is discarded. The following outputs from a pair of routers running Cisco IOS software illustrates.

Routers A and B are configured to exchange iBGP routing information.

```
!
hostname router-a
....
!
interface serial 3/0
 ip address 10.1.1.3 255.255.255.254
 ....
!
interface loopback 0
 ip address 192.168.1.1 255.255.255.255
 ....
!
router bgp 65500
 neighbor 10.1.1.2 remote-as 65500
 network 10.2.0.0 mask 255.255.0.0
 ....

!
hostname router-b
....
!
interface serial 2/1
 ip address 10.1.1.3 255.255.255.254
 ....
!
interface loopback 0
 ip address 192.168.1.1 255.255.255.255
 ....
!
router bgp 65500
 neighbor 10.1.1.2 remote-as 65500
```

From these configurations, everything looks fine. On router A, we see

```
router-a#show ip bgp neighbors 10.1.1.3 advertised-routes
BGP table version is 2, local router ID is 192.168.1.1
  Network          Next Hop          Metric LocPrf Weight Path
*>i10.2.0.0         0.0.0.0                 0   100      0 I
```

So router A is advertising the 10.2.0.0/16 route to router B. On router B, however, we see

```
router-b#show ip bgp 10.2.0.0

router-b#
router-b#show ip bgp neighbors 10.1.1.2 routes
Total number of prefixes 0
```

So router B is not accepting the 10.2.0.0/16 route for some reason. To find out what is happening, we can do some debugging on router B.

```
router-b(config)#access-list 101 permit ip host
  10.2.0.0 host 255.255.0.0
router-b#debug ip bgp update 101

router-a#clear ip bgp 10.1.1.2

router-b#
*10:28:48: BGP(0): 10.1.1.2 rcv UPDATE w/ attr: nexthop 10.1.1.2,
origin i, localpref 100, metric 0, originator 192.168.1.1, clusterlist
10.1.1.2, path , community , extended community
10:28:48: BGP(0): 10.1.1.2 rcv UPDATE about 10.2.0.0/16 — DENIED due
to: ORIGINATOR is us;
```

This output clearly shows the originator ID is the same as the local router ID, so router B is rejecting the update for 10.2.0.0/16. To check this, we can run show ip bgp summary on both router A and router B.

```
router-a# show ip bgp summary | include identifier.
BGP router identifier 192.168.1.1, local AS number 65500.

router-b# show ip bgp summary | include identifier.
BGP router identifier 192.168.1.1, local AS number 65500.
```

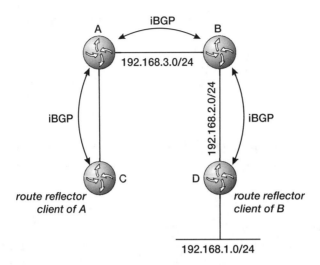

Figure 8.6
Missing routes in a partial route reflector mesh.

Duplicate Cluster IDs

A similar problem occurs with route reflectors; Figure 8.6 illustrates.

While router B has 192.168.1.0/24 in its BGP and routing tables, routers A and C do not. Since router D is a route reflector client of B, B should be advertising routes learned from D to its iBGP peers, including router A, which would then advertise the route to router C. Router B is advertising the route to A, but router A isn't receiving it, as shown in **show ip bgp neighbors.**

```
router-b#show ip bgp neighbors 192.168.3.1 advertised-routes
BGP table version is 2, local router ID is 192.168.3.1
   Network         Next Hop          Metric LocPrf Weight Path
*>i192.168.1.0    192.168.2.2            0    100      0 I

router-a#show ip bgp neighbors 192.168.3.2 routes
Total number of prefixes 0
```

Using debug ip bgp update on router A, we can determine why it isn't accepting the update.

```
router-a(config)#access-list 101 permit ip host
   192.168.1.0 host 255.0.0.0
router-a#debug ip bgp update 101
```

```
14:28:57.208: BGP(0): 192.168.3.2 rcv UPDATE w/ attr: nexthop
192.168.2.2, origin i, localpref 100, metric 0, originator 192.168.2.2,
clusterlist 0.0.0.10, path , community , extended community
14:28:57.208: BGP(0): 192.168.3.2 rcv UPDATE about 192.168.1.0/24 --
DENIED due to: reflected from the same cluster;
```

Routers A and B both have the same route reflector cluster ID, so router A is rejecting the advertisement from B. To resolve this, you should always follow the general rule that all route reflector clients must peer with each route reflector in the same route reflector cluster.

Troubleshooting Tools for Update Problems in Cisco IOS Software

We've used a number of tools in the previous section to troubleshoot various problems; Table 8.2 provides a list of these troubleshooting tools.

Table 8.2

Command	Explanation
show ip route x.x.x.x y.y.y.y longer	Useful for finding out what components of a summary are in the local routing table.
show ip bgp x.x.x.x y.y.y.y longer	Useful for finding out what components of a summary are in the local BGP table.
show ip bgp neighbor x.x.x.x advertised-routes	Displays the routes advertised to a peer; shows whether a route has been properly advertised or not.
show ip bgp neighbor x.x.x.x routes	Displays the routes learned from a specific peer; useful for determine if a route you know has been advertised is being received and accepted.
show ip bgp neighbor x.x.x.x received-routes	If soft reconfiguration is configured, shows all the routes received from a peer, including those denied by local policy or other reasons. This will also work if route-refresh(new) is available. You can check this with **show ip bgp neighbor a.b.c.d.**

(continued)

Table 8.2 *(cont.)*

Command	Explanation
debug ip bgp update	Displays information about route updates received, and why they were
	denied or dropped; should always be used with a limiting access list.
debug ip bgp x.x.x.x update	Provides the same information as **debug ip bgp update,** but only for information received from a specific peer.
show ip bgp filter-list	Shows the routes from the local BGP table matching the specified filter list.
show ip bgp regexp	Shows the routes from the local BGP table with AS Paths matching the specified regular expression.
show ip bgp community-list	Shows the routes from the local BGP table with communities matching the specified community list.
show ip bgp prefix-list	Shows the routes from the local BGP table with communities matching the specified prefix list.
show ip bgp route-map	Shows the routes from the local BGP table matching the specified route map.

Inconsistent Routing

There are two common reasons for inconsistent routing within BGP: holes in the BGP specification, and vendors modifying the best path algorithm (to reduce the rate of flapping routes in the Internet, for instance). We'll examine two of these issues here, the indeterminism of the multiple exit discriminator and a simple change to the best path algorithm that places the older route over the route learned from the peer with the highest router ID.

Multiple Exit Discriminator Indeterminism

> The MULTI_EXIT_DISC attribute may be used on external (inter-AS) links to discriminate among multiple exit or entry points to the same neighboring AS. [RFC1771].

According to RFC 1771, the multiple exist discriminator is not always compared between two paths; it is only compared when

- The local preference of the two routes is the same.
- The paths are both locally originated or both not locally originated.
- The length of the AS Path is the same.
- Both paths have the same origin code (either IGP, EGP, or unknown).
- The first (neighboring) autonomous system in the AS Path is the same; in other words, the multiple exit discriminator is only compared if both paths are received from the same neighboring autonomous system.

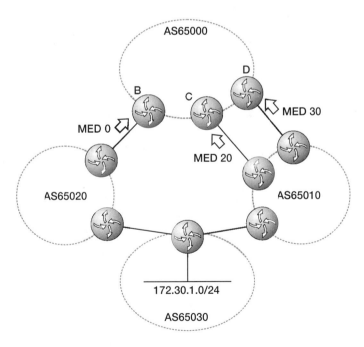

Figure 8.7
Inconsistent multiple exit discriminator.

Because the multiple exit discriminator is not always compared, the BGP table in most implementations is not ordered based on the MED; instead, BGP tables are ordered on the age of the routes as they are received. This can lead to indeterminate results when the MED comparison takes place. Figure 8.7 illustrates a network where the ordering of paths by the age of the route can impact the best path computation.

In the initial state, on router B, we see the path through AS65020 has been chosen as the best path.

```
router-b#sh ip bgp 172.30.1.0
BGP routing table entry for 172.30.1.0/24, version 40
Paths: (3 available, best #3, advertised over iBGP, eBGP)
  65010 65030
    192.168.1.1 from 192.168.1.1
      Origin IGP, metric 20, localpref 100, valid, internal
  65010 65030
    192.168.2.1 from 192.168.2.1
      Origin IGP, metric 30, localpref 100, valid, external
  65020 65030
    10.1.1.1 from 10.1.1.1
      Origin IGP, metric 0, localpref 100, valid, internal, best
```

The route learned from AS65020 is chosen as the best path because

- The first two paths in the table are compared, the routes learned through 192.168.1.1 (from router C) and 192.168.2.1 (from router D). The Local Preference is the same (100), both routes are learned from a peer (neither of them or originating on this router), the AS Paths are the same length (2 hops), and both routes have the same origin code (IGP). The neighboring autonomous system is the same, so the multiple exit discriminators are compared; when this comparison takes place, the path through 192.168.1.1 wins.
- The path learned through 192.168.1.1 (from router C) is now compared to the path learned through 10.1.1.1 (from router B). Again, the Local Preference is the same; both routes are learned from a peer, the AS Paths are the same length, and both routes have the same origin code. The neighboring autonomous system is not the same, so the multiple exit discriminator is not compared. They are both learned through iBGP, and we are assuming that they both have the same interior gateway protocol

metric, so the decision algorithm comes down to the last step. The router ID. 10.1.1.1 is lower than 192.168.1.1, so the path through 10.1.1.1 wins.

Now, the path through 10.1.1.1 is lost and relearned, so the table is reordered as follows:

```
router-b#sh ip bgp 172.30.1.0
BGP routing table entry for 172.30.1.0/24, version 40
Paths: (3 available, best #3, advertised over iBGP, eBGP)
  65020 65030
    10.1.1.1 from 10.1.1.1
Origin IGP, metric 0, localpref 100, valid, internal
  65010 65030
    192.168.1.1 from 192.168.1.1
      Origin IGP, metric 20, localpref 100, valid, internal
  65010 65030
    192.168.2.1 from 192.168.2.1
      Origin IGP, metric 30, localpref 100, valid, external, best
```

The path through 192.168.1.1 is now the best because

- The path learned through 10.1.1.1 (from router B) is compared to the path learned through 192.168.1.1 (from router C). The Local Preference is the same, both routes are learned from a peer, the AS Paths are the same length, and both routes have the same origin code. The neighboring autonomous system is not the same, so the multiple exit discriminator is not compared. They are both learned through iBGP, and we are assuming that they both have the same interior gateway protocol metric. The next step in the decision algorithm is the router ID, and 10.1.1.1 is lower than 192.168.1.1, so the path through 10.1.1.1 wins.
- The path learned through 192.168.2.1 (from router D) is now compared to the path learned through 10.1.1.1 (from router B). The Local Preference is the same, both routes are learned from a peer, the AS Path is the same length, and both routes have the same origin code. The neighboring autonomous system is different, so the multiple exit discriminators are not compared. 192.168.2.1 is an eBGP peer, while 10.1.1.1 is an iBGP peer, so the path through 192.168.2.1 wins and becomes the best path. Table 8.3 summarizes these decision paths.

Table 8.3

	Before Reordering Due to Route Flap			
	First Comparison		*Second Comparison*	
Route	192.168.1.1	192.168.2.1	192.168.1.1	10.1.1.1
Local Preference	100	100	100	100
Locally Originated	No	No	No	No
AS Path Length	2	2	2	2
MED	Compared because the first AS in the AS Path is the same.		Not compared because the first AS in the AS Path is not the same.	
	20	30		
iBGP vs. eBGP			iBGP	iBGP
IGP Cost			Equal	
Router ID			192.168.1.1	10.1.1.1

	After Reordering Due to Route Flap			
	First Comparison		*Second Comparison*	
Route	10.1.1.1	192.168.1.1	10.1.1.1	192.168.2.1
Local Preference	100	100	100	100
Locally Originated	No	No	No	No
AS Path Length	2	2	2	2
MED	Not compared because the first AS in the AS Path is not the same.		Not compared because the first AS in the AS Path is not the same.	
iBGP vs. eBGP	iBGP	iBGP	eBGP	iBGP
IGP Cost	Equal			
Router ID	10.1.1.1	192.168.1.1		

From the preceding explanation and Table 8.3, you can see that the ordering of the paths in the local BGP table can have a large impact on the decision algorithm. In order to alleviate this inconsistency, the table needs to be ordered in some deterministic way, including the multiple exit discriminator in the ordering process, so the paths that would have their multiple exit discriminators compared would always be placed next to one another. The command **bgp deterministic-med** causes the BGP process in Cisco IOS software always to order paths based on the next hop autonomous system rather than the age of the routes, so the decision process is always the same. Once **bgp deterministic-med** is enabled, the paths from the preceding example will always be ordered:

```
router-b#sh ip bgp 172.30.1.0
BGP routing table entry for 172.30.1.0/24, version 40
Paths: (3 available, best #3, advertised over iBGP, eBGP)
  65010 65030
    192.168.1.1 from 192.168.1.1
      Origin IGP, metric 20, localpref 100, valid, internal
  65010 65030
    192.168.2.1 from 192.168.2.1
      Origin IGP, metric 30, localpref 100, valid, external
  65020 65030
    10.1.1.1 from 10.1.1.1
      Origin IGP, metric 0, localpref 100, valid, internal, best
```

Some vendors use deterministic MED by default, while other vendors require a knob to enable it. If two routers within the same autonomous system treat the MED differently, one with deterministic MED enabled, and another with it disabled, a permanent routing loop can form in the network. It's important for all routers within an autonomous system to have deterministic MED enabled or disabled.

Oldest Route versus the Highest Router ID

In Figure 8.8, the best path for 192.168.1.0/24 chosen at router A will always be through router B, since its router ID is lower than router C's router ID.

All of the metrics on the routes learned through routers B and C are the same at router A; the Local Preference, AS Path length, and so on. We begin with the path through router C being preferred, since the router ID is lower.

```
router-a#show ip bgp 192.168.1.0/24
BGP routing table entry for 192.168.1.0/24, version 17
Paths: (2 available, best #2)
  Not advertised to any peer
  65501 65503
    10.2.2.2 from 10.2.2.2
      Origin IGP, metric 0, localpref 100, valid, external
  65502 65503
    10.1.1.1 from 10.1.1.1
      Origin IGP, metric 0, localpref 100, valid, external, best
```

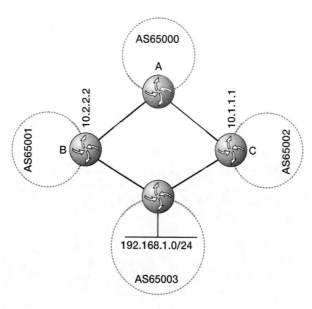

Figure 8.8
Lowest router ID versus the oldest route.

Now, the link between routers A and C flaps, and even though the route through router C has the lower router ID, the route through router B is preferred, being the older route.

```
router-a#show ip bgp 192.168.1.0/24
BGP routing table entry for 192.168.1.0/24, version 18
Paths: (2 available, best #2)
  Not advertised to any peer
  65502 65503
    10.1.1.1 from 10.1.1.1
      Origin IGP, metric 0, localpref 100, valid, external
  65501 65503
    10.2.2.2 from 10.2.2.2
      Origin IGP, metric 0, localpref 100, valid, external, best
```

This behavior was introduced into Cisco IOS to prefer the more stable path along the border of an autonomous system; it may be disabled using the command **bgp bestpath compare-router-id** within BGP router configuration mode.

Next Hop Recursion Oscillation

Under some circumstances, all the routes (or a large number of routes) in the local BGP table will either switch from one next hop to another next hop or be installed in the routing table and then removed from the routing table; this is most likely next hop recursion oscillation, one of the most common problems we see and troubleshoot in BGP deployments. Since this problem is so common, we will describe two different ways in which next hop oscillation presents itself, and solutions for each of these problems, in the following sections.

Oscillating between Two Next Hops

In some cases, next hop recursion oscillation can cause a BGP speaker to rapidly choose between two different exit points. Figure 8.9 illustrates a situation where this occurs.

Router A will learn two routes to 10.1.0.0/16; one through router C, with a next hop of 10.3.3.3 and Local Preference of 110, and one through router D, with a next hop of 10.4.4.4 and a Local Preference of 90. When router A first learns these paths, it will install both paths in

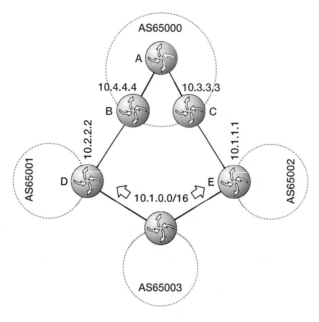

Figure 8.9
Oscillating between two next hops.

the local BGP table and choose the route through router C as the best
path, installing that path in the routing table.

```
router-a#show ip bgp 10.1.0.0/16
BGP routing table entry for 10.1.0.0/16, version 100
Paths: (2 available, best #2)
  Not advertised to any peer
  65502 65503
    10.2.2.2 from 10.4.4.4
      Origin IGP, metric 0, localpref 90, valid, external
  65501 65503
    10.1.1.1 from 10.4.4.4
      Origin IGP, metric 0, localpref 110, valid, external, best
```

Cisco IOS software's implementation of BGP has a process called
the *BGP Scanner,* which, by default, runs once a minute and performs a
variety of functions on the BGP table. One of the actions this scanner
takes is to check the next hop of each route in the routing table and
make certain it does not recurse into itself; in other words, the next hop

used is not learned through the BGP route that has been installed. If we look at the route to 10.1.1.1 on router A, we find it does, in fact, recurse into the 10.1.0.0/16 route learned from router C.

```
router-a#show ip route 10.1.0.0
Routing entry for 10.1.0.0/16
  Known via "bgp 65500", distance 200, metric 0
  Routing Descriptor Blocks:
   * 10.1.1.1, from 10.3.3.3, 00:00:53 ago
       Route metric is 0, traffic share count is 1
       AS Hops 2, BGP network version 474
```

When the scanner runs, the dependence of the longer prefix next hop on the shorter prefix route will be discovered, the next hop will be marked as unreachable, and the route removed from the routing table.

```
router-a#show ip bgp 10.1.0.0/16
BGP routing table entry for 10.1.0.0/16, version 100
Paths: (2 available, best #1)
  Not advertised to any peer
  65502 65503
    10.2.2.2 from 10.4.4.4
      Origin IGP, metric 0, localpref 90, valid, external
  65501 65503
    10.1.1.1 (inaccessible) from 10.3.3.3
      Origin IGP, metric 0, localpref 110, valid, external, best

router-a#show ip route 10.1.0.0
Routing entry for 10.1.0.0/16
  Known via "bgp 65500", distance 200, metric 0
 Routing Descriptor Blocks:
  * 10.2.2.2, from 10.4.4.4, 00:00:26 ago
      Route metric is 0, traffic share count is 1
      AS Hops 2, BGP network version 474
```

The BGP process will then revert the route back to the bestpath through router C, and the next time the BGP scanner process runs, the route will switch the router to the path through router B. This will continue, every 60 seconds.

The problem here is not that the route to the next hop is learned via iBGP, but rather the route to the next hop recurses through the route itself, which is impossible. There are several possible solutions to this problem:

- Include the next hop, in this case 10.1.1.1, in the interior gateway protocol so it is not learned through iBGP. This breaks the recursion of the route onto itself.
- Create a static route to the next hop from router A. This also breaks the recursion by providing another path to the route's next hop than through the route itself.
- Configure router C to set the next hop for all routes it is advertising to itself using the Cisco IOS software command neighbor <x.x.x.x> next-hop-self. This breaks the recursion of the route by changing the next hop so it's not part of the route being learned.

Oscillating between Installing and Removing the Routes from the Local Routing Table

Another common symptom of route oscillation on the next hop is the insertion and removal of routes from the routing table, as the next hop route is installed in the routing table and then removed by the BGP scanner process. Figure 8.10 illustrates a common situation.

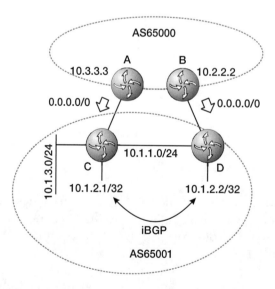

Figure 8.10
Route installation and removal next hop oscillation.

We begin with the link between routers C and D up, and the iBGP session between the two routers running through this link. The 10.1.2.1 network is reachable through a static route on router D, through the 10.1.1.0/24 network, and the 10.1.3.0/24 network is reachable through 10.1.2.1.

```
router-d#show ip route 10.1.2.2
Routing entry for 10.1.2.2/32
  Known via "static", distance 1, metric 0
  Routing Descriptor Blocks:
  * 10.1.1.11
      Route metric is 0, traffic share count is 1

router-d#show ip bgp 10.1.3.0
BGP routing table entry for 10.1.3.0/24, version 22
Paths: (1 available, best #1, table Default-IP-Routing-Table)
  Not advertised to any peer
  Local
    10.1.2.2 from 10.1.2.2 (10.1.1.11)
      Origin IGP, metric 0, localpref 100, valid, internal, best
```

When the link between routers C and D fails, we would expect the iBGP session between the routers to fail as well. However, we find that it doesn't; from router D with the router C to D link failed:

```
router-d#show ip bgp neighbor 10.1.2.2
BGP neighbor is 10.1.2.2, remote AS 65001, internal link
  BGP version 4, remote router ID 208.0.13.11
  BGP state = Established, up for 00:23:23
  Last read 00:01:23, hold time is 180,
  keepalive interval is 60 seconds
....
```

Why hasn't this iBGP session failed? Because 10.1.2.2 is still reachable; as long as the peer is reachable, the session will stay up. We see this on router D, after the router C to D link has failed.

```
router-d#sho ip bgp nei 10.1.2.2
BGP neighbor is 10.1.2.2, remote AS 65001, internal link
  BGP version 4, remote router ID 10.1.2.2
  BGP state = Established, up for 00:13:47
```

```
Last read 00:00:47, hold time is 180,
   keepalive interval is 60 seconds

router-d#ping 10.1.2.2

Type escape sequence to abort.
Sending 5, 100-byte ICMP Echos to 10.1.2.2, timeout is 2 seconds:
!!!!!
Success rate is 100 percent (5/5), round-trip min/avg/max = 8/8/9 ms
```

Router D can still ping 10.1.2.2, because the traffic is following the default route (0.0.0.0/0) learned from router C. The iBGP session between routers C and D is actually passing traffic through the external autonomous system, AS65000, so the peers are staying up, as Figure 8.11 illustrates.

What impact does this have on the routes being learned from router C on router D?

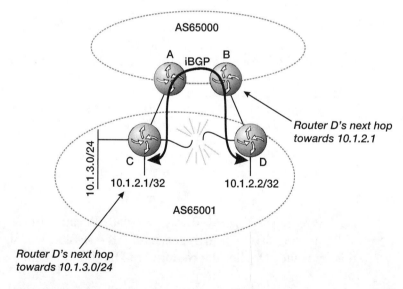

Figure 8.11
The iBGP session running through the external path.

```
router-d#sho ip bgp 10.1.3.0
BGP routing table entry for 10.1.3.0/24, version 291
Paths: (1 available, best #1, table Default-IP-Routing-Table)
Flag: 0x820
    Local
    10.1.2.2 from 10.1.2.2 (10.1.2.2)
      Origin IGP, metric 0, localpref 100, valid, internal, best

router-d#sho ip bgp 10.1.3.0
BGP routing table entry for 10.1.3.0/24, version 293
Paths: (1 available, no best path)
Flag: 0x820
  Not advertised to any peer
  Local
    10.1.2.2 (inaccessible) from 10.1.2.2 (10.1.2.2)
      Origin IGP, metric 0, localpref 100, valid, internal
```

These two conditions occur within every sixty-second cycle, as the BGP scanner process marks the next hop as inaccessible and the BGP process reinstalls the route. The easiest way to resolve this issue is with a *floating static route* on both routers C and D. When there are several protocols have a route to the same destination, Cisco IOS software installs the route with the best *administrative distance,* leaving the other routes as *backup routes,* which are used in cases where the route with the lowest administrative distance is removed from the table for any reason. You can think of this administrative distance as a protocol metric with a minimum value of 0 (connected routes) and a maximum value of 255 (not accessible), allowing the routing table to decide between several different protocols whose metrics are not comparable.

To create floating static routes, put an administrative distance higher than the distance of the protocol through which the route is normally learned. Since no routing protocol has an administrative distance higher than 200, giving the static routes a distance of 240 normally works. You can create a floating static route on both routers B and C so when the link between them fails, the packets transmitted from the BGP process to the other peer are discarded rather than delivered.

```
router-d#config terminal
router-d(config)#ip route 10.1.2.2 255.255.255.255 null0 240
```

When the link between the routers fails, the best path to the other peer will be this static route rather than the default route (0.0.0.0/0) learned through eBGP. The destination interface, **null0,** indicates that the packets should be discarded rather than delivered. With this static route in place, when the router B to router C link fails, the keepalives and other packets transmitted between the peers will be discarded, causing the iBGP session to fail.

Troubleshooting Next Hop Recursion Oscillation

The first step in troubleshooting next hop route recursion is to recognize it is happening; we've only provided two situations where this type of problem shows up, but there are numerous others. The first clue, however, is a number of routes in the routing table that are either switching next hops, or being removed and reinstalled, every sixty seconds. You can see this by examining the route timers in the routing table.

```
router#show ip route 10.1.0.0
Routing entry for 10.1.0.0/16
  Known via "bgp 65000", distance 200, metric 0
  Routing Descriptor Blocks:
    * 192.168.1.1, from 192.168.1.1, 00:00:53 ago
        Route metric is 0, traffic share count is 1
        AS Hops 2, BGP network version 474
```

If this timer never exceeds sixty seconds for a BGP learned route, you should begin further troubleshooting, since this is a definite sign of next hop recursion oscillation. Once you've discovered an oscillating route, you should monitor the output of **show ip bgp** to see if at least one path is alternately marked the best path and inaccessible.

```
router#show ip bgp 10.1.0.0
BGP routing table entry for 10.1.0.0/16, version 474
Paths: (2 available, best #1)
  65000 65001
    192.168.1.1 from 192.168.1.1 (192.168.1.1)
    Origin IGP, localpref 100, valid, internal, best
  65002
    192.168.10.2 (inaccessible) from 192.168.2.2 (192.168.2.2)
    Origin IGP, metric 0, localpref 100, valid, internal
```

If you find a route acting in this way, then you should examine the next hop by checking the routing table to find out if the next hop is a part of the route itself. Once you discovered the recursion, you can take one of the actions outlined previously–advertising the next hop through an interior gateway protocol, installing a floating static route to force the peering session to fail under certain circumstances, and so on–to stop the recursion and resolve the problem.

Route Churn

The combination of indeterministic multiple exit discriminator and route reflectors can cause a condition where the BGP table on a set of routers will constantly churn between two different best paths; Figure 8.12 illustrates a network in which this will occur.

The costs shown along each link are the interior gateway protocol costs; we'll assume the cost of the links between AS65000 and the other autonomous systems are all 5. So the interior gateway protocol cost of router E to reach 10.2.2.2 will be 23. Examining the path to 172.17.1.0/24 at the routers along the edge of AS65000, routers C, D, and E, we find

```
router-c#show ip bgp 172.17.1.0
BGP routing table entry for 172.17.1.0/24, version 500
Paths: (1 available, best #1)
  65001 65003
    10.2.2.2 from 10.2.2.2 (10.2.2.2)
      Origin IGP, metric 10, localpref 100, valid, external, best

router-d#show ip bgp 172.17.1.0
BGP routing table entry for 172.17.1.0/24, version 126
Paths: (1 available, best #1)
  65002 65003
    10.3.3.3 from 10.3.3.3 (10.3.3.3)
      Origin IGP, metric 1, localpref 100, valid, external, best

router-e#show ip bgp 172.17.1.0
BGP routing table entry for 172.17.1.0/24, version 985
Paths: (1 available, best #1)
  65002 65003
    10.4.4.4 from 10.4.4.4 (10.4.4.4)
      Origin IGP, metric 0, localpref 100, valid, external, best
```

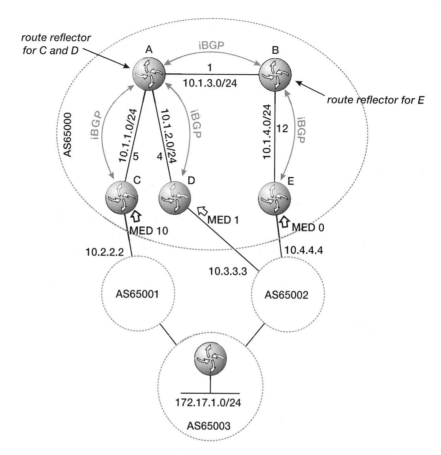

Figure 8.12
A network with persistent route churn

When we begin, router A has two paths to 172.17.1.0/24:

```
router-a#show ip bgp 172.17.1.0
BGP routing table entry for 172.17.1.0/24, version 326
Paths: (2 available, best #2)
  65002 65003
    10.3.3.3 from 10.1.2.13 (10.1.2.13) // Router D
      Origin IGP, metric 1, localpref 100, valid, external
  65001 65003
    10.2.2.2 from 10.1.1.12 (10.1.1.12) // Router C
      Origin IGP, metric 10, localpref 100, valid, external, best
```

Examining the network diagram, however, we see the interior gateway protocol cost through router D is lower than the interior gateway protocol cost through router C, so the path through C should be the best path. The BGP process on router A catches this and switches over to the path through router D.

```
router-a#show ip bgp 172.17.1.0
BGP routing table entry for 172.17.1.0/24, version 327
Paths: (2 available, best #1)
  65002 65003
    10.3.3.3 from 10.1.2.13 (10.1.2.13) // Router D
      Origin IGP, metric 1, localpref 100, valid, external, best
  65001 65003
    10.2.2.2 from 10.1.1.12 (10.1.1.12) // Router C
      Origin IGP, metric 10, localpref 100, valid, external
```

Since router A has changed its best path, it needs to send an update to each of its peers, including router B, to notify them of the change. If we look in router B's BGP table when it receives this update, it has the following routes:

```
router-b#show ip bgp 172.17.1.0
BGP routing table entry for 172.17.1.0/24, version 518
Paths:
  65002 65003
    10.4.4.4 from 10.1.4.14 (10.1.4.14) // Router E
      Origin IGP, metric 0, localpref 100, valid, external
  65002 65003
    10.2.2.2 from 10.1.2.13 (10.1.2.13) // Router D
      Origin IGP, metric 1, localpref 100, valid, external
```

Examining these two routes, it's apparent that the path through 10.1.4.14, router E, should be preferred, since the multiple exist discriminator is lower, and the neighboring autonomous system is the same (AS65002). Once router D has run its bestpath and marks the path through router E the best path, it will send updates to each of its peers about this change, including router A. On receiving this update, router A has the following routes in its BGP table:

```
router-a#show ip bgp 172.17.1.0
BGP routing table entry for 172.17.1.0/24, version 328
Paths:
```

```
65002 65003
  10.4.4.4 from 10.1.4.14 (10.1.4.14) // Router E
    Origin IGP, metric 0, localpref 100, valid, external
65002 65003
  10.3.3.3 from 10.1.2.13 (10.1.2.13) // Router D
    Origin IGP, metric 1, localpref 100, valid, external
65001 65003
  10.2.2.2 from 10.1.1.12 (10.1.1.12) // Router C
    Origin IGP, metric 10, localpref 100, valid, external
```

Using the BGP bestpath algorithm on the routes available, we can see the first path is better than the second path; the multiple exit discriminators are compared, because the next hop autonomous system (AS65002) is the same, and the MED on the first path is lower than the MED on the second path. Next the first path is compared to the third path, and the third path wins. The multiple exit discriminators are not compared, and the interior gateway protocol cost to reach 10.2.2.2 (10) through router C is lower than the interior gateway cost to reach 10.4.4.4 (18) through router E.

On deciding the path through router C is the best path, router A now sends an update to each of its peers, including router B. This actually causes the route through router D, which router A had advertised to router B in the last step, to be withdrawn; router A replaces the path through router D with the path through router C. On router B, then, we now have the following paths in the local BGP table:

```
router-b#show ip bgp 172.17.1.0
BGP routing table entry for 172.17.1.0/24, version 519
Paths:
  65001 65003
    10.2.2.2 from 10.1.1.12 (10.1.1.12) // Router C
      Origin IGP, metric 10, localpref 100, valid, external
  65002 65003
    10.4.4.4 from 10.1.4.14 (10.1.2.14) // Router E
      Origin IGP, metric 0, localpref 100, valid, external
```

Examining these paths, we find the multiple exit discriminators will not be compared, since the next hop autonomous system is not the same, so the best path will be decided based on interior gateway protocol metrics. The IGP metric from router B to 10.2.2.2, through router C, is 11, while the IGP metric through router E to 10.4.4.4 is 17, so the path through router C is chosen as the best path. Router B sends router A an update about this change in its best path, which then leaves router A with the following routes in its local BGP table:

```
router-a#show ip bgp 172.17.1.0
BGP routing table entry for 172.17.1.0/24, version 329
Paths: (2 available, best #1)
  65002 65003
    10.3.3.3 from 10.1.2.13 (10.1.2.13) // Router D
      Origin IGP, metric 1, localpref 100, valid, external, best
  65001 65003
    10.2.2.2 from 10.1.1.12 (10.1.1.12) // Router C
      Origin IGP, metric 10, localpref 100, valid, external
```

This is exactly where we started from, so the process will repeat it-self forever. Figure 8.13 illustrates the entire process.

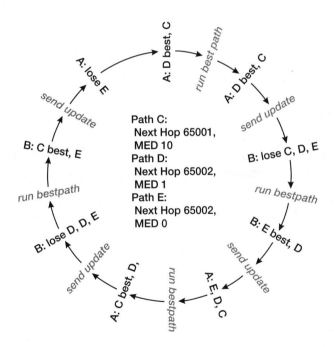

Figure 8.13
An overview of route churn.

Troubleshooting Route Churn

The easiest way to troubleshoot route churn in Cisco IOS software is to use the **show ip route** and **show ip BGP commands,** combined with the ability to filter the output of these commands on a regular expression to see quickly just the parts you want. Using **show ip route | include , 00:00,** you can find all of the routes in the local routing table that have changed within the last minute. Using this command several times, over a period of minutes, will show you those routes that are constantly changing in the routing table.

```
router#show ip route bgp | include , 00:00
B 10.1.1.0/22 [200/1] via 192.168.1.18, 00:00:58
....
router#
router#show ip route bgp | include , 00:00
B 10.1.1.0/22 [200/1] via 192.168.1.18, 00:00:46
....
router#
router#show ip route bgp | include , 00:00
B 10.1.1.0/22 [200/1] via 192.168.1.18, 00:00:57
....
router#
```

Once you've discovered some set of BGP routes that are constantly changing, then you can employ the output of show ip bgp <network> | include include best # to discover if the best path is changing constantly and which paths the best path is oscillating between.

```
router#show ip bgp 10.1.1.0 | include best #
Paths: (3 available, best #1)
router#show ip bgp 10.1.1.0 | include best #
Paths: (3 available, best #1)
router#show ip bgp 10.1.1.0 | include best #
Paths: (3 available, best #2)
router#show ip bgp 10.1.1.0 | include best #
Paths: (3 available, best #2)
router#show ip bgp 10.1.1.0 | include best #
Paths: (3 available, best #3)
router#show ip bgp 10.1.1.0 | include best #
Paths: (3 available, best #1)
```

You can see that among the three possible best paths, the best path chosen by this router is switching among all three of them; this is a certain sign of churn in the BGP table and should be investigated further.

Resolving Route Churn

The best option for resolving route churn is to use one of the following methods:

- Make certain the interior gateway cost between any pair of route reflectors is always higher than the interior gateway cost of reaching the route reflector clients from those route reflectors.
- Do not accept the multiple exit discriminator from any of your external BGP peers.
- Force the BGP best path algorithm to never reach the multiple exit discriminators; this can be accomplished, for instance, by setting the local preference on all routes received from external peers so every exit point has a different local preference.
- Enable bgp always-compare-med in Cisco IOS software. This forces the multiple exit discriminator always to be compared, even when the next hop autonomous system is not the same.
- Discontinue the use of route reflectors, and use a full iBGP mesh instead.

Of these options, most network operators will choose the first option, along with configuring their routers to compare the multiple exit discriminators deterministically (using **bgp deterministic-med** in Cisco IOS software).

> Route churn is described in RFC 3354, *Border Gateway Protocol (BGP) Persistent Route Oscillation Condition.*

Review Questions

1. With most BGP implementations, what is the source address of the TCP packets sent to a peer? How can this cause a problem for eBGP sessions built between nonconnected interfaces?

2. How many IP hops does BGP normally assume will be between two eBGP peers? How is this condition normally checked within BGP implementations?

3. Which open parameters can cause a BGP session to fail?

4. What three common problems can cause a peering session to flap between two BGP speakers?

5. What problem is synchronization between BGP and interior gateway protocol learned routes supposed to prevent? What methods are used to prevent these problems from occurring without synchronization being enabled?

6. BGP speakers do not normally change the next hop when readvertising a route learned from an external peer to an internal peer. How can this cause routes to be missing from a BGP speaker's tables?

7. When is the multiple exit discriminator compared between two routes?

8. Can the multiple exit discriminator comparison rules cause issues with route selection process?

9. What rules can you follow in network design with regard to the interior gateway protocol metric between route reflectors to prevent persistent route churn?

9

BGP and Network Security

Security has become, in recent years, a very large concern within networks; it's increasingly difficult to consider any change to a protocol, or any change to a network, without also considering the implications on the security of the network. BGP, as the protocol that "runs the Internet backbone," is a major focus of the efforts that have been made towards producing a secure routing protocol.

In the following sections, we'll discuss some various issues impacting BGP. We'll begin by considering the protection of BGP peering sessions at the edge of the network, and then we'll discuss other security issues at the edge of the autonomous system. Finally, we'll discuss two proposed methods of securing the information propogated through the BGP protocol, soBGP and S-BGP.

Protecting Peering Relationships

The edge of the network, where two autonomous systems meet, is the most critical juncture in the BGP protocol. Here is where the network administrators of two different networks, managed by two different entities, with different goals, ideas, and concerns, must work together to provide security for both networks without compromising the network's utility or performance. The edge of the network is the place where most attacks are likely to be launched, and the BGP speaker on the edge is probably one of the most logical places to try and get into the network and impact the network's control plane.

There are several methods available to counter the threats of attacking the BGP speaker itself; we discuss traffic filters, MD5 authentication, Generalized TTL Security Mechanism, and some other options in this section.

Infrastructure ACLs (iACLs)

The first line of defense that should be raised to protect a BGP control plane is basic packet filtering. Packet filters can be used to prevent hosts other than the legitimate BGP speakers that a router is peering with from being used as a base to launch attacks against the BGP speaker itself.

It's generally a good idea to filter all packets at all network perimeter points if they are destined for infrastructure elements within the network. For example, if your network's router and circuit addresses are all numbered out of 172.16.0.0/22, don't allow any packets to enter the network destined for that block of address space. This can be problematic, however, especially when considering the impact of such policies on diagnostic capabilities. For example, although traceroute to a destination through the network would remain operational, a network engineer outside the network trying to ping a router or interface within your network would fail. Thus, you may be required to permit ICMP or other protocols access to these addresses, though you should be explicit about what you permit, and then implicitly deny all other protocols and services access to your infrastructure addresses.

In addition, all networks should configure packet filters at the network perimeter that deny packets from entering the network if the source address of those packets falls within your infrastructure address space. With the above 172.16.0.0/22 address range as an example, this would mean denying all packets from entering the network if their source address is within the infrastructure address range. This will remove the ability for a miscreant to inject packets into the network in order to inject data or disrupt a TCP session between to internal BGP speakers. Note that even with these filters, it is still possible to receive packets sourced through an external BGP peer's network with a source address of that peer and a destination address of the associated local external BGP speaking router, potentially disrupting the peering sessions between you and that peer. If your peer applies infrastructure ACLs as well, this should not be as much of a concern. However, in this specific example the BGP TTL Security Mechanism, discussed in a following section, can help complete your BGP TCP Transport connection's session protection.

MD5 Authentication

BGP can also take advantage of MD5 within TCP to authenticate a specific peer transmitted packets. MD5 authentication is not intended to protect the contents of the packet (preventing them from being altered) nor hide the information transmitted in the packet; instead, it is designed to verify a given device sent to a packet.

> *Protection of BGP Sessions via the TCP MD5 Signature Option,* RFC 2385, describes the use of MD5 signatures with BGP. MD5 digest signatures are described in RFC 1321.

MD5 authentication is based on a *key,* also commonly referred to as a *shared secret,* which can be changed periodically, shared between the two BGP peers. Each router uses this key, along with a set of mathematical computations described in the MD5 specifications, to find a number. This number, called the digest signature, is included in the packet when it's transmitted. The receiver can use a local copy of the key and perform the same mathematical computations and arrive at the same number the transmitter included in the packet. If the receiver does not arrive at the same number as the transmitter, using the same key and performing the same math, then the packet is discarded.

The key is not transmitted over the connection on a periodic basis, so the network administrators who manage the BGP devices must manually configure it. If periodic key changes are required, the keys must be changed manually (or through some local system which automatically configures the routers on both ends of the connection, such as a script). The use of MD5 authentication isn't negotiated at session startup; it's a matter of local configuration on each router. A new option header is added to the TCP header, as illustrated in Figure 9.1, to carry this MD5 digest signature.

- Kind: Indicates the type of TCP option header included. In this case, this indicates to the TCP software an MD5 message digest is included in the TCP header.
- Length: This is always set to 18 for a TCP MD5 digest authentication header.
- MD5 Signature: This is set to the MD5 authentication digest, as calculated by the sender. It is always set to 16 octets.

kind	length
MD5 signature	

Figure 9.1
The TCP MD5 option header.

The MD5 digest is calculated over the following fields in the TCP header:

- The source IP address
- The destination IP address
- The protocol number
- The length of the TCP segment
- The TCP header (excluding optional headers)
- The data carried in the TCP segment
- The key itself

Care must be taken in building an MD5 authentication key; the key must not be guessable, and it should be at least strong enough to prevent the key being broken between key changes. For instance, if the key is going to be used for a month or two at a time (since its difficult, presumably to change keys very frequently when they are manually configured), it should be at least 96 octets in length.

> Suggestions for building MD5 authentication digest keys are given in Security Requirements for Keys Used with the TCP MD5 Signature Option, draft-ietf-idr-md5-keys.

Some consideration has been given to automating the process of changing keys used for MD5 authentication between peers, but no standards have been written at this point. The following configurations illustrate the use of TCP MD5 authentication between two BGP peers running Cisco IOS software.

```
router-a#sho run
....
interface serial 0/1
```

```
 ip address 10.1.1.14 255.255.255.0
!
....
router bgp 65501
 bgp log-neighbor-changes
 neighbor 10.1.1.3 remote-as 65500
 neighbor 10.1.1.3 password anmd5password
!

router-b#sho run
....
interface serial 0/1
 ip address 10.1.1.3 255.255.255.0
!
....
router bgp 65500
 no synchronization
 bgp log-neighbor-changes
 neighbor 10.1.1.14 remote-as 65501
 neighbor 10.1.1.14 password anmd5password
 no auto-summary
....

router-b#sho ip bgp neighbors
BGP neighbor is 208.0.5.14,  remote AS 65501, external link
  BGP version 4, remote router ID 208.0.11.14
  BGP state = Established, up for 00:05:43
....
SRTT: 221 ms, RTTO: 832 ms, RTV: 611 ms, KRTT: 0 ms
minRTT: 0 ms, maxRTT: 300 ms, ACK hold: 200 ms
Flags: passive open, nagle, gen tcbs, md5

Datagrams (max data segment is 1440 bytes):
Rcvd: 13 (out of order: 0), with data: 10, total data bytes: 216
....
```

Employing the TCP MD5 Signature Option for BGP provides session protection from potential disruption that may incur from spoofed packets (e.g., TCP SYNs or RSTs) or potential data injection that may occur. It was for quite some time assumed that injecting spoofed segments into a TCP transport connection was extremely difficult without some inside knowledge regarding the session. That is, not only would an attacker need to know the source and destination IP addresses and corresponding TCP port numbers, he or she would need to be aware of the TCP segment sequence number expected by the receiver, which represents a value of $2^{\wedge}32$. However, it has recently been widely discussed that an attacker doesn't actually need to know the exact sequence number, he or she only needs the sequence number value to fall within the TCP receive window range on the receiver. Recall in earlier chapters that increasing this value helps improve the TCP Transport connection convergence properties of BGP; in addition it should be noted that it also lessens the difficulty of injecting spoofed segments into the session, because the TCP receive window size is much larger. As such, it is highly recommended that TCP MD5 Signature Option be employed to protect against this vulnerability.

BGP over IPsec

The next step beyond simply authenticating the data in the data stream passing between two BGP peers is to encrypt the data stream passing between two BGP peers. The most commonly implemented and deployed method for encrypting data streams in the Internet is IPsec.

IPsec encrypts the data itself, which means the data carried inside the IP packets is not readable by anyone who does not have the key to decrypt it with. This protects the integrity of the data and prevent outsiders from using information gleaned by snooping in on BGP streams from using the information gained through snooping (such as TCP sequence numbers and networks advertised) to attack either of the BGP speakers or the networks they represent.

> Securing BGPv4 Using IPsec, draft-ward-bgp-ipsec, describes in detail the use of IPsec sessions to secure BGP peering relationships. This draft will most likely be generalized to cover all routing protocol and republished.

The following configurations illustrate the use of IPsec to secure a BGP session between two peers running Cisco IOS software.

```
router-a#show running-config
Building configuration...
....
!
crypto ipsec transform-set bgp-ipsec esp-des
 mode transport
```

```
!
crypto map encrypt-bgp 1 ipsec-manual
 set peer 10.1.1.1
 set session-key inbound esp 256 cipher
  deadbeefdeadbeefdeadbeefdeadbeef
 set session-key outbound esp 256 cipher
  deadbeefdeadbeefdeadbeefdeadbeef
 set transform-set bgp-ipsec
 match address 101
!
....
!
interface FastEthernet6/0
 ip address 10.1.1.2 255.255.255.0
 duplex half
 crypto map encrypt-bgp
!
router bgp 65501
 bgp log-neighbor-changes
 neighbor 10.1.1.1 remote-as 65500
!
....
!
access-list 101 permit tcp host 10.1.1.2 host 10.1.1.1
!
....
router-a#sho crypto engine connections active

  ID Int   IP-Address State  Algorithm         Encrypt Decrypt
2000 FA6/0 10.1.1.2   set    DES_56_CBC             14       0
2001 FA6/0 10.1.1.2   set    DES_56_CBC              0      23
....

router-a#show ip bgp neighbors
BGP neighbor is 10.1.1.1,  remote AS 65500, external link
  BGP version 4, remote router ID 147.28.255.1
  BGP state = Established, up for 00:08:11
....

router-b#show running-config
Building configuration...
....
!
```

```
crypto ipsec transform-set bgp-ipsec esp-des
 mode transport
!
crypto map encrypt-bgp 1 ipsec-manual
 set peer 10.1.1.2
 set session-key inbound esp 256 cipher
  deadbeefdeadbeefdeadbeefdeadbeef
 set session-key outbound esp 256 cipher
  deadbeefdeadbeefdeadbeefdeadbeef
 set transform-set bgp-ipsec
 match address 101
!
....
!
interface FastEthernet6/0
 ip address 10.1.1.1 255.255.255.0
 duplex half
 crypto map encrypt-bgp
!
....
!
access-list 101 permit tcp host 10.1.1.1 host 10.1.1.2
!
....
router-b#show crypto engine connections active

   ID Int    IP-Address State  Algorithm              Encrypt  Decrypt
2000 FA6/0 10.1.1.1    set    DES_56_CBC                  38        0
2001 FA6/0 10.1.1.1    set    DES_56_CBC                   0       25
....
router-b#sho ip bgp nei
BGP neighbor is 10.1.1.2,   remote AS 65501,  external link
  BGP version 4, remote router ID 208.0.11.14
  BGP state = Established, up for 00:12:07
```

BGP may also be run over an IPsec tunnel, as well as in transport mode, but since BGP is already within a TCP data stream, unless you are trying to hide the actual peer addresses, it's simpler to run it in transport mode, as the preceding example shows. IPsec can also interact with Internet Key Exchange, IKE, to manage the keys used by peers in an encryption session. This greatly simplifies key change and other events. IKE, however, is not commonly run between routing domains.

IKE is described in RFC 2409, *The Internet Key Exchange (IKE)*.

The Generalized TTL Security Mechanism

As we've already discussed, one of the major vulnerabilities suffered by BGP is in its use of TCP as a transport mechanism. This means that unicast packets, which can be sourced from almost any host on the Internet, can be used to launch attacks against a router running BGP. To counter this, some method of preventing hosts that are not "close" to a BGP speaker from directing packets at it would be useful. The Generalized TTL Security Mechanism, described in RFC 3682 is a method of ensuring no packets transmitted by hosts outside the range of known peers are accepted by a BGP speaker. Figure 9.2 illustrates.

Suppose an attacker would like to break into router A. Under normal circumstances, the attacker could use host C and send unicast packets toward router A's IP address. If he can find the right combination of keys, TCP sequence number, and other information, the attacker can either disrupt the session between routers A and B, or he can simply inject false information into the routing system by hijacking the session between A and B.

However, suppose router A now determines B is directly connected, and if router B were to set the time to live on each packet it

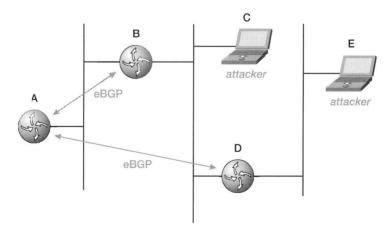

Figure 9.2
The Generalized TTL Security Mechanism.

transmits to 255, A should receive these packets with the same time to live, or possibly one less, 254. Once this is configured on both routers, C is no longer a location from which an attack against A can be made. The only way for C to attack A would be to set the time to live on packets it transmits to something greater than 255, which isn't possible.

This sort of defense against attacks can be extended to multihop BGP sessions as well. For instance, if router A knows D is two hops away, it can set its inbound filtering so only BGP packets with a time to live of 253 or higher will be accepted. Thus, E would no longer be a location from which an attack against the BGP speaker on router A could be made. Of course, opening up the acceptable time to live to account for multihop sessions does pose some risk; once A reduces its minimum acceptable time to live, so it can peer with D, C becomes an available attack point again, if it can spook router D's address.

> This method of providing security is described in RFC 3682.

You might be wondering at this point why the time-to-live value isn't simply set to 1 instead. The reason is quite simple, actually. If the IP header time-to-live value is set to 1, an attacker could craft packets with a transmit TTL value that results in packets landing on the target with a value of 1. However, if the value is set to 255, as long as intermediate nodes in the network are decrementing the TTL value of the packet as it's forwarded through the network, there's no way for the attacker to craft a packet that can land on the target router with a value of 255.

Preventing Spoofing at the Edge

Not all security at the edge of an autonomous system focuses on protecting the BGP sessions running and the BGP speakers; there are a lot of other precautions that can be taken at the edge of the network to protect the network itself as well. One primary area of concern is preventing attackers who are spoofing IP addresses, using an IP address other than their own, to launch an attack against some other network. Figure 9.3 illustrates.

The laptop, which is temporarily connected to 10.3.1.0 network, is requesting a traffic stream from 10.2.1.10, but it's doing so using

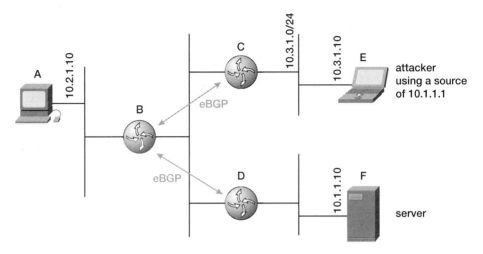

Figure 9.3
Using spoofing to launch an attack against a server.

10.1.1.10 as its source address. Each of these traffic streams will be transmitted to 10.1.1.10, which didn't request them, eating up resources on the server. If enough traffic streams are requested from different hosts on a large network, the server could become overwhelmed and fail (either permanently, or for some period of time). How could this be prevented using routing information provided through BGP at the network level?

Through BGP, router B learns that 10.3.1.0/24 is reachable through router C. When router B receives packets from C, it can compare the networks it knows are reachable through C to the source of the packet and discard the packet if the route to the source isn't through the interface its receiving the packet on. In this case, when router B receives a packet sourced from 10.1.1.1 from C, it can check its local routing information and see the path to 10.1.1.1 is actually through router D. Since router A doesn't use C as its next hop toward 10.1.1.10, it can discard the packet.

This method of checking the source address using local routing information is called a Reverse Path Forward (RPF) check. The main problem with using an RPF check to prevent spoofing is that a path may be valid and not appear in the local routing table. This is common in the case of dual-homed customers to a single Internet service provider, as shown in Figure 9.4.

While the 10.1.1.0/24 network is actually reachable through both routers D and E, only one of these two paths will be chosen as the best

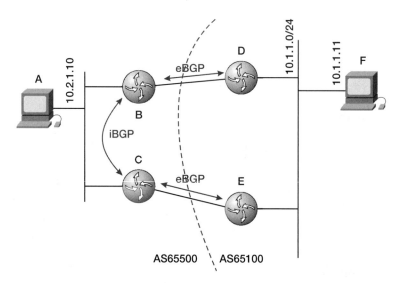

Figure 9.4
A simple dual-homed network.

path within AS65500; either both routers B and C will choose the path through D, or they will both choose the path through E. Assume they both choose the path through router D as the best path and install this path in their local routing tables.

From the other side of the network, F is using router E as its default gateway, so any packets it generates are routed through C to reach A. When router C receives these packets, it will examine them, note the source is reachable through B rather than E, and discard them, even though this is a valid path. This presents a large obstacle in deploying reverse path forwarding checks.

One possible solution to this problem is to widen the scope of the RPF checks; instead of checking the route to the source in the local routing tables and comparing the interface the packet is received on to the interface the source would be reached through, just check the source of each packets to make certain it is actually reachable through any route in the local routing tables. This allows spoofing, as long as the attacker chooses some real, reachable address to use as its source.

```
router(config-if)#ip verify unicast source ?
  reachable-via    Specify reachability check to apply to the
                   source address
router(config-if)#ip verify unicast reverse-path ?
```

```
<1-199>              A standard IP access list number
<1300-2699>          A standard IP expanded access list number
                     allow-self-ping  Allow router to ping itself
                     (opens vulnerability in verification)
<cr>
```

> **Whitelist Virtual Routing Tables and RPF Checks**
>
> Another option for resolving this problem is to allow BGP to install valid routes that are not the best path to a destion into a seperate routing table, and then perform RPF checks against this secondary routing table, called a whitelist table. For instance, in the network in Figure 9.4, router C could run the best path algorithm and determine the path through B is the best path to the 10.1.1.0/24 network. The alternate path that is available could be marked through a BGP community and placed in a separate routing table, which is consulted while performaing a reverse path forwarding test.
>
> When the RPF check is performed, this whitelist table is checked, and since the 10.1.1.0/24 network is reachable through router E, the packets will be allowed.

Infrastructure ACLs, the TCP MD5 Signature Option, and the Generalized TTL Security Mechanism are all widely deployed throughout networks in the Internet today. Taking these basic steps to protect your infrastructure should be considered critical to any network engineer.

Securing Routing Information within BGP

Beyond protecting the sessions between BGP peers and filtering of data based on the information learned through BGP, there is the issue of protecting the data carried inside BGP itself. Any security system attempting to secure the information carried within BGP faces a very high set of requirements. For instance, the BGP packet formats have been carefully designed and optimized over a number of years to allow the transmission of large amounts of routing data with the smallest possible load on the transmitting and receiving router, and so on.

Consideration must also be given to what can actually be secured within BGP. The primary two areas we will focus on in our discussions of the proposed mechanisms for securing the information carried within BGP are protecting the origin of the routing information and validating the transmitter of any given routing information actually has a feasible path to the destinations advertised.

soBGP

Secure Origin BGP, or soBGP, has been proposed by a group of routing protocols and security experts through the IETF in the form of several drafts; each of these drafts covers a separate part of the protocol specification or operation. In this section, we'll provide an overview of how soBGP works and how it provides for the validation of the origin of any given piece of routing information, and how it allows the originator of a prefix to set certain policies toward those prefixes and the receiver of a prefix to validate the existence of at least one valid path from the origin.

soBGP consists of three pieces that interoperate to provide security information:

- A database of valid autonomous systems in the internetwork and their keys
- A database of prefixes, matched with the autonomous systems authorized to originate them
- A directed graph describing all known valid paths through the internetwork

There are three types of keys used by soBGP to provide this information:

- The *EntityCert,* which describes an entity, or an autonomous system, and the entity's public key
- The *PolicyCert,* which describes the connections to an autonomous system, and the policies of an autonomous system in regard to particular prefixes it is advertising
- The *AuthCert,* which describes the set of autonomous systems authorized to advertise a given prefix

Each of these certificates is described in the following sections, and a section follows that describes how soBGP builds the correct databases and how these databases are used to validate the routing information received through BGP. The final section briefly discusses the ways in which soBGP may be deployed in a large scale network.

The Entity Database and the EntityCert

Each autonomous system (entity) begins by creating a public/private key pair, having its public key signed by some other member of the internetwork, and advertising its public key through an EntityCert. Each EntityCert contains

- A unique identifier for the entity, the autonomous system number
- A public key generated by the entity, the counterpart of a private key used to sign other certificates
- A unique identifier of the entity signing this certificate, an autonomous system number
- A signature created using the private key of the signing entity

As long as the signer is a trusted member of the internetwork, the public key advertised in the EntityCert may me trusted as well. Through the EntityCerts advertised from each member of the internetwork, a web of trust is built that provides the means to trust all the public keys advertised; Figure 9.5 illustrates this principle.

As each EntityCert is received, the current database of known trusted EntityCerts is checked to see if the public key of the signing autonomous system is already known. If it is, then the EntityCert's signature is checked, and if it's found to be valid, the certificate is placed in the database of known valid EntityCerts. EntityCerts contain serial numbers allowing them to be revoked by issuing newer EntityCerts, or allowing a single autonomous system to have several outstanding certificates at any given time.

There are several number of possible combinations for signing EntityCerts:

- Autonomous systems may self-sign their keys; this will probably be most useful and accepted from well-known autonomous systems, such as regional Internet registries, various government agencies, and top-level service providers.
- Autonomous systems may cross sign keys; again, this would be most useful for well-known entities within the internetwork.

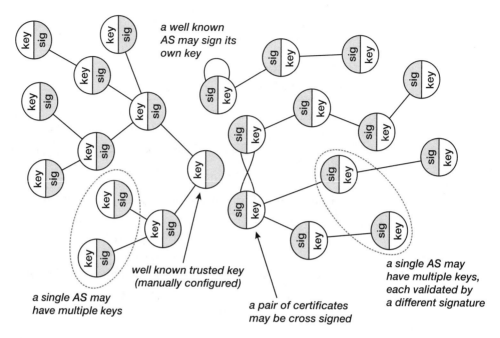

Figure 9.5
Interrelating EntityCerts through signatures.

- Any given autonomous system may have several outstanding keys, signed by the same or different validators.
- Outside agencies, such as well-known key signing authorities, may also participate as a well-known and trusted key signing authority as long as they have an autonomous system number.

Network operators may determine what level of trust they will have in any given key. For instance,

- Self-signed keys from certain entities may be trusted, while the self-signed keys of other entities are not trusted.
- Some keys may be manually trusted and configured on the device
- Some entities may be trusted to sign keys while others may not be.

The Directed Graph and the PolicyCert

Once a device has a set of valid public keys, one for each autonomous system operating in the internetwork, it can then use the information contained in the PolicyCerts advertised by each AS to build a directed graph of the existing interconnections in the internetwork. Each PolicyCert contains

- A list of the autonomous systems the advertising AS is attached to
- A set of policies the advertising autonomous system applies to the prefixes it originates, or requests receiving autonomous systems to apply to prefixes it advertises
- A signature created using the private key of the origination autonomous system

As each PolicyCert is received, the EntityCert database is searched for the public keys of the originating autonomous system, and the signature in the PolicyCert is validated against at least one of these public keys. Once the PolicyCert has been validated, the list of autonomous systems the advertiser is attached to can be used to build a directed graph of the topology of the internetwork. For instance, suppose we have the following valid PolicyCerts:

- AS65500: attached to 65501, 65502
- AS65501: attached to 65500, 65504, 65503
- AS65502: attached to 65500, 65504
- AS65503: attached to 65501, 65506
- AS65504: attached to 65501, 65507, 65506
- AS65505: attached to 65506, 65508
- AS65506: attached to 65503, 65505, 65504, 65507, 65509
- AS65507: attached to 65504, 65506
- AS65508: attached to 65505, 65509
- AS65509: attached to 65506, 65508

From this information, a directed graph can be built describing the entire topology of the internetwork and each possible valid path in the internetwork. For instance, starting from AS65500,

- AS65500 claims to be connected to 65501; 65501 also claims to be connected to 65500, so this path is valid.
- AS65500 claims to be connected to 65502; 65502 also claims to be connected to 65500, so this path is valid.

Using this sort of two way connectivity check at every point, the graph illustrated in Figure 9.6 can be built.

The PolicyCert also contains other information about the policies of the advertising autonomous system, such as the longest prefix the AS will ever advertise within a given range of prefixes, whether or not path checks should be done on prefixes received from this autonomous system, and whether or not second hop checks should be done.

The Address Block Database and the AuthCert

The AuthCert ties the originating autonomous system to the prefixes they advertise; it contains

- A range (or set of ranges) of addresses, within which this autonomous system may advertise prefixes
- The autonomous system of the entity authorized to advertise prefixes within these blocks of addresses
- The autonomous system of the entity validating this entity may advertise prefixes within these blocks of addresses
- A signature computed using the private key of the entity validating this autonomous system may advertise prefixes within these blocks of addresses
- A bit indicating whether or not this AuthCert was signed by the autonomous system authorized to assign these addresses, or some third party

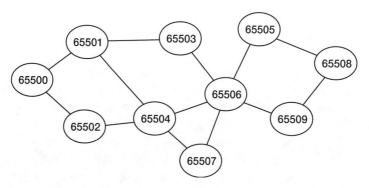

Figure 9.6
A simple graph built from PolicyCert information.

Blocks of addresses are carried within AuthCerts rather than actual prefixes to reduce the size of the database built from this information. Each valid AuthCert is placed in a local database or table of address ranges and the autonomous systems authorized to advertise prefixes within those address ranges.

An authorization tree may be built with the information contained within the AuthCerts; Figure 9.7 illustrates.

- The AuthCert allowing AS65500 to advertise 10.0.0.0/8 is signed by AS65500 itself; presumably AS65500 is well known to anyone who receives this AuthCert and thus can be trusted to sign their own AuthCert (as in the case of a well-known top-level service provider).
- The AuthCert allowing AS65501 to advertise 10.4.0.0/16 is signed by AS65500. Since the signer of the AuthCert is trusted to advertise the addresses within the 10.0.0.0/8 block, this AuthCert can be trusted.
- The AuthCert allowing AS65503 to advertise 10.4.1.0/24 is signed by AS65501. Since the signer of the AuthCert is trusted

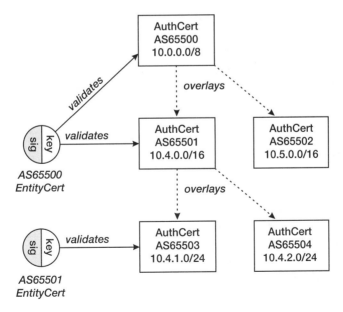

Figure 9.7
A tree of AuthCerts.

to advertise the addresses within the 10.4.0.0/16 block, this AuthCert can be trusted.

The only point at which this chain of AuthCerts is broken is where the originator of the AuthCert indicates the certificate is not signed by the authorizer, but rather the signature is from some third party or the certificate is self-signed. The receiver must determine its level of trust for any AuthCert not signed by the authorizer. For instance, a top-level well-known autonomous system, such as a tier 1 service provider, may be trusted to self-sign its certificates. If some "out of band" business arrangement exists between two autonomous systems, they may trust each other's self-signed AuthCerts as well.

Validating Received Routing Information

When a BGP speaker begins receiving BGP updates, it may validate the information in these updates using the information contained in the AuthCerts and PolicyCerts. Let's work with the small network illustrated in Figure 9.8, and set of certificates, and follow the process from the advertisement of the certificates to the validation of each piece of information contained in the updates carried in BGP.

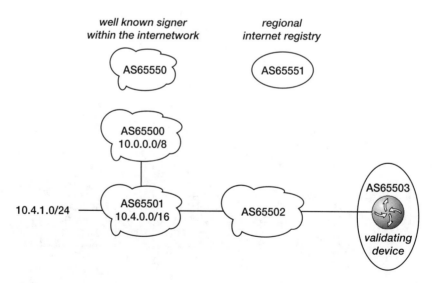

Figure 9.8
A simple network running soBGP.

In this network, we have

- The public key of AS65550, a well known entity within the internetwork
- An EntityCert from AS65500, signed by 65550
- An EntityCert from AS65501, signed by 65500
- An EntityCert from AS65502, signed by 65550
- An EntityCert from AS65551, signed by 65550
- An AuthCert authorizing AS65500 to advertise anything within 10.0.0.0/8, signed by AS65501
- An AuthCert authorizing AS65501 to advertise anything within 10.4.0.0/16, signed by AS65500
- PolicyCerts from AS65500, 65501, and 65502 describing their connections

From this set of certificates, given the certificate from AS65550 is already trusted, the validating device can validate each of the public keys available, building a database of each autonomous system within the internetwork and each of the public keys. These public keys can then be used to validate other received certificates. Figure 9.9 illustrates the relationships built using this information.

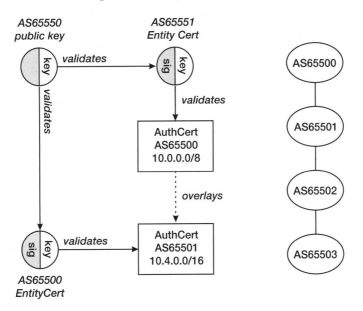

Figure 9.9
Certificate relationship.

- The manually configured well-known key validates the public keys of AS65551 and AS65500.
- AS65551's key validates the AuthCert authorizing AS65500 to advertise prefixes within the 10.0.0.0/8 block of addresses.
- AS65500's key validates the AuthCert authorizing AS65501 to advertise prefixes within the 10.4.0.0/16 block of addresses.
- The authority of AS65500 to allow AS65501 to advertise the 10.4.0.0/16 block of addresses can be checked as well. The next shorter length AuthCert overlapping the AuthCert for 10.4.0.0/16 is the 10.0.0.0/8 certificate. The 10.4.0.0/16 AuthCert is signed by the autonomous system authorized to advertise the 10.0.0.0/8 addresses, validating the 10.4.0.0/16 certificate as well.

If an update for the 10.4.1.0/24 network is received by a validating device in AS65503 with an AS Path of {65501, 65502}, it can be validated by

- The originating autonomous system can be checked against the database of validated AuthCerts to make certain the originator is authorized to advertise this destination. In this case, the originator is AS65501, which has been authorized to advertise prefixes within this address block 10.4.0.0/16.
- The AS Path contained in the update can be checked to ensure the peer from whom the update was received is known to have at least one valid path to the destination. In this case, the update is received from AS65502, which is connected to AS65501, the originator, as verified through the two-way connectivity check run over the connectivity information contained in the Policy Certs.

Route Validation and the Security Preference

Routes are not simply validated as good or bad within soBGP; there can be many levels of trust, depending on the types of validation possible on any given route received. Rather than simply marking a route as "bad," then, soBGP offers the concept of a *security preference,* which can be set on a route when it is validated. There is no security preference within the BGP protocol or the metrics used in the best path calculation; the local system administrator may choose to set the local preference, cost community, or some other metric on each route based on the authentication level available. The only caveat is, as with all other changes to the BGP decision algorithm, the algorithm used to set the security preference must be consistent throughout an autonomous system. For instance, one possible way of setting the security preference could be

- Set the security preference to 0 to indicate a neutral security preference.
- Examine the known validated AuthCerts, and determine if this range of addresses falls within the block of addresses described.
  - If the prefix falls within one of these blocks of addresses but the originating AS does not match the autonomous systems authorized to advertise this route, the route should be discarded.
  - If the prefix falls within one of these blocks of addresses, examine the policies advertised by the originating autonomous system for this block of addresses. If any of the policies indicate the route is invalid, discard it. For instance, an autonomous system may indicate that it will not advertise prefixes longer than 20 bits in length, so if this prefix has a length of 21 bits, the prefix should be discarded.
  - If the prefix falls within one of these blocks of addresses and the originating AS does match the one of the autonomous systems authorized to advertise this route, increase the security preference by 100.
- Examine the topology of the internetwork and compare it to the AS Path listed in the learned route.
  - If the AS Path contained in the route is known to be invalid (passes through an intersection between two autonomous systems known not to exist, based on the information contained in the directed graph), the route should be discarded.
  - If the second hop of the AS Path is not contained in the set of autonomous systems connected to the originating AS, the route should be discarded.
  - For each known valid intersection the AS Path passes through, increase the security preference by 10.

From this example, you can see the level of control over the trust for each route received is very flexible.

Propagating the Certificates

soBGP is transport agnostic; the certificates described above can be transported in any way possible, as long as the keys interlock in the ways described. However, there are two specific certificate transport mechanisms we will mention here. The first is a new BGP message type, the Security message type, defined in the soBGP extensions to BGP draft, which can carry various types of security information, including soBGP certificates.

The ability to exchange BGP Security messages and when those messages should be exchanged are both negotiated at session startup. Normal routing information may be exchanged first, after which Security messages are exchanged, or Security information may be exchanged, followed by routing information. This allows the network to converge first, before updates are validated; security can be preferred over faster convergence times, or faster convergence times can be preferred over security.

Another option for obtaining the certificates necessary is to gather them from well-known http servers. AuthCerts have the capability of carrying a uniform resource locator where the EntityCert containing the public key, which may be used to validate the AuthCert, can be obtained. The inherent danger in using servers to hold these certificates is, though, that the server can only be reached through routing, and the routing can only be validated using the information contained on the servers. This sort of mutual dependency may be acceptable for some small number of certificates within the system, or within an autonomous system when validating the routing between autonomous systems, but it does rule out using centralized servers for validating routing information on a large scale.

It's important to note the order of processing—security information first, or routing information first—is under local administrative control. A system administrator may determine that high-speed convergence is more important than forwarding a few packets down an invalid route, so they can set the routers to install routes, then determine the security preference for each route, and withdraw or change routes as needed. On the other hand, the system administrator may determine that security is of paramount concern and not allow any route to be accepted until it is validated and a security preference set.

Partial Deployment of soBGP

Is it possible to gain some value by partially deploying soBGP? For instance, in Figure 9.10, AS65500 and AS65503 would like to validate the routing information between their autonomous systems, although AS65501 and AS65502 are not running soBGP.

Assume AS65500 and AS65503 have some way to exchange certificates; they could, for instance, set up a multihop eBGP connection passing through AS65501 and AS65502 directly connecting their autonomous systems just for certificate exchange, or they may pass their certificates to one another using some other method, such as a physically mailed disk. Assume these two autonomous systems have some sort of a business relationship allowing them to trust each other; AS65503 may be willing to allow AS65500 to sign its certificates or to trust AS65500's certificates as valid if received through some specific means.

With these two assumptions in place, some trust model may be set up in which soBGP can be used to validate the routing information between the two autonomous systems. AS65500 and AS65503 could begin by exchanging the following certificates:

- An EntityCert validating AS65500's public key, self-signed, signed by some trusted third party, or signed using AS65503's private key
- An EntityCert validating AS65503's public key, self-signed, signed by some trusted third party, or signed using AS65500's private key
- An AuthCert authorizing AS65500 to advertise 10.1.0.0/16, self-signed, or signed by some trusted third party

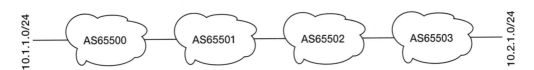

Figure 9.10
Can partial deployment of soBGP help here?

- An AuthCert authorizing AS65503 to advertise 10.2.0.0/16, self-signed, or signed by some trusted third party
- A PolicyCert originated by AS65500 describing AS65500's connection to AS65501
- A PolicyCert originated by AS65503 describing AS65503's connection to AS65502

When AS65503 receives an update from AS65502 for the 10.1.1.0/24 network, it can

- Validate that the prefix is being advertised by an autonomous system that is authorized to advertise the prefix; in this case AS65500.
- Validate that the second hop of the AS Path passes through an autonomous system the originator claims to be connected to. This validates the second AS Path hop, AS65501.

Since AS65503 should be able to trust the path through AS65502, it can validate or trust the path through all four autonomous systems listed in the AS Path. AS65503 cannot know, however, if any autonomous system inserted between AS65501 and AS65502 is valid or invalid. If AS65501 were to being running soBGP, however, the length of the AS Path that can be validated is increased by one.

Thus, soBGP can be incrementally deployed in a useful manner; each participating autonomous system increases the security of the routing system as a whole, but even partial information can be useful in ensuring the validity of the information in the system.

Edge-to-Edge Deployment of soBGP

The simplest soBGP deployment option is to deploy soBGP along the edges of each autonomous system, and exchange certificates through the BGP peering sessions. Figure 9.11 illustrates.

Each BGP speaker in the internetwork runs soBGP, building a full database of certificates, a web of EntityCerts, a directed graph of the internetwork topology, and a database of prefixes and the autonomous systems that are authorized to originate them.

Routes and certificates that are learned from an iBGP peer may be trusted, since the BGP speaker transmitting them should have validated

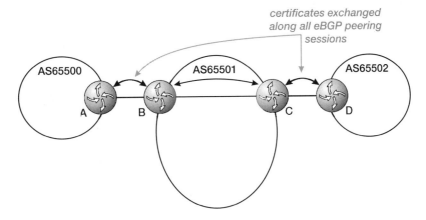

Figure 9.11
Edge-to-edge soBGP deployment.

the information in the certificate before advertising it to its iBGP peers. In other words, an EntityCert learned by C from B may be able to be trusted as valid without the signature on the EntityCert being validated.

> Within the BGP Security message negotiation process, there is an exchange to confirm this trust. C can state, during this negotiation phase, that B should not send any certificates that are not valid, and B can state that it will not send C any certificates that are not valid. If both of these signals are present, then C can trust all certificates transmitted from B as already validated and can place them immediately in its local databases.

This deployment model requires that each edge router validate any certificates received, which means that the processing required to validate certificates is done on the edge routers. If the edge routers are not capable of supporting this processing or the network administrators do not want them to spend their time doing this processing, it's also possible to offload the processing of validating certificates to a server within the autonomous system and allow the routers at the edge to interact with this server. Figure 9.12 illustrates.

In this configuration, routers B and C simply pass through any certificate they learn; they do not validate certificates or hold databases

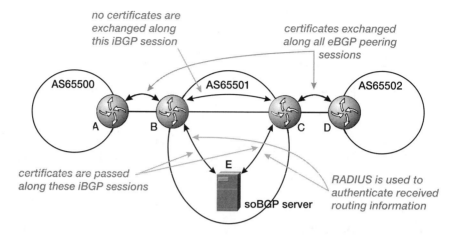

Figure 9.12
Edge-to-edge soBGP deployment using a central soBGP server within the autonomous system.

locally at all. To better understand how this works, let's examine how a certificate transmitted by router A is handled.

- Router A advertises some certificate to B using the BGP Security message type.
- Router B forwards this certificate to each of its iBGP peers with which it is exchanging BGP Security messages. This only includes E, the soBGP server.
- The soBGP server, E, receives this certificate, validates it, and adjusts its local databases as required. E will then advertise this certificate to router C.
- Router C, when it receives this certificate, will advertise it to each of its eBGP peers with which it is exchanging BGP Security messages. This includes router D.

Now, assume router A advertises some prefix to B; how would router B know this prefix is valid?

- Router A advertises some routing information to B.
- Router B queries E, the soBGP server, using RADIUS.

- The soBGP server then replies, using RADIUS, and indicates the preference level of this routing information.

Server to Server Deployment of soBGP

If two autonomous systems, both using centralized soBGP servers, are peering, do they need to actually exchange BGP Security messages along their edge? No; they could pass BGP Security messages directly between their security servers, as Figure 9.13 illustrates.

Again, let's follow the flow of certificates through the internetwork.

- Certificates are exchanged between the soBGP servers A and D directly through an eBGP multihop session.
- Certificates received by D are validated and forwarded to router E.
- Router E, on receiving these certificates, advertises them to its eBGP peer, F, without validating them in any way.

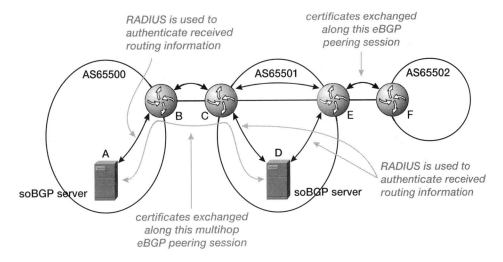

Figure 9.13
Server-to-server certificate exchange.

The process of validating routing information is similar to the centralized server model described previously:

- When router B receives advertised routes, it will use RADIUS to communicate with the local soBGP server, A, which will provide a route preference for each route received.
- When routers C and E receive advertised routes, they will use RADIUS to communicate with the local soBGP server, D, which will provide a route preference for each route received.

Extending the concept of server to server certificate exchange, you could imagine certificate services, where a network may connect to a service which provides an eBGP multihop session through which all known certificates are transmitted. Figure 9.14 illustrates a certificate service.

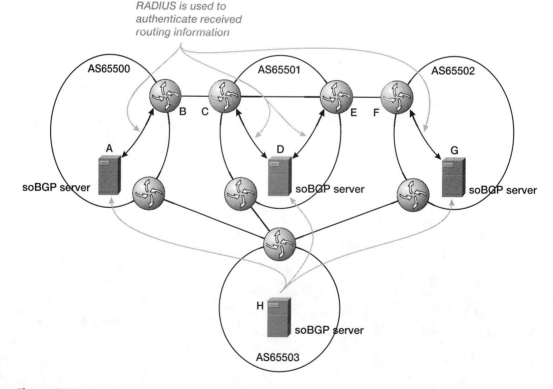

Figure 9.14
Using eBGP multihop sessions to a third party certificate service.

Key Rollover and Certificate Revocation in soBGP

One of the major issues confronting any security system is allowing participants in the system to change keys periodically, and allowing the revocation of certificates once they have been advertised. This is made more difficult in a routing system; in most systems, an interruption in the flow of data may be acceptable, while keys are changed, and so on. But in a routing system, disruptions because of key changes are unacceptable; there simply is no way to have a "flag day" in a very large scale routing system when the keys can be changed, and the certificates are replaced to reflect these new keys.

To facilitate key changes and the revocation of certificates, soBGP has a set of interlocking serial numbers within each certificate and a temporary certificate revocation list AuthCerts. First, let's review the fields related to serial numbers included in each certificate and how they work in relation to each other.

- Each EntityCert has a serial number.
- Each EntityCert has a number indicating the lowest valid serial number for all other EntityCerts from this autonomous system.

These two serial numbers work together to allow an autonomous system to have more than one outstanding EntityCert at any time, and thus more than one valid public key that can be used for validating other certificates it issues. For any autonomous system, the valid EntityCert with the highest serial number defines the valid serial number range for the remaining EntityCerts available. Any EntityCert with a serial number lower than the lowest valid serial number in the EntityCert with the highest serial number should be discarded. Figure 9.15 illustrates.

- Assume the autonomous system has created EntityCert A, and distributed it, with the serial number 1272.

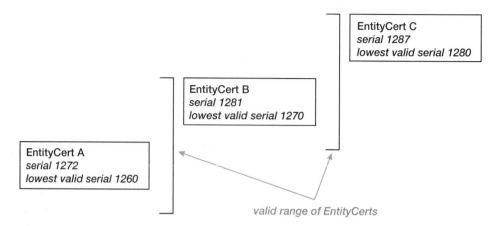

Figure 9.15
Interaction between the EntityCert's serial number and the lowest valid serial number.

- When EntityCert B is issued and validated, it now defines the range of acceptable EntityCerts for this autonomous system. The lowest acceptable EntityCert serial number is 1270, and EntityCert A's serial number is 1272, so EntityCert A is still valid for this autonomous system.

- When EntityCert C is issues and validated, it again defines the range of acceptable EntityCert serial numbers for this autonomous system. The lowest acceptable EntityCert serial number is 1280, so EntityCert B is still valid. However, EntityCert A has a serial number lower than the current lowest acceptable serial number, so it is discarded.

Now let's look at how the serial numbers in the AuthCert interlock with the information carried in the PolicyCert and the EntityCert:

- Each PolicyCert has a serial number. The valid PolicyCert with the highest serial issued by any given autonomous system is considered valid, so there can only be one valid PolicyCert per autonomous system at any time.

- Each AuthCert has a serial number.
- Each EntityCert has a start and end valid AuthCert serial number, which defines the range of valid AuthCerts.
- Each PolicyCert has a list of revoked AuthCert serial numbers.

The serial numbers carried in the AuthCert, the start and end AuthCert serial numbers carried in the EntityCert, and the list of revoked AuthCerts carried in the PolicyCert allow the list of valid AuthCerts advertised by a given autonomous system to be closely regulated; Figure 9.16 illustrates the interlocking nature of these three pieces of information.

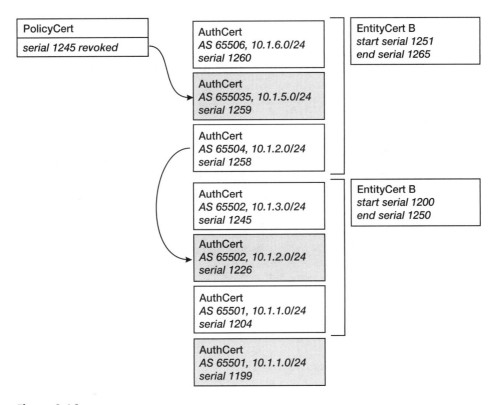

Figure 9.16
The relationship between the AuthCert serial numbers, and the information carried in the other certificates.

- The public key in EntityCert A is used to validate the AuthCerts with the serial numbers 1204, 1226, and 1245, while the public key in EntityCert B is used to validate the AuthCerts with the serial numbers 1258, 1259, and 1260.
- AuthCert serial 1199 is not validated, and thus should be discarded, since there is no EntityCert with a serial number range to cover it.
- AuthCert serial 1245 has been revoked, so it is no longer valid, and should be discarded.
- AuthCert serial 1258 authenticates the same block of addresses as AuthCert 1226; the one with the higher serial number is kept, and the older one discarded.

Now that we've examined the certificates and how they interlock, let's work through how an autonomous system can change their private/public key pair without impacting routing information in the internetwork. We begin with a simple set of keys, as illustrated in Figure 9.17.

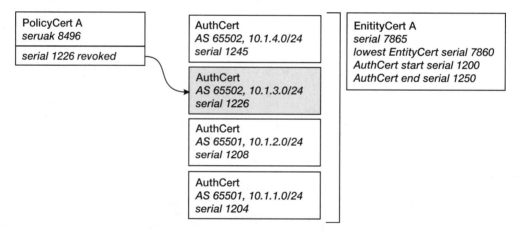

Figure 9.17
The certificates at the beginning of a key rollover.

NOTE WELL: Do not attempt anything of significant impact without first having at least two cups of a caffeinated beverage (unless prohibited by health or religious observence). You should also call your mother. The authors and contributors to this document don't feel anything technical will be gained from that conversation (unless your mother is very technical, a possiblity we do not wish to discount), but the conversation will get your mind working. And we all think getting your mind working and calling your mother are both really nice things to do.

The autonomous system has a single EntityCert and four AuthCerts that it has signed for other autonomous systems, allowing them to advertise various blocks of addresses. The autonomous system's PolicyCert has revoked one of those AuthCerts, serial number 1226. The first step in a key rollover is to issue a new EntityCert with the new public key, signed by some third party. Once this is done, a new set of AuthCerts is issued within the new EntityCert's serial number space, as illustrated in Figure 9.18.

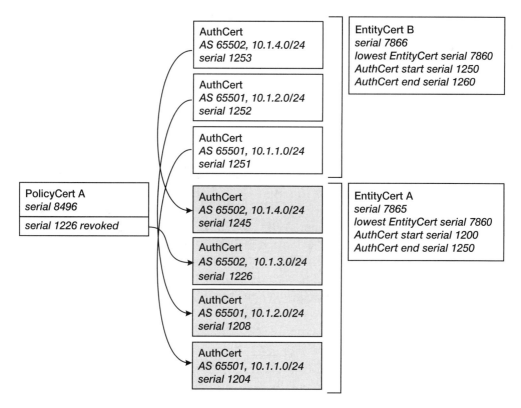

Figure 9.18
The certificates after issuing a new EntityCert.

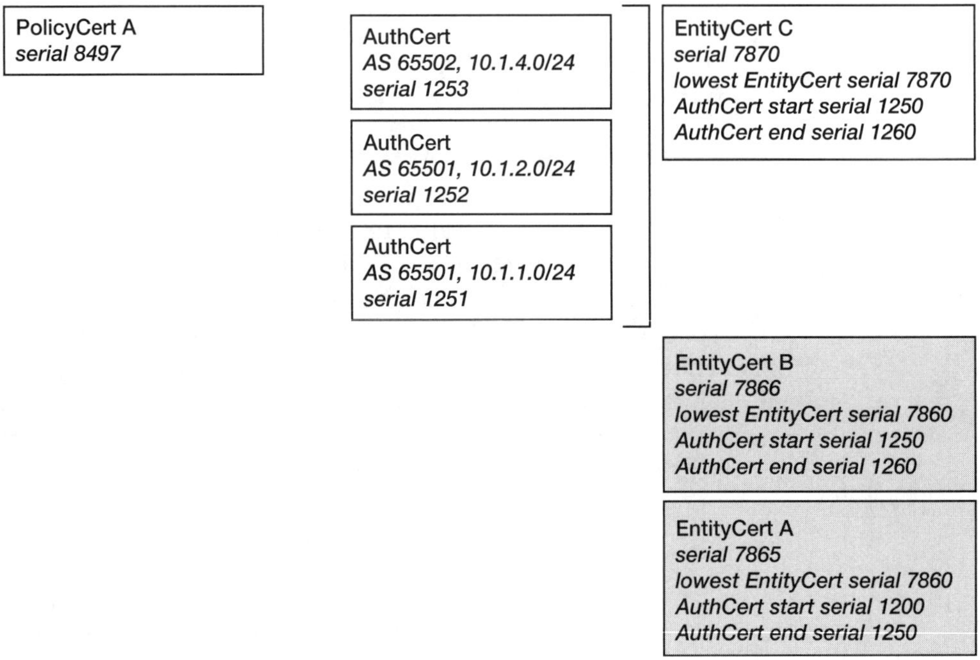

PolicyCert A
serial 8497

AuthCert
AS 65502, 10.1.4.0/24
serial 1253

AuthCert
AS 65501, 10.1.2.0/24
serial 1252

AuthCert
AS 65501, 10.1.1.0/24
serial 1251

EntityCert C
serial 7870
lowest EntityCert serial 7870
AuthCert start serial 1250
AuthCert end serial 1260

EntityCert B
serial 7866
lowest EntityCert serial 7860
AuthCert start serial 1250
AuthCert end serial 1260

EntityCert A
serial 7865
lowest EntityCert serial 7860
AuthCert start serial 1200
AuthCert end serial 1250

Figure 9.19
The final stage of key rollover.

Now that EntityCert B has been issued and new AuthCerts have been issued, all the AuthCerts being validated by EntityCert A are discarded. Each of them is either revoked through the PolicyCert or replaced with an AuthCert of a newer serial number. Finally, a new EntityCert is issued using the same public/private key pair as EntityCert B, but with a lowest EntityCert serial number range invalidating all other EntityCerts. A new PolicyCert is issued, as well, with an empty revocation list. Figure 9.19 illustrates this final phase, with the key rollover completed.

soBGP Summary

From the previous sections covering soBGP, you can see soBGP can deployed incrementally and in a variety of configurations. It provides protection against spoofed and modified paths, allowing attackers to only modify the path in ways that leave the path valid. Beyond these attributes, soBGP has several other important attributes:

- Private keys are well protected; they are not configured in devices, nor are they transported through the network in any way.
- The trust model is decentralized, so there is no single point of failure or single point of attack to gain control of the security system.
- The BGP protocol itself is not changed, in terms of the decision process, update processing, or even packet formats. Any and all existing optimizations within the BGP protocol would work within soBGP as well.
- The ability to expand the types of policies advertised by, and preferred by, the originator of any autonomous system is provided.
- The authority of any given autonomous system to advertise any given prefix can be validated.

Secure BGP

Secure BGP, S-BGP, is another proposal, based on the analysis of BGP security vulnerabilities described in *BGP Security Vulnerabilities Analysis,* by Sandra Murphy, and the protection methods described in *BGP Security Protections,* also by Sandra Murphy. Essentially, S-BGP secures the information carried in BGP through the use of private key signatures created at each edge between autonomous systems, which can then be verified using the public key of each autonomous system. Figure 9.20 illustrates the process of advertising a prefix through S-BGP.

- When AS65500 requests a prefix from the Regional Internet Registry, it also requests a certificate, signed with the Registry's private key. This certificate contains the originating AS, 65500, and the prefix, 10.1.1.0/24, signed using the Registry's private key.
- AS65500, at the edge with AS65501, adds AS65501 as the autonomous system it is authorizing to advertise this prefix and signs the resulting data set with its private key.
- AS65501, at its edge with AS65502, adds AS65502 as the destination it is authorizing to advertise this prefix and signs the resulting data set with its private key.

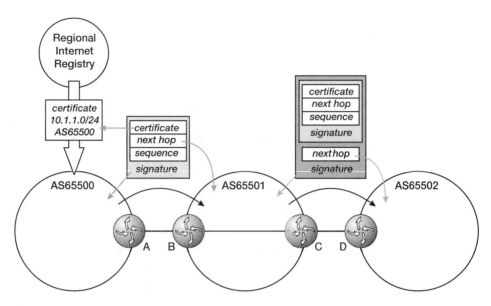

Figure 9.20
S-BGP route advertisement.

Thus, S-BGP relies on the principle that each autonomous system must authorize its neighboring autonomous systems to advertise a prefix, and each autonomous system must authorize any given prefix from the autonomous system from which it receives the prefix. The chain of signatures may be validated using the public key of each autonomous system found in the path, allowing the AS Path to be validated against tampering in route. These signatures are carried in a new attribute, added to the information carried inside the BGP packet.

The mechanisms used to distribute the public keys between autonomous and the method of distributing private keys to each device at the edge of the network (which must sign each update advertised) are beyond the scope of the S-BGP drafts themselves. The basic semantic of S-BGP is that including AS65501 in the signed portion of the update, AS65500 is authorizing AS65501 to readvertise the 10.1.1.0/24 prefix to its peers, whoever those peers might be.

Cryptographic Optimizations

Since there is a great deal of cryptographic work that must be done at each edge, verifying a number of signatures, and signing a large number of outbound updates, S-BGP provides several optimizations:

- Each device may choose to receive all prefixes and run the best path algorithm over them before validating any of the signatures. Only those paths that are actually installed in the local routing table, and readvertised to BGP peers, need to be validated.

- Each device may cache the results of previous cryptographic operations; this allows the device to verify a signature against an older computation rather than being forced to revalidate the signature on each received route.

- Each device should probably have some form of cryptographic equipment installed, which will perform these operations in specialized hardware, and protect the private key, which is distributed among all the devices at the edge of the network, from being compromised.

One other optimization for cryptographic operations, which is also impacts the number of updates a BGP speaker must build, is the ability to add more than one target autonomous system to the certificate before it is advertised. Figure 9.21 illustrates.

Router C needs to transmit an update to three different peers, routers D, E, and F, each in a different autonomous system. It could build three different updates, one for each peer, but this would require signing the certificate three separate times, resulting in a different signature on each certificate. Instead, router C can place three target autonomous systems in the certificate, sign it, and send the same certificate to routers D, E, and F. This saves cryptographic work on router C, and allows router C to send the same update to all three peers rather than being forced to build a separate update for each peer.

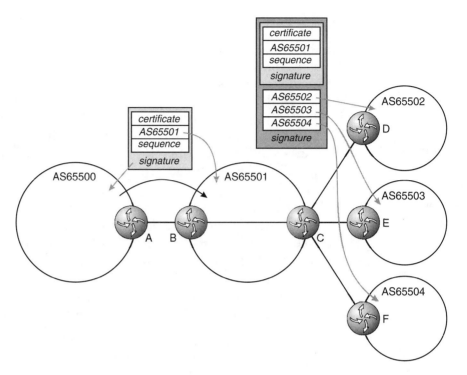

Figure 9.21
Multiple target or authorized autonomous systems in the certificate.

Review Questions

1. Are MD5 keys periodically transmitted over the link between two BGP peers? How are keys managed when using MD5 to authenticate a session between two BGP speakers?

2. At what level within the BGP packets is the MD5 authentication inserted? Is it an IP option, a TCP option, or a BGP option?

3. What type of protection does the BTSH security hack provide?

4. What types of attacks do reverse path forwarding checks prevent?

5. What three types of certificates does soBGP use to validate the information carried within the BGP protocol?

6. What two pieces of information does the EntityCert tie together?

7. What three pieces of information does the PolicyCert tie together?

8. What type of check is used in building soBGP's directed graph to prevent the advertising of false connectivity information?

9. What two pieces of information does an AuthCert tie together?

10. What is the security preference used for in soBGP?

11. How are security certificates transported in soBGP?

12. Must soBGP processing be done on every edge device within an autonomous system?

13. Are private keys transmitted through the network, or configured on any edge device, when running soBGP?

14. What semantic does S-BGP rely on to provide authorization?

15. How does S-BGP optimize for the case where there are multiple peers, in different autonomous systems, an update needs to be transmitted to?

10

Deploying BGP/MPLS Layer-3 VPNs

There is a great deal of interest in deploying virtual private networks within service provider networks to provide virtual circuits to a large-scale enterprise network. Conceptually, using virtual private networks (VPNs) to interconnect geographically separated networks can save money, since the service provider's network is shared among many customers, and at the same time allow the service provider to take on some of the routing and network design complexity rather than forcing the enterprise customer to work on these things.

In this chapter, we'll look at deploying layer-3 MPLS VPNs using BGP to signal tunnel setup and carry the customer's routing information through the VPN. We'll begin by discussing fundamental concepts of layer-3 VPNs, introducing and explaining the operation of the BGP-based MPLS approach, and then delve into different deployment topologies, explaining how the control and data planes operate. Finally, we advanced uses for MPLS VPNs, such as carrier's carrier topologies.

What Is a Virtual Private Network?

The term virtual private network (VPN) is widely used; in fact, it's so widely used, it means different things to different people. Let's look at the three words involved:

- *Virtual* indicates the network topology isn't tied to a physical topology but rather a logical topology which is defined through a physical network. The network equipment used for forwarding traffic along a virtual network isn't owned or operated by the end user but rather by some service provider.

- *Private* indicates that the security, addressing, and routing of the network (or logical topology) are completely independent of the network security, addressing, and routing of other networks running across the same physical topology.

- A *network* is nothing but a system interconnecting other systems to allow data to be exchanged between those systems. A network isn't necessarily in one physical location but rather can be dispersed geographically.

In this chapter, a VPN is a set of sites able to communicate with each other via one or more service provider networks while maintaining their own set of policies (including quality of service), security, addressing, and routing without regard to the physical topology of the service provider's network or other customers using the same physical network to transit traffic.

Overlay and Peer-to-Peer VPNs

From an implementation perspective, VPNs can be classified into *overlay* and *peer-to-peer* VPNs. From a connectivity perspective, VPNs can be classified into intranet and extranet VPNs. Lets look closer at these classifications.

The Overlay Model

In a VPN based on *overlay model,* the service provider provisions a set of emulated leased lines called virtual circuits (VCs), and the customer establishes router-to-router communications between its sites over these VCs. The service provider neither has knowledge of the customer's network nor participates in routing with the customer; the VPN is simply a layer-2 circuit from the customer's point of view.

The service provider backbone may have many such VPNs running across the same physical circuits and devices, but each customer's traffic appears to be traveling across a completely separate layer-2 infrastructure from the customer's point of view. In Figure 10.1, customer sites A, C, and E build neighbor adjacencies with one another via the VPN while B, D, F, and G form neighbor adjacencies with one another over another VPN, both overlaid on an SP network infrastructure.

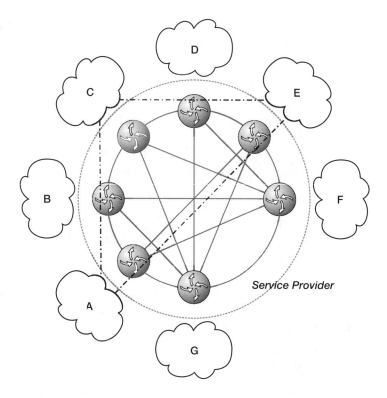

Figure 10.1
An overlay model VPN.

Overlay VPN networks can be implemented with a number of switched WAN layer-2 technologies, such as frame relay or ATM. Recently, IP-over-IP tunneling methods, like Generic Route Encapsulation (GRE) and IPSec encryption, have been used to implement VPNs based on the overlay model.

The Peer-to-Peer Model

In a VPN based on peer-to-peer model, sites are interconnected via a service provider in the same way they are interconnected in an overlay model, but rather than the customer running routing protocols over the VPN VCs, the customer actually injects their routing information into the service provider's routing table. The service then provider takes responsibility for conveying the customer's routing information from one customer site to another, providing layer-3 connectivity between them, as Figure 10.2 illustrates.

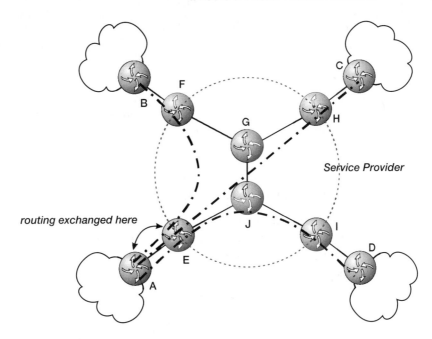

Figure 10.2
A peer-to-peer VPN.

In this network, rather than router A peering direction with routers B, C, and D to receive routing information from them, it only peers with router E. Router A can inject routing information learned from the site it's attached to into the ISP's routing tables at router E. Information injected by router A is then pulled from the ISP's routing table at F, H, and I, and given to routers B, C, and D, at the other customer sites.

Peer-to-peer VPN networks can be implemented via shared or dedicated routers on the service provider end, with access control lists controlling the routing information advertised toward the customer. BGP/MPLS-based VPNs fall into the peer-to-peer VPN category.

Which Model Is Best?

There are advantages and disadvantages to VPN networks built based on either of these two models. Overlay VPN networks place the burden of routing on the customer, so they can be difficult to manage if the number of sites increases—especially in the case where there is a need to connect from a site to every other site (full mesh intersite connections are required). Further, the service provider is now just a layer-2 provider and isn't able to add much value to the customer's network.

Peer-to-peer VPN networks only require the customer to peer with the service provider—regardless of how many sites are interconnected using the VPN, the customer only has to manage one peering session for each site. The tradeoff is that the service provider has to now manage multiple routing clouds, thus affecting scalability of the service provider's infrastructure. In the next section we will focus on BGP/MPLS-based VPNs and see its advantages over other VPN solutions.

Intranet and Extranet VPNs

If a VPN is only used to interconnect a single company's sites, it's considered an intranet VPN. For instance, in Figure 10.2, if routers A, B, C, and D are all connected to a single customer's sites, the VPN interconnecting them across the service provider's network would be considered an intranet VPN. In an intranet VPN, all the sites connected to the VPN are under the administrative control of a single entity, such as a company or government agency. An intracnet VPN, then, is analgous to a single autonomous system in BGP.

An extranet VPN, on the other hand, interconnects multiple networks. Extranet VPNs can be used to provide private connectivity between two autonomous systems—for instance, two partnering companies may want to share inventory information between their sales systems. They could do this by setting up an extranet VPN rather than purchasing a private link of some type.

Other Terms

Other terms you will see on a regular basis when discussing MPLS/BGP VPNs include the following:

- A *site* is a collection of systems that can access each other without any external provider connectivity.
- A *customer edge* (CE) router is the customer owned and managed router that connects to the service provider's network. Routers A, B, C, and D in Figure 10.2 are CE routers.
- A *provider edge* (PE) router is the service provider owned and managed router connected to the customer's network. Routers E, F, H and I are PE routers in Figure 10.2.

- Routers within the service provider's network, providing connectivity between the PE routers, are called *provider* (P) routers, such as routers G and J in Figure 10.2.

The BGP/MPLS-Based VPN

In the peer-to-peer model, service providers are responsible for propagating routing information between the customer's sites, so a service provider who provides peer-to-peer VPNs for multiple customers will end up participating in routing for every one of those customers. This means that

- There is a heavy burden on the service provider's routers to maintain multiple routing and forwarding tables, one for each customer using a peer-to-peer VPN across the service provider's network.
- Each customer may use the same address space (in fact, many probably will, since most large networks are addressed out of one of the private, or nonroutable, IP address spaces).

BGP/MPLS-based VPNs solve these two problems and provide other advantages over other traditional peer-to-peer model–based VPN solutions. Figure 10.3 shows a VPN service provider network and its connectivity to its customers.

The following lists some of its salient features.

- The BGP/MPLS-based VPN defines the administrative boundary between the customer and service provider networks. Each customer site is modeled as a separate autonomous system, so the customer's interior routing protocol runs independently at each site. This means the customer can actually run different routing protocols at each site. The service provider's PE routers will learn routing information from the customer's sites by forming adjacencies with the CEs at each customer site.
- An address conversion scheme is used to make every customer VPN route unique within the service provider's network, allowing VPN customers to have a common addressing scheme.

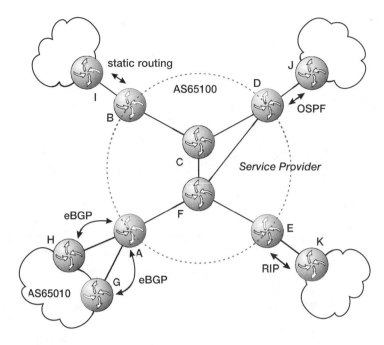

Figure 10.3
An MPLS/VPN network.

- Multiple routing and forwarding tables are supported on each PE router, maintaining separation between different customer's routing information.
- It employs BGP as a signaling protocol to setup of VPN connectivity among the customer's sites.
- It employs hierarchical MPLS to keep the service provider core free of all customer VPN routing information.
- The level of security it provides to VPN customers is equivalent to that provided by overlay VCs based on frame relay or ATM networks.

You can be see BGP/MPLS-based VPNs offer many advantages over other commonly available VPNs. Customers generally prefer VPNs built using BGP/MPLS techniques because such techniques can simplify their networks and connectivity requirements, directly impacting their operational expenses. The service provider, on the other hand, adds value to its customer's networks not only through providing a simpler solution for its customers but also in possible gains through the deployment of traffic engineering, fast reroute, and other technologies.

CE to PE routing

One of the critical components in the BGP/MPLS architecture is the PE router; it must learn routes through various routing protocols from the customer site CE and provide routing information back to the customer site CE router through those same routing protocols. Various customer side routing protocols need to be supported, such as eBGP, RIPv2, OSPF, IS-IS, EIGRP, and even static routes, making the PE's job more complex, and some extensions to existing routing protocols are required to provide the features required for the protocol to work in this environment.

- Using static routes is simple; the CE is configured with the list of routes reachable via the PE, and the PE router is configured with the list of routes reachable via the CE.
- BGP is the protocol used in today's Internet for exchanging routing information across administrative boundaries. If a customer is already using BGP in his network, it makes more sense to use the same protocol also to exchange routing information with their VPN service provider. Note that eBGP is used in this role, rather than iBGP, so the customer's and service provider's networks are in two different autonomous systems.
- OSPF, RIPv2, EIGRP, and IS-IS are all widely deployed routing protocols. From a customer's perspective, it is beneficial to have very little or no extra routing requirement as imposed by the VPN service provider. As long as the PE can exchange routing information through one of these protocols, and the customer and service provider have software installed that supports the features required for the protocol to work in this environment, the customer can simply continue using the protocol and feature set they are accustomed to in their network.

Using any of these protocols, a CE router at a local customer site advertises its routing information to the locally attached PE router. The PE router then takes care of propagating routing information learned from the customer's CE through the service provider's network and thus to the relevant remote PE router(s) in the service provider's network. The remote PE learns this routing information through the service provider's network, and then advertises the routing information to the remote CE router. Thus, routing information between two customer sites of a VPN are exchanged and the two sites will be able to access one another over the service provider network.

> The extensions to routing protocols we've mentioned here revolve around preventing loops in the BGP/MPLS environment. We'll discuss these extensions in later parts of these chapters and provide some information on how they are used.

Supporting Overlapping Addresses

In our description of BGP/MPLS VPNs, we stated that they can support multiple customers with overlapping address spaces; why is this important, and how does it work? Most large network administrators use private, or nonroutable, address space from the ranges specified in RFC 1918, 10.0.0.0/8, 172.16.0.0/19, and 192.168.0.0/16. Typically, these addresses are used for two reasons:

- They prevent hosts outside the network from reaching internal addresses without first passing through a network address translator, which provides for security choke points along the edge of the network.
- They are easy to allocate and manage since they are large address spaces and don't require allocation or management through some outside agency, such as an Internet addressing authority.

When an enterprise network addressed using private addressing connects sites using a BGP/MPLS VPN through a service provider, it will advertise those private addresses into the service provider's routing tables, expecting them to be communicated to the customer's other sites. It's possible for the service provider to learn the same private address space from more than one VPN customer network, each of which needs to be routed differently.

Once a PE router learns a set of reachable destinations from a customer's CE router, it should distribute that routing information to re-

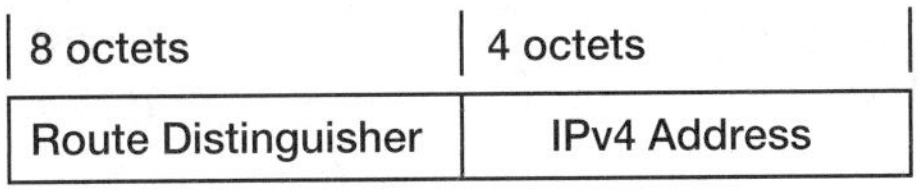

8 octets	4 octets	
Route Distinguisher	IPv4 Address	

Figure 10.4
VPN-IPv4 address format.

mote PE routers, but it needs to make certain there is no overlap between this customer's address space and any other customer's address space. Rather than requiring the customer to translate its addresses or requiring the service provider to assign private addresses to each customer, BGP/MPLS VPNs add an additional identifier to each route received so BGP can tell the difference between routes received from two customers, even if the prefixes are the same.

The BGP/MPLS-based VPN solution prepends the customer's IP address with a 64-bit quantity called "route distinguisher" (RD), creating a VPN-IPv4 address that will be unique no matter what the actual prefix learned from the CE is. BGP treats each unique IP address/RD pair as a different prefix, inserting each one in the routing table, and forwarding each one on to its peers. The minimum length of a VPN-IPv4 address is 8 octets (8 octets of RD + default) and the maximum length is 12 octets (8 octets of RD + 4 octets of IPv4 address). Figure 10.4 shows the format of VPN-IPv4 address.

RDs are structured so service providers can administer their own numbering space without conflicting with other service provider assignments. Figure 10.5 shows how the 8 octets of RD are organized.

The value of the Type field determines how the administrator and assigned fields are interpreted. At the time of this writing, only two types are supported by vendors, and type 0 is deployed predominantly.

- Type 0
  - Administrator Field: 2 octets.
  - Assigned Number Field: 4 octets

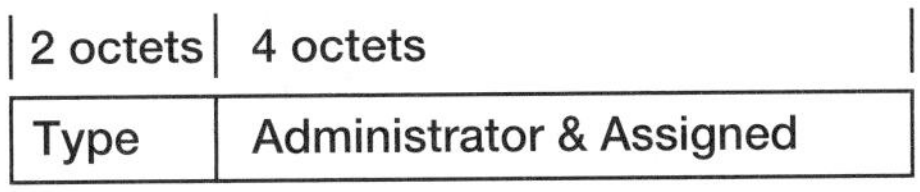

2 octets	4 octets	
Type	Administrator & Assigned	

Figure 10.5
The structure of a route distinguisher.

The Administrator field is the IANA assigned public Autonomous System Number (AS). The Assigned Number field is a number from a numbering space administered by the service provider (or enterprise) to which IANA has assigned that AS. The type 1 RD is structured using the same fields but with different lengths.

- Type 1
  - Administrator field: 4 octets
  - Assigned Number field: 2 octets

The Administrator field is the IANA assigned public IPv4 address. The Assigned Number field is a number from the numbering space administered by the enterprise to which IANA has assigned that IPv4 address.

The RD is used to make an IP address unique; it has no influence on how sites are interconnected to form a VPN. The distribution of VPN-IPv4 addresses is not governed by the RD. One may choose to associate each site with a unique RD even though all the sites belong to the same Intranet VPN. On the other hand, a single RD can be used for all the sites of a Intranet VPN.

In Figure 10.6, customer 1's two sites form VPN-1 while customer 2's two sites form VPN-2.

Let's also assume that the sites use private addresses in their network and they wish to advertise them in their respective VPNs. Each PE on which a customer is connected to would be configured with a set of virtual routing and forwarding (VRF) tables—which will be explained in the following section—and each VRF would be configured with the RD. The <cust-1, site-1> is connected to PE router A, and the corresponding VRF on router A has been assigned the RD of 100:2. Similarly, other customer sites are connected to other PEs in the VPN service provider network. The <cust-1, site-1> wants to advertise 10.0.0.0/24 to other sites in VPN-1. Similarly, <cust-2, site-1> wants to advertise 10.0.0.0/24 to other sites in VPN-2.

The RD router A attaches to routes it has learned from router F, 65100:2, is interpreted as a Type 0, with an Administrator field of 65100, and Assigned Number field of 2. The Administrator field value is the service provider's IANA assigned public autonomous system number, and the Assigned Number field value is a 32-bit number assigned and managed by the service provider.

When router F in (customer 1, site 1) advertises 10.0.0.0/24, router A learns the IPv4 unicast prefix and converts it into the VPN-IPv4

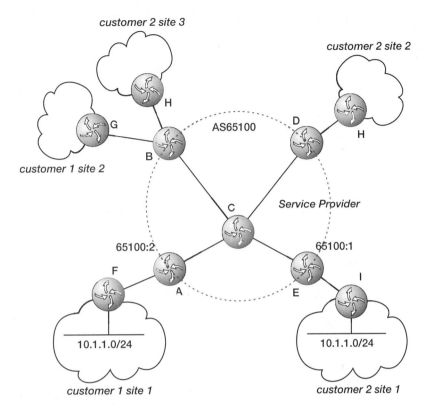

Figure 10.6
A BGP/MPLS network illustrating the use of the RD.

address 65100:2::10.0.0.0/24. Similarly, the PE router E converts the 10.1.1.0/24 prefix it learned from (customer 2, site 2) into VPN-IPv4 address 65100:1::10.0.0.0/24. Within the service provider network, the two VPN-IPv4 address are unique, even though the IPv4 addresses within them are not. Similarly, router B, upon receiving the VPN-IPv4 address 65100:2:10.0.0.0/24 through BGP, will convert the address from the VPN-IPv4 format to the IPv4 formatted 10.1.1.0/24 for local forwarding of traffic to and from router G.

> BGP/MPLS VPNs allow a pair of sites within an enterprise to communicate with one another regardless of their addressing scheme. It doesn't allow the enterprise using private addresses to communicate outside their network onto the Internet—for this, some sort of network address translator (NAT) is still required.

Multiple Routing and Forwarding Tables

In many cases, the PE router may connect to multiple customer sites—such as router B, which connects to router G in (customer 1, site 2), and router H in (customer 2, site 3). How can the PE keep the routes it has learned from different customers from being mixed up and forward the right traffic to the right customer site? By using multiple routing and forwarding tables. Each separate routing and forwarding table pair are called a *virtual routing and forwarding* instance, or a VRF. Multiple VRFs reside on the same router, so there is a logical separation and a logical link between these VRFs. Addresses stored in VRFs are IPv4; routing information present in the VRFs is used to forward of VPN traffic.

Each customer site, connected through a CE to a PE, is associated with a singe VRF on the PE. For instance, router G in (customer 1, site 2) will have an associated VRF on router B. Any routes received on the interface that connects to router G will be installed in that VRF, and any traffic received from the interface connecting to router G will be forwarded based on that VRF. In the same way, router H is associated with a separate VRF at router B, containing routing information received from router H through some interior gateway protocol, or through static configuration.

Routes learned from the CE are tagged using an RD, transmitted through iBGP to other PEs as VPN-IPv4 routes, such as router A. This is called *exporting* the route from the IGP into the service provider's BGP (since you are exporting the routes from the VRF). Some other PE, say router A, where the RD, along with other configured policies, is used to determine which VRF the route should be installed in on the PE, and the routes are installed as standard IPv4 routes in the correct VRF. This operation is called *importing* the routes (since the routes are being imported into a VRF). We will explain importing and exporting routes in more detail later in this chapter.

BGP as the Signaling Protocol

We probably don't need to discuss how widespread BGP deployment is in the Internet today—BGP is the routing protocol that connects the routing domains making up the Internet. Because of this wide deployment, BGP is the ideal protocol to distribute VPN information within (or between) autonomous systems. In this section, we'll discuss how iBGP is used to distribute VPN information imported from VRFs on PE routers at the edge of the network and carried through iBGP to other PE routers within the same autonomous system.

Carrying Reachability Information

We have previously described how IPv4 address are converted into VPN-IPv4 address by adding a route distinguisher, but how is this route distinguisher carried, and how are VPN destinations carried separately from public, or Internet reachable, destinations? BGP carries routes imported from a VRF on a PE router as a new type of address, or a new address family, using the multiprotocol BGP extensions outlined in RFC 2858. When a BGP speaker first brings up a session with another BGP speaker, it negotiates the exchange of VPN-IPv4 addresses; a PE exporting routes from a VRF into BGP would negotiate the exchange of VPN-IPv4 addresses with each of its iBGP peers, for instance.

The actual routes are carried in *multiprotocol reachable* (MP-REACH) and *multiprotocol unreachable* (MP-UNREACH) TLVs within the address family, much as normal IPv4 prefixes are carried within BGP update packets; Figure 10.7 illustrates.

Fields in the multiprotocol reachable unreachable attributes include the following:

- AFI: The Address Family Identifier, set to 1 for IPv4 addresses.
- SAFI: The Subsequent Address Family Identifier.
- Next Hop Length: Notes the length of the Network Address of Next Hop field in octets.
- Network Address of Next Hop: The network address of the next router in the path toward this destination; this is a 12-octet address, with the last four octets containing an IPv4 address. This field isn't used to convey the router that just forwarded this advertisement to its peer, but rather the next hop from the router that exported the route into BGP at the edge of the network (the next hop from the PE router).
- Number of SNPAs: The number of subnetwork point of attachments included for the device listed in the Network Address of the Next Hop field.
- Length of SNPA: The length, in octets, of the SNPA that follows this field.

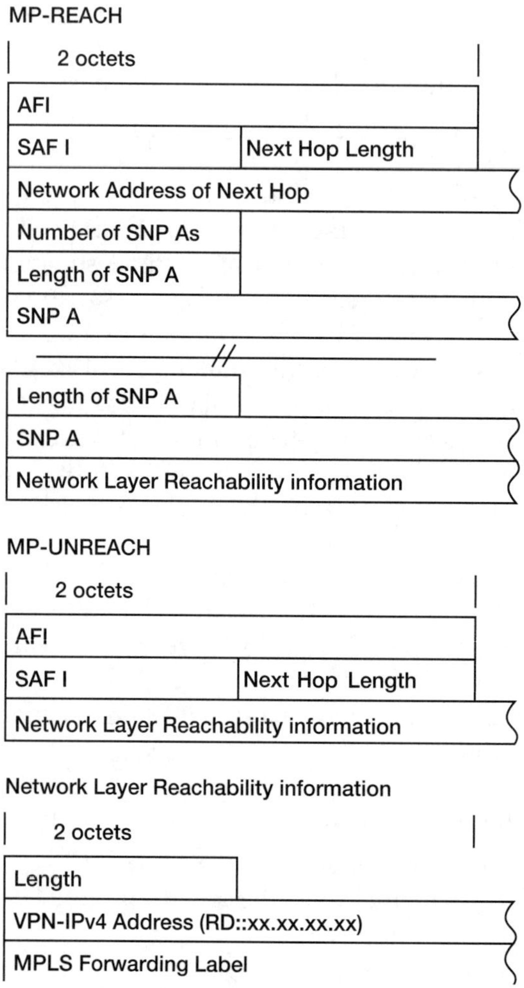

MP-REACH

| 2 octets |

| AFI |
| SAF I | Next Hop Length |
| Network Address of Next Hop |
| Number of SNP As |
| Length of SNP A |
| SNP A |

———————//———————

| Length of SNP A |
| SNP A |
| Network Layer Reachability information |

MP-UNREACH

| 2 octets |

| AFI |
| SAF I | Next Hop Length |
| Network Layer Reachability information |

Network Layer Reachability information

| 2 octets |

| Length |
| VPN-IPv4 Address (RD::xx.xx.xx.xx) |
| MPLS Forwarding Label |

Figure 10.7
MP-REACH and MP-UNREACH attributes for carrying VPN-IPv4 routes in BGP.

- SNPA: A subnetwork point of attachment for the device listed in the Network Address of the Next Hop field. Any number of SNPAs may be included for the next hop device, including 0; each one represents some point at which the next hop device attaches to the network.

Note that the multiprotocol unreachable attribute doesn't contain the SNPAs, and the network layer reachability information doesn't need to contain the MPLS label either. An extended community attribute, used to provide VPN membership information, is also carried in the VPN-IPv4 address family. The next section delves into more detail about the usages of this attribute.

Extended Communities Carried with VPN-IPv4 Routes

We discussed the concept of extended communities in the Extended Communities section of Chapter 1, The Border Gateway Protocol. Extended communities are used by BGP/MPLS VPNs to carry information about which VPN a specific route belongs to. BGP/MPLS VPNs use extended communities with the type code 16; these communities are *transitive* and *optional*.

> By *transitive*, we mean BGP speakers can announce this attribute to other BGP speakers. By *optional*, we mean no BGP speaker is expected to support or interpret this attribute. Please note that any new attribute introduced in BGP must be transitive and optional, given the wide deployment of BGP in the internet today.

For BGP/MPLS VPNs, two classes of extended communities are used: *route target* (RT) and *site of origin* (SOO); the structures of these two communities are shown in Figure 10.8.

As the name suggests, the g*lobal administrator* makes the route target and site of origin unique across all the providers within the Internet, by tying the issuing service provider's autonomous system to the route target. The *local administrator* is assigned by the service provider to make the route target and site of origin unique within their network. To understand how route targets are used, we first need to understand VPN specification and management. BGP/MPLS VPNs use the concept of a colored topology to indicate VPN membership.

VPN Colors

Each customer's network (or set of VPNs through the service provider network) is associated with a color. In Figure 10.9, for example, *red* is used to define the VPN for customer 1, with the routes originating from each of customer 1's sites being marked. Within the service provider's

Route Target

Type	Sub-Type	Global Administrator	Local Administrator
0x00	0x02	2 octet AS Number	4 octets

Type	Sub-Type	Global Administrator	Local Administrator
0x01	0x02	4 octet public IP	2 octets

Site of Origin

Type	Sub-Type	Global Administrator	Local Administrator
0x00	0x03	2 octet AS Number	4 octets

Type	Sub-Type	Global Administrator	Local Administrator
0x01	0x03	4 octet public IP	2 octets

Figure 10.8
The route target and site of origin extended communities.

network, the VPN-IPv4 routes learned from the two customer 1 sites are colored *red*. This coloring describes how those routes should be handled within the service provider's network.

The route target is represents a color expressing the VPN relationship among sites. By assigning route targets to the routes as they are imported into BGP at the PE routers, the service provider defines the set of colors used in their network. A single VPN-IPv4 prefix can be associated with a number of different colors within the service provider's network, by adding more route targets to the route.

Exporting and Importing VPN-IPv4 Routes

How are routes learned on a PE tagged with the right route destination and then advertised through BGP? By exporting the routes into BGP and then importing them back into a local routing table, the VRF. Figure 10.10 illustrates VRFs and the import and export process.

It's easiest to think of exporting and importing routes in terms of the VRF tables on the PE routers. Routes are *exported* from the VRFs into BGP and *imported* from BGP into a VRF. An import route target, then, will always apply to routes being taken from the local BGP table and placed in a VRF associated with a specific customer site. An export

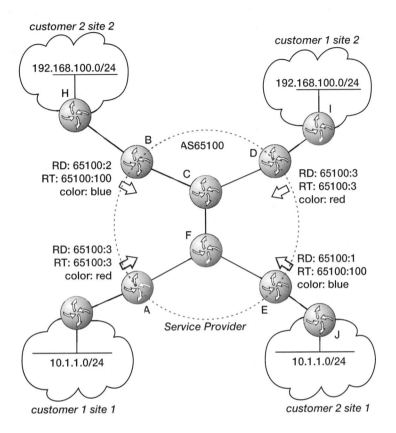

Figure 10.9
An illustration of VPN colors.

route target will always take traffic from a VRF and pull it into the BGP table, along with the right route target and route distinguisher information, so the routing information can be transported to other provider edge routers connecting to that same customer.

MPLS Forwarding

We've now seperated the routes and routing information, through VRFs, at the provider edge, we've imported them into BGP, marking them with the information needed to separate them out at the egress provider edge, but how do we actually forward packets across the service provider's network? MPLS, the other half of the MPLS/BGP VPN architecture. Figure 10.11 illustrates the problem we face.

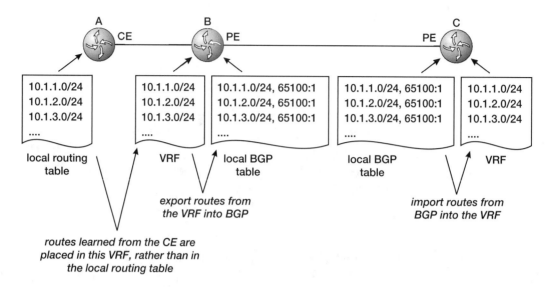

Figure 10.10
Importing and exporting routes into and out of BGP.

Router A receives a packet from some customer attached device, examines its local routing table, and finds the best path toward 10.1.1.1 is through router B. Router B receives this packet and finds the best path is through router C. Now, when router C receives this packet, it finds there are two paths to 10.1.1.0/24, both of which are good matches for the IP address in the packet it needs to forward. Since there's no way to determine which destination is correct, based on the information available in the packet itself, how can we resolve this problem? By not using the information in the IP packet's header to determine the correct

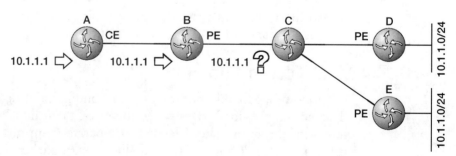

Figure 10.11
Forwarding through a VPN.

forwarding path through the network. Instead, we can use MPLS, which attaches a label onto the front of the packet, to forward the packet. Using MPLS decouples the information used for packet forwarding–the MPLS label–from the information carried in the IP header. So we can bind label switched paths (LSPs) to VPN-IPv4 routes and then forward the IP packets along these paths using MPLS.

We don't want to spend too much time explaining how MPLS works here, but at a high level, MPLS forwarding consists of the following:

- Pushing a label onto the incoming data packets at the ingress (also called head-end) of the MPLS cloud. This is the PE in the MPLS/BGP VPN network.
- Swapping the initial label for a new label describing the next hop toward the destination at every inetermediate node or router. This isn't important from the MPLS/BGP VPN perspective. Each label swap is one for one; the new label is determined strcitly by the old label and not based on the information in the IP header of the packet.
- Pop the label off the data packet at the egress (also called as tail-end) of the MPLS cloud. Again, this is the PE in an MPLS/BGP VPN.

In BGP/MPLS-based VPN networks, LDP (Label Distribution Protocol) is used to establish label switched paths within the network. Since the nexthop of all the VPN-IPv4 addresses is going to be a PE router, the label switched path is set up for the PE via LDP. Heirarchical MPLS forwarding can be used (each MPLS frame can have more than one label in the label stack) for VPN forwarding. Figure 10.12 illustrates this concept at a high level.

To simplify this example, we're going to discuss just the edge operation and ignore the operation of the interior routers in terms of label swapping.

- Router D builds a label switched path to router B using LDP. To reach router D, router D can forward packets labeled 2000 to router B, which will then swap the labels as needed, and forward the packets on to Router D.
- Router B learns 10.1.1.0/24 from router A, through some interior gateway protocol (OSPF, IS-IS, EIGRP, or a manually

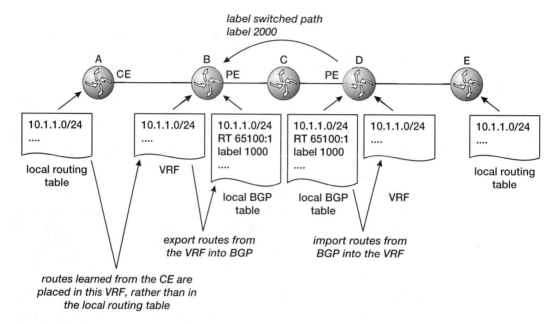

Figure 10.12
MPLS forwarding through a VPN.

configured static route). Because this route is learned from a customer edge router, it's placed in a VRF dedicated to that customer's routes.

- Router B then imports the information from the customer's VRF to the local BGP table. While importing the route, router A tags it with a route target, indicating the VPN (or the route color), and it inserts a label that can be used to forward traffic to this destination, 1000.

- Router B builds a corresponding entry in its forwarding table, so any packets received with a label of 1000 will be forwarded to router A.

- Router E receives the routing update with information about 10.1.1.0/24, with the route target and label included, through iBGP. Either router D is a route reflector, or routers B and D are configured as iBGP peers.

- Router E now receives a packet destined to 10.1.1.0/24. In this case, a VRF is tied to the interface the packet is received on, so router E knows which VRF to look the destination up in.

- Router E finds the route and finds that the exit point is router B. It first pushes this label, 1000, onto the MPLS label stack.

- Router E now finds the path to router B, and finds that this is through the MPLS tunnel with the label 2000 will allow it to reach router B. So it pushes this label, 2000, onto the MPLS label stack and forwards the packet to router D.

- Router D switches the packet based on the outer label, 2000, forwarding it to router B. It pops this topmost label off the MPLS label stack before forwarding the packet, leaving just the label router B originally advertised, 1000, as the only remaining MPLS label.

- When router B receives this packet, it examines the MPLS label and finds the label that indicates it should forward the packet to router A. Router B pops the last MPLS label and forwards the IP packet on to router A.

In an MPLS/BGP VPN network, then, every VPN-IPv4 address is not only associated with a route target, it is also associated with an MPLS label. One MPLS label is assigned by the PE router for every VPN-IPv4 address it creates and is used to identify the circuit or interface of the PE router to which the CE's site is attached.

In this environment, we often tie a single VRF to a single interface, to make easier the PE's job of sorting out which table in which to look up a given destination. However, there are several technologies that don't tie a VRF to an interface, so you shouldn't tie these two together logically.

Putting It Together: An MPLS/BGP VPN Example

At this point, we've examined each piece of the puzzle—BGP for signaling and MPLS for forwarding—and discussed how they are used together. To make these concepts clear, we'll provide an example of how an PMLS/BGP VPN would actually be configured and deployed in the real world.

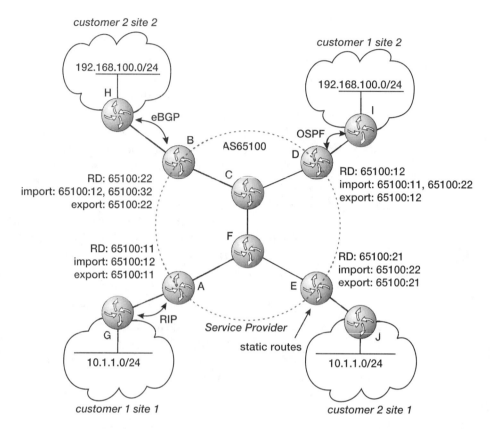

Figure 10.13
An example of an MPLS/BGP VPN.

Examining the Control Plane

In Figure 10.13, we have two intranet VPNs and one extranet VPN. BGP, RIP, and OSPF are used for exchanging routes between PE-CE, and some manually configured (static) routes are included as well.

There are three VPNs defined in this network:

- Intranet VPN VPN-1: customer1-site1 and customer1-site2
- Intranet VPN VPN-2: customer2-site1 and customer2-site2
- Extranet VPN VPN-3: customer2-site2 and customer1-site2

There is also a full mesh of MPLS tunnels between the PE routers, only a few of which we are concerned with for this example:

- Between B and A, with a label of 210
- Between B and D, with a label of 220
- Between B and E, with a label of 230

Router B and router E's configurations are as follows:

```
!
hostname router-b
!
ip vrf customer2-site2
 rd 65100:22
 route-target import 65100:12
 route-target import 65100:32
 route-target export 65100:22
!


!
hostname router-e
!
ip vrf customer2-site1
 rd 65100:21
 route-target import 65100:22
 route-target export 65100:21
!
ip route 10.1.1.0 255.255.255.0 pos0/1/0 crf customer2-site1
```

Let's examine VPN-2's control plane operation in some detail so we can understand the process completely. Prefix 10.1.1.0/24 is present in customer2-site1, and 192.168.100.0/24 is present in customer2-site2; the two sites want to exchange reachability of the these two prefixes. Router B, the provider edge, has been configured with a VRF for customer2-site2, and router E, another provider edge router, has been configured with a VRF for customer2-site. The configured route distinguisher, imported route targets, and exported route targets are shown in the diagram and router configurations.

Router H, a customer edge, peers with router B, the provider edge, using eBGP to exchange routing information. Router H advertises 192.168.100.0/24 over its eBGP session to the VPN service provider. Routes are not being dynamically exchanged between routers E and J (there's no routing protocol running between these two routers), so the service provider's system administrator configures static routes at router E to inject information about 10.1.1.0/24 into the correct VRF. From there, the routes are imported into BGP–there is no difference between static routes being injected into the VRF and a dynamic proto- col injecting them, from the MPLS/BGP VPN point of view, other than the administration required on the PE router.

When router B receives the prefix 192.168.100.0/24, it converts the converts the preifx into the VPN-IPv4 address 65100:22::192 .168.100.0/24, by adding the export route target extended community 65100:22. It also assigns an MPLS label, let's call this 1000, for the PE-CE interface between routers H and B. This label is added to the forwarding table so incoming MPLS packets can be forwarded towards router B (the label is popped off the packet before it's forwarded). Router H then advertises the VPN-IPv4 address plus the label to all the iBGP speakers it's exchanging VPN-IPv4 addresses with–routers A, B, D and E.

Router E, a provider edge, after receiving this advertisement for 65100:22::192.168.100.0/24, checks to see if the route target extended community attached to the route matches one of the import route tar- gets with the one of its locally configured VRFs. Since there is a match for this route target, the VPN-IPv4 advertisement is accepted, and the VPN-IPv4 address, 100:22::192.168.100.0/24, is converted back to an IPv4 address and added to customer2-site1's VRF. The MPLS label, 1000, is added to the forwarding entry just created, so packets for- warded using this entry will have the correct label pushed onto their label stack.

A separate label switched path is also set up between all the PE routers, crossing through the P routers (such as routers C and F), using LDP. This, in effect, creates two full meshes of tunnels (each full mesh being unidirectional) between all of the PE routers in the network. So to each PE router at the edge of the network, it appears there is a tunnel to each possible exit from the network, and it only needs to know the cor- rect label to push onto the packet's label stack to forward the traffic to the correct egress PE.

Examining the Forwarding Plane

At this point, we've advertised reachability information for 192.168 .100.0/24, within customer2-site1, from router H, through B, where the prefix is converted into a VPN-IPv4 route, then finally to router E, where the prefix is converted back into an IPv4 entry in the correct

VRF, along with an associated MPLS label. Now, lets take a quick look at the state of forwarding table on routers H, B, C, F, E, and J.

- Router J has a local routing table entry, learned via a static route (manually configured), that to reach 192.168.100.0/24 it should forward traffic to router E.

- Router E has a local entry in the VRF associated with customer2-site1 for 192.168.100.0/24, learned through iBGP. This entry has a label of 1000 associated with it.

- Router E has a local routing table entry for router B's IP address, learned through the autonomous system's IGP, associated with a label of 2000.

- Router C has a local routing table entry for router B's IP address, learned through the autonomous system's IGP, associated with a label of 2000.

- Router B has a VRF table entry for 192.168.100.0/24, pointing to router H's address, with an associated label, 1000.

Assume some host behind router J transmits a packet to 192.168.100.50; what is the process to switch this packet through the network? The routers within customer2-site1 forward the packet toward the exit point, following the route toward 192.168.100.0/24 injected at router J. When Router J receives the packet, it examines its local routing table and finds the best path is toward router E, so it forwards the packet to router E.

Router E looks up 192.168.100.50 in the VRF associated with the interface connecting to router J and finds the correct entry. This entry points to router B, across the mesh of MPLS tunnels built between the PE routers, as the next hop, and has an associated label of 1000. Router E pushes the label, 1000, onto the label stack and then examines its local tables to determine the best path to reach router B, through the MPLS tunnel. It finds the next hop along this tunnel is through router F, and it needs to push another label, to carry the packet through the MPLS tunnel, onto the label stack. The associated label is 2000, so router E pushes 2000 onto the label stack and forwards the packet to Router F.

At the other end of the tunnel, router C receives the packet, with two labels on the label stack, 2000 on the top, and 1000 on the bottom. Using this label, router C examines its forwarding table and determines that the next hop is router B and that the tunnel ends at router B. Router C then removes the top label, 2000, leaving just the single label on the stack (1000), and forwards the packet to router B.

When router B receives this packet, it uses the label to look up the next hop. B determines that the next hop is router H and that router B is, itself, the last hop along the MPLS path, so router B pops the remaining label and forwards the packet to router H, the CE connected to customer2-site2.

VPN Topologies

Up to this point, we've discussed how MPLS/BGP VPNs work, from both the control and data planes, and what their advantages are. In this section, we'll examine some MPLS/BGP VPN deployment scenarios. Before discussing each type of topology, we'll discuss some of the customer requirements that might drive the use of the topology.

VPNs can be broadly classified as hub and spoke, any-to-any (full mesh), and partial mesh topologies. Let's take a closer look at each of these topologies—we'll generally find each one similar in scope and use to a physical topology we are already familiar with.

Hub and Spoke

Hub and spoke VPN toplogies are similar to, and used in similar situations as, traditional hub and spoke topologies carried across nonbroadcast multiaccess media, such as frame relay. Generally, there is one hub, with many spokes, and communication is only possible between a spoke and the hub (not from spoke to spoke). If spoke to spoke communication is required, any traffic must cross the VPN network twice, once while being forwarded from the spoke to the hub and once while being forwarded from the hub to the spoke. Hub and spoke topologies can be constructed in either intranet or extranet VPN scenarios. Figure 10.14 illustrates a hub and spoke MPLS/BGP VPN.

In this MPLS/BGP VPN, each remote site is configured with the the same import route target, 65100:200, and the same export route target, 65100:100. When 10.1.3.0/24 is originated from customer1-site3, then, it will be converted to the VPN-IPv4 route 65100:100::10.1.3.0/24, which the other customer sites will not import. Only at router A are routes from the sites imported and forwarded through the local routing protocol to router K.

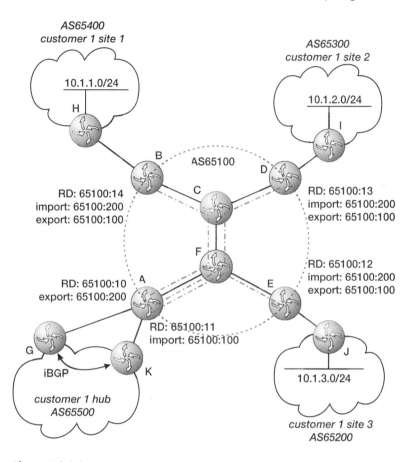

Figure 10.14
A hub and spoke MPLS/BGP VPN.

It might appear to be odd that router K only imports routes and doesn't export them, but this is done for a reason. When 10.1.3.0/24 is learned at router K, it is can be filtered and checked for other policies within the customer's network. Once it has passed these checks, 10.1.3.0/24 is then advertised via iBGP to router G, where it is again advertised to router A.

Router A will now convert the route to a VPN-IPv4 route again, this time 65100:200::10.1.1.0/24, and transmit it via iBGP to PE routers B, D, and E. These routers will convert the route back into an IPv4 route, and send it to their respective CEs, which connect to the customer sites. In this way, the remote sites may send traffic to one another, but only through the hub site.

Traffic, of course, will follow the same route. Suppose some host, 10.1.3.1, sends a packet to 10.1.2.1. The packet would first be forwarded to router J; router J would look the destination up in its local routing table and find the best path is through router E, so it would forward the packet to router E. Router E would, in turn, find the best path is through the MPLS/BGP VPN, with a next hop of router A. The packet is tagged appropriately and forwarded to router A. Router A would forward the packet to router K, based on exmaning the local tag tables. Router K would then send the packet to router G; in between these two routers the packet could be filtered or otherwise examined to make certain the intranet's policies are met. Finally, the packet arrives at G, where it is again forwarded to router A, tagged as needed, and forwarded to router D, then to router I, and finally the destination host.

One interesting side effect of the route looping through routers K and G is that we must disable BGP's loop detection mechanism at router A for BGP routes learned through router G, because routers G and K are running iBGP between them. When 10.1.3.0/24 is learned at Router K, it has an AS Path of (65200, 65100). Router K, on receiving the route, adds 65300 to the AS Path and updates router G on the newly learned reachability information. When router G readvertises 10.1.3.0/24 to router A, it will have an AS Path of (65200, 65100, 65300)—since AS65100 is already in the path, router A will reject the prefix. We obviously need to get around this if this hub and spoke MPLS/BGP VPN is going to work, but how?

Most BGP implementations provide a knob allowing the rules for AS Path checking to be relaxed. In Cisco IOS software, we can configure **neighbor <a.b.c.d> allowas-in <asn-limit>** on router A, allowing routes with AS65100 in the AS Path to be accepted, although there is an apparent loop, from BGP's perspective. If routers G and K are using some other routing protocol, an IGP, to exchange routes, rather than iBGP, this isn't a problem, since the AS Path would be completely different when router G advertises 10.1.3.0/24 to router A.

If remote site to remote site communication isn't required, the second router connecting to the service provider isn't required.

Any to Any (Full Mesh) Topology

In some cases, a network will have a number of sites that intercommunicate about equally; there is no defined "hub site" where most of the traffic concentrates or where most of the services are located. This would be typical if the MPLS/BGP VPN is used as a network core, or the WAN connectivity between a number of large sites, where the sites communicate equally, and the traffic and routes being exchanged between sites aren't monitored or controlled in any way. Figure 10.15 illustrates an any to any (full mesh) topology.

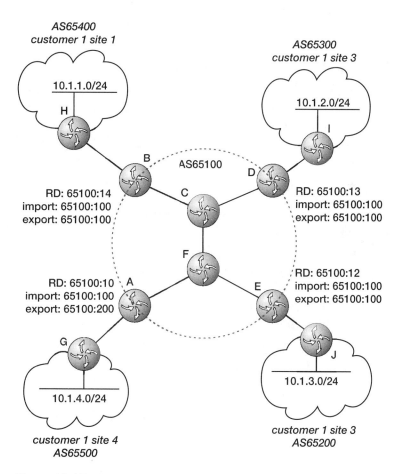

Figure 10.15
An MPLS/BGP VPN any to any (full mesh) topology.

On each of the PE routers, VRFs are created such that each has unique RD. The export Route-Target extended community is the same as Import Route-Target extended community. This lets every route from a site to be distributed to all other sites, thus enabling any to any connectivity. Note that intranet and extranet are overlapping in this example.

10.1.1.0/24 advertised by H becomes VPN-IPv4 address 65100:100::10.1.1.0/24 with 65100:100 as a Route-Target extended community prepended on it. When routers A, D, and E receive this VPN-IPv4 address, they will accept this route due because their configured import route targets. The corresponding IPv4 address is retrieved from the VPN-IPv4 address and then advertised to the attached CE routers.

Partial Mesh Topology

In this scenario, a combination of hub-spoke and partial mesh connectivity between sites is configured, which might be used in a network where a large number of remote sites are combined with a smaller number of central sites on the same MPLS/BGP VPN. The topology and configurations will be a combination of the previous two sections.

VPN Service Provider Deployment Considerations

In previous chapters, we've discussed three basic deployment options for BGP within an autonomous system:

- Running iBGP full mesh between all of the BGP speakers within the autonomous system.
- Running route reflectors to reduce the full mesh while maintaining full routing information at every BGP speaker in the autonomous system.
- Breaking the autonomous system up into subAS's, creating a confederation of autonomous systems that appear to be a single AS to external networks.

Routes with additional attributes to support MPLS/BGP VPNs are exchanged in the normal way between BGP speakers, so we are going to have the same issues with scaling and deployment. While a full mesh of

BGP peers are the simplest to manage, from the perspective of network design, it's the most difficult to manage from the perspective of configuration and maintenance. Route reflectors and confederations are used to reduce the configuration and maintenance requirements for managing a large-scale autonomous system, but they introduce some design considerations. We'll consider each of these, route reflectors and confederations, as they relate to MPLS/BGP VPN networks.

MPLS/BGP VPNs and Confederations

Since BGP attributes are unchanged when a route is exchanged between autonomous systems with a confederation, propogating VPN-IPv4 routes through the confederation, from PE to PE, isn't a problem. However, the interior gateway protocols are generally separated between the autonomous systems, which means MPLS VPN connectivity between the provider edge routers is disrupted. Figure 10.16 illustrates.

For router B to set up an MPLS tunnel to router D, the other edge PE for a specific customer, it will need to have specific reachability information in its local routing table to reach router D. The problem is that since the BGP next hops are changed at the confederation subAS border between AS65100 and AS65200, router B doesn't have this connectivity information. There are two options to resolve this problem:

- Provide prefix reachability all the way through the network, either using a single IGP, or by specifically injecting a route to router D into BGP.

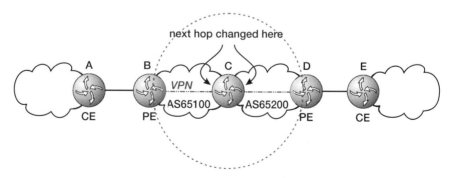

Figure 10.16
MPLS/BGP VPNs and confederations.

- Create an MPLS tunnel from router B to C, and then from C to D, so router B has a single tunnel all the way through the confederation.

The second method is widely deployed in the BGP/MPLS-based Layer-3 VPN for service providers who have deployed confederations.

Route Reflectors

Route reflection, as explained earlier in the book, can be used in to reduce the n^2 iBGP peering problem within the autonomous system. Generally, any BGP speaker can be configured to act as route reflector, however, as described earlier in the book, care must be taken to ensure that proper heirarchy in forwarding is maintained.

The route reflector topologies we've discussed in this book are based on building heirarchy using route reflector clusters. When a network is built using a hierarchy of reflection cluster, every router in the network will have the same routing information for all the prefixes any BGP speaker has leaned along the edge of the network. This architecture can run up against scaling issues in a network providing MPLS/BGP VPN services to a large number of customers, however, because the number of VPNs, and the routes within each VPN, can be huge. For instance, suppose a service provider has 1000 customers, each with 1000 routes advertised into a separate VPN. The service provider's routers will be carrying the full Internet tables, about 150,000 routes, plus each customer's full routing table, which is about 500 x 1000 = 500,000 routes—so the total number of routes would be about 650,000! Clearly, we need to find some way to reduce the amount of routing information carried through the service provider's network.

To solve this problem, we need to begin by noting that route reflection is per address family/sub address family. In other words, a BGP speaker acting as a route reflector for IPv4 unicast routing information need not be a route reflector for VPN-IPv4 unicast routing information. Figure 10.17 illustrates.

Both IPv4 and VPN-IPv4 have been deployed in this network, but they don't completely overlap; we don't need the VPN-IPv4 routes at routers A or E. In this case, we don't need full mesh iBGP peering for both address families, then, so we can configure router C as a route reflector for both VPN-IPv4 and IPv4 routes while configuring router F as just a reflector for IPv4 routes.

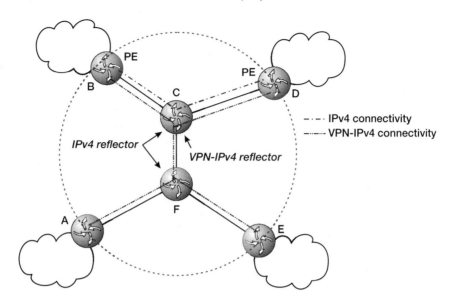

Figure 10.17
Route reflection in an MPLS/BGP VPN network.

Using this capability—a single route reflector can be used for each address family/subaddress family—we can resolve the scaling problem by partitioning the service provider's network into multiple groups, where each group is defined to be a collection of route targets. Each group can have two route reflectors, providing failover through redundancy. A route reflector contained within such a group will store only those VPN-IPv4 unicast prefixes that are associated with the respective route target, and the route reflector client PE routers store a subset of the VPN-IPv4 prefixes within the address family/subaddress family set the route reflector is reflecting.

Let's examine how PE routers and route reflectors can be deployed to limit the set of VPN-IPv4 prefixes each one needs to store and advertise (Figure 10.18).

In this network, the route reflector configurations follow the physical topology, so

- Router A is a route reflector client of router E
- Router B is a route reflector client of router F
- Router C is a route reflector client of routers E and F
- Router D is a route reflector client of routers E and F

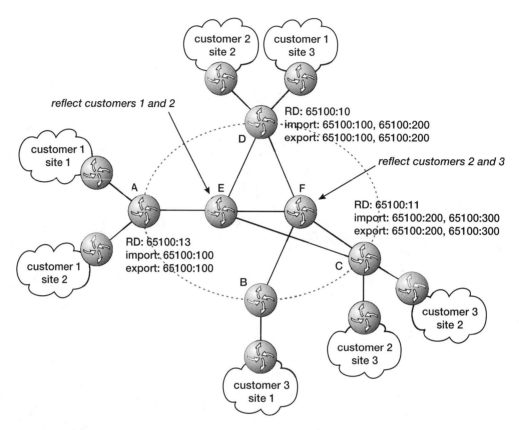

Figure 10.18
Scalable deployment of MPLS/BGP VPN networks.

To simplify the network further and concentrate on the example at hand, we will consider both customer 1; and customer 2's VPNs as any to any (full mesh) VPNs; any site within customer 1's network may communicate with any other site within customer 1's network, and likewise for customers 2 and 3. Customer 1 is marked using route target 65100:100 throughout, customer 2 is marked using route target 65100:200 throughout, and customer 3 is marked using route target 65100:300 throughout.

Without any controls on the routes being propagated through the network, routers A through F will carry the entire Internet routing table, all of customer 1's, 2's and 3's routes. We can, however, configure the route reflectors so they split the reflection load, and we can configure the PE routers so they only accept the routes for locally attached customers.

At the route reflectors, we would set up sessions so each route reflector reflects routes for a limited set of customers rather than for all the customers attached to the network and using MPLS/BGP VPNs. So here, router E is reflecting routes for customers 1 and 2, and router F is reflecting routes for customers 2 and 3. At the edge of the network, we can mark all Internet routes (routes without a route target) with a special community, say 65100:1000, so we can distinguish these routes from routes carried for a specific VPN. In our configuration for router E, then, we can filter the routes it's learning so it only accepts routes with extended communities 65100:100, 65100:200, and 65100:1000 attached. In the same way, router F can be configured only to accept routes with extended communities 65100:22, 65100:300, and 65100:1000.

The PE routers can filter their routes based on the locally attached customers, or rather the set of route targets they are configured to import from BGP into some local VRF. Router B could be configured to only accept routes with extended communities 65100:300 and 65100:1000, while router C would accept routes with extended communities 65100:200, 65100:300, and 65100:1000.

If the configured route targets are modified, the PE or P router can rebuild its routing information around the new routes it should be accepting by simply issuing a route refresh, which causes its BGP peers to resend all the routing information they have in their tables. This might seem inefficient, but changes in which extended communities a router filters on shouldn't be all that common on an individual router basis.

> Another option, should it become available at some in the future, is to use outbound route filters (ORFs), described in Chapter 7, New Features in BGP. Extended community-based ORF is not available at this time.

Carrier's Carrier

So far, we have talked about customer sites interconnected through a single VPN service provider network to form a VPN. It's possible, however, that a customer could want a VPN through multiple providers. The carrier providing service to other sites outside the primary provider's autonomous system is called a carrier's carrier; Figure 10.19 illustrates a sample interprovider extranet VPN.

Customer 1 is connected to AS65100, while customer 2 is connected to AS65200. The routes advertised by the customer sites will be converted to VPN-IPv4 addresses within their respective service provider networks and tagged with the respective route target extended communities defining the VPNs within each service provider's network. The following needs to be done to be able to provide connectivity between these two customer sites.

- VPN-IPv4 addresses need to be exchanged between the service providers. Note that the VPN-IPv4 addresses should not be converted into IP format as we will run into the IP address nonunique problem.
- Exchanging the VPN-IPv4 addresses requires the remapping of the route distingauishers on each route. Note that the RD contains the SP identifier in the Administrator field at the route exchange point.

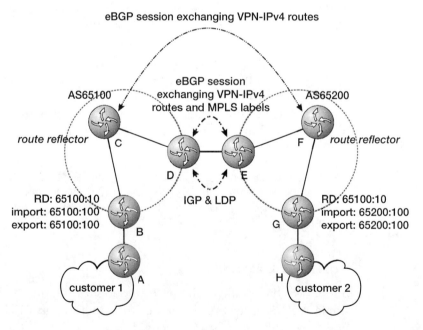

Figure 10.19
An interprovider BGP/MPLS VPN.

- VPN membership rules need to be mapped. The route target defining the VPN membership has Global and Local Administrator fields that require mapping at the route exchange point.
- To avoid the overloading of routers at the provider exchange point, the next hop should not changed when VPN-IPv4 addresses are exchanged between the providers. This means that a MPLS LSP needs to be set up from the PE router within one service provider's network to the PE router of the other service provier's network.
- LDP can be used at the DMZ between providers to exchange the FEC bindings for all the PEs.
- A new subaddress family under the IPv4 address family is used to carry the VPN-IPv4 prefixes with labels, to reduce the load on the DMZ with LDP and IGP.

The routes from customer 1 are advertised by router A to router B. Router B converts the IPv4 prefixes to the VPN-IPv4 format, adding the local VPN label, and advertises it to all PEs and RRs in AS65100, as we have seen earlier in the chapter. Similarly, routers G and H populate the routing tables in the PE and route reflectors in AS65200. The eBGP session between routers C and F leaks these VPN-IPv4 routes from one autonomous system to another—but doesn't change the next hop in the route advertisements. And IGP or eBGP carrying IPv4 and the MPLS labels between routers D and E leaks the label bindings for the FECs from one autonomous system to the other.

Customer traffic from router A is forwarded to router B, which then pushes the MPLS label originated by router G onto the packet's label stack. This traffic will then follow this MPLS tunnel to router G, where the labels are popped. Router G looks up the incoming label, pops it, and forwards the traffic to router H, where it is forwarded to customer 2's Internet network.

Conclusion

Routing protocols are designed to solve certain problems. BGP, for instance, is used for managing and exchanging huge set of routes within intra- and inter-autonomous domains. Providers and vendors gained experience while vendors implemented new features in BGP and tweaked its performance. The current deployment of BGP today in the

Internet has proven its scalability and performance—an important advantage of BGP when used in an MPLS/BGP VPN environment. Using the tools available in BGP, a service provider can give customers highly efficient and well-managed VPN services throughout their network, and beyond their network through any partnering service provider in the world.

Review Questions

1. What problems are solved by the BGP/MPLS-based approach that other peer-to-peer models don't?
2. What is the difference between a route distinguisher and a route target?
3. Is it possible to send prefixes that belong to multiple <address-family, sub-address-family> with the same set of attributes? How?
4. Is BGP required in the core of the MPLS networks? If not, how is reachability achieved?
5. How is partial mesh topology created in BGP/MPLS-based VPNs?

Appendix A

Answers to the Review Questions

Chapter 1

1. What is a routing domain from BGP's perspective? How is this different from a routing domain within IS-IS?

   A routing domain, from BGP's perspective, is a group of routers or networks under a single administrative control. In IS-IS, a routing domain is the area within which topology information is flooded.

2. What are the two primary differences between an interior gateway protocol and an external gateway protocol?

   Interior gateway protocols are generally concerned with fast convergence and assume uniform policies throughout the routing domain (although this is changing with policy propagation and other additions to interior gateway protocols). Exterior gateway protocols focus on propagating policy and stability.

3. What types of policies would you normally see implemented through BGP?

   Always take the closest exit point, always take the exit closest to the customer, take the cheapest exit point, don't traverse certain networks, and don't accept unstable or invalid routing information from a peer.

4. For what does BGP use the path information it carries through the network?

To detect and eliminate routing loops.

5. Why does BGP treat each autonomous system as a point on the connectivity graph? What does this imply about BGP's usefulness within an autonomous system?

By treating each autonomous system as a point, BGP hides the details of each autonomous system's internal connectivity. Since BGP doesn't change the AS Path within the autonomous system and ignores the internal structure of the autonomous system, it's difficult to use for interior routing.

6. What transport does BGP use to build a session to another BGP speaker? What local port number and remote port number does BGP use when initiating a connection?

BGP relies on TCP to reliably transmit data between BGP peers. The local port is ephemeral, some port number chosen randomly above port 1024, and the destination port is 179.

7. How is a collision between two BGP speakers attempting to open a connection at the same time resolved?

When the collision is detected, the BGP speaker with the higher router ID drops the passive session, and the BGP speaker with the lower router ID drops the active session.

8. Define *prefix, NLRI,* and *attribute.*

A prefix, or NLRI, provides network layer reachability information, or a layer-3 destination. An attribute provides information about the path, desirability, and policies attached to a given path to a destination within the internetwork.

9. How many sets of attributes can a single BGP update contain? How many prefixes?

A BGP update can contain a single set of attributes and a large number of prefixes or NLRIs that share that set of attributes.

10. What are the four primary differences between eBGP peering relationships and iBGP peering relationships?

Routes learned from an iBGP peer are not normally advertised to other iBGP peers, the attributes of routes learned from iBGP peers are not normally modified before the routes are readvertised, the AS Path of a route is not normally modified when a route is readvertised to an iBGP peer, and the next hop is not normally modified when a route is readvertised to an iBGP peer.

11. Why does BGP include the concept of notifications; what types of errors can a notification indicate has occurred in the BGP session?

BGP normally shuts down a session when an error is detected, including malformed packets being received. A notification can indicate that an error has occurred in the message header, an open message, an update message, the hold timer expired, an error has occurred in the neighbor finite state machine, or the peer should stop sending data (a cease).

12. What purpose do BGP capabilities server? What sorts of capabilities can be negotiated?

Capabilities allow a pair of BGP speakers to advertise their optional capabilities and negotiate which optional capabilities will be used in a session. Capabilities include the ability to refresh routing information, the ability to send multiprotocol routing information, the ability to support cooperative route filtering, and the ability to gracefully restart the session.

13. Describe the four classes of BGP attributes.

Well-known mandatory attributes, which must be recognized by all BGP speakers and must be carried in each update that is advertised. Well-known discretionary attributes, which must be recognized by all BGP speakers but are not required in all BGP updates. Optional transitive attributes, which may not be recognized by all BGP peers but must be kept with a prefix when transmitted to a BGP speaker's neighbors. Optional nontrasitive attributes, which may not be recognized by all BGP speakers, and a BGP speaker is not required to send to its peers when readvertising a route.

14. What is a community? What are some well-known communities?

Communities are a way to group routes (or BGP speakers) into groups, or communities, that share common policies. Some well-known communities include NO_EXPORT, which indicates that a route should not be readvertised outside the autonomous system, and NO_ADVERTISE, which indicates that a route should not be readvertised to any peer by the router receiving the route.

15. What is the atomic aggregate bit used for?

To indicate that a route is an aggregate and that attribute information may have been lost or that attributes have been aggregated and some attributes may not apply to some more specific parts of the aggregated route.

Chapter 2

1. What is the point at which the responsibility for a network connection transfers from the service provider to the customer?

The demarcation point, or the DEMARC, for short.

2. Where would you normally get a block of addresses from if you are connecting to the Internet for the first time?

The Internet service provider you are contracting for connection service with. You could also request a block of IP addresses from a regional Internet Registry (RIR), but these organizations typically only provide address blocks for very large customers, such as Internet service providers, large governmental organizations, and large corporations.

3. What are the primary advantages of dual homing to the Internet through the same Internet service provider?

You can more closely control the service level agreement, and you only need to deal with one set of engineers and other contacts when trying to resolve technical or contractual problems.

4. How many routers should you use to peer with when dual homing to a single Internet service provider?

You should use two routers to peer, rather than one, since the capital outlay of the second router is going to be easily offset by the gains in connection uptime.

5. What is the primary disadvantage of dual homing to the same Internet service provider rather than to two different Internet service providers?

If the Internet service provider's upstream connection fails, you will lose all connectivity to the Internet, even though you are dual homed. It's also possible that a regional disruption may cause you to lose all connectivity to the Internet.

6. What other type of diversity is just as important as logical diversity?

   Physical diversity; making certain that all traffic to and from two logically diverse connections are not traveling through a common set of physical cables.

7. What types of records can you request from your Internet service provider to determine whether or not you have enough diversity of the right types?

   Design layout records (DLRs).

8. What are the primary considerations that would cause you to run eBGP with your Internet service provider?

   Traffic flow considerations and optimal routing to locations connected to the Internet.

9. How can you run BGP to an Internet service provider without a registered autonomous system number?

   You can use a private autonomous system number assigned by your Internet service provider, which the ISPF then strips out of the AS Path at the edge of its network.

10. What is the most common problem preventing traffic from flowing inbound on two links when dual homed to two different Internet service providers?

    The Internet service provider you received the IP address block from is advertising an aggregate of that space, while your second Internet service provider is advertising the more specific prefix they are learning through your connection with them.

11. Can you control inbound traffic flow by controlling outbound traffic flow?

    No; IP traffic is forwarded based on the best hop in each local router through which it passes. In fact, it's very difficult to ensure symmetric traffic flow through dual homed connections to the Internet.

12. What methods could you investigate to balance outbound traffic flow through two different connections to the Internet?

    You can consider iBGP Multipath within the Internet service provider's network if you are dual homed to the same ISP. You can set the multiple exit discriminator on the routes you advertise, but many Internet service providers reset or ignore the MEDs on routes they receive. You can set a community that causes the Internet service provider to set the Local Preference to some value, or you can add length to the AS Path by prepending the same autonomous system number onto the AS Path several times. You can advertise two different sets of routes out the two connections, so all the traffic destined to one block of addresses is preferred because of longer prefix matching.

13. What options could you consider if you only wanted to use one connection to an Internet service provider and only send traffic along a backup link when the primary link fails?

Conditional advertisement.

14. What are the primary means you have to control outbound traffic flow when dual homed to the Internet?

Controlling traffic flow through the Interior Gateway Protocol metric; filtering the routes received along each link; iBGP multipath, using an eBGP multihop session across the parallel links.

15. What is one of the major considerations when determining how to control outbound traffic flow across several connections to the Internet?

How far back, or deep, into your network you want to run BGP.

16. Why is it sometimes important to force traffic to enter and exit your network symmetrically?

Most often symmetric entry and exit points are important for firewalls and other network security devices.

17. What options can you consider when attempting to force traffic to enter and exit your network symmetrically?

Using two different blocks of IP addresses; each IP address block is only advertised to the Internet service provider it was provided by. Network address translation is used to ensure traffic leaving a given exit will always come back into the same entry point.

18. How should you prevent your network from becoming a transit autonomous system if you are dual homing to the Internet?

Using AS Path filtering so that only locally originated prefixes are advertised to external peers.

Chapter 3

1. What are some common reasons for splitting up a large enterprise network using BGP?

   To divide the administration of the network among several different groups, to allow the network to be rebuilt one small piece at a time, to handle situations where there are a large number of routes, and very little can be done in the way of aggregation or other techniques to reduce pressure on the interior gateway protocol.

2. When merging two networks, should you consider using a BGP core as a permanent solution or a short-term solution?

   It depends on the way the merger is being accomplished and what the desired final results are. For instance, if a larger company is taking over a smaller company and would like to leave the smaller company somewhat autonomous, a BGP core merging the two networks could be considered a permanent solution. On the other hand, if the final goal is to merge all operations, then a BGP core may be considered a temporary solution until the two networks can be merged at each point where it makes sense.

3. What is the primary advantage of using eBGP within the core of an enterprise network versus iBGP?

   The ability to implement policies between each section of the network.

4. What is one of the primary advantages of using iBGP to build a BGP core within an enterprise network?

   It's much easier to load share across iBGP connections than eBGP connections.

5. What is the primary reason a BGP core will still need to run an IGP?

   To provide next hop reachability information for BGP.

6. What are the three primary ways of originating routes into BGP?

   Redistribution, aggregation, and reorigination.

7. What is one important consideration to consider when using two points of mutual redistribution between two routing protocols?

   Filtering or some other technique should be used to prevent routing loops from forming between the routing domains.

Chapter 4

1. Why do iBGP peers only advertise routes learned from other iBGP peers to eBGP peers?

   To prevent routing loops; BGP relies on the AS Path to prevent routing and forwarding loops, and the AS Path does not change within an autonomous system.

2. In an network with 100 iBGP peers, fully meshed, with a single peer receiving 1000 routes from an eBGP peer, how many routes would each iBGP peer receive and store?

   100 peers × 1000 routes, so each peer would receive and store 100,000 routes. Each iBGP speaker would only use 1000 of these routes, however, since there are actually only 1000 reachable destinations, or prefixes.

3. If a route reflector receives a route from a nonclient peer, which peers would the route be reflected to?

   The route would be reflected to all client peers.

4. If a route reflector receives a route from a client peer, which peers would the route be reflected to?

   The route would be reflected to all nonclient and client peers.

5. What is the Cluster ID?

   A 32-bit number that uniquely identifies a route reflector (or a route reflector cluster). It is generally the router ID of the route reflector.

6. What is the Cluster List?

   The list of the route reflector clusters a route has passed through, expressed as a set of Cluster IDs.

7. What does the Cluster List provide?

   Information about the path a route update has traversed within the autonomous system, to prevent routing and forwarding loops when using route reflectors.

8. Why should no other attributes be modified when a route reflector reflects a route?

   To prevent routing or forwarding loops between route reflector clusters. This is especially true of the next hop attribute.

9. How can we resolve issues with route reflectors being a single point of failure?

By setting up redundant route reflector clusters, with matching sets of clients.

10. What is the primary disadvantage to consider when configuring each route reflector in a pair of redundant route reflectors with different Cluster IDs?

Each route reflected from each reflector will be considered a different route; each one will be stored and processed separately, undoing some of the savings gained by using route reflectors.

11. What is the primary disadvantage to consider when configuring each route reflector in a pair of redundant route reflectors with the same Cluster ID?

It's possible to lose reachability to specific destinations in certain failure modes, even though physical reachability still exists.

12. Why is it important to match the physical and logical topologies when using route reflectors?

To prevent routing or forwarding loops from forming within the route reflector cluster.

13. What does a group of autonomous systems organized as a confederation appear as to routers outside the confederation?

A single autonomous system.

14. What is the AS Confederation Sequence used for?

The AS Confederation Sequence is used as an AS Path within a confederation, to prevent loops between autonomous systems within a single confederation. The AS Confederation Sequence is not transmitted outside the confederation boundaries.

Chapter 5

1. How should you judge the performance of BGP in your network?

You need to judge the performance of BGP in your network within the context of the network itself. You should baseline the current performance rather than assuming some absolute baseline.

2. What inefficiency does grouping peers by outbound policy overcome?

The cost of copying information from one place in a computer's memory to another place in a computer's memory.

3. What provides configuration grouping for outbound BGP policy without impacting BGP performance?

Peer templates.

4. What provides BGP performance by grouping peers with similar outbound policies without impacting peer configuration?

Update groups.

5. How are BGP updates packed?

All the prefixes with a common set of attributes are packed into the same update.

6. Which timer paces how often a BGP speaker will attempt to reconnect to a peer?

The connect retry timer.

7. Which timer paces how often a BGP speaker will originate a route?

The minimum origination interval.

8. What is the minimum route advertisement interval supposed to suppress?

Rapid changes in the network from passing throughout the entire network, and causing the network to fail to converge.

9. What property of the Transport Control Protocol does the input queue size of an interface interact with to impact BGP convergence times?

TCP slow start; each time an acknowledgment is dropped due to an input queue overflow, the TCP session will revert to a very small window, slowing data transfer across the link and causing BGP top converge more slowly.

Chapter 6

1. What routes would you differentiate between using Local Preference?

   Service providers often differentiate between routes learned from customers and peers and those originated within their own networks using Local Preference.

2. What is the MED often set to when a route is advertised to another autonomous system?

   The interior gateway protocol's cost to reach the next hop (the exit point from the local autonomous system).

3. What application of Communities described in RFC 1998?

   Directing the receiving autonomous system to set their Local Preference to a value that either prefers or does not prefer the received route. This can be useful in controlling inbound traffic flow when an autonomous system is connected to two different upstream service providers.

4. What are commonly accepted prefix lengths when peering to routers connected to the Internet?

   Greater than /8 and less than /24.

5. What problems can filtering based on the address allocation tables provided by the Internet Registries cause?

   If a dual-homed autonomous system loses the link through the upstream service provider that assigned its addresses, it will lose connectivity with all networks not directly attached to the other service providers' network.

6. Which RFC describes private address space which cannot be routed to or advertised on the Internet?

   RFC 1918.

7. Beyond private address space, what other address spaces should be filtered at the edge of an autonomous system?

   Multicast addresses (224.0.0.0/5) and unallocated address space.

8. How does outbound route filtering reduce the number of prefixes advertised between two peers?

By allowing one BGP speaker to tell its peer it will not accept a certain set of routes (based on the AS Path or the prefix itself) so the sender can filter them out before transmitting them.

Chapter 7

1. What capability does the cost community add to BGP?

The ability to customize the BGP decision process by inserting an administratively defined cost at any point.

2. What capability does the redistribution community add to BGP?

The ability to control redistribution at a peering point outside your local autonomous system.

3. Where is the redistribution community most useful for implementing policy?

In an internetwork where the immediate surrounding connectivity is well known and the redistribution community can be used to influence traffic flow in to the local autonomous system.

4. What capability does the No Peer community add to BGP?

The ability to determine which of your peer's peers a given prefix will be advertised to, allowing the local autonomous system to limit the ability of remote autonomous systems to transit their traffic.

5. What capability does iBGP multipath load sharing add to BGP?

Normally BGP implementations only choose one path to install in the local routing table, which means the router will only forward traffic along one path. If more than one path equal cost path is available, iBGP multipath allows a number of available paths (depending on the implementation) to be installed in the local routing table and traffic to be load shared across them.

6. What capability does the DMZ Link Bandwidth community add to BGP?

The ability to load share over multiple unequal cost exit points, in proportion to the bandwidths of those exit points.

7. In what situations can BGP graceful restart be used to minimize the impact of a control plane restart on the network?

   When the data and control plane are separated on the restarting router and the surrounding routers can support the signaling required for the restarting router to recover its routing information.

8. What new signaling methods are added to BGP to support graceful restart?

   A new capability signaling the ability of the BGP speaker to support graceful restart, a graceful restart bit in BGP messages, and an end of RIB marker to indicate the completion of the routing information being transmitted by a peer.

9. What two important issues do we need to consider when deploying BGP graceful restart?

   That the BGP speakers peered with the speaker we are deploying graceful restart on can support graceful restart signaling, and that the interior gateway protocol through which the next hops are being learned can support graceful restart as well.

10. Why would we want an interior gateway protocol to wait on BGP to converge before allowing its peers to route through the local router?

    To prevent traffic from being dropped while BGP is converging.

11. What problem within the Internet does inbound route summarization solve?

    The growth of the Internet routing table due to dual-homed autonomous systems requiring unaggregated address space.

Chapter 8

1. With most BGP implementations, what is the source address of the TCP packets sent to a peer? How can this cause a problem for eBGP sessions built between nonconnected interfaces?

   The source address of the TCP packets transmitted to a peer is normally the IP address of the interface used to reach the peer's address (the destination address of the packets). This can cause problems for a pair of eBGP peers communicating over nondirectly connected addresses because it can mean the expected source of the packets doesn't match the real source of the packets.

2. How many IP hops does BGP normally assume will be between two eBGP peers? How is this condition normally checked within BGP implementations?

The BGP specification states that there will only be one IP hop between two eBGP peers; BGP implementations normally check this by making certain the peer's IP address is on the same subnet as the local peering IP address and by setting the time to live on all packets sent to an eBGP peer to 1, so they cannot be forwarded beyond directly connected interfaces. Most implementations allow these two checks to be overridden, allowing eBGP peers to be formed over multihop sessions.

3. Which open parameters can cause a BGP session to fail?

The BGP version number, the autonomous system number, the hold time, and the route identifier.

4. What three common problems can cause a peering session to flap between two BGP speakers?

Traffic shaping, rate limiting, and other forms of quality of service configured between two peers that are not configured in such a way to account for BGP traffic and maximum transmission unit mismatches.

5. What problem is synchronization between BGP and interior gateway protocol learned routes supposed to prevent? What methods are used to prevent these problems from occurring without synchronization being enabled?

Synchronization between the interior and interior BGP protocol tables prevents routing black holes, where traffic is discarded in the center of a network by a router with less than full routing tables. Synchronization isn't normally used any longer, because interior gateway protocols are not designed to handle efficiently the number of routes carried within BGP. Instead of using synchronization, a full mesh of BGP is maintained between all the routers over which the traffic could pass when transiting the network.

6. BGP speakers do not normally change the next hop when readvertising a route learned from an external peer to an internal peer. How can this cause routes to be missing from a BGP speaker's tables?

If a BGP speaker receives a route with a next hop outside the autonomous system doesn't have a route to that next hop, it will consider this route as unreachable.

7. When is the multiple exit discriminator compared between two routes?

   Only when the autonomous systems the two routes were learned from are the same.

8. Can the multiple exit discriminator comparison rules cause issues with route selection process?

   It can cause the path chosen to forward traffic along to be chosen in a different way at different times, causing inconsistent routing through an autonomous system. This inconsistent routing can lead to route churn in some situations.

9. What rules can you follow in network design with regards to the interior gateway protocol metric between route reflectors to prevent persistent route churn?

   You can prevent persistent oscillation with route reflectors by adjusting the interior gateway protocol metrics so the cost between the route reflectors is always higher than the cost of reaching any edge from the route reflectors.

Chapter 9

1. Are MD5 keys periodically transmitted over the link between two BGP peers? How are keys managed when using MD5 to authenticate a session between two BGP speakers?

   Keys are not periodically exchanged between BGP speakers when using MD5 as an authentication method; they must be manually managed, including manual periodic key changes.

2. At what level within the BGP packets is the MD5 authentication inserted? Is it an IP option, a TCP option, or a BGP option?

   MD5 authentication strings are included as a TCP option header.

3. What type of protection does the BTSH security hack provide?

   It prevents the attack of BGP speakers from further away than the farthest known peer. For instance, if all the peers of a BGP speaker are directly connected, then any attacker would need to be directly connected, as well, to attack that BGP speaker.

4. What types of attacks do reverse path forwarding checks prevent?

   Attackers using some address other than their own as a source address (spoofing).

5. What three types of certificates does soBGP use to validate the information carried within the BGP protocol?

   The EntityCert, which provides information about the entities within the routing system; a PolicyCert, which provides information about connections between entities and policies preferred by entities; and the AuthCert, which provides information about which entities are allowed to originate which prefixes.

6. What two pieces of information does the EntityCert tie together?

   An EntityCert ties an autonomous system's public key and autonomous system number together.

7. What three pieces of information does the PolicyCert tie together?

   A PolicyCert ties together an autonomous system, the list of peers it is connected to, and a list of policies that autonomous system prefers.

8. What type of check is used in building soBGP's directed graph to prevent the advertising of false connectivity information?

   soBGP uses a two-way connectivity check; this verifies that both sides of a peering relationship are advertising the relationship, so no single autonomous system can advertise false information.

9. What two pieces of information does an AuthCert tie together?

   An autonomous system and the blocks of address space it is allowed to send.

10. What is the security preference used for in soBGP?

   To indicate the level of trust a given received prefix has, based on whether or not the prefix is covered by an entry in the authorization database, the path can be validated, and other information.

11. How are security certificates transported in soBGP?

   Any form of transport may be used; however, a new BGP message type, SECURITY, is proposed as one method of transporting certificates.

12. Must soBGP processing be done on every edge device within an autonomous system?

No, all cryptographic processing can be done on a set of servers within the autonomous systems. The edge routers can communicate with these servers using RADIUS or some other method.

13. Are private keys transmitted through the network, or configured on any edge device, when running soBGP?

No, private keys are only used to create certificates, which are then transmitted through the network. Public keys are the only keys that are transmitted through the network.

14. What semantic does S-BGP rely on to provide authorization?

By signing an update with the target autonomous system in the signature, you are authorizing the receiving autonomous system to advertise the update to its peers.

15. How does S-BGP optimize for the case where there are multiple peers, in different autonomous systems, to which an update must be transmitted?

By allowing the insertion of multiple target autonomous systems in the signed update.

Chapter 10

1. What problems are solved by the BGP/MPLS-based approach that other peer-to-peer models don't solve?

In an MPLS/BGP VPN-based model, the service provider can take on some of the management of the customer's network connectivity while allowing the customer to manage their own address space and separating the customer's traffic and routes. Other VPN options either require the customer to build the entire network out, treating the VPNs as a simple layer 2 connection (like a circuit), or require the service provider to manage the customer's network address space as well.

2. What is the difference between a route distinguisher and a route target?

A route distinguisher distinguishes two routes with the same prefix that are within two different VPNs. A route target indicates which local routing tables a given prefix should be installed into.

3. Is it possible to send prefixes that belong to multiple <address-family, sub-address-family> with the same set of attributes? How?

By using different route distinguishers.

4. Is BGP required in the core of the MPLS networks? If not, how is reachability achieved?

No. Reachability is achieved through the use of MPLS tunnels through the core of the network, built from provider edge to provider edge.

5. How is partial mesh topology created in an MPLS/BGP based VPN?

By configuring the route targets full mesh and hub and spoke topologies are combined.

Index

A

access lists. See also prefix lists
  addressing, 186–187t
  application, 189
  AS Path, 206–208
  Cisco IOS software, available in, 188t
  entry matches, 189t, 191t
  extended, 190–191
  nonexistent, application of, 192–193
  parameters, 188–190
  standard IP syntax, 185
  usage, 185
ACLs. See access lists
Address Family Identifier, 35
address pools
  separate, as routing possibility, 79–80
  splitting, 80–81
advertisement length, acceptable, 225–227
aggregate-address-summary-only, 119
aggregation
  aggregate-address-summary-only, 119
  AS path, relationship between, 36–37
  atomic, 37–38
  BGP routes, 117–119
  example code, 118, 119
  router, 43
aggregation router, 4. See also aggregation, 43
AS Confederation Sets, 155
AS Path, 11–12, 25. See also autonomous
      systems
  access lists. (see access lists)
  aggregation, interaction with, 36–37
  common filters, 234
  filters, 235–238
  first AS, enforcing, 232–233
  loop prevention, 127
  policy setting, 231–232
  private AS, removing, 232
atomic aggregation. See aggregation
AuthCert, 344, 348–350, 351, 354, 355, 356
  certification list, 361
  serial numbers, 363
autonomous systems, 3. See also AS Path
  AS Path. (see AS Path)
  filters, 224, 235–238
  local preference
    default, 209
    route maps, 209–215
  number, need for, 49
  safety nets. (see safety nets)
  usage issues, 3–4

B

balance-list, 75
Bellman-Ford algorithm, 9
best-exit routing, 6
BGP. See Border Gateway Protocol
bgp confederation identifier 65100, 129
bgp confederation peers, 129
bgp deterministic-med, 251, 313, 329
bgp enforce-first-as, 233
bgp fast-external-fallover, 177
BGP/MPLS-based VPN
  addresses, overlapping, support for, 380–383
  carrier considerations, 407–409
  CE to PE routing, 379–380
  colors, 387–388
  confederations, relationship between, 403–404
  control plane, 394–396
  example, 393–398
  features, 377, 378–379
  forwarding plane, 396–398
  forwarding, MPLS, 389–393
  full mesh topologies, 401–402
  hub and spoke topologies, 398–400
  multiple forwarding tables, 384
  multiple routing tables, 384
  network address translator, 383
  overview, 377
  partial mesh topologies, 402
  reachability information, 385–387
  route reflectors, 404–407
  routes, exporting and importing, 388–389
  service provider considerations, 402–409
  signaling protocol, 384–387
bogon filters
  announce mailing list, 230
  classes of, 227
  CYMRU, 228–230
Border Gateway Protocol
  attributes, 21, 23. (see also specific attributes)
  autonomous system, 3
  best path algorithm, 38–40
  confederations. (see confederations, BGP)
  cores. (see cores, BGP)
  custom decision process. (see custom decision process, BGP)
  decision algorithm, 31
  dual homing. (see dual homing)
  exterior (eBGP). (see eBGP)
  external connections, 123–129. (see also eBGP)
  firewall, opening hole in to operate, 48
  graceful restart. (see graceful restart, BGP)
  Indentifier. (see Identifier, BGP)

429

Register Your Book

at www.awprofessional.com/register

You may be eligible to receive:

- Advance notice of forthcoming editions of the book
- Related book recommendations
- Chapter excerpts and supplements of forthcoming titles
- Information about special contests and promotions throughout the year
- Notices and reminders about author appearances, tradeshows, and online chats with special guests

Contact us

If you are interested in writing a book or reviewing manuscripts prior to publication, please write to us at:

Editorial Department
Addison-Wesley Professional
75 Arlington Street, Suite 300
Boston, MA 02116 USA
Email: AWPro@aw.com

Addison-Wesley

Visit us on the Web: http://www.awprofessional.com